In this new and much-expanded edition of his classic study, John Vasquez examines the power of the power politics perspective to dominate inquiry, and evaluates its ability to provide accurate explanations of the fundamental forces underlying world politics. Part I of the book reprints the original 1983 text of *The Power of Power Politics*. It examines classical realism and quantitative international politics, providing an intellectual history of the discipline and an evaluation of statistical research guided by the realist paradigm. Part II provides six new chapters covering neorealism, post-modernism, the neotraditional research program on balancing, Mearsheimer's analysis of multipolarity and institutionalism, the debate on the end of the Cold War, and neoliberalism. Through the use of comparative case studies these chapters analyze the extent to which the realist paradigm has been progressive (or degenerating), and empirically accurate, and the extent to which it remains a relevant and explanatorily powerful theoretical approach for our current era.

John Vasquez is Professor of Political Science at Vanderbilt University. His work focuses on international relations theory and peace research. His books include *The War Puzzle* (1993), *In Search of Theory: A New Paradigm for Global Politics* (with Richard Mansbach, 1981), *The Power of Power Politics: A Critique* (1983), and *Classics of International Relations* (3rd edition 1996). He has published articles in *International Studies Quarterly*, *World Politics*, *American Political Science Review*, *Review of International Studies*, *Journal of Peace Research*, and *Journal of Politics*, among others.

The Power of Power Politics

CAMBRIDGE STUDIES IN INTERNATIONAL RELATIONS

The Power of Power Politics
From Classical Realism to Neotraditionalism

John A. Vasquez

CAMBRIDGE
UNIVERSITY PRESS

PUBLISHED BY THE PRESS SYNDICATE OF THE UNIVERSITY OF CAMBRIDGE
The Pitt Building, Trumpington Street, Cambridge CB2 1RP, United Kingdom

CAMBRIDGE UNIVERSITY PRESS
The Edinburgh Building, Cambridge CB2 2RU, UK
http://www.cup.cam.ac.uk
40 West 20th Street, New York, NY 10011–4211, USA   http://www.cup.org
10 Stamford Road, Oakleigh, Melbourne 3166, Australia

First published 1998

Printed in the United Kingdom at the University Press, Cambridge

Typeset in Palatino 10/12½ pt [CE]

A catalog record for this book is available from the British Library

Library of Congress Cataloging in Publication data
Vasquez, John A., 1945–
The power of power politics: from classical realism to neotraditionalism /
John A. Vasquez.
    p.   cm. – (Cambridge studies in international relations : 63)
Includes bibliographical references and index.
ISBN 0 521 44235 4 (hardbound)
1. International relations – Research.
2. Balance of power – Research.
I. Title.   II. Series.
JZ 1234.V37   1998
327.1'072–dc21   98–20166   CIP

ISBN 0 521 44235 4 hardback
ISBN 0 521 44746 1 paperback

For Barbara
Some things, although understood,
still passeth all understanding.

Contents

Contents

Figures

Tables

Preface

Longer ago than I care to relate, I thought it would be nice to have a paperback edition of this book released with perhaps an epilogue addressing some issues facing international relations theory since the original publication. From this whimsical idea, the volume before you has emerged. It has fully six new chapters, each with its own research design and argument. In part, this is a function of the fact that it proved impossible to treat the question of the power of the realist paradigm to guide inquiry and adequately explain it since the publication of Kenneth Waltz's *Theory of International Politics* (1979) in just one or two chapters, let alone an epilogue. It is also partly a result of the change in historical events that resulted in the end of the Cold War and that has led to much rethinking (with new historical perspective gained with the passing of an era) about the nature of world politics and the ability of our theories to explain it. However, the main reason behind the expansion of the book can be found in the richness and variety of the discourse on international relations that has emerged since I worked on the original text. Many of the topics I treat in the new chapters, from neorealism to the debate over the end of the Cold War, simply did not exist when I wrote the dissertation (1974) that gave rise to the original text (completed in 1980, but not released until 1983 because of problems at the original press).

While these intellectual currents have expanded the book, the new chapters are not just a hodge-podge of essays reflecting recent trends. From the outset I made the commitment to make the new chapters a logically tight self-contained unit. They, like the original text, are linked into an overall argument that seeks to appraise the adequacy of the realist paradigm. They also seek to complement the original text by examining a new body of evidence and by applying some additional criteria of adequacy. Whereas the original text examined quantitative evidence quantitatively to make an evaluation, the new chapters examine neotraditional research through the use of comparative case studies to make an appraisal. The old and the new form a unified whole, even though they are separated by about seventeen years.

Every book you write takes part of your life and part of the lives of those close to you; you can only hope that it returns more than it takes. When it does so, it tends to give back more to you as author than to those close to you. Nevertheless, I have learned a great deal writing the new chapters and seeing how they relate to the original chapters written in a very different time and different place. I hope readers, both the original ones and new ones, will also learn from this work.

I have been fortunate that the person closest to me has been able to provide not only emotional support for my work but also intellectual support and criticism that has improved it. Marie T. Henehan read the entire manuscript more times than she would like to count and offered numerous emendations and comments. I remain, as always, in her debt. My thanks also to several others. John Haslam, my editor at Cambridge University Press, waited patiently for this manuscript. After it was promised several times, I still kept adding things here and there. Steve Smith, the series editor, was supportive of the project from the initial idea to the review of the final product. I much appreciate his critical reading of the manuscript, and the conversation (mostly by reading each others' work) on international relations theory we have had over the years. My new colleague at Vanderbilt, James Lee Ray, also read the manuscript and offered counsel, which I always find valuable. Fred Chernoff generously provided a detailed reading of about 100 manuscript pages for which I am enormously grateful. A special thanks goes to Matthew Evangelista who was kind enough to review the chapter on the Cold War for me. As always it has been a pleasure working with the editorial and production staff at Cambridge, particularly Dr. Anne Dunbar-Nobes who copy-edited the manuscript professionally and expeditiously. Needless to say, none of the above individuals should be held responsible for my own errors.

Parts of this book draw upon two of my previously published pieces. An early version of Chapter 10 appeared in Ken Booth and Steve Smith (eds.) *International Relations Theory Today* (Cambridge:

Polity Press, 1995) as "The post-positivist debate," pp. 217–240. The chapter here is longer and its theme more focused on the need for theory appraisal and how to conduct it. A shortened version of chapter 11 appeared in the *American Political Science Review* 91 (December 1997): 899–912 with responses by Kenneth Waltz, Thomas Christensen and Jack Snyder, Colin Elman and Miriam Fendius Elman, Randall Schweller, and Stephen Walt. The chapter here is more tightly linked with the theme of the book and structured as one of several case studies. In this chapter, I have also taken the liberty of replying mostly, but not exclusively, in the footnotes and in the section on "Shirking the evidence" to the points made by my critics.

Let me also state here that the criticisms I make of realist and other scholars in this book should not be taken as meaning that I find their work without value – just the opposite is the case. It should come as no surprise that I still use Morgenthau's *Politics Among Nations* as the main text in my freshman international relations course, and that I use Waltz (1979) in my core graduate course in international relations theory. Criticism remains one of the main ways (but not the only way) by which knowledge in the field grows. One of my greatest debts is to the scholars I criticize in this book, for they have made me think (and rethink) the most fundamental questions currently facing international relations theory.

Support for this project was provided by Vanderbilt University in the form of paid leaves both to start this work and later to complete it. Without that released time and support from the University Research Council, this work would have taken even longer. Most of what is new in this book was completed on Block Island, which proved once again to be a congenial place for reflection and for the arduous labor of transforming thoughts into written arguments.

Introduction

This is an unusual book in that it is not simply a revised or updated edition of a work that in certain quarters has become well known; it is really two books in one. The first part contains the original text of *The Power of Power Politics: A Critique*. This provides a theoretical intellectual history of international relations inquiry, applying and testing several propositions about scientific disciplines initially presented by Thomas Kuhn (1962). Its argument is that realism, specifically the work of Hans J. Morgenthau, has provided a paradigm for the field that guides theory and research. It then goes on to review systematically the statistical findings in the field to show that the paradigm has not been very successful in passing such tests and concludes that this evidence along with well-known conceptual flaws indicates that the realist paradigm is a fundamentally flawed and empirically inaccurate view of the world.

Since the original text has acquired a life of its own, I have not sought to revise it so as to make the views of someone who was starting out in the profession accord with someone who is now in his mid-career. It is published as it was in its first printing except for the deletion of a few minor citations and about eighty pages from chapter 4 – pages which provided a detailed review of international relations theory in the 1950s and 1960s but which is less relevant now. This slight abridgement actually makes the text closer to the dissertation that gave rise to it in that the main revisions were in chapter 4 and the addition of chapter 8, which provided a new conclusion.

Nor was it ever my intention to truly update the text. Done properly that would involve new data analyses that would essentially replicate chapters 4–7. That would require an immense effort and is certainly worth doing, but it is not clear that this sort of additional evidence would change anyone's mind about the argument, even though a key part of the argument is empirical.

The reason for this is that an increasing portion of the field, even within North America, has, until quite recently, moved further and further away from quantitative analysis. The crest in this anti-quantitative sentiment was perhaps reached with the publication of Puchala's (1991) "Woe to the Orphans of the Scientific Revolution." Since then the tide has turned the other way with the findings on the democratic peace increasing the interest in scientific research even among senior scholars who had long been hostile to such modes of analysis. It was these non-quantitative scholars whom I wanted to reach, and I knew that another data-based analysis would not do it. Many of these scholars had already reacted to the quantitative evidence presented in the original text by saying that all that this indicated was that quantitative analysis is a flawed method that cannot produce knowledge; not that the realist paradigm is inaccurate. I therefore decided to employ a mode of analysis more amenable to them and to focus on current non-quantitative theory and research. This research, which is often conducted by realists, but not confined to them, is best known for its use of comparative case studies, historical analysis, and theoretical argumentation, while at the same time eschewing quantitative analysis. Because the roots of its work can be traced back to Hedley Bull's (1966) defense of traditionalism, I have labeled this approach *neotraditionalism*. Among the major journals neotraditionalists dominate are *International Security*, *International Organization*, *Political Psychology*, and *Security Studies*.

Among realists, this approach reflects a third generation of contemporary scholars working within the central core of the realist paradigm, with Morgenthau and the early realists (like E. H. Carr, Reinhold Niebuhr, and George Kennan) being the first generation and the neorealists Kenneth Waltz and Robert Gilpin being the second. Within North America the third generation of realists include John Mearsheimer, Stephen Walt, Joseph Grieco, Randall Schweller, Michael Mastanduno, and Barry Posen, as well as those, who, while critical of certain aspects of realism, remain within that larger paradigm. Most prominent among these are Jack Snyder, Kenneth Oye, and Stephen Van Evera. There are also a number of nonrealists who reflect a neotraditional orientation in their research and mode of discourse, i.e. an emphasis on history, case studies, and a de-emphasis on quantitative findings. Among those who have pioneered the case method are the more senior Alexander George, as well as third-generation scholars Richard Ned Lebow and Janice Stein.

The best way to address the objection that the conclusion of the original text could not be accepted (because it focused on quantitative findings and quantitative scholars) was to look at non-quantitative research. Examining this research would be a logically compelling way of demonstrating that the anomalies the realist paradigm needs to explain away are not exclusively associated with the use of a particular method. Empirical research that is done well should not produce different results depending on the research techniques employed; statistical, historical, and comparative case studies should produce convergent findings.

In addition to examining non-quantitative research, I wanted to provide at least an overview of international relations theorizing in light of the changing intellectual and historical context of the last two decades of the twentieth century. The original text had been written before the rise of neorealism; before post-positivism, post-modernism, and feminist discourse; before the end of the Cold War; and before the widespread attention devoted to findings on the democratic peace and the concomitant rise of the liberal Kantian paradigm. How did these movements and events affect the claims made for and against the realist paradigm in the original text?

At the same time, I felt the need to appraise the quality of realist theorizing, especially since one of the claims in favor of the realist paradigm was that it was, by far, more theoretically robust and fruitful than possible alternatives. I also wanted to examine the connection between realist theory and realist practice. If it were true that the realist paradigm was both as dominant and as fundamentally flawed as argued in the original text, then this should have some impact on realist ability to provide an understanding of contemporary events and guide practice. It was my suspicion that neotraditionalists make their greatest errors when they ignore all research and seek to deduce knowledge on the basis of realist understandings and then use this "knowledge" to derive policy prescriptions.

Obviously, such an agenda was much too ambitious, and I settled instead on doing some carefully selected case studies on the most important questions. The end result is a sequel to the original text that constitutes Part II of this volume. This "new" text complements the original both historically and logically. Historically, it traces and appraises the major trends in realist work from Waltz (1979) through neotraditionalism; it examines the rise of post-positivism and post-modernism in terms of its implications for paradigm evaluation, and it looks at the impact of the major historical event of the current era – the end of the Cold War – on realist inquiry.

Logically, this second part is meant to complement the first by employing a different and new body of theory and research and by applying a broader set of criteria to evaluate the paradigm. If this effort is to be successful, the logic of this research design and how it complements that of the original text must be made explicit. In terms of comprehension of coverage, the original text examined classical realism and quantitative international politics, and the sequel examines neorealism and neotraditional research. In this manner, all relevant realist variants are covered and both quantitative and non-quantitative evidence is included.

Unlike the original text, where all statistical findings in a given period were analyzed, not all neotraditional research will be examined. Instead, case studies of different areas of inquiry will be selected, and then the most appropriate research will be brought to bear to deal with the criteria being applied. In order not to bias the results, it is important that the topics of inquiry that are selected be central to the realist paradigm and indicative of some of the best work done on realism. An evaluation of peripheral areas or of straw men will not do much to reaffirm the original thesis on the inadequacy of the realist paradigm.

Identification of the most important and best realist work in the last fifteen to twenty years is not difficult and is not very controversial. Clearly, the single most important work in terms of its intellectual impact on the field, the attention it has received, the research to which it has given rise, and its use to inform policy analyses has been Waltz's (1979) *Theory of International Politics* (see Buzan et al. 1993: 1). To this, one might want to add Gilpin (1981), the most politically oriented (as opposed to economic-oriented) of his works. Together these are the heart of neorealism and respectively have informed much of realist-guided work in international politics and international political economy. Since the former is of main concern here, only that aspect of Gilpin's work that has had a major impact on questions of war, peace, and political conflict will be included. Because neorealism has been such a major force within the field, it was decided to devote an entire chapter to it to see what this new theoretical version of realism could tell us about the power of power politics thinking to guide inquiry and accurately explain phenomena.

4

Waltz (1979) focuses on two major subtopics of inquiry: an explanation of what he regards as the major law in international politics – the balancing of power – and an analysis of the comparative stability of bipolarity and multipolarity. Each of these was selected as a focus of separate case studies, once it was determined that a body of relevant research or discourse had been devoted to them by prominent neotraditionalists.

Waltz's ideas about balancing of power have actually spurred a great deal of neotraditional research and theoretical innovation in light of that research. Research by Stephen Walt (1987), Christensen and Snyder (1990), Schweller (1994), Rosecrance and Stein (1993), and the historian Paul Schroeder (1994a, 1994b) has been quite extensive on the questions of balancing, bandwagoning, chain-ganging and buck-passing. In fact, one could argue that this has been one of the most researched areas by neotraditionalists in the last several years. For this reason alone, it is worthy of a case study. In addition, the rise of neorealism and this subsequent theoretical growth have been widely lauded and seen by many as an indicator of the fertility of the realist paradigm and a satisfaction of Lakatos's criterion that research programs should be progressive (see Hollis and Smith 1990: 60).

The work on multipolarity and bipolarity has produced considerably less neotraditional research, but it has been the focus of a major debate about the future of the post-Cold War world. John Mearsheimer's (1990a) article used Waltz's analysis in a theoretically insightful fashion to make predictions and policy prescriptions about the coming multipolar world that attracted wide attention and spurred debate among neotraditionalists. Subsequently, he used realism proper to attack the "false promise" of liberal institutionalists' prescriptions of peace. Although many have disagreed with Mearsheimer's (1990a) policy advice, no one has claimed he has misused Waltz or provided an illegitimate version of realism. Given the prominent attention his work has received within the field and its influence outside the field (see Mearsheimer 1990b, 1993), his work was taken as the focus for another case study. This also provided an opportunity to examine how realists use theory to guide practice and to evaluate the empirical soundness of that policy advice.

The case studies on neorealism, balancing, and polarity cover the major intellectual currents within realism and neotraditionalism. There remains, however, one other major intellectual debate relevant to realism and the paradigm debate – the debate spurred by the end of the Cold War. Even though it is not directly related to Waltz's work proper, it does involve that of Gilpin (1981), which is the main realist text used by neotraditionalists to explain the end of the Cold War (see Oye 1995: 58). Beginning with Gaddis' (1992/93) indictment of the entire profession for failing to anticipate the end of the Cold War and the collapse of the Soviet Union, a debate quickly developed over the failure of realism and neorealism to provide an adequate explanation of the Cold War (Lebow and Risse-Kappen 1995). Since realism has placed great emphasis on the ability of international relations theory to comprehend and explain historical events, like World War I and World War II, and rose to ascendency in many ways because of the failure of idealism to prevent the coming of World War II, it was felt that including a case study of the ability of realist and non-realist theories to explain the major historical event of our own time was highly appropriate.

Four intellectual topics, then, will serve as the sample, so to speak, for the case studies – neorealism, neotraditional research on balancing power, Mearsheimer's work, and the debate over the end of the Cold War. This seems to be a representative sample of the most important work in realism since 1979, includes the most prominent thinkers on security questions, and does not leave out any work that would bias the study against the realist paradigm.

Certain areas, of necessity, could not be covered, even where they might be relevant to the major thesis of the book. I have confined the "second part of this volume" to inquiry that has focused on the central questions defined by the realist paradigm – the study of war, peace, conflict, and the foreign policy of "high politics." I have done this because one of the points I want to make is not just that an alternative nonrealist paradigm would look at different questions, but that it would frame realism's central questions in a manner that would provide better and more empirically accurate answers. For this reason, as well as my own expertise, I do not, on the whole, deal with the now rather vast literature on international political economy. This is not too serious an omission because much of the debate over realism in this area of inquiry has been adequately covered in the literature (see, for example, Baldwin 1993).

For reasons of space, I have not been able to go beyond an epistemological discussion of post-modernist approaches in chapter 10. This is regrettable because the theorizing and research of post-structuralists has been one of the more innovative and imaginative areas of inquiry in the last ten years. Similarly, initial criticisms of realism and patriarchy by early feminists, especially those that relied on deconstruction as a technique, have provided some new insights (e.g., Tickner 1992; Cohn 1987; Sylvester 1994), but I have not been able to give this literature the full attention it deserves. At some point, however, feminist discourse in international relations will make an interesting case study of the difficulties of fulfilling critical theory's research agenda in the context of a broader political movement and of balancing concerns about self-interest with the search for truth – ethical and empirical. Nevertheless, omission of research not included in the study – political economy, post-modernist, and feminist research – should not bias the results against the realist paradigm.

The next major question to be decided is what criteria to select to evaluate the realist paradigm. This poses a major epistemological problem because many post-positivists and most post-modernists would object to the kind of scientific (positivist) appraisal conducted in the original text. This necessitates a chapter that comes to grip with the post-modernist and post-positivist critiques. In chapter 10, I discuss the promise of post-modernism and review some of its major insights about theory. I then raise the question of the danger of relativism posed by post-modernism and of the need for theory appraisal. In the chapter, I attempt to reconstruct the foundations of the scientific study of world politics, broadly defined, and to offer a number of criteria for the appraisal of empirical and normative theories. I concede to post-positivists that such criteria cannot be logically justified, but following Lakatos (1970) and Toulmin (1950) I argue that there are "good [instrumental] reasons" for *choosing* them, even if scholars are not logically compelled to do so. These criteria then serve as a basis for the paradigm evaluation in the case studies. In order to make the chapters reflect the chronological order of the history of the field, the chapter on post-modernism follows the chapter on neorealism.

The original text employed only one criterion for evaluating paradigms – the ability to pass empirical testing – although it recognized the existence of several. While this criterion must always be at the center of any serious appraisal, I wanted to supplement it with others in the second study. In particular, I wanted to have at least one case study applying the most important of Lakatos' (1970) criteria not applied in the original text – the idea that research programs must be progressive, as opposed to degenerating. Not all bodies of research are amenable to appraisal with this criterion, because in order to apply this criterion, there has to be a considerable body of research available, and it needs to be fairly cumulative. Mearsheimer's work cannot be evaluated along these lines simply because very little neotraditional research has been conducted on multipolarity. Conversely, neotraditional research on balancing of power is an excellent case in which to examine the question of theoretical fertility and progressive/degenerating research programs: first, because the non-quantitative research has been extensive and individual works attempt to build on each other in a cumulative fashion, and second, because this work is often cited as a strength of the paradigm. This criterion will be employed in chapter 11 and provides one of two major studies on whether non-quantitative work will expose realist theories as inaccurate and inconsistent with the evidence.

Mearsheimer's (1990a) work on multipolarity deals with the possibility of peace and the risk of war in the future; it is the focus of chapter 12. Since he uses theory to derive important policy prescriptions, the most appropriate criterion to apply is the criterion of empirical soundness, which maintains that the empirical theory upon which prescriptions are based must be empirically accurate (see ch. 10 in this volume). Unfortunately, there has not been much non-quantitative work on this question or on the question of the effect of norms and institutions on peace. However, there is a considerable amount of quantitative research, and this is consistent with what is known historically about the pertinent periods. Although the use of this evidence makes this case not relevant to the question of whether non-quantitative research will produce the same results as quantitative work, the differences in nonrealist and realist predictions about the immediate future sets up an important "real world" crucial test to resolve this debate. In the meantime, this case exposes the danger of relying too heavily on theoretical deduction and ignoring an entire body of research.

The debate on the end of the Cold War also brings together empirical and policy themes. Here, the most appropriate criteria for theory and paradigm appraisal are explanatory power and relevance. Can the realist paradigm provide a plausible explanation for one of the major historical events of our time and can it provide an intellectual understanding that is *relevant* to the new historical era we seem to be entering? These are the main questions addressed in chapter 13. Non-quantitative and neotraditional research and argumentation are the evidence used to analyze this question, thus providing a second case study to see whether non-quantitative evidence will produce a different conclusion from statistical evidence.

The new text applies the following criteria to appraise the adequacy of recent realist theories, explanations, and prescriptions: empirical accuracy, theoretical fertility (progressive vs. degenerating research programs), empirical soundness, explanatory power, and relevance. In the late 1940s, classical realism claimed to do well on all of these criteria. The original text claimed that quantitative testing raised serious questions about the empirical accuracy of the realist paradigm, as well as pointing out numerous conceptual flaws that weakened its explanatory power. Neorealism and neotraditional realists claim once again to satisfy all of these criteria, and certainly to satisfy them better than any non-realist alternative. The case studies in the new analysis attempt to provide some non-quantitative, but rigorously derived, evidence relevant to each of these criteria. In doing so, it will not provide evidence as systematic as that in the original text, but it will raise a greater variety of questions and potential anomalies than were raised in the original book.

No single case study can ever be definitive; this is a defect of the case study method. Nevertheless, several case studies are more conclusive than one or two. Chapter 14 looks at the collective impact of the case studies conducted in this book for appraising the merits of the realist paradigm and its various branches that have been investigated in the new study. It then reviews the cases and the original text for what they suggest about the promise of a nonrealist paradigm and what problems a nonrealist paradigm would need to resolve in order to produce better and more accurate theories than the realist paradigm has produced. Problems with the major alternative to realism – the Liberal Kantian paradigm – are surveyed. The chapter concludes with a plea for a closer connection between theory construction and research and some ideas to make each more rigorous.

Part I

The Original Text: Classical Realism and Quantitative International Politics

Preface to the Original Text

This book is concerned with two aspects of the power of power politics. The first deals with the ability of power politics perspectives to dominate the field of international relations inquiry; that is, to guide and direct the theory and research of most of the practitioners of the discipline. The second deals with the ability of power politics to explain phenomena adequately. Although power politics "theory"; can be found as far back as the ancient civilizations of Greece, India, and China, this analysis will deal only with its twentieth-century manifestation, the realist paradigm. This book will seek to demonstrate two controversial claims: that the realist paradigm has dominated the field of international relations since the early 1950s, and that this paradigm has not been very successful in explaining behavior.

The analysis has a descriptive and an evaluative component. In its descriptive section it will demonstrate empirically that the realist paradigm has indeed dominated the field. This will be accomplished by showing that the paradigm has guided theory construction, data making, and research. In its evaluative section it will demonstrate that the realist paradigm has been a scientifically inadequate approach for explaining behavior in international relations. This will be accomplished by applying criteria of adequacy for paradigm and theory evaluation developed by various philosophers of science. The major criterion to be employed is that paradigms, in order to be adequate, must produce significant findings after a reasonable period of time and research.

The analysis presented here is important for two reasons. First, the descriptive component, in providing a sketch of the research agenda of the field and a report on how systematically that agenda is being followed, allows practitioners and students of the discipline to form a gestalt out of the welter of events occurring in the field. As the number of scholars and their output increase within a field, communication becomes a problem because of information overload. In order to deal with that problem, part of the scholarly effort of any discipline must be devoted to describing the activities of other scholars. Consequently, in any discipline there can always be found bibliographies, abstracts, book reviews, inventories, and overviews.[1] The descriptive component of this book stems from this tradition. What differentiates the description reported herein from other recent efforts is that it attempts to delineate long-term trends by the use of quantitative analysis. Second, the analysis is important because the evaluative component provides practitioners and students with a review of what hypotheses have been statistically tested, what findings have been produced, and how useful certain fundamental conceptions of international relations are for explaining behavior scientifically. It will be demonstrated in the descriptive component that most scholars in the field share a fundamental view of the world that was promulgated by the realist scholars. If this view is indeed pervasive, then it is extremely important to assess its scientific utility. One of the fundamental principles of the scientific method is that theories should be tested against empirical evidence and in light of that evidence be either rejected, reformulated, or accepted. By reviewing tests of hypotheses that have been made, the evaluative component provides the evidence and analysis required by that scientific principle.

The evaluation is particularly important now because there has been no systematic attempt to evaluate the adequacy of the realist paradigm in light of the extensive quantitative research that has been conducted.[2] It has been over thirty years since the publication of Morgenthau's *Politics Among Nations* (1948), and at least twenty-five since the publication of the first mainstream article attempting to test statistically an explanatory hypothesis about international relations

---

[1] Examples of such work are Dougherty and Pfaltzgraff (1971); Jones and Singer (1972); Porter (1972); Alker and Bock (1972); McGowan and Shapiro (1974); Greenstein and Polsby (1975); Zinnes (1976); and Taylor (1978b).

[2] There have of course been numerous conceptual critiques of Morgenthau's work. Typical of the best of this work are Tucker (1952); Claude (1962); and E. B. Haas (1953). There have also been tests on specific propositions; see J. D. Singer, Bremer, and Stuckey (1972); and J. D. Singer (1980).

(Deutsch 1956).[3] It would appear that this amount of time has been sufficient to produce enough evidence on the adequacy of the realist paradigm to warrant review, but not so much evidence that a review would be unmanageable.

The scope of this analysis is limited by two parameters. First, only empirical and nomothetic work – that is, work concerned with constructing highly general and scientific theories of international relations behavior – will be systematically reviewed. Work that is primarily devoted to normative concerns, such as policy prescriptions, or to idiographic analysis, such as historical descriptions, will not be reviewed unless it bears directly on a nomothetic work. Second, the analysis is intended to apply only to the United States branch of the field of international relations. Scientific work outside the United States is only referred to when it has had a major impact on the develoment of the field within the United States.

In order to substantiate its claims, the analysis will be organized along the following lines. In chapter 1, a conceptual framework that can be used to describe and evaluate scholars' activities will be developed. The concept of a *paradigm* will be defined and its utility demonstrated. An empirical theory of how scientific inquiry is conducted, most notably associated with the work of Thomas Kuhn, will be outlined. Finally, a set of principles that can be used to evaluate the adequacy of paradigms will be presented and justified. Chapter 2 will employ the conceptual framework presented in chapter 1 to interpret the activities of international relations scholars. An historical theory of the role the realist paradigm played in international relations inquiry will be elaborated. In chapter 3, the realist paradigm will be defined and operationalized. The propositions crucial to the claims of the analysis will be specified and a justification of the research design of the book presented. Chapters 4 through 6 will test the proposition that the realist paradigm has dominated international relations inquiry. Chapter 4 will test the proposition that the realist paradigm has guided the theory-construction activities of scholars. Chapter 5 will test the proposition that the realist paradigm has directed the data-making efforts of scholars. Chapter 6 will test the proposition that the realist paradigm has guided the quantitative research of scholars.

---

[3] Jones and Singer (1972: vii) list Deutsch (1956) as the earliest data-based correlational/ explanatory article in the field of international relations. They do not include such forerunners of the quantitative movement as Lewis Richardson.

Chapter 7 will provide a data-based evaluation of the adequacy of the realist paradigm in light of the statistical findings it produced in the 1950s and 1960s. Chapter 8 will supplement this synoptic analysis with an in-depth review of two of the major areas of research in the 1970s, foreign policy and war, to identify the main anomalies that have emerged to undercut the fundamental assumptions of the paradigm.

Acknowledgments

A scholar's first book often begins as a doctoral dissertation, and that is the case with this work. Of the many people who have aided me a special place must be reserved for Bill Coplin, my dissertation advisor, who inspired the topic and encouraged me to investigate its feasibility. Without his steadfast support and intellectual stimulation, the dissertation, which gave rise to this book, could not have been written. Several other persons have aided me. Michael K. O'Leary, with whom I collaborated in an earlier critique of the realist paradigm, provided important guidance in making this a scholarly work. After the dissertation was completed, J. David Singer and Harold Guetzkow, although they hardly agree with all that is presented here, provided aid and encouragement in getting the work published and offered a number of specific criticisms that saved me from several errors. Marie Henehan, both student and friend, proved invaluable in discussing revisions and in preparing the manuscript for publication, often taking more care and showing more concern for the finished product than did I, and working down to the wire at great personal sacrifice. Diane Wallace and Diane Swartz respectively typed the initial and final drafts of the manuscript with care and patience. Finally, the Syracuse University International Relations Program provided financial assistance for the data collection, and the Rutgers University Research Council provided funds for reviewing research published in the 1970s and for typing the manuscript.

A number of other individuals, although they have not directly assisted me in this book, have had such a profound influence on my development that they deserve mention. Fred Frohock first introduced me to the writings of Thomas Kuhn and to philosophy of science. Frank Nevers and Raymond Duncan first introduced me to the realist paradigm. Howard Zinn shattered the hold the realist paradigm had had on my early conception of politics, and in doing so provided me with a critical perspective on both scientific theory and national policy. Finally, a note of thanks to my sister, Margie, who got me through some difficult times in 1976–1977. Although all of the above have influenced me, I have not always heeded their instruction; therefore the final responsibility for this work is my own.

Of all the people who helped me throughout the years of my graduate education, the most important was Barbara Vasquez. She gave as much of her life to this work as I did my own. When I entered graduate school she left a highly rewarding position to come with me. Without her at my side I could never have finished. To her I dedicate this work with love for the time together and sorrow for the time wasted. εὐκαρίστω.

1 The role of paradigms in scientific inquiry: a conceptual framework and a set of principles for paradigm evaluation

The work of Thomas Kuhn (1962, 1970a) has attracted much interest from historians and philosophers of science because it offers a way to describe and evaluate scientific inquiry. For this reason it provides a framework for determining whether the realist paradigm has adequately guided inquiry in international relations. Before the framework can be applied, a number of questions that have been raised by critics of Kuhn must be addressed.[1] The three most important are: how to define *paradigm*; whether Kuhn's description of scientific change is correct; and how paradigms can be evaluated. Each of these will be examined in this chapter.

Defining the concept of *paradigm*

Despite its wide use, the paradigm concept remains very difficult to define. The reason for this stems from its original usage by Thomas Kuhn in *The Structure of Scientific Revolutions* (1962). A textual analysis of that work by Margaret Masterman (1970) has shown that the concept of *paradigm* was used by Kuhn in at least twenty-one different ways. In the postscript to the second edition of the book, Kuhn (1970a: 174–191) recognized this criticism and attempted to clarify the definition. He maintains that most of the varying usage is due to stylistic inconsistencies but concedes that even after these inconsistencies are removed, the concept is used in two distinct ways:

> On the one hand, it stands for the entire constellation of beliefs, values, techniques, and so on shared by the members of a given

[1] For a criticism of work in political science that has failed to take note of Kuhn's different definitions see J. Stephens (1973).

community. On the other, it denotes one sort of element in that constellation, the concrete puzzle-solutions which, employed as models or examples, can replace explicit rules as a basis for the solution of the remaining puzzles of normal science.

(Kuhn 1970a: 175)

The first definition is what Kuhn (1970a: 181) has called "the constellation of group commitments." In this first definition, it is the shared constellation which is the basis of classifying an aggregate of scholars as a community (Kuhn 1970a: 176–178, 182). Kuhn (1970a: 182; 1971: 462–463; 1977: xvi–xxiii) has suggested that this use of the concept *paradigm* may be too broad in scope to support the central thesis of his book. He has therefore chosen to call this notion of paradigm a *disciplinary matrix*, the chief components of which are: (1) symbolic or theoretical generalizations, such as $f = ma$; (2) metaphysical beliefs or beliefs in certain models, such as heat kinetic energy of the constituent parts of bodies; (3) values, such as predictions should be accurate, what constitutes accuracy, what is inconsistency, what is plausibility, what is parsimonious, etc.; (4) an exemplar, which is the element in the disciplinary matrix that by itself forms the second definition of paradigm (Kuhn 1970a: 184–186; 1971; 464).

The second definition is what Kuhn (1970a: 187) has called the *paradigm as exemplar*, or *shared example*. In order to understand what an exemplar is and why it has such force within a scholarly community, it is necessary to examine how future professionals of a discipline are educated. According to Kuhn (1970a: 187–189) scientific education involves primarily "problem-solving." Problem solving is a central component of scientific education in two ways. First, the ability to solve new problems is the primary educational objective of scientific training. Second, the basic means of achieving this objective is to have students solve problems to which the correct answers are already known. The assumption behind this philosophy of education is that if students are capable of arriving at the correct solution to old but difficult problems, they will acquire the ability to solve current and new problems. According to Kuhn (1970a: 189), these sets of problems function to inculcate the student with a fundamental way of viewing the world (see also Kuhn 1971: 472–482). In addition to providing sets of solved problems, the exemplar is used in scientific education to inform the student about the existing unsolved problems or puzzles in the field. The latter bit of information tells the student what is worth knowing. These sets of problems constitute the concrete manifestation of the exemplar. But the paradigm as exemplar consists not of the problems themselves but of the elements that are used to perceive, define and solve problems.

Unfortunately, this reformation of the concept has not satisfied most of Kuhn's critics (see Shapere 1964, 1971; Toulmin 1967, 1970; Watkins 1970). Their original criticisms can be reduced to two points: that the concept is ambiguous in that it refers to so many aspects of the scientific process that his thesis is almost nonfalsifiable; and that it is so vague that it is difficult to identify (in operational terms, for example) the specific paradigm of a discipline (Shapere 1964: 385–386). The problem of ambiguity is quite severe. At times it seems that the paradigm concept refers to a set of research questions, the publication of a seminal work that changes inquiry in the field (exemplar), a particular theory, an epistemological viewpoint, or a method of investigation (Masterman 1970: 61–65).

Clearly, focusing on one of these elements while ignoring the others will produce a very different description of a discipline. Kuhn's selection of puzzle solutions attempts both to solve this problem and produce an operational indicator. Yet this notion is not adequate. In any science, there are numerous puzzle solutions, and Kuhn does not provide any criteria for distinguishing among or classifying these solutions. Are puzzle solutions to be defined on the basis of their method, their dependent variables, their independent variables, or their connection to an exemplar? Kuhn does not address these questions adequately, and it is not surprising that, of the original critics (compare Shapere 1964 and 1971; Toulmin 1967 and 1970), none is satisfied with his response.

These conceptual problems have led some of the scholars who have applied Kuhn's concept in describing inquiry within political science to produce very different and sometimes contradictory analyses (cf. Stephens 1973). Lijphart (1974) argues that within international relations behavioralism is a paradigm, whereas Beal (1976) argues that Lijphart places too much emphasis on method and ignores the fact that many quantitative scholars have tested traditional propositions. Lijphart and others such as Wolin (1968), who view behavioralism as a paradigm, see it as the attempt to employ the scientific method to study politics and distinguish this approach from traditional and normative methods. Keohane and Nye (1972) are more concerned with the substantive focus and have argued that international relations is dominated by a state-centric paradigm, whereas Handelman et al. (1973) have argued that a realist paradigm has dominated the field. While Keohane and Nye (1974, 1977) have more recently spoken of the realist rather than the state-centric paradigm, others, for example Ashley (1976), have argued that international relations is in a pre-paradigm stage, and that there are many different conceptual approaches and "theories" in the discipline (see also Alker 1971). Such disagreements are primarily a function of emphasizing different aspects of Kuhn's conception of paradigm.

If Kuhn's concept and his subsequent analysis are to be employed, they must be defined more precisely, and procedures must be established for operationalizing them. Since Kuhn has not adequately resolved these problems, this analysis must provide its own stipulative definition. Stipulative definitions are neither correct nor incorrect, since they are not empirical statements (see Ayer 1946; Wilson 1956); rather, they can be evaluated on the basis of their ability to conceptualize a set of phenomena in a way that clarifies rather than obscures relationships. In this sense, the most useful stipulative definition of *paradigm* is one that can utilize most of Kuhn's insights and provide an adequate account of how science proceeds.

To provide such a definition, it is important to stipulate what is not a paradigm. A paradigm is neither a method nor a theory. In the first instance, the scientific method and its various modes of testing (experimentation, simulation, statistical analysis, comparative case studies) cannot constitute a paradigm in any Kuhnian sense, because all the physical sciences share this method and would be dominated by a single paradigm. Clearly, Kuhn is not interested in the shared elements of the physical sciences, but in what makes them individual and coherent disciplines.

The heart of the paradigm concept must be substantive and not methodological, but a paradigm is not necessarily the same thing as a dominant theory. First, there can often be more than one theory in a field or shifts in accepted theories without producing what Kuhn would call a paradigm shift. Second, a paradigm is in some sense prior to theory. It is what gives rise to theories in the first place. Toulmin (1967) in particular is intrigued by the question of what exists in a field when there is no theory (a question certainly relevant to international relations inquiry), and suggests that Collingwood's (1940) notion of absolute presuppositions serves the same function as Kuhn's notion of paradigm.

The concept of *paradigm*, then, could be stipulatively defined as *the*

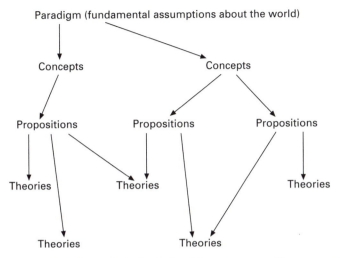

Figure 1.1. The analytical relationship among paradigms, concepts, propositions, and theories

fundamental assumptions scholars make about the world they are studying. These assumptions provide answers to the questions that must be addressed before theorizing even begins. For Kuhn, as Masterman (1970: 62) points out, such questions are: What are the fundamental units of which the world is composed? How do these units interact with each other? What interesting questions may be asked about these units? What kinds of conceptions will provide answers to these inquiries? By responding to these questions, the fundamental assumptions form a picture of the world the scholar is studying and tell the scholar *what is known about the world, what is unknown about it, how one should view the world if one wants to know the unknown, and finally what is worth knowing.*[2]

---

[2] This stipulative definition differs considerably from the components of a research paradigm that are identified by Alker (1971, reprinted in Ashley 1976: 154). Alker's list is not used here because its requirements are so stringent that only very narrow research efforts, like work on the Richardson arms race model, would be seen as having a paradigm. Ashley (1976: 155) is even more restrictive. Such a position comes close to the notion that the paradigm concept should be employed only to distinguish the narrowest scientific community, the invisible college. At times, in his revisions, Kuhn (1971: 461–462) comes close to saying this, but he recognizes that there are different levels of a scientific community. Each of these in some sense may have its own shared-examples. Clearly, however, classics such as Newton's *Principia* function at the broad disciplinary level and provide an exemplar or paradigm for the

The preceding definition has been stipulated to distinguish a paradigm from a conceptual framework or theory. To clarify this distinction, figure 1.1 specifies the analytical relationships. A paradigm consists of a set of fundamental assumptions of the world. These assumptions focus the attention of the scholar on certain phenomena and interpret those phenomena via concepts. Propositions, in turn, are developed by specifying relationships between concepts. Finally, theories are developed by specifying relationships between propositions.

It can also be seen from figure 1.1 that a pyramid effect is in operation. For example, if A, B, C are concepts, the following propositions, among others, can be logically derived:

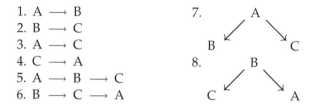

Likewise, as shown in figure 1.1, a given set of propositions can be linked in different ways to give rise to a variety of theories. Therefore it follows that one paradigm can give rise to more than one theory. On the basis of this analysis, it can be stipulated that a paradigm only changes when its fundamental assumptions or view of the world changes.[3] "New" concepts, propositions, or theories that do not change the assumptions of the paradigm do not constitute new paradigms, but only the elaborations, or what Kuhn (1970a: 24, 33–34) calls articulations, of the old one.

disciplinary matrix and not just for the invisible college. As will be seen later, the primary difference between the role of realism in the international relations field and that of other approaches, like decision making or systems, is that some of the fundamental assumptions of realism are shared by most scholars in the discipline, whereas the shared-examples of the other approaches are confined to a narrower group. In this analysis, *paradigm* is defined in a very broad (but not necessarily imprecise) manner. For a recent reconstuction of Kuhn that attempts to delineate how assumptions lead to a picture of the world and then to a research program, see Tornebohm (1976). For an attempt to delineate invisible colleges within international relations, see Russett (1970).

[3] This statement agrees with Kuhn (1970a: ch. 10, "Revolutions as changes of World View").

One of the main advantages of this stipulative definition is that, by reducing the ambiguity of the term, it does not affect most of Kuhn's propositions about scientific inquiry, yet it specifies clearly the conditions under which paradigms change, thereby permitting Kuhn's thesis to be falsified. Throughout the remainder of this analysis, unless otherwise indicated, whenever the concept *paradigm* is employed, including references to Kuhn's use of the term, it should be thought of in terms of the stipulative definition given here.

Describing scientific inquiry

The utility of the paradigm concept can be demonstrated by showing how Kuhn uses the concept to describe scientific inquiry. Kuhn's description is concerned with how paradigms dominate a field and how they are displaced. A dominant paradigm is usually provided by a single work, which is viewed as so unprecedented in its achievement that it becomes an exemplar of scientific analysis in a particular field:

> Aristotle's *Physica*, Ptolemy's *Almagest*, Newton's *Principia* . . . these and many other works served for a time implicitly to define the legitimate problems and method of a research field for succeeding generations of practitioners. They were able to do so because they shared two essential characteristics. Their achievement was sufficiently unprecedented to attract an enduring group of adherents away from competing modes of scientific activity. Simultaneously it was sufficiently open-ended to leave all sorts of problems for the redefined group of practitioners to resolve. (Kuhn 1970a: 10)

Once a paradigm dominates a field, scholarship enters the stage Kuhn (1970a: 10, 23–25) calls *normal science*. Scholarly behavior in this stage is characterized by extensive articulation of the paradigm by a research program that guides the theory construction, fact gathering, and research of scholars (Kuhn 1970a: 34). Theory construction in normal science is not haphazard, but highly systematic because the paradigm constrains scholars to the elaboration of theories that do not violate the fundamental assumptions of the paradigm (Kuhn 1970a: 24).

In addition to suggesting what are legitimate theories, the paradigm also suggests what, out of the welter of phenomena, are theoretically significant facts (Kuhn 1970a: 25). Much of normal science consists of gathering these facts. Before "facts" can be gathered, however, scientists must create tools that will permit the facts to be measured, just as the thermometer had to be invented in order to observe and measure heat. Finally, having gathered the facts, the theory is tested by matching it with the facts. After the tests, the theory is further elaborated and refined.

Theory construction, fact gathering, and research, then, are systematically linked through a feedback process. This does not mean that there will not be drastic changes in theories. There will be, as theories are tested, but any "new" theories will never violate the assumptions of the paradigm (Kuhn 1970a: 33–34). When a truly new theory emerges, it signals the existence of a new paradigm(s) and may under certain conditions result in what Kuhn (1970a: 52–53) calls *scientific crisis and revolution*.

Normal science begins to come to an end when an anomaly – "the recognition that nature has somehow violated the paradigm-induced expectations" – is unable to be removed by paradigm articulation (Kuhn 1970a: 52–53). The persistence of the anomaly(ies) results in a crisis in the field. Crisis is met by devising "numerous articulations and ad hoc modifications of . . . theory in order to eliminate any conflict" between fact and theory (Kuhn 1970a: 78). However, if the anomaly can be accounted for only by seeing the world in a new and different way (i.e., by the creation of a new paradigm), then the stage is set for a struggle between the adherents of the competing paradigms (Kuhn 1970a: 53, ch. 10). If the struggle results in the displacement of the old paradigm and the dominance of the new paradigm, then this period is viewed with hindsight as a period of scientific discovery and revolution. New textbooks rewrite the history of the field, students are trained to see the world according to the new paradigm, and the process repeats itself.

Some critics (Shapere 1971: 706; Toulmin 1970: 41) have questioned this description of scientific inquiry by challenging the sharp distinction between normal science and revolutionary science (what might be better termed extraordinary science [see Kuhn 1970a: 34]), arguing that the distinction is really a matter of degree and that such discontinuities are not as common as Kuhn implies. This criticism underlines the more general point that within paradigms there can be considerable variations and disagreement, and out of this process there can evolve what Kuhn would call revolutions. For Toulmin, these "revolutions" tend to be a product of many earlier changes; he therefore finds the process of change described by Kuhn incomplete because it does not explain how knowledge evolves through learning (1967: 339–346; 1970: 46). Blachowicz (1971: 182–183, 186–188) goes further, arguing that Kuhn so underestimates the amount of learning and changes that he must see theories as arising from a random process.

Kuhn has in part responded to the criticism by granting that there might be microrevolutions, but he is unwilling to abandon the more fundamental distinction between normal and revolutionary science and insists that normal science can involve considerable conceptual jettisoning without any rejection of the paradigm (see Kuhn 1970b: 249–259, 1970a: 250). He thereby rejects the more evolutionary notion of progress implied by Toulmin, maintaining instead that only certain anomalies and conceptual changes are revolutionary. Paradigm shifts, not variation and microrevolutions, bring about fundamental changes in thought.

These criticisms of Kuhn are primarily empirical and can only be answered by further research. It must be remembered that Kuhn's thesis is based on generalizing from his earlier work on the Copernican revolution (Kuhn 1957) and may not in fact apply to all other cases, as some have readily pointed out in the case of theories of matter (Shapere 1964: 387; Popper 1970: 55; Watkins 1970: 34). Yet one exception is hardly a disconfirmation. Kuhn's thesis needs systematic investigation in the physical sciences and should not be seen as having been "confirmed" or refuted by the discussion it has generated (L. P. Williams 1970: 50).

Keeping in mind the various qualifications and caveats that have been introduced, it should be clear that Kuhn provides a theoretically interesting and general conceptual framework for describing scientific inquiry. For international relations inquiry it suggests questions such as: Is the field dominated by a single paradigm? What is that paradigm? How did it displace the old one if there was an old paradigm? How does it guide theory construction, data making, and research? How do conceptual variation and change occur yet still remain within the paradigm? More important, Kuhn's framework provides a way of asking the major questions of this analysis – Is the dominant paradigm adequate? Is it producing knowledge? Before these last two questions can be addressed, a set of criteria for evaluating paradigms must be developed. Here Kuhn provides little aid.

Evaluating scientific inquiry

Evaluation differs from description in that its purpose is to apply a value criterion to a situation or object, whereas the purpose of description is empirical veracity.[4] Therefore, in order to evaluate scientific inquiry, some acceptable value criteria must be employed. Philosophers of science have spent a great deal of time attempting to delineate and justify such criteria. Although there are many disagreements among these philosophers, there is a certain minimal content on which they all agree. Part of this content includes a set of criteria for evaluating theories. Although there is dispute over the logical status of these criteria, there is not a dispute among either philosophers or practicing scientists about what these criteria actually state (see Braybrooke and Rosenberg 1972). It is upon this basis that criteria for evaluating paradigms can be erected.

The main criteria that these scholars accept rest on the assumption that science can produce knowledge. Part of Kuhn's analysis, however, led to a debate in philosophy of science over whether science is a rational enterprise that can claim to be producing knowledge. The part of Kuhn's analysis that caused the debate was his discussion of paradigm comparability and displacement. Kuhn appeared to argue that paradigms were not disproven but discarded on the basis of a struggle for power between the adherents of competing paradigms. Many critics took this argument to mean that Kuhn was maintaining that science was irrational and subjective.[5] In a later work, Kuhn attempted to defend himself by saying that although he maintained that paradigm displacement is a matter of persuasion, he did not mean to suggest "that there are not many good reasons for choosing one theory rather than another . . . These are, furthermore, reasons of exactly the kind standard in philosophy of science: accuracy, scope, simplicity, fruitfulness, and the like" (Kuhn 1970b: 261; see also 1977: 320–339). Kuhn (1970a: 186) maintained that what makes these reasons good is determined by the value component of the disciplinary matrix. This clarification makes it clear that Kuhn is willing to evaluate paradigms by employing the standard criteria

---

[4] On the differences and similarities of evaluative and empirical analysis see Toulmin (1950); on the relationship between evaluation and value criteria see Urmson (1968: ch. 5) and Frohock (1974: ch. 3).

[5] See Scheffler (1967); Lakatos and Musgrave (1970). Also see Shapere (1964, 1971); Popper (1970); and Shimony (1976).

used in science to determine the adequacy of theories. Therefore, the basic criterion that a paradigm must produce knowledge can be employed to evaluate paradigm adequacy. In order to determine exactly how this basic criterion can be applied and to understand what the debate between Kuhn and his critics has been about, it is necessary to review briefly some of the epistemological arguments that have been made about the confirmation of theories.

The earliest respectable view about confirmation was that theories are proven when there are a sufficient number of facts to support them.[6] The basic fallacy of this position is known as *the riddle of induction*. This debate over induction goes back at least to the time of John Stuart Mill. The debate was replayed in the twentieth century when Rudolph Carnap attempted to derive a logical position asserting that hypotheses could be proven.[7] Carnap, however, was unsuccessful in this effort; the consensus of philosophers of science is that such confirmation is impossible to achieve.

Sir Karl Popper (1935) attempted to place confirmation of theories on a firmer logical foundation by introducing the principle of falsification. According to Popper, a theory is a theory only if it specifies in advance what would be accepted as disproof of the theory. Experimentation in Popper's view never proves a theory but simply fails to falsify it. Popper's principle provides a clear, precise, and logically sound rule for evaluating theories. It was not until Kuhn introduced the concept of paradigm that the principle was seriously challenged.

Despite the fact that Kuhn's claim of paradigm incommensurability has been rejected in part because of the work of Scheffler (1967), the challenge to Popper has carried more weight (see Lakatos 1970). Kuhn (1970a: 146–148) has attempted to show that Popper's rule is simply not followed in the physical sciences. Theories and the paradigms out of which they arise do not stipulate what will count as falsifying evidence. Furthermore, when falsifying evidence is encountered, it does not lead to a rejection of the paradigm. Finally, according to Kuhn no paradigm has ever been "rejected" unless there is a competing paradigm ready to take its place. Popper's (1970: 52–53, 56–58) response is not that this does not occur, but that it need not necessarily occur and will not if scientists are trained properly. What

---

6 An excellent history of this debate is Lakatos (1970).
7 This is obviously a simplification of Carnap's work. The two books that adequately summarize his early work on this question are Carnap (1952, 1962).

most of the debate has been about, then, is how to confirm competing theories that may emerge from competing paradigms and their research programs.

On what basis can one decide to follow one research program rather than another? Lakatos (1970) has attempted to solve the problem by synthesizing Kuhn's work with the standard view of philosophy of science. He has given a major concession to Kuhn in that he admits that confirmation is a matter of decision and not logic.[8] He comes to this conclusion because he maintains that theories and paradigms can produce an infinite number of plausible ad hoc hypotheses to account for falsifying evidence. Nevertheless, he does think that the decision can be based on rules that are clearly stipulated in advance. Among the most important rules are the following: (1) T' (rival theory) has excess empirical content; that is, it predicts novel experimental outcomes (anomalies) that are improbable or forbidden by T (original theory); (2) T' explains all the unrefuted content of T; and (3) some of the excess content of T' is corroborated (Lakatos 1970: 116). Lakatos has thus provided a set of principles that can be used to compare theories. In this scheme, paradigms and their research programs can be evaluated on the basis of the theories they produce.

The philosophical problem over which there is much contention is whether there is some logical foundation for rules that tell scientists when to stop introducing ad hoc explanations or theories, or whether the foundation is merely sociological consensus (see Worrall 1978; Musgrave 1978; Koertge 1978; and Feyerabend 1976). The latter position saves science as a rational enterprise, but whether science can have a more solid logical foundation is a matter of hot debate. At a minimum, the justification of Lakatos' rules could rest on the kind of instrumentalist argument often associated with Toulmin (1953, 1972: 478–503).

This justification rests on the acceptance by philosophers of science and scientists of the following type of argument: (1) the purpose of science is to produce knowledge; (2) knowledge itself is a semantic concept; that is, one can determine whether something is known by stipulatively defining what is meant by knowledge and establishing decision-rules on how to employ the word;[9] and (3) what is meant by knowledge is (at least in part) empirical corroboration of hypotheses.

---

[8] Some argue that this grants too much to Kuhn; see Musgrave (1976: 482).

[9] For a justification for this position in regard to the word *truth* see Tarski (1949).

A theory or a research program that has the most corroborated hypotheses and the least anomalies is obviously the best or the most promising one to use in order to achieve the purpose of science.

In social science, particularly in international relations inquiry, the problem of evaluating paradigms turns not so much on comparing the corroborated empirical content of rival theories and their research program but on finding any theory with a corroborated content of any significance. Since a paradigm is used to produce theories, it is possible to evaluate the adequacy of a paradigm in terms of the corroborated hypotheses it produces. This is the basic criterion that will be used here to evaluate paradigms. However, as Lakatos suggests, applying this criterion is a matter of decision. How many corroborated hypotheses must there be? How much paradigm-directed research must there be, and for how long must this research continue before a paradigm can be declared inadequate? All of these are unanswered questions in the field of international relations. But it does seem reasonable to assume that if various theories and hypotheses produced by the use of a paradigm fail over time to produce a significant number of findings, the problem may very well be that the picture of the world being used by scholars is simply inadequate. If the science of international relations is to be systematic, it is incumbent upon scholars to examine periodically what paradigm (if any) is dominating the field and to evaluate its usefulness in the terms outlined. In a discipline where there are very few corroborated hypotheses, there will always be disagreements over whether a paradigm and its research program are useful. But attempts at evaluation are important because they provide empirical evidence that scholars can use to come to a rational conclusion. As more research is conducted and more evaluations of it are made, a trend may become clear and the disagreements will probably subside. It is in this spirit that the present evaluation is offered.

2 The role of the realist paradigm in the development of a scientific study of international relations

Kuhn's analysis implies that a proper understanding of the historical development of any science involves identifying the rise of a paradigm and how it is displaced. In this chapter, a historical interpretation of how the scientific study of international relations is conducted will be offered by drawing on a number of Kuhn's insights. Although the study of international relations can be said to go back at least to the time of Thucydides, the starting date of this analysis will be the formal creation of international relations inquiry as an institutionalized discipline. This is commonly taken to have occurred in 1919, with the creation of "the world's first Chair in International Politics . . . at the University College of Wales, Aberystwyth" (Porter 1972: ix).[1]

In the interpretation, emphasis will be placed on delineating the role the realist paradigm has played in international relations inquiry, and the relationship between that paradigm and idealism and the behavioral revolt. The resulting analysis shows how the idealist paradigm helped institutionalize the discipline and instill it with purpose, how the anomaly of World War II led to the displacement of the idealist paradigm and to the dominance of the realist paradigm, and how the behavioral revolt did not change the paradigm of the field but provided a conception of scientific methodology. Only historical examples will be given here to demonstrate the plausibility of the interpretation, but systematic evidence will be presented in chapters 4 through 6.

---

[1] See Morgenthau and Thompson (1950: 3); W. Olson (1972: 12) and Kirk (1947: 2–5) for similar justifications.

The idealist phase

The twentieth-century history of international relations inquiry can be roughly divided into three stages: the idealist phase; the realist tradition; and the "behavioral" revolt (see Bull 1972: 33). The first stage of international relations inquiry was dominated by the idealist paradigm.[2] The immediate origins of this paradigm stemmed from the experience of World War I and the belief that such a conflagration could and must be avoided in the future (Kirk 1947: 3–4; Fox 1949: 68). Its fundamental belief was that by using reason, humans could overcome such problems as war (Carr 1939 [1964: 25–27]; Dunn 1949: 81). All humans were seen as having a common interest that formed a "nascent world community" (Wolfers 1951 [1962: 86]). Given a basic harmony of interest among all people, a system of peace could be established under the proper conditions. The scholar's purpose was to reveal this fundamental truth and to delineate those conditions so that it would be possible to establish a set of institutions that by their very structure would force nations to act peacefully and thereby cause a revolution in the way international politics was conducted (Carr 1939 [1964: 27–31]).

The best-known intellectual force behind this paradigm was, of course, Woodrow Wilson, and his specific theory of democracy as the cause of peace and dictatorship as the cause of war formed the heart of the paradigm.[3] According to this theory, the masses never benefit from war, and with proper enlightenment they will realize this. Through education and contact with others, ignorance and prejudice would be eliminated. Through the spread of democracy, the masses would prevent sinister interests from promulgating wars. Finally, the institutions that prevented violence at the domestic level could be created at the global level to resolve disputes nonviolently.[4] These ideas were embodied in the League of Nations, the Permanent Court of International Justice, and in the emphasis on international law,

---

[2] The terms *idealists* and *utopians* were never used by those scholars who were guided by the paradigm. It was applied to them by the realists, particularly by E. H. Carr (1939).

[3] Carr (1939 [1964: 8, 14, 27, 32–38]); Wolfers (1962: 81–82, 234); Kirk (1947: 3); Fox (1949: 68–77); Dougherty and Pfaltzgraff (1971: 6–7). For a general review of the sources of the paradigm see Carr (1939 [1964: ch. 2]). For Wilson's theory of democracy see Wolfers (1951 [1962: 86]); and Waltz (1959: 110–123).

[4] For documentation on the role of education, contact, democracy, and global institutions in idealist thought see Fox (1949: 70) and Bull (1972: 34).

arbitration, disarmament, collective security, and peaceful change (Fox 1949: 74–75). Together, these theory-laden beliefs constituted a research program for idealist scholars.

Wilson's ideas were widely shared by others in the United Kingdom and the United States and adopted by a group of scholars whose conscious purpose was the investigation of the major tenets of the paradigm in order to better promote its normative goals. They attempted to create an analytical model of a system characterized by peace and then to show how the present world system deviated from that model (Fox 1949: 77; Dunn 1949: 93). Among the major scholars sharing this paradigm were Alfred Zimmern, S. H. Bailey, Philip Noel-Baker, and David Mitrany of the United Kingdom and James T. Shotwell, Pitman Potter, and Parker T. Moon of the United States (Bull 1972: 34).

Inquiry under this paradigm was of two kinds: historical and legal-institutional. The historical aspect at times emphasized the "mistakes" of history in the hope that rational knowledge of these mistakes would prevent their reoccurrence. James Bryce's *International Relations* (1922) was one of the popular texts of the time and reflected this historical emphasis (Fox 1949: 75–76; W. Olson 1972: 19). Knowledge of the past was only part of the answer to the problem of peace. If history provided a negative example, the study of international organization was to provide the positive example. Since the idealist paradigm guided scholars toward a normative and prescriptive analysis, the study of international organization consisted of the role international institutions should and could play in establishing an era of peace (Kirk 1947: 4–5). The best reflection of this view was Alfred Zimmern's *The League of Nations and the Rule of Law* (1936).[5] The dominance of the paradigm is reflected by the fact that the two most popular approaches to teaching international politics in the United States during the interwar period were current events and diplomatic history and international law and organization (Thompson 1952). In addition, there was a strong emphasis on interdisciplinary study, including anthropology, sociology, economics, demography, geography, law, psychology, and even animal behavior (see Kirk 1947: 14–21).

The idealist phase was important in terms of institutionalizing the

---

[5] Cited in Bull (1972: 35). For a short introduction to the idealist perspective see Alfred Zimmern, "Introductory Report to the Discussions in 1935," in Zimmern (1939: 7–13); reprinted in Morgenthau and Thompson (1950: 18–24).

field and creating the emphasis on peace and war. The idealist phase reflects characteristics of many of the early forerunners of a scientific discipline – for example, alchemy. Both idealism and alchemy share the common characteristic of establishing a separate field of inquiry and making the major purpose of that field highly practical and valuable to laymen. In many ways, the purpose of the idealist paradigm was to provide a panacea for the major problem of the early twentieth century – war.

The realist tradition

Since the idealists tested their "theories" not in the laboratory but in the real world, by attempting to guide policy, the anomaly that led to a scientific crisis and eventual displacement of the paradigm was the inability of international law and organization to prevent World War II (see Kirk 1947: 6–7; Fox 1949: 67–68). It was the background of the war that made E. H. Carr's *The Twenty Years' Crisis* (1939) a devastating and seminal critique of idealism. He began by calling for a true science of international politics and maintained that in order to have a science, inquiry must take account of how things actually are (i.e., of "reality") and not solely of how things should be (1939 [1964: 9]). He stated that it was the idealists' inability to distinguish aspiration from reality that made idealism an inappropriate perspective for either the study or conduct of international politics. Carr maintained that the purpose of realism is to understand and adapt to the forces that guide behavior and warned that such a perspective might lead to a conservative acceptance of the status quo, but that in this stage it was a "necessary corrective to the exuberance of utopianism" (1939 [1964: 10; also ch. 6]). He then went on to shatter systematically the "illusions" of the utopians, or idealists, by employing a type of Marxist analysis that became more evident in his later work and by pointing out the need to consider the importance of power in international relations.[6] Carr's work, however, was essentially a critique and offered only the vaguest outline of an alternative picture of the world (see W. Olson 1972: 19).

Others besides Carr were reacting to the same events, and it was these other writers along with Carr who began to develop the realist

---

[6] For examples of Marxist influence in Carr's later work see E. H. Carr (1947, 1951); on the importance of power see Carr (1939: ch. 8).

paradigm. These leading writers and their most influential works were: Frederick Schuman, *International Politics* (1933); Harold Nicolson, *Diplomacy* (1939); E. H. Carr, *The Twenty Years' Crisis* (1939); Reinhold Niebuhr, *Christianity and Power Politics* (1940); Georg Schwarzenberger, *Power Politics* (1941); Nicholas Spykman, *America's Strategy in World Politics* (1942); Martin Wight, *Power Politics* (1946); Hans J. Morgenthau, *Politics Among Nations* (1948); George F. Kennan, *American Diplomacy* (1951); and Herbert Butterfield, *Christianity, Diplomacy and War* (1953).[7]

These writers represent the attempt of an entire generation to understand and express their most fundamental beliefs about international politics. Together they were successful in displacing the idealist paradigm by accounting for the anomaly of World War II in terms of power politics.

Hans J. Morgenthau best expressed, promulgated, and synthesized the work of these writers. Because his *Politics Among Nations* (1948) was so comprehensive, systematic, and theoretical, it became the exemplar of this group. With the advantage of hindsight, there can be no doubt that Morgenthau's work was the single most important vehicle for establishing the dominance of the realist paradigm within the field. Recent historians of the field all agree on this point. Stanley Hoffmann, writing in 1960 (p. 30), maintained that Morgenthau's realist theory had occupied the center of the stage in the United States for the previous ten years.

Dougherty and Pfaltzgraff (1971: 12, 15) assert that *Politics Among Nations* was the most influential textbook within the field. Finally,

---

[7] This list is taken basically from Bull (1972: 38). It agrees fairly closely with the classification of Dougherty and Pfaltzgraff (1971: 1–30 and ch. 3). I have taken the liberty of adding Frederick Schuman to the list; W. Olson (1972: 19) lists his work as one of the "landmarks" in the field, and Dougherty and Pfaltzgraff (1971: 74–75) appropriately classify it as realist. Also, I have substituted Niebuhr's *Christianity and Power Politics* (1940) as the most influential of his realist work for Bull's selection of *The Children of Light and the Children of Darkness* (1945). Because it played a prominent role in debunking utopianism and pacifism in American Protestantism, Niebuhr's early work was more influential. On this question see Bingham (1961) and Meyer (1960). Finally, I have removed F. A. Voight's *Unto Caesar* (1939) from the list; Bull (1972: 38) himself admits this has not stood the test of time. With these three exceptions the list is the same as that of Hedley Bull. Schuman (1933), Carr (1939), Wight (1946), and Morgenthau (1948) were labeled by W. Olson (1972: 19) as landmarks in the field. These works can be viewed as the most influential works within the field in both the United Kingdom and the United States in the early post-World War II period.

William C. Olson, writing in 1972, states that *Politics Among Nations* "was by all odds the most influential textbook of the early post-war period and is thought by many, if indeed not most, *to have transformed the field from idealist advocacy to realist analysis*" (Olson 1972: 19–20), emphasis added).

In order to account for the anomaly of World War II, Morgenthau attempted to delineate those realistic laws of behavior that Carr claimed the idealists had ignored. He maintained that all politics was a struggle for power, that nations strived to protect their national interests, and that the power of a nation(s) could be most effectively limited by the power of another nation(s) (Morgenthau 1960, 1973: chs. 1 and 11).[8] In delineating these general "laws," Morgenthau provided a view of the world the international relations scholar was investigating and provided answers to what Masterman (1970: 62) has said are the major questions of any paradigm: What are the fundamental units of which the world is composed? How do these units interact with each other? What conception of the world should be employed to answer these questions? Morgenthau's answers provided a view of the world that made three fundamental assumptions:

1. Nation-states or their decision makers are the most important actors for understanding international relations.
2. There is a sharp distinction between domestic politics and international politics.
3. International relations is the struggle for power and peace. Understanding how and why that struggle occurs and suggesting ways for regulating it is the purpose of the discipline. All research that is not at least indirectly related to this purpose is trivial.

The picture of the world provided by the realist paradigm has been aptly summarized by numerous scholars in the field (see K. W.

---

[8] The third edition of *Politics Among Nations* is used throughout this book for purposes of direct quotation. The changes in the various editions are minor, consisting mostly of updating the analysis with current events and analyzing those events in light of the paradigm. For example, Morgenthau writes in the preface to the third edition: "I have felt the need to change the emphasis here or there while leaving assumptions, tenets, and theoretical structure intact." In order to ensure that the quotes are central to Morgenthau's analysis, the fifth edition (1973) will also be cited. The most recent edition is the 5th revised edition (1975), which removes a number of minor changes in the 5th edition, thereby making it even more similar to the 3rd (see preface to the 5th revised edition).

Thompson 1960; Tucker 1952; T. W. Robinson 1967; Platig 1967; and Taylor 1978a) and will be discussed in chapter 3. What is important at this point is that acceptance of the three assumptions in the World War II period constituted, in Kuhn's terms, a revolution in the way scholars viewed their world. The idealists, for example, did not believe that nations were the most important actors (Wolfers 1951 [1962: 86]). To them, the most important actors were individuals and the emerging international organizations that would replace the nation-states as the organizing unit of civilization (Fox 1949: 68–71; see Bryce 1922: lectures 7 and 8). Studying these institutions and improving their processes would bring about peace. Nor did the idealists accept the second assumption. Indeed, their entire purpose was to make international politics more like domestic politics, as was emphasized by Wilson's hopes for a League of Nations (Carr 1939: ch. 2). Finally, the assumption that international politics consisted of a struggle for power and peace was not accepted. Although the idealists believed that some selfish persons acted in terms of power politics, they did not believe that the real world worked this way. They did not believe such behavior was in harmony with the real world, because it led to war. What was in harmony with the real world could be determined by using reason to establish a new global order (Wolfers 1951 [1962: 86]). This, of course, was the way to achieve the goal of the field – the establishment of peace.

By the early 1950s, however, Morgenthau and the other realists succeeded in getting their assumptions about the world accepted by other scholars in the United States and the United Kingdom. The acceptance of the new paradigm led the field to develop the normal science characteristics of a discipline. Having settled on a picture of the world that emphasized certain phenomena and ignored others, scholars began to develop and test alternative theories and propositions about international politics that rested on the (untested) validity of the paradigm's three fundamental assumptions. These theoretical explanations, of which Morgenthau's was only one, were used to explain contemporary and past events and were periodically revised on the basis of the adequacy of these explanations. As research continued, the field became more specialized, with fewer attempts at "grand theory" à la Morgenthau and more investigations of the limited topics originally delineated by Morgenthau and the other early realists as legitimate research areas. In the 1950s and 1960s this division of labor, which is often confused with competing schools of thought, consisted of: the study of foreign policy; the study of systemic processes such as the balance of power; the related study of the causes of war; the study of bargaining and strategy such as deterrence; and the study of supranationalism, including integration and international law and organization. Each of these topics or subfields, and the way they have been handled, can be interpreted as attempts to articulate the realist paradigm and make that picture of the world more detailed.

The contribution of the realist paradigm to the development of a scientific study of international relations has been, first, to point out that science must be empirical and theoretical, not normative and narrowly historical, and second, to provide a picture of the world (i.e., a paradigm) which has permitted the field to develop a common research agenda and to follow it systematically and somewhat cumulatively. The power of the realist paradigm to guide the development of the field toward normal science has been overlooked by scholars because of a preoccupation with and misunderstanding of the "behavioral" revolt. The nature of that revolt and the relationship between it and the realist paradigm will now be examined.

The realist tradition and the behavioral revolt

The term *behavioral revolt* is somewhat inappropriate to describe the conflict that arose between the traditionalists and nontraditionalists in international relations inquiry, since traditionalists also study behavior, not just legal documents and institutional flow charts. The debate is not over whether behavior should be the focus of inquiry; nor is it really a debate over empirical versus normative concerns. Rather, as will be shown, the debate is over scientific methodology. In this light it is often tempting to call the nontraditionalists the scientific-oriented, which is occasionally done (see J. D. Singer 1972b). This would be unfair to the traditionalists, however, who long ago claimed the scientific label (see Carr 1939). Since the term *behavioralists* has been widely used in international relations inquiry, and everyone seems to understand who are the behavioralists and who are the traditionalists, the term will be used here despite some of its confusing connotations.[9]

---

[9] On the use of the term in international relations see J. D. Singer (1966) and Klaus Knorr and James N. Rosenau (1969a).

In the late 1950s and early 1960s the behavioral revolt began to make its influence felt.[10] Among the first major scholars reflecting this new emphasis were Morton Kaplan and Karl Deutsch. Their work reflected the three main characteristics of the new approach: a concern with philosophy of science; an attempt to borrow from the physical and more "developed" social sciences; and an attempt to apply mathematical, particularly statistical, analysis to international relations inquiry. Kaplan's *System and Process in International Politics* (1957), for example, reflected the first two characteristics.[11] The concern with philosophy of science led Kaplan to attempt to develop models of the international system. The attempt to achieve the rigor of physical science led him and many others to borrow conceptual frameworks from these other fields and apply them to international relations (Bull 1972: 40). Kaplan borrowed the systems language of W. Ross Ashby's *Design for a Brain* (1952).[12] Deutsch also borrowed from the physical sciences, using communications and cybernetics theory.[13] Unlike Kaplan, however, Deutsch (1956) attempted to employ statistical tests as a means of determining whether the evidence supported a hypothesis. The work of Kaplan and Deutsch, taken together, can be seen as setting the pattern for the type of analysis conducted by the adherents of the new behavioral approach.[14]

What the behavioralists wanted was a more systematic way of testing explanations. They believed that if their procedures were

[10] For example, Knorr and Rosenau (1969b: 5) state: "the impact of the behavioral revolution upon the international field was delayed. Not until the 1960s did its vitality and practices become prominent." This delay occurs despite the call of Guetzkow (1950) for a more scientific approach.

[11] It should be noted that some behavioral scholars, although they grant that Kaplan claims to be scientific, maintain that his understanding and application of scientific procedure is faulty. See in particular M. Levy (1969).

[12] Kaplan acknowledges the influence of Ashby in Kaplan (1967: 150).

[13] See Karl W. Deutsch (1964, 1953) and Karl Deutsch et al. (1957). The influence of cybernetics on Deutsch came from Norbert Wiener. For an overview of cybernetics theory proper see Wiener (1954).

[14] Kaplan's and Deutsch's work is taken as an indicator because it gave rise to a sustained movement that adopted the scientific or behavioral approach to international relations. Earlier mathematical work such as that of F. W. Lancaster (1916) or Lewis Richardson (re-issued 1960a, 1960b) did not give rise to a sustained movement (see Burns [1972: 73ff.]). Likewise Quincy Wright's *A Study of War* (1942), while clearly employing the behavioral approach, is better seen as a forerunner of the movement, since the type of analysis he employed was not greatly copied until the 1960s. Guetzkow's (1950) early call clearly stems from his social psychology training, and hence can be seen partly as an outside influence.

followed, truly scientific and cumulative knowledge could be gained. The procedures, which were most controversial, consisted of the use of quantitative analysis to test hypotheses. In addition, many behavioralists were not willing to grant that the traditional method produces scientific knowledge, but at best only untested conjecture (see J. D. Singer 1969: 70–72).

From the behavioralist perspective, what was in contention was not the three fundamental assumptions of the realist paradigm but how the realists had conceived of science, particularly scientific methodology. The traditionalists agreed; Hedley Bull (1966: 361), speaking for the traditionalists, characterized the debate as one between "explicit reliance upon the exercise of judgment" and "strict standards of verification and proof"; he maintained that confining the field to the latter would make it impossible to say anything of significance.[15]

If the conclusion that the debate was over method and not substance is accurate, then in Kuhn's terms it would be incorrect to think of the behavioral revolt as a paradigm-displacing event.[16] The picture of international relations provided by the realist paradigm has not been displaced, nor for that matter has it been seriously challenged. Klaus Knorr and James Rosenau provide evidence that the picture has not changed. They state that the scholars engaged in the debate do not challenge each other about the way they identify international phenomena (1969a: 4).[17] Knorr and Rosenau (1969a: 13) say that while authors have similar conceptions of the subject matter they do not have at all similar conceptions of scientific methodology. Therefore, Knorr and Rosenau (1969a: 12) rightly conclude that "it is the mode of analysis, not its subject matter, that is the central issue." If it is the mode of analysis and not the subject matter that is the central issue,

---

[15] Morgenthau's position is generally in agreement with Bull. See Morgenthau (1973: vii–viii, 1967).

[16] For the view that behavioralism is a new paradigm see Lijphart (1974). Lijphart (1974: 61), however, agrees that behavioralism did not introduce new substance in the field when he asks, "Can we regard behaviorism as a paradigm-based school if it does not possess any substantive content?" Unfortunately, Lijphart never seriously addresses this question. It is necessary to distinguish the world view of a field from its use of the scientific method; otherwise all the physical sciences would have the same paradigm.

[17] For additional exchanges in the debate see the other essays in Knorr and Rosenau (1969a), particularly those by Kaplan, Levy, Vital, M. Haas, and Jervis. Also see Wight (1966); O. R. Young (1969); and Russett (1969). For a review of the debate see Finnegan (1972b).

then it cannot be said that the behavioral revolt displaced the realist paradigm. What the behavioralists attempted to displace was not the paradigm but the methods used to determine the adequacy of the paradigm.

The amount of attention the behavioral revolt has received has tended to obfuscate the role the realist paradigm has played and continues to play in international relations inquiry. With the exception of the methodological debate, much of the work in the field since 1948 bears a remarkable resemblance to what Kuhn has called "normal science." In this interpretation international relations inquiry in the last thirty years or so can be viewed as an attempt to articulate the realist paradigm in light of research, while at the same time learning and debating what constitutes scientific research. This view suggests that the field has been far more coherent, systematic, and even cumulative than all the talk about contending approaches and theories implies (see Knorr and Rosenau 1969b; Dougherty and Pfatzgraff 1971; and Starr 1974: 339, 351).

The basis of this coherence stems from the dominance of the realist paradigm. That paradigm provided a picture of the world that scholars in the 1950s and 1960s used to focus upon certain phenomena out of all possible events and to create a manageable enterprise. Morgenthau provided a particular set of concepts, explanations, and topics of inquiry that articulated the paradigm. Scholarly activity in the 1950s and 1960s can be interpreted as clarifying and systematizing Morgenthau's concepts and explanations; providing alternative concepts and explanations that, while at times very different from those employed by Morgenthau, are still with few exceptions consistent with the three fundamental assumptions of the realist paradigm; and conducting research in either the traditional or scientific mode that was then used to advance the conceptual and theoretical work. The behavioralists can be interpreted as systematizing realist work according to their own criteria of adequacy and then quantitatively testing the hypotheses they derived from the paradigm.

While the application of Kuhn's analysis contributes to the preceding insights, it should also be clear that Kuhn's own analysis is quite limited when applied to embryonic sciences such as international relations. Of equal importance to paradigm development and displacement, in terms of the energy they command and the debates they generate, are discussions of what it means to be a science. While Kuhn would probably claim that such debates subside once a science

42

matures, one may suspect that he underestimates the impact of methodological and measurement changes in the physical sciences and mathematics.

Conclusion

This survey of the history of the field since 1919 has shown that each of the three stages – the idealist stage, the realist stage, and the behavioral revolt – has had an impact on developing a science of international relations. The idealist phase helped institutionalize the field and established the emphasis of the discipline on questions of peace and war. The realist challenge to idealism was to state that "wishing for peace does not make it occur." The realists pointed out that the development of utopian strategies to end war could not hope to succeed, because they ignored basic laws of human nature and behavior. The implication of the realist critique was that in order to eliminate war it is first necessary to discover the laws that govern human behavior and the idealists were not aware of these laws or had a misconception of what they were. The realists attempted to move the field from purely normative analysis to more empirical analysis. They did this by displacing idealism and providing a paradigm that clearly specified a picture of international politics and a set of topics of inquiry that if properly researched would delineate the laws of international behavior. The most comprehensive list of those laws appeared in Morgenthau's "theory" of power politics. The behavioral revolt challenged not the picture of the world that the realists had provided but the realist conception of what constitutes an adequate scientific theory and the procedures used to "verify" that theory. Borrowing from the more advanced social and natural sciences, the behavioralists attempted to apply the principles of philosophy of science accepted in these other fields to international relations. The behavioralists asserted that explanations should be stated in such a form as to be both falsifiable and testable, that evidence should be systematically collected to test them, and that in light of the tests, explanations and the theories from which they were derived should be evaluated and reformulated. The behavioralists' own work was essentially to apply these procedures to the subject matter, but within the confines of the realist paradigm. The behavioralists then attempted to bring the scientific practices of the field more into line with the practices of the physical sciences, and most observers would probably agree that they have been fairly successful in this attempt. Keeping in mind that summaries are always oversimplifications, it can be concluded that the idealists provided the goal of the discipline, the realists provided the paradigm, and the behavioralists provided the scientific principles.

3 Research design: defining and operationalizing the realist paradigm

While the Kuhnian interpretation of the intellectual history of the field, presented in the previous chapter, appears plausible, its accuracy has not been tested in a systematic and falsifiable fashion. This is important because some critics of Kuhn (e.g., Shapere 1964, 1971) have argued that the paradigm concept is so vague and ambiguous that a specific paradigm cannot be easily identified in a discipline. In this chapter these potential problems will be addressed by explicitly deriving testable propositions that must be true if the Kuhnian interpretation of international relations inquiry is true; demonstrating that the definition of the realist paradigm employed in this analysis is valid; and operationalizing that definition so that it is possible to determine which works are guided by the paradigm.

Deriving propositions

If an interpretation is to be adequately tested, it is necessary to ensure that important and not trivial propositions are logically derived from the interpretation and that the research design constitutes a valid test of the proposition. A number of propositions can be found in the interpretation presented in chapter 2. If the more important or controversial propositions in the interpretation are corroborated, there is more confidence in the adequacy of the interpretation than if some less controversial propositions (such as the proposition that the realist displaced the idealist paradigm) were corroborated. The most controversial and important proposition in the historical interpretation is that the realist paradigm has guided international relations inquiry after the behavioral revolt.

In order to test this claim, it is necessary to define more precisely the time period to which it applies, and what is meant by *international relations inquiry*. To assess the claim that the behavioral revolt was not a paradigm change, the 1950s and 1960s (the major period of the revolt) will be examined in the data-based tests. To incorporate all of the 1970s would make a more comprehensive test but would involve so much data that it would not be feasible to collect it at this time. Nevertheless, the literature reviews in chapters 4, 5, and 8 will deal with the more recent research.

A more precise definition of international relations can be constructed by examining the major activities of scholars. Kuhn (1970a: ch. 3) points out that there are three major activities of any discipline – theory construction, data collections, and research. Therefore, if the major proposition of this analysis is true, one would expect the following three propositions to be true:

1. The realist paradigm guided theory construction in the field of international relations in the 1950s and 1960s.
2. The realist paradigm guided data making in the field of international relations in the 1950s and 1960s.
3. The realist paradigm guided research in the field of international relations in the 1950s and 1960s.

These three propositions specify much more clearly the spatial–temporal domain of the major proposition and what is meant by the realist paradigm "dominating" international relations inquiry. Since the essential activities of any science are theory construction, data making, and research, it can be concluded that if the realist paradigm guides these three activities, then it is dominating international relations inquiry.

A second problem that has to be solved is how to test the three propositions so that it is possible to determine if behavioralists as well as traditionalists have been guided by the realist paradigm. This problem can be solved by sampling. The first proposition on theory construction will be tested in such a manner that both traditional and behavioral work will be included. The second and third propositions on data making and research will be tested only on behavioral work, because there is more doubt that behavioralists have been guided by the realist paradigm. Also, given the method of the traditionalists, it is difficult to distinguish operationally when the traditionalist is engaged in theory construction, data collection, or research (hypothesis testing). This research design reflects the behavioral assertion that traditional work is really just theory construction through the use of argument and impressionistic evidence without the attempt to collect data systematically and test hypotheses (see Singer 1969: 68). Although traditionalists strongly disagree with this assertion, accepting it here is necessary to simplify the testing procedure and does not bias the results of the tests. This is because traditional work is adequately covered in the first proposition, and the findings of the second and third propositions apply only to the work of the behavioralists.

Defining the realist paradigm

Since a paradigm involves a set of fundamental assumptions made in the exemplar, the realist paradigm can be defined by delineating the fundamental assumptions in *Politics Among Nations*, as was done in the previous chapter. This is a valid procedure if *Politics Among Nations* was the most influential of all realist writings. A recent survey by Richard Finnegan (1972a) of international relations scholars confirms this assertion.

Finnegan (1972a: 8–9) finds that the leading scholarly work cited by more scholars than any other is *Politics Among Nations*. Over one-third of the scholars chose this book. The next ranking book was Kaplan (1957), which received only 14 percent of the choices. Likewise, when asked to choose the single scholar who has contributed more to the field than any other person, more respondents chose Morgenthau (46.7 percent). The scholar who received the second greatest number of choices was Karl Deutsch, but he was chosen by only 25.2 percent of the respondents.

It was also shown in chapter 2 that *Politics Among Nations* had the three characteristics of an exemplar; namely, recognition as an unprecedented work (that displaces a competing paradigm); attraction of an enduring group of followers; and use as a textbook.[1] Since this is the case, it appears reasonable to assume that *Politics Among Nations* is a valid indicator of the realist paradigm.

The realist paradigm can be defined by delineating the fundamental assumptions made in that text. Because Morgenthau's text provides a theoretical explanation of international politics, it makes many

---

[1] Kuhn (1970a: 10). For its "recognition as an unprecedented work" see W. C. Olson (1972: 19–20). "Attraction of an enduring group of followers" should be an obvious fact to anyone familiar with the field. For evidence of its "use as a textbook" see Dougherty and Pfaltzgraff (1971: 12, 15).

assumptions. Not all of these assumptions are *fundamental* assumptions. For example, Morgenthau's (1960: 173–223; 1973: 172–221) assumption that the balance of power can sometimes be a useful mechanism for maintaining peace is not a fundamental assumption, because it rests on certain prior assumptions – for example, only nations can balance power. A fundamental assumption is one that forms the foundation upon which the entire edifice of a discipline is built. In order to define the fundamental assumptions of the realist paradigm, it is necessary to delineate the phenomena it focuses upon.

Morgenthau focuses on two phenomena: nation-states and the struggle for power and peace. In doing so, he makes three fundamental assumptions delineated in chapter 2.

The first assumption Morgenthau makes is that nation-states are the most important actors for understanding international relations. Why Morgenthau makes this assumption can be demonstrated by a simple syllogism:

1. Politics consists of a struggle for power, and in order to be a political actor a person or group must wield significant political power (true by definition).
2. In international politics, during the modern state system, only nations wield significant power (empirical statement).
3. Therefore, in international politics, during the modern state system, only nations are actors (conclusion).

Given the first two premises, the conclusion follows logically.[2]

Morgenthau's second assumption is that there is a sharp distinction between domestic politics and international politics. The use of the concept *international politics* as a way of demarcating the field assumes by its definition that there is something about politics that occurs outside nations that makes it different from politics that occurs inside nations. Morgenthau makes the distinction throughout *Politics Among Nations* (1960: 27, 38–39, 435–440, 501–518; 1973: 27, 40, 429–433, 481–497). In *Dilemmas of Politics*, Morgenthau (1958: 47) maintains that

---

[2] In order to determine whether Morgenthau actually makes these premises and the conclusion (which is assumption 1), a textual analysis, reported in Vasquez (1974: 70–74), was conducted. That analysis demonstrates that Morgenthau accepts not only the two premises but the conclusion of the syllogism as well. The appropriate quotations can be found for the first premise in Morgenthau (1960, 1973: 27); for the second premise, Morgenthau (1960: 9–10; 1973: 10; 1958: 67–68); and for the conclusion, Morgenthau (1960, 1973: 27–28).

the distinction "exerts a persuasive influence on the practice of international politics as well as upon its theoretical understanding." Morgenthau points out in the same work that it is specifically the decentralized or anarchic system of international society that makes domestic politics different from international politics. Domestic politics is played in an arena where the government can legitimately and effectively regulate the actions of the actors, but in the world arena no such regulation occurs (Morgenthau 1960: 501–509 and ch. 19; 1973: 481–489 and ch. 19). In international politics, only nations have power, and their power can only be limited by the power of other nations. The sovereignty of nations, therefore, has an important effect on the way politics is played; hence a theory of international politics cannot be the same as a theory of domestic politics. It can be concluded that Morgenthau does in fact make what was delineated as the second assumption.

Morgenthau's third assumption is that international relations is the struggle for power and peace. Morgenthau (1960: 23; 1973: 24) clearly states that the two concepts around which *Politics Among Nations* is planned are power and peace. It is evident from the following quotation that to Morgenthau (1960: 38; 1973: 40) international relations is a struggle for power and peace: "All history shows that nations active in international politics are continuously preparing for, actively involved in, or recovering from organized violence in the form of war." The fact that Morgenthau defines the purpose of international relations inquiry in these limited terms and excludes other forms of international behavior by definition is evident from the following statement:

> Two conclusions follow from this concept of international politics. First, not every action that a nation performs with respect to another nation is of a political nature. Many such activities are normally undertaken without any consideration of power, nor do they normally affect the power of the nation undertaking them. Many legal, economic, humanitarian, and cultural activities are of this kind. Thus a nation is not normally engaged in international politics when is concludes an extradition treaty with another nation, when it exchanges goods and services with other nations, when it co-operates with other nations in providing relief from natural catastrophes, and when it promotes the distribution of cultural achievements throughout the world. In other words, the involvement of a nation in international politics is but one among many types of activities in which a nation can participate on the international scene.
>
> (Morgenthau 1960: 27–28; 1973: 27–28)

By defining the purpose of his work in this manner, Morgenthau is doing what Kuhn has stated is the prerequisite of all scientific inquiry, that is, focusing on and magnifying certain phenomena while allowing other phenomena to disappear from the picture. There is nothing wrong with this procedure, and, as a number of philosophers of science point out (Kuhn 1970a: ch. 5; Hanson 1965: ch. 1; Popper 1970: 51–52), it would be logically impossible for science to proceed in any other manner. By providing a definition of international politics, Morgenthau states what he is going to study, what he is not going to study, and by implication what is important and not important (or less important) to study.[3]

Up to this point, the type of evidence presented to support the accuracy of the three fundamental assumptions of the Morgenthau paradigm has been citation from his texts. The problem with this kind of evidence is that it assumes that the author being cited is fairly consistent and that the passages quoted are representative of his work. Furthermore, it does not allow a hypothesis about an author to be easily and openly falsified, since readers who object to the evidence must find their own counterquotations. In order to deal with these three problems, a content analysis of the index and table of contents of *Politics Among Nations*, which is fully reported in Vasquez (1974a: 80–95), was conducted.

If Morgenthau accepted the first and second assumptions, it would be expected that he would tend to use concepts that referred primarily to nations or the relationships among nations. A content analysis of all common nouns in the index of the third edition found that 72.3 percent of the common nouns referred primarily to nations ($n = 159$). When only nouns that have at least fifteen pages devoted to them were included in the sample, then 77.7 percent of the common nouns referred to nations ($n = 27$). The evidence that Morgenthau accepted the third assumption was that of the ten section titles in the table of contents, eight referred directly to either the struggle for power or the

---

[3] It should be pointed out that Morgenthau is not simply making the distinction between international relations and international politics. Because his work became an exemplar, his originally stipulative definition is accepted as defining the scope of the entire field. International relations becomes international politics by definition. What is not international politics is simply irrelevant. Whether or not Morgenthau intended this to occur, it is, according to this theory, the result of his procedure. See Kuhn (1970a: ch. 2) for the general process by which the working definitions of a great scholar become the working definitions of an entire field.

struggle for peace. These eight sections constituted 85.8 percent of the pages in the third edition.

Although the preceding analysis demonstrates that Morgenthau makes the three assumptions, there might be some question as to whether other scholars also made the same assumptions. A review of one of the leading realists of the time, Arnold Wolfers, who did most of his work after the publication of *Politics Among Nations*, should eliminate any doubts. Wolfers provides even better evidence for the three assumptions than does Morgenthau's own work, primarily because Wolfers was very interested in exploring the basic questions. His acceptance and justification of the first assumption is clear and even goes to the extreme of saying that the decision-making approach is irrelevant because all official decision makers will behave in the same manner given the structure of the current nation-state system (Wolfers 1951 [1962: 82]). Likewise, he accepts the third assumption on the struggle of power and maintains that the roles of anarchy and power are so great that domestic politics is fundamentally different from international politics (Wolfers 1949, 1951 [1962: 103–116]).

In defining the realist paradigm it is important to distinguish it from the power politics conceptual framework that Morgenthau, Wolfers, and others have employed. For the purposes of this analysis, scholars who employ that conceptual framework will be referred to as adherents of the power politics school or of real*ism*. These last two terms will be employed the way they are commonly understood in the discipline. The term *realist paradigm*, however, is used in a technical sense and refers only to the three delineated fundamental assumptions, which adherents of realism happened to make, but it does not include all their conceptual baggage or their explanations. This analysis does not deny that there are important theoretical differences between realism (narrowly defined) and other schools such as decision making and systems. It does want to say that realism has provided to the discipline as a whole, and thus to these other schools, a critical shared-example which provides the paradigm of the disciplinary matrix.[4]

The three delineated assumptions make the meaning of the realist paradigm much clearer, but the assumptions do not provide an

---

[4] The adjective *realist* is always used [in the original text] as a shorthand for realist paradigm and not for realism in the narrow sense, unless otherwise specified.

operational definition. An operational definition requires a set of rules that can be used to determine whether a scholar is guided by the three fundamental assumptions.

Operationalizing the realist paradigm

This section tests whether a scholar accepts these three assumptions by use of the coding scheme shown in table 3.1. The coding scheme was developed by selecting indicators of each of the three assumptions. The first two assumptions of the realist paradigm are that nation-states are the most important actors for understanding international relations and that the sovereignty of nations makes domestic politics different from international politics. Given this emphasis on the nation, it is reasonable to expect that a scholar who accepted the first two assumptions of the realist paradigm would study primarily nation-states and neglect other actors, since these nonnational actors would be of only minor importance. Therefore, in order to see if a scholar employs the first two assumptions, one simply examines the actors he or she studies.

The first part of the coding scheme lists all the possible actors an international relations scholar could study. If a scholar's work – whether it be a theory, collected data, or a hypothesis – referred primarily to nations and not to any other actor, then the work was coded in category 3 and taken as evidence that the scholar employed the first two realist assumptions. If a scholar studied any other actor or the nation in conjunction with nonnational actors, then the work was coded in categories 1, 2, 4–6, or 7 and taken as evidence that the first two assumptions of the realist paradigm had been rejected.

The use of the nation-state as the actor is only an indicator of acceptance of the first two assumptions. In order to determine if a scholar accepts the critical third assumption, it is necessary to determine whether his or her studies follow the research program established by the exemplar. Kuhn argues that the major influence of a paradigm is the establishment of a research program. Even critics of Kuhn who do not employ the concept of paradigm (e.g., Worrall 1978) recognize the importance of alternative or competing research programs within a discipline. If *Politics Among Nations* is an exemplar, then the topics of inquiry discussed within it constitute a set of dependent variables that followers would seek to investigate empirically and explain theoretically. Similarly, the key independent variables

Table 3.1. *Coding scheme*

Code	Item
	ACTOR
1	Intergovernmental organization (IGO)
2	International nongovernmental organization (NGO)
3 [a]	Nation-state
4	Subnational group or individuals
5	No actor
6	Any combination of 1, 2, 4
7	The nation and any other combination of actors
	TOPIC OF INQUIRY
10 [a,b]	Conflict-cooperation
11	Non-conflict-cooperation and non-power perceptions of decision makers
12	Non-(war/peace or power issues), issue positions of actors, and issue salience
13 [a,b]	Alignment and alliances
14 [a]	Integration and regionalism
15	Magnitude of transactions (target specific)
16 [a,b]	National power and/or weakness – including social, cultural, economic, political, and geographic characteristics; penetration, dependence, prestige, success, and failure
17 [a]	Isolationism-involvement
18	Miscellaneous
19	Sociological characteristics of actors – age, party, education, religion, etc.
20 [a]	Propaganda
21 [a]	Supranationalism – support and participation in United Nations, League, or International Courts

Notes: [a] Indicators of the realist paradigm
[b] Central topics of the realist paradigm.

would provide a focus of inquiry because they hold the promise of solving existing puzzles. A review of Morgenthau's *Politics Among Nations* revealed that all topics in table 3.1 marked *a* were present.

Some topics are, of course, more central than others. Clearly, Morgenthau's major dependent variable is inter-nation conflict-cooperation. In order to understand this topic more clearly, Morgenthau delineated a set of topics of inquiry that, if researched successfully, would provide a scientific understanding of the international struggle for power and peace. He thought a proper understanding of the role of national power would ultimately explain inter-nation conflict-cooperation. This provided the heart of his own theoretical explanation and conceptual framework. He went to great lengths to identify the elements of national power. The geographical, political, economic, and sociocultural characteristics of a nation were all viewed as important elements (Morgenthau 1960, 1973: chs. 8 and 9). In addition to explaining inter-nation conflict-cooperation, national power was used to account for general patterns of foreign policy. Morgenthau submitted that weak nations were being best served by isolationism if they were not threatened (1960: 36–37, 159, 196; 1973: 37–38, 196); otherwise an alliance with a stronger power would serve their interests (Morgenthau 1960: 173–178; 1973: 172–178). Conversely, stronger nations were seen as more likely to be active and opt for the policies of the status quo, imperialism, or prestige (Morgenthau 1960, 1973: 28, chs. 4–6). Which of these policies a nation selects, Morgenthau implied, is a function of the historical context and power relationships among the elite.

Closely related to the topic of national power is Morgenthau's concern with the balance of power and alliances. Whereas national power considerations have an impact on all forms of global behavior, alliances and the balance of power are seen as directly related to the maintenance of peace and the outbreak of war (Morgenthau 1960, 1973: chs. 11–14, 21).

These three topics – national power, alliances, and inter-nation conflict-cooperation – constitute the central core of the realist paradigm. This conclusion is supported by a rank order of the common nouns in the index of *Politics Among Nations*, which showed that the three most frequently used nouns were *balance of power* (86 pages), *national power* (69 pages), and *war* (62 pages). (See Vasquez 1974a: 89–90, 92 for the data and evidence.)

Even though these three concepts provide the conceptual framework for Morgenthau's own theoretical explanations, they also provide a research program for other scholars. Any exemplar provides not so much answers as the promise of answers if scholars work to improve the conceptual frameworks and theoretical explanations given in the exemplar. One would expect considerable attention to be devoted by adherents of the realist paradigm to clarifying major concepts like national power and the balance of power and specifying precise relationships between these concepts and various dependent variables. New definitions, measures, and alternate hypotheses all would constitute part of a systematic investigation into every aspect of the topics and their connection to each other.

A group of scholars that accepted the third assumption would be expected to study more frequently the topics in the research program that Morgenthau saw as more promising, and to study these in the manner he suggested until the research showed that these leads no longer must be followed up, either because they proved fruitless or because they had been fully exhausted.

While inter-nation conflict-cooperation, national power, and alliances provided the central core, Morgenthau saw other topics as important for a complete understanding of the field even if they were not central. Because Morgenthau was writing in opposition to the idealists and at a time when many Americans hoped the United Nations could become, at some point, the foundation for a world government, supranationalism was an interesting topic to him. He had two main concerns with it. The first was to debunk illusions about the United Nations and argue that the United Nations simply reflected existing power relationships and the struggle for power. The second was to stipulate the conditions that create a stable supranational entity. He dwelt on what forces created a nation and how a world community (and from there a world state) might be created (Morgenthau 1960, 1973: chs. 27, 29, 30). It is because of this last concern that inter-state integration is labeled as part of the realist research program, even though Morgenthau's own purpose was to show that the proper conditions for supranationalism did not exist. Finally, Morgenthau (1960: 338–345; 1973: 332–339) used the concept of propaganda to explain some of the verbal acts of states, although his concern with it was marginal.

The following topics of inquiry were taken as indicators of work outside the realist paradigm: non–conflict-cooperation and non–power perceptions of decision makers; non–war/peace issues, issue positions of actors, and issue salience; magnitude of transactions; sociological variables of actors – age, size, party, education, etc.; and finally a miscellaneous category to make the classification logically exhaustive. A scholar who studied one of these topics would be said to have rejected the third assumption.

Studying aspects of decision making other than inter-nation power relationships suggests a topic of inquiry that sees decision making itself as the primary dependent variable. Such a perspective implies a rejection of all three assumptions. If individuals other than leaders of nation-states are studied, then the first two assumptions are violated, particularly if the explanations are psychological and/or social psychological, since this implies a single theory at the individual, group, and state level. The third assumption is also violated because the unique nature of global anarchy is not seen as affecting behavior.

Studying issues other than war/peace is seen as a rejection of the second and third assumptions, because Morgenthau (1960, 1973: 27) explicitly states that all substantive goals can be reduced to the struggle for power. To study different kinds of issues is to imply that the realist paradigm is applicable only to one aspect of the global system, and hence incomplete.

Studying transactions is a vestige of the idealist paradigm, particularly Mitrany's (1943) functionalism. Finally, sociological characteristics usually violate the second assumption because, by borrowing from other social sciences (not just sociology), they imply that there need not be a special theory of international politics or even a special theory of politics, but perhaps only a theory of various aspects of human behavior (e.g., decision making, conflict, perception, bargaining, etc.).

A scholar's work was coded as realist only if *all* the actor and topic categories were realist. For example, if a scholar studied nation-states but did not study them in the context of a realist topic of inquiry, then the entire work was coded as nonrealist, because the third assumption was rejected. In other words, all three assumptions had to be employed before a work was coded as realist.

A strong case for the validity of this coding scheme can be made. The central validity question is whether the three delineated assumptions of the realist paradigm are indeed the fundamental assumptions made by that paradigm. It has been shown that Morgenthau's *Politics Among Nations* is a valid indicator of the realist paradigm and that it is based on those three assumptions. The second validity question is whether the indicators employed in the coding scheme actually measure a scholar's acceptance of the three realist assumptions. It has been shown that Morgenthau emphasized certain actors and topics of inquiry which have been taken as indicators of the realist assumptions in the coding scheme. It seems reasonable to expect that scholars who accept the assumptions of the realist paradigm would also tend to employ the same actors as Morgenthau and follow his research agenda. The third validity question deals with the mechanical problem of whether it is easy or difficult to code a work as realist. Because the coding scheme requires that both actor and topic categories must be realist before a work is coded as realist, it is more difficult, mechanically, for a work to be coded realist than nonrealist. Since only one actor category is labeled realist, there are only seven possible ways in which a work could be coded realist. Conversely, there are thirty possible ways a work could be coded as nonrealist. Also, anything with a miscellaneous topic is coded as nonrealist.

A more serious criticism is that the coding scheme is so broad that any work about world politics would be coded as within the realist paradigm. The Marxist paradigm, however, shows that this is not the case, in that class is the most important actor and the distinction between domestic and international politics is not emphasized. Nations are viewed as an artificial creation and inter-nation conflict as bogus; only classes and class conflict are real. Likewise, the Marxist paradigm does not accept the third assumption, in that it considers the most important set of questions to be the evolution of economic production and its effect on behavior whether or not that behavior leads to inter-state war.

Finally, it might be argued that the coding scheme is too imprecise because it might code substantive power politics propositions in the same categories as propositions derived from game theory or systems analysis if they studied only nations and conflict-cooperation. This criticism misconstrues the purpose of the coding scheme, which is not to make distinctions among propositions or theories that share the same fundamental assumptions about the world but to make distinctions among propositions that have very different views of the world. To insist on the former distinctions is to reduce the realist paradigm to Morgenthau's specific power politics conceptual framework. This would be like saying that because Marx, Kautsky, Lenin, Mao, and Marcuse are all different, they cannot share the same paradigm. Since the coding scheme is intended to provide an analysis of the effect of accepting or rejecting realist paradigmatic assumptions, to criticize it for not analyzing the dominance and adequacy of various realist elaborations within the dominant paradigm and research program is to suggest an analysis that is not directly relevant to the thesis being tested here.

Nevertheless, the coding scheme does label certain topics as central, so that it is possible to identify the degree to which a proposition within the paradigm is near the core or at the periphery

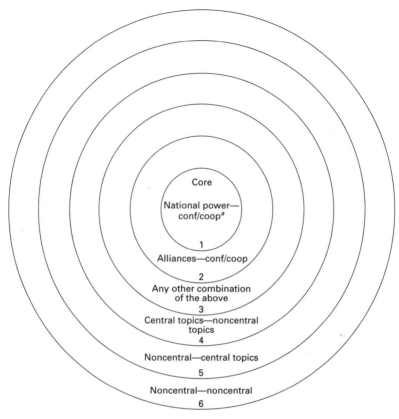

Outside paradigm:
Any central or noncentral topic coupled with a nonrealist topic
Any topic not studied exclusively on nation-states

[a]First topic is an independent variable; second is a dependent variable

Figure 3.1 Rank order of propositions within the realist paradigm according to centrality

of the paradigm (see figure 3.1). The most central are those propositions that claim that national power explains inter-nation conflict-cooperation. Next come those that state that alliances are related to inter-nation conflict-cooperation. Other interrelationships among these three central concepts would be farther from the core. They are followed by those propositions that employ the central topics to explain a noncentral one. Next come the inverse relationships; finally, propositions that relate noncentral concepts are at the periphery of the paradigm.[5]

The coding scheme has been found to be quite reliable. It has been applied to different documents (books, abstracts, data files, and hypotheses) in a series of tests employing various coders with reliability scores ranging from 0.86 to 0.93.[6] Specific reliability scores are reported in chapters 4 through 6.

Because the coding scheme appears to be valid and has been found to be reliable, it will be employed to determine whether the realist paradigm has guided theory construction, data making, and research in the field. This will be done respectively in chapters 4 through 6 by coding the theories that have been articulated in the field, the data that has been collected, and the hypotheses that have been tested. Since each of these chapters has its own research design, there is no need for further methodological discussion here.

[5] A more refined treatment of differences within the paradigm is presented in chapter 4. See also Russett (1970).

[6] The formula used to calculate reliability was the number of successes divided by the number of decisions.

4   Theory construction as
a paradigm-directed activity

Introduction

The proposition

Kuhn's notion that theory construction is a paradigm-directed activity
has both an analytical and an empirical meaning. Analytically, the
proposition means that it is logically impossible to construct theories
without the prior existence of a paradigm (Kuhn 1970a: 15–17). This
aspect of Kuhn's notion is substantiated by definition, since it is
impossible to have a theory that does not make certain fundamental
assumptions. Empirically, the proposition means that a single specific
paradigm guides theory construction (Kuhn 1970a: 10–11). It is this
empirical aspect that is embodied in the proposition that will be tested
in this chapter: *The realist paradigm guided theory construction in the field
of international relations during the 1950s and 1960s.*

According to Kuhn, theory construction in normal science involves
clarifying the concepts presented in the dominant paradigm and
employing them in light of research to elaborate theories. Kuhn calls
theory construction *paradigm articulation* because the process is conducted by a division of labor, with different scholars working in
specialized problem areas suggested by the research agenda of the
paradigm. In a sense, the paradigm provides an outline, and theory
construction articulates the paradigm by filling in the details. The
paradigm provides guidance in that it focuses scholars' attention on
certain problems and provides them with a set of fundamental
assumptions that the new theoretical work never violates.

The need for paradigm articulation presupposes that the work that
originally presented the paradigm did not provide all the answers.

Kuhn (1970a: 23–24) states that a paradigm often does not provide any answers at all, only the promise of answers. How much and what type of articulation is necessary depends on the specific paradigm and the state of the science or field. In some fields, very little new conceptual formulation is needed. In other cases, particularly when the science is in qualitative stage, conceptual reformulation may dominate efforts at paradigm articulation (Kuhn 1970a: 29, 33).

It is clear to most people that international relations inquiry has been in a qualitative stage. Consequently, it should come as no surprise that a great deal of emphasis has been placed on developing alternative conceptual frameworks. Such an emphasis in the field, however, does not mean in itself that the realist paradigm has not directed theory construction. That would only be the case if the various conceptual frameworks did not employ the three fundamental assumptions of the paradigm. It is claimed in this chapter that most of the conceptual and theoretical work within the field and the research that has given rise to it has accepted those three fundamental assumptions, and, as a result, various aspects of the realist paradigm have been articulated fairly systematically and somewhat cumulatively.

This does not mean, however, that there will be no conceptual change or innovation. Indeed, to the extent to which critics of Kuhn like Toulmin (1967, 1970, 1972) and Shapere (1964, 1971) are correct (and they seem to be, in part), the paradigm should evolve as well as be articulated. Since Kuhn has conceded that microrevolutions can occur in normal science, the debate between Kuhn and his critics is partially semantic. Nevertheless, if Kuhn's emphasis is correct, one would expect innovation to pull back from challenging paradigmatic assumptions, unless anomalies persist. In this sense, the main difference between Kuhn and his critics is over the presence of some sharp discontinuities in the intellectual development of a field.

In terms of the proposition being examined in this chapter, it is important to distinguish Morgenthau's own specific conceptual framework and theoretical explanations (what can be called *power politics* or *realism* in the narrow sense) from the broader set of fundamental assumptions of the realist paradigm itself. The paradigm (see figure 1.1) can be consistent with a number of theories and conceptual frameworks. New conceptual frameworks, even if brought in from sister disciplines, may not necessarily contradict the assumptions of the dominant paradigm and are adapted if they do. Thus, while new frameworks like decision making, systems analysis, game theory, and cybernetics constitute breaks with the power politics framework, they do not necessarily reject the three fundamental assumptions of the realist paradigm. Only if they do can they be said to be outside the paradigm.

Nevertheless, they do constitute real change and evolution, and the further away in time scholars get from the exemplar, the more likely are drastic changes in the original concepts (Kuhn 1970a: 28–34). Thus, even among those who saw national power as the key concept and employed a power politics conceptual framework, there were major differences. Morgenthau did not give the same explanation as Schuman (1933), Niebuhr (1940), Spykman (1942), Wight (1946), Kennan (1951), Claude (1956; 1962), Organski (1958), or Wolfers (1962). Yet they all were regarded as working on a power politics theory (see Bull 1972; T. Taylor 1978a).

While early work on the paradigm will tend to follow the theoretical explanations given in the exemplar, later work will be bolder in developing new concepts, particularly if the central ones in the exemplar pose conceptual, theoretical, methodological, or empirical problems. These new concepts will at first appear as radically new approaches, but in fact they evolve out of the concerns of the paradigm, the logic of its own assumptions, and the problems posed by its research program. The more difficulty scholars have in understanding their world, the more drastic the changes they make and the more concepts evolve. If anomalies persist, they may lead to a crisis that may produce a new paradigm.

At what point does the evolution of new conceptual frameworks and theoretical explanations constitute a new paradigm? Only when a theory violates one or more of the fundamental assumptions can a new paradigm be said to exist. Although the latter becomes an operational indicator of a paradigm shift, the discontinuity is clearly not as sharp and surprising as Kuhn implies with his imagery of crisis and revolution. Toulmin's notion of variation and evolution seems a more precise description not only of innovation within normal science, but of the shift from normal science to revolutionary science as well. Kuhn, however, is probably more accurate for describing the transition from revolutionary science to a new normal science. Thus, one can note the collapse of the specific theoretical explanation of the examplar, then a reconceptualization of a key independent or dependent variable, then the abandonment of the original conceptual framework, then the introduction of new frameworks that get further and further away from the original one, then perhaps the introduction of new metaphors or analogies (maybe from other disciplines or paradigms), then the modification of a fundamental assumption, then calls for a new paradigm, and finally the rejection of all or most of the assumptions and the picture of the world they provide in favor of a new paradigm.

Toulmin's (1967, 1970, 1972) analysis probably best describes all but the last two steps, which, because they are sharp and conscious breaks, are better seen as discontinuities or thresholds rather than just evolutionary products. At any rate, they are certainly perceived by scientists as sharp breaks in retrospect, and for this reason alone Kuhn's analysis should be modified rather than abandoned entirely. Toulmin, however, is certainly justified in pointing out that the activities of most scientists do not differ that much from normal science to revolutionary science.

Research design

The problem now is how to test the proposition. Testing such a broad proposition requires at least some prediction or statement that would be accepted as clearly falsifying the proposition if the evidence did not agree with it. At the same time, the developmental aspect of the proposition requires that it be able to make sense and coherence out of the intellectual development of the field. These are obviously very difficult tasks to accomplish in a single test or mode of testing. To resolve this problem, two different methods will be employed. The falsifiability requirement will be satisfied by conducting a preliminary empirical test, and the plausibility requirement (sometimes referred to as *face validity*), will be satisfied by a lengthy but necessarily cursory review of the field's intellectual development since Morgenthau.

The preliminary empirical test makes three predictions. If the realist paradigm indeed dominates the field, then scholars in the discipline should recognize the significance of Morgenthau's contribution and should agree on what work has been the most influential in the field. In addition, other leading works in the field should articulate important problems in the paradigm and should at minimum not challenge the paradigm's assumptions. By making such explicit predictions, problems of nonfalsifiability can be limited.

The problem with such a test, however, is that it loses much of the richness and complexity of the proposition because it looks only at a few predictions, which, while observable, may not be very important or interesting. In particular, a quantitative test cannot adequately assess the development of normal science and the role of conceptual innovation. To resolve these problems, a case study of the intellectual development of the field since the 1948 publication of *Politics Among Nations* will be presented to demonstrate that the literature of the field can be interpreted to show that theory construction has been fairly systematic and somewhat cumulative in articulating the realist paradigm. Such a review will also permit an assessment of the disagreement between Kuhn and Toulmin over the role of change and innovation in normal science.

The works reviewed will include those that have made major theoretical, as opposed to idiographic or policy, contributions to the understanding of international relations. The review will describe how each of the works articulated major aspects of the realist paradigm, how the works embodied the three fundamental assumptions of the paradigm, and how change and innovation were brought about. Finally, the review will discuss works outside the paradigm and indicate why they do not falsify the proposition. There have, of course, been many reviews of the field. This chapter does not represent an attempt to redo this work, but to use it in order to delineate the cumulative nature of work within international relations.

Preliminary empirical tests

The most obvious way to test the proposition is to ask scholars in the field what scholarly works and thinkers have been most influential in the study of international politics. If the analysis presented here were correct, then the following two hypotheses would be true:

1a. International relations scholars perceive Hans J. Morgenthau as the most influential scholar in the field.

1b. International relations scholars perceive the exemplar of realist scholarship, *Politics Among Nations*, as the most important theoretical work in the field.[1]

Although a survey was not conducted as part of this analysis, an

---

[1] These hypotheses are numbered 1a and 1b because they test the first proposition in this analysis.

Table 4.1. *Ranking of scholars mentioned by respondents (hypothesis 1a)*

Scholar	Number[a]	Percentage of total respondents[b]
H. Morgenthau	100	46.7
K. Deutsch	54	25.2
Q. Wright	49	22.9
S. Hoffmann	34	15.8
M. Kaplan	33	15.4
R. Aron	26	12.2
I. Claude	26	12.2
R. Snyder	25	11.7
E. Haas	19	8.9
J. Rosenau	18	8.4
T. Schelling	16	7.5
A. Wolfers	16	7.5
J. D. Singer	16	7.5
H. Lasswell	15	7.0
H. Sprout	13	6.1
C. McClelland	10	4.7
E. H. Carr	9	4.2
W. T. R. Fox	8	3.7
R. Niebuhr	8	3.7
B. Russett	8	3.7
H. Guetzkow	7	3.2
G. Kennan	7	3.2
H. Kissinger	7	3.2
G. Almond	6	2.7
J. Herz	6	2.7
K. Boulding	5	2.2
M. Sprout	5	2.2
K. Waltz	5	2.2

Source: Finnegan (1972a: 9). Reprinted with the permission of the publisher.
Notes: [a] Scholars mentioned by four or fewer respondents are omitted.
   [b] Percentages do not add to 100 percent because of multiple responses.

earlier survey by Richard Finnegan (1972a) provides evidence to support both hypotheses.[2] Finnegan's survey was based on a random sample of international relations scholars in the American Political Science Association. In a question that is relevant to hypothesis 1a, Finnegan asked the respondents "to list the scholars they felt had

---

[2] Technically, the use of the Finnegan survey to support hypotheses 1a and 1b does not constitute a valid test because the hypotheses were developed ex post facto. Nevertheless, the findings are reported here because they are highly relevant to the analysis.

Table 4.2 *Ranking of scholarly works mentioned by respondents (hypothesis 1b)*

Work	Number[a]	Percentage of total sample[b]
Politics Among Nations (Morgenthau 1948)	76	35.5
Systems and Process in International Politics (Kaplan 1957)	30	14.0
Peace and War (Aron 1966)	21	9.8
The Study of International Relations (Wright 1955)	21	9.8
International Politics and Foreign Policy (Rosenau 1961, 1969)	19	8.9
The Twenty Years' Crisis 1919–1939 (Carr 1939)	18	8.4
Contemporary Theory in International Relations (Hoffmann 1960)	14	6.5
A Study of War (Wright 1942)	13	6.1
Man, the State, and War (Waltz 1959)	12	5.6
Foreign Policy Decision-Making (Snyder et al. 1962)	12	5.6
Power and International Relations (Claude 1962)	11	5.1
The Strategy of Conflict (Schelling 1960)	10	4.7
Political Community and the North Atlantic Area (Deutsch et al. 1957)	9	4.2
Nationalism and Social Communication (Deutsch 1953)	8	3.7
The Nerves of Government (Deutsch 1964)	8	3.7
International Behavior (Kelman 1965)	8	3.7
Quantitative International Politics (Singer 1968)	8	3.7
Swords into Plowshares (Claude 1956)	7	3.3

Source: Finnegan (1972a: 8–9). Reprinted with the permission of the publisher.
Notes: [a] Works mentioned by six or fewer respondents are omitted.
[b] Percentages do not add to 100 percent because of multiple responses.

made a great contribution to the study of international relations" (1972a: 9). No specific number of nominations was requested. The findings, which are reported in table 4.1, fail to falsify the hypothesis. The table shows that Morgenthau is the most frequently nominated scholar, receiving almost twice as many nominations (46.7 percent) as the second most frequently nominated scholar (Karl Deutsch, 25.2 percent).

In a question relevant to hypothesis 1b, Finnegan asked respondents to nominate what they considered the three works that had contributed the most to the field. The findings, reported in table 4.2, fail to falsify hypothesis 1b. Finnegan (1972a: 9) notes

> . . . the marked domination of the list by one work, *Politics Among Nations*, which is mentioned by one third of the respondents and is mentioned by more than twice as many as the second ranked work. In addition, Morgenthau's book is often listed first on the questionnaires indicating for many of the respondents it is the first book to come to mind.

The findings on hypotheses 1a and 1b lend credence to the proposition on theory construction by demonstrating that Morgenthau and *Politics Among Nations* are regarded as the most influencial scholar and book in the field.

A final way to test the propositions is to examine whether other leading theoretical works in the field articulate aspects of the realist paradigm. Since this is a legitimate expectation, the following hypothesies will be tested.

> 1c. Works that are viewed by scholars in the field as having made a major contribution will tend to employ the conceptual framework of the exemplar, or, failing that, will not violate the three fundamental assumptions of the paradigm.

The works listed in table 4.2 provide evidence to support each of the above predictions. Before the evidence can be presented, there must be some way to reliably classify each of the works. This is somewhat problematic, because the coding scheme developed in chapter 3 is not easily applied to an entire book. To resolve this problem, two decisions were made. First, edited books were deleted, since they might employ different approaches in different articles. In addition, there was no easy way of determining which articles prompted a respondent to nominate the book. Second, each book was judgmentally classified into three categories: (1) whether it employed the power politics conceptual framework; (2) whether it accepted the three fundamental assumptions; (3) whether it was outside the paradigm because it rejected one of the assumptions.

The works of Carr (1939), Claude (1956, 1962), Waltz (1959), and

Aron (1966) were all classified as employing a power politics conceptual framework. This assessment agrees with that of T. Taylor (1978a: 123, 130–140), who classified all these books, except Claude (1956), which was not reviewed, as part of the power politics tradition. Claude's (1956) work is clearly a power politics critique of international organization. The works of K. Deutsch (1953) and Deutsch et al. (1957), Snyder et al. (1954), Wright (1955), Kaplan (1957), and Schelling (1960) tended to employ other conceptual frameworks but did not violate the three fundamental assumptions of the paradigm. With the exception of Wright (1955), the primary contribution of each of these works was to introduce and apply a new conceptual framework. For Deutsch it was cybernetics or communication theory, for Snyder, Bruck, and Sapin it was decision making, for Kaplan it was systems language, and for Schelling it was game theory. In this manner, conceptual innovation was introduced, but each of these new frameworks, which were consciously borrowed from other disciplines, had to be adapted to fit global politics. In doing so, each scholar, at least subconsciously, employed the picture of the world provided by the realist paradigm. They believed that nation-states were the most important actors, that domestic politics was fundamentally different from international politics, and that international relations consisted of the struggle for power and peace. Each of these authors looked primarily at nation-states as the most important actors; the only possible exception is Snyder, Bruck, and Sapin (1954), who looked at decision makers, but they defined a state as its official decision makers. Each of these books embodied the third assumption of the realist paradigm in that it studied, at least indirectly, inter-nation conflict-cooperation. Kaplan studied alliances and their stability, Schelling analyzed deterrence and bargaining, R. C. Snyder and Paige (1958) applied their framework to the decision to intervent militarily in Korea. Deutsch investigated the old idealist propositions that integration and communication could be paths to peace. In this sense, Deutsch's work, although not idealist, reflects nonrealist tendencies and is somewhat on the periphery of the paradigm. However, his strong empirical emphasis and analysis of nation-states saved him from moving too far in a nonrealist direction (see his textbook [Deutsch 1968] for evidence of his agreement with the three fundamental assumptions of the paradigm).[3]

---

[3] To a certain extent, the edited works of Kelman (1965), J. D. Singer (1968), and Rosenau (1961, 1969) are similar to the books in the second category in that each

Finally, two books, Wright (1942) and K. Deutsch (1964), are seen as outside the paradigm. Wright employed both idealist and realist assumptions in his study of war, focusing on individuals as well as states, and attempting to develop a single theory of conflict and violence rather than one unique to the international system. Deutsch presented a general theory of government that violated the second assumption of the paradigm and wrote on a topic not directly relevant to the research agenda of the field. Indeed, most people in the field would probably say that it was a book about comparative politics, not international politics.

On the basis of the above classifications, it can be stated that six of the fourteen leading non-edited books (including Morgenthau 1948) employ a power politics conceptual framework and that an additional six do not violate the three basic assumptions and do study a topic of inquiry central in the realist paradigm. The first six can be seen as reflecting realism in the narrow sense as well as being traditional in methodology. The second six are behavioral and attempt to rework power politics propositions in a more scientific manner and to introduce new concepts to aid this task. Since only two books out of fourteen do not reflect work guided by the realist paradigm, it can be tentatively concluded that hypothesis 1c has failed to be falsified.

Although preliminary, the tests in this section have shown that the scholar seen as contributing more to international relations inquiry than any other scholar is Hans J. Morgenthau; the work most frequently nominated by scholars as the leading work in the field is Morgenthau's *Politics Among Nations*; and twelve of the fourteen books nominated by scholars in a sample survey as leading works in the field do not violate the three fundamental assumptions of the realist paradigm. All these findings provide support for the proposition that the realist paradigm guided and directed theory construction in the field in the 1950s and 1960s.

---

introduces a new approach. For Kelman it is social psychology, for Singer it is statistical testing of hypotheses, and for Rosenau it is scientific (or "behavioral") theorizing. Hoffman (1960) is primarily a reader combining power politics approaches and some of the new conceptual frameworks with commentary that is an expanded version of his (1959) essay. The essay is respectful of power politics approaches and does not violate any of the three fundamental assumptions of the paradigm.

Continuity and change in the intellectual development of the field: an interpretive review of the literature

This literature review attempts to demonstrate that theory construction in international relations inquiry has followed a fairly coherent research program that has even built cumulatively on the work of others. This research program can be divided into five subfields, linked to each other by the paradigm's overall goal of understanding the struggle for power and peace. The articulation of the realist paradigm has centered around five subfields: (1) foreign policy; (2) systemic processes; (3) the causes of war; (4) deterrence and bargaining; and (5) supranationalism. Although each of these five areas introduced major new concepts and explanations to the field that were not found in the writings of early power politics theorists, most of the work in each subfield did not challenge the assumptions of the paradigm.

[This seventy-nine page review has been eliminated in this edition. The review of each subfield describes how Morgenthau and other early realists set the intellectual agenda for the field and how conceptual variation was introduced, typically by borrowing from other disciplines. Underlying this variation, however, was a fundamental view of the world which posed a number of research problems that were investigated in somewhat systematic and even cumulative manner over the long term, thereby giving the field a normal science character.]

Conclusion

The preceding survey seems to support several general points. First, there is a basic agreement within the field about the nature of international politics and how it should be studied. Second, this agreement has provided a general underlying coherence to work in the field by providing a research program for each subfield that has linked them together. Third, this division of labor has allowed five areas within the realist paradigm to be articulated systematically and somewhat cumulatively. Fourth, articulation of the paradigm has consisted of four types of activities: conceptual clarification in the traditional mode; conceptual clarification in the behavioral mode (i.e., the attempt to operationalize and measure concepts); tests of explanations in either the traditional or behavioral mode; and the reformulation of explanations in light of these tests and the work on conceptual clarification. Fifth, the various approaches and conceptual frameworks that have become popular in the field at different times do not constitute different paradigms but are better interpreted as elaborations of different aspects of the realist paradigm, since they do not reject the three fundamental assumptions of the paradigm. Finally, prior to the 1970s no attempt was made within the field to seriously challenge the assumptions of the realist paradigm, and those who used the major alternative paradigm available, Marxism, were viewed as being outside the field. Since the literature review supports these points, the proposition that the Realist paradigm has guided theory construction within the field during the 1950s and 1960s is given a certain amount of credence. It can be concluded therefore that the findings of the "face validity test" do not falsify the proposition.

From the review of the field several insights can also be derived about the nature of change in normal science. While these are not directly relevant to the proposition, they are interesting in terms of the larger question raised in the debate between Kuhn (1970b: 249–259) and Toulmin (1967, 1970, 1972) over normal science. One of the major sources of innovation in the field has been the application of scientific criteria of assessment to traditional explanations. The attempt to apply rigorous scientific analysis made scholars more sensitive to the ambiguity, lack of operational criteria, nonfalsifiability, and absence of explicit propositions in much of the traditional wisdom. As a result, many scholars consciously searched for new concepts by borrowing from other disciplines. This became an established way of attempting to solve puzzles generated through the use of the new methodological criteria. The decision-making approach solved the problem of anthropomorphizing the nation-state. Game theory, because of its deductive quality, gave strategic analysis more explanatory power. Systems analysis helped reformulate discussions of the balance of power and global structure into explicit, testable propositions. Cybernetics elucidated part of the mystery of community formation by pointing to the importance of communication and transaction flows for building ties. While each of these frameworks introduced new rigor and pointed to propositions that were not easily grasped by the power politics framework, the methodological concerns must be seen as the ultimate source of innovation within the field. This is something that Kuhn entirely overlooked in his work.[4]

Of all the frameworks, the one that introduced the most innovation was that of decision making. This was primarily because with the emphasis on decision making came an interest in social psychology, and then cognitive psychology, that began to challenge the assumptions of the paradigm. The introduction of social and cognitive psychology appeared to have a more radical impact because those who introduced these approaches were not political scientists borrowing from other fields, but social psychologists who either remained within psychology or came into international relations but still adhered to a psychological paradigm. Because of this coherence and professional identity, social psychology was the least changed by the realist paradigm in the process of being "adapted" to explain world politics. Throughout, it has undercut more than the other frameworks the emphasis of power politics on rational actors, the use of coercion, and the need to balance power as the only way to live with the security dilemma.

This review of the field has shown that, despite the introduction of conceptual change, there is a remarkable degree to which propositions or conceptual frameworks will not be given up. Rare is the instance in which someone who has actually employed a framework has given it up because of someone else's criticism. Change seems to occur not so much from conversion or changing another scholar's perspective but from adding new approaches or propositions to old ones, which, rather than being refuted, simply seem to run out of new and interesting things to say. From Morgenthau on, every scholar who introduced a new approach never gave it up. Each just kept writing until people stopped reading. Cumulative "knowledge" developed not so much from rejection and real advancement but from seeing things from a new perspective. Because there is no real rejection based on testing, the emergence of a consensus on any framework could make the field highly susceptible to dogma and ideology. This was particularly the case with deterrence theory, which, because it enhanced the explanatory power of power politics, was never really questioned or even tested by any of its proponents. Often the policy

---

[4] This is probably because basic methodological questions are much more easily settled in the physical sciences. Kuhn (1970a: 27–28) does, however, discuss the importance of innovation in measurement for bringing about theoretical change.

relevance of an explanation seemed to be a more important criterion for its acceptance than its accuracy. For example, when deterrence theory was questioned by Rapoport (1964), the criticism was rejected as too moralistic. Eventually, empirical investigations in the 1970s began to have an impact, and the accuracy of deterrence theory was finally doubted.

The main contribution of the behavioral revolt has been to save the field from this dogmatic tendency (see Vasquez 1976b: 200–203). If anything, quantitative tests have shown that the field knows considerably less than most of its members think. Theorists' unwillingness to specify what will count as falsifying their explanation or demonstrating the inutility of their approach is the main potential source of ideological rigidity, and only insistence on testing provides any guard against it. If any real cumulative knowledge results from rejection of "false" or inadequate explanations, it will be because quantitative tests have rejected incorrect and imprecise hypotheses.

The danger of ideology is particularly important in international relations because it seems that one of the major sources of fundamental (paradigm-producing) change in the field comes not from laboratory anomalies but from current events. Idealism was rejected because of the failure of the League of Nations and the coming of World War II. Realism was accepted not only because it could explain the anomaly that the idealist paradigm could not, but also because it provided a guide to the United States as it emerged as the world's most powerful state. Marxism was rejected primarily because the United States was capitalist and its opponent happened to be communist. The realist paradigm itself began to be questioned because of the Vietnam War, and because, while it seemed able to explain the struggles for power in the two world wars and in the Cold War, it appeared at a loss to explain détente. This is similar to major climatic changes or earthquakes bringing about paradigm shifts in physics.

The intrusion of such events makes decisions about the adequacy of explanations, theories, and paradigms difficult for several reasons. First, it is more difficult to be dispassionate about the evidence, and second, even though the truth value of an explanation is separate from its normative value, explanations may be accepted because of their political consequences or policy relevance rather than the evidence. This will be particularly the case when testing is not rigorous, or the evidence is mixed. When such tendencies occur, it is difficult to separate science from ideology. One of the ways to avoid this problem is to be more laboratory oriented. In the rush to be policy-relevant, the field has overlooked the fact that most physical sciences and even advanced social sciences do not directly predict or explain real world events, only indicators or experimental outcomes. Once these "artificial" phenomena can be predicted and explained, then it may be possible to deal with their more complex (because they are less pure) counterparts in the "real world." At any rate, decisions about data can be more rigorous and based primarily on scientific criteria. In terms of these issues, it must be concluded that an application of Kuhn to the social sciences is limited because he does not provide much role for nonlaboratory evidence and does not speak directly about ideologcial considerations.

Finally, the literature review provides some clues about the relationship between normal science and the process by which old paradigms are rejected and new ones accepted (i.e., the debate between Kuhn [1970b: 249–259] and Toulmin [1967, 1970, 1972]). Paradigm change and articulation seem to be incremental, even though considerable innovation may occur. This change does not evolve into a new paradigm, because when innovation challenges an assumption in the paradigm, the author either pulls back or others reject or ignore the suggestion. Rosenau (1966) and Rummel (1977) are two major examples of scholars who introduced changes that they later abandoned because they challenged the paradigm. After Rosenau's (1966) use of penetration broke down the notion of unitary and sovereign states, he returned to the realist assumptions by introducing the theory of adaptation. Rummel (1979) moved away from status explanations that challenged the second and third assumptions of the paradigm and moved back to balance of power notions.

Kuhn, then, is partially correct about discontinuities being present in a field. Paradigm shifts are seen as radical. There is much debate and argument about them. They do not simply evolve, as Toulmin implies. The reason for this is that every possible alternative – conceptual changes, ad hoc explanations, new testing procedures – is tried before fundamental questioning occurs.

Kuhn also seems to be correct in arguing that younger scholars or those on the periphery are responsible for bringing about paradigm shifts. Those who called for paradigm change in international relations often were younger, more junior members of the discipline. They also tended to work at the periphery of the field and/or had experience outside it. Those who called for a transnational paradigm

(Keohane and Nye 1971; Burton 1972) were working in an area, international organization and integration, that had been most influenced by the idealist paradigm. Others, like Coplin (1966), had done work in international law, an area of little concern to the realists, and had worked on social and cognitive psychological approaches.

Such individuals seemed to have a hostile attitude toward the realist paradigm that made them look for things that would refute its tenets. For this reason, they could see things that others could not. But others ignored them (see McClelland 1977) because they were aware of the hostility and suspected the critics of being latent idealists. Such biases are not necessarily irrational, since they make paradigm critics prove their case beyond a shadow of a doubt. Due compensation is provided, however, because fame and accolade come to the critics if they are successful. This in itself may provide a nonacademic incentive for criticizing paradigms. Within the field, then, the rewards and punishments for fundamental change are fairly well balanced, but they tend to make discontinuities inevitable, if a paradigm shift is to occur.

Toulmin appears to be more relevant for explaining nonparadigmatic change within normal science. Normal science is much more innovative and diverse than Kuhn implied. In addition, Toulmin made an important point by suggesting that conceptual innovation can lead to discoveries that may be anomalous and thereby help bring about a paradigm shift. The use of social and cognitive psychology in the field may be having this effect. This use of a theory from another field's paradigm has had a devastating effect on the rational-actor model in explanations of global state behavior. In addition, as the Cold War waned, social psychological models seemed more relevant for explaining processes to which scholars had not paid much attention because they were so concerned with power struggles. In the presence of anomalies, outside conceptual frameworks can make a subfield more susceptible to a paradigm shift.

These points on normal science are inductive conclusions that have been derived from the review of the field and can be used to make more precise some of the general points Kuhn and Toulmin make about intellectual change. They are, however, somewhat tangential to the main purpose of this chapter, which is to assess the extent to which the realist paradigm had guided theory construction in the field. In that regard, the evidence presented in the preliminary tests and the literature review is very consistent with the proposition, and it can be concluded that not only has the proposition passed a preliminary test, but it also is able to offer a plausible interpretation of normal activity within the field to account for change, continuity, and overall coherence. The next chapter will examine the extent to which the realist paradigm guided data making in the field.

5   Data making as a paradigm-directed activity

The proposition

Kuhn's analysis

Kuhn (1970a: ch. 3) explicitly states that fact gathering (i.e., data making) in normal science is guided by the dominant paradigm in the field; such guidance is necessary because the world consists of numerous phenomena, and phenomena only take on meaning to the extent that they are conceptualized. Conceptualization, as pointed out earlier, is a function of theory construction or paradigm articulation. Facts, then, presuppose a paradigm that sifts through the welter of phenomena to focus on what is important. In the pre-paradigm stage of science, fact gathering tends to be random because there is no single paradigm to distinguish the chaff from the wheat (Kuhn 1970a: 16–17). In normal science, however, fact gathering becomes highly directed, not only because the paradigm focuses on certain phenomena, but because fact gathering usually "consumes much time, equipment, and money" (Kuhn 1970a: 25). Consequently, the gathering of facts becomes a highly selective activity.

According to Kuhn (1970a: 25–27), three types of facts are gathered. The first consists of those that the paradigm has shown to be of great importance for revealing the nature of things. The second, which is a smaller set, consists of those facts that, although they are not intrinsically important, can be used to test certain predictions from paradigm theory. Finally, the third class of facts, which Kuhn considers most important, consists of those facts that were not originally central to the paradigm but subsequently become important because of paradigm articulation. Before applying this analysis to international relations inquiry, it is important to specify just what is meant by data making in the field and indicate why it occurred.

Data making: what it is and why it occurs

Data making is the process by which facts are measured and quantified so that they can be used for hypothesis testing (see J. D. Singer 1965, 1968: 2). This definition is similar to that of Kuhn (1970a: 25–28), who defines fact gathering as not only the observation and recording of facts, but their transformation by measurement techniques into a form that allows them to be used to test hypotheses.

Data making is a central activity of any science not only because it provides the evidence for evaluating propositions but also because it is conducted by following specified rules and procedures. Part of the methodology of any discipline is devoted to the rules that should be followed and the techniques employed in converting facts into data. One of the primary rules is that the process should be replicable and reliable; that is, the procedures employed should be clear and precise enough that another scholar can independently follow those procedures and obtain the same results (J. D. Singer 1968: 2). The term *data* is usually applied only to the product of an activity that has followed this rule.

It is clear from this analysis that it would be possible to predict attempts at data making on the basis of knowing the amount of concern with hypothesis testing in a given field. This conclusion seems to be supported by the fact that it has only been on the two occasions when hypothesis testing became a concern to international relations scholars that data-making projects were initiated. The first occasion occurred with the independent studies of war initiated by Lewis Richardson and Quincy Wright just after World War I, the second with the behavioral revolt of the 1960s.

To say that data making arose out of a concern for hypothesis testing does not explain why the latter suddenly became a matter of concern. Lewis Richardson, who was a physicist, aptly summarized why he became concerned with hypothesis testing and data making in two letters to Wright:

> There is in the world a great deal of brilliant, witty political discussion which leads to no settled convictions. My aim has been different:

> namely to examine a few notions by quantitative techniques in the hope of reaching a reliable answer. . . .
>
> I notice that many of those who are considered to be experts on foreign affairs do not base their opinions on historical facts, but on some sort of instinctive reasoning.   (cited in Richardson 1960b: v)

Wright expressed a similar concern (1942: ch. 16 and appendix 25). Other scholars in the field, however, did not share this concern and were occupied instead with the debate over idealism and realism. As a result, Richardson's work was not recognized within the field until the 1960s, and, although Wright's work was lauded, it was not imitated. Data making died as suddenly as it had been born.

It was not until the beginning of the behavioral revolt of the 1960s that the concern with data making and hypothesis testing was resurrected. Indeed, one of the chief characteristics of the revolt was the initiation of data-making projects. This time, data making did not die out; it grew for over a decade and shows no signs of disappearing. What transpired in the interval between the late 1930s and the 1960s were two decades of intense theoretical activity. It may have been the existence of this theoretical analysis that allowed data making to become a concern in the field. Charles McClelland provides some hints as to why this may have happened:

> So many interesting concepts applicable to international relations were brought to attention in the 1950's and 1960's that the most urgent problem often seemed to be coordinating the concepts rather than testing them against data. . . . Theory has tended to become doctrine and the facts have been expected to conform to the doctrine. . . .
>
> A new research movement has arisen very recently apparently in reaction to the long preceding period. . . . The movement centers on the collection of international event data and the analysis of that data.   (McClelland 1972b: 16–17)

If McClelland is correct, and there is much impressionistic evidence to suggest that he is, then the second data movement in the field, along with the general concern with scientific method, arose out of the conviction that the kind of theorizing that had been conducted after World War II had gone about as far as it could and it was now time to collect data systematically and test some of the explanations suggested by the theorizing.

Data making in international relations during the pre-realist and behavioral periods

The appearance of two distinct periods of international relations data making, before the 1950s and during the 1960s, provides an opportunity to examine the validity of the proposition that data making in the field has been guided by the realist paradigm in the 1950s and 1960s. It would be expected that data making in the 1960s would be guided by the realist paradigm while data making prior to the 1950s would not. In addition, since the two pre-1950s projects are both on wars and Wright's was conducted in the field and Richardson's outside the field, an opportunity is provided to assess Kuhn's idea that different fields will employ different paradigms to study the same phenomena. Since Wright collected his data during the idealist–realist debate he would be expected to incorporate assumptions of both paradigms in his project. Conversely, Richardson, who was outside the field and had a certain disdain for its analysis, would be expected to employ a totally different paradigm. A review of the major data-making projects in the field will demonstrate that the expectations about Wright, Richardson, and data making in the 1960s support Kuhn's analysis.

Wright's project reflected the idealist–realist debate by taking assumptions from both idealism and realism. Idealism is apparent in his emphasis on the interdisciplinary approach and on legalism. His use of an interdisciplinary approach was evident in his devotion of large sections of his work to non-national war (e.g., animal and primitive warfare) and to reviewing the relevant literature in biology, psychology, sociology, and anthropology.[1] His emphasis on legalism was illustrated by the fact that he defined contemporary war in part as a "legal condition" (Wright 1965a: ch. 2, p. 8). However, Wright also reflected the realist emphasis on nation-states, power, and empirical analysis. He stated that the legal definition given at the beginning of the study is not scientific, but derived from the literature (Wright 1965a: 685), and a scientific definition would have to emerge from an examination of war itself. Finally, when he came to defining war operationally so he could collect data, Wright

---

[1] Compare Wright (1965a: chs. 5, 6, and 15) with the idealist approaches of Zimmern (1939).

combined assumptions of both the realists and idealists by limiting his data to:

> all hostilities involving members of the family of nations, whether international, civil, colonial or imperial, which were recognized as states of war in the legal sense or which involved over 50,000 troops. . . . The legal recognition of the warlike action, the scale of such action, and the importance of its legal and political consequences have, therefore, all been taken into consideration in deciding whether a given incident was sufficiently important to include in a list of wars. (Wright 1965a: 636)

Other uses of armed force, such as revolutions and interventions, were not included (Wright 1965a: 636), and participants in a war were only included if they were actually independent (*sovereign* in the realist paradigm) before or after the war. Participants with only de facto status in the war itself were not included (Wright 1965a: 637). Thus, Wright employed assumptions of the two paradigms to decide how to collect data on war.

Given the struggle between the idealist and realist paradigms, Wright's procedure seemed legitimate and obvious. To Richardson, who was outside the field, it did not appear at all obvious, and he opted for a very different operational definition. Richardson wanted a definition that would allow him to compare and measure specific wars. Taking assumptions from astronomy and psychology, he replaced the notion of *war* with the concept of a *deadly quarrel* and measured it as one would measure the magnitude of a star. His reasoning is worth quoting at length:

> CRITIC: . . . And how have you counted wars? . . . Are all to be counted alike?
>
> ASTRONOMER: Fortunately the logical problem of how to count unequal things has been solved. We should count wars as astronomers count stars, by first arranging them in order of magnitude. To ask whether "civil wars have been rarer than international wars" is indeed about as crude as to ask whether "red stars are rarer than blue stars." You can take another hint from the astronomers: as they have replaced red and blue by "spectral type," so you will probably have to reconsider the meanings of civil and international. Before the counting can begin we need to form a collection or list of wars of all kinds. The less conspicuous incidents are the more numerous – as among stars – so that it is impossible to make a list of them all. Some rule is therefore necessary for excluding the smaller incidents.

> Wright's selection rule . . . is however hardly satisfactory for statistical purposes. . . .[2]

> An essential characteristic of a war may be said to be casualties. . . . From a psychological point of view a war, a riot, and a murder, though differing in many important aspects . . . have at least this in common, that they are all manifestations of the instinct of aggressiveness. . . . By a deadly quarrel is meant any quarrel which caused death to humans. The term thus includes murders, banditries, mutinies, insurrections, and wars small and large; but it excludes accidents, and calamities.   (Richardson 1960b: 1, 4–6)

Thus, Richardson rejected the dominant notions about war within the field of international relations inquiry, whereas Wright reflected the emphases in the field. The first occasion of data making, then, tends to support Kuhn's analysis of fact gathering as a paradigm-directed activity.

The second occasion of data making in the field occurred in the early 1960s and continues through the present. In the 1960s, data making was centered on three areas – national attributes, foreign policy behavior, and war. As a result of the articulation of the realist paradigm that had been conducted in the 1950s, these three areas were the most obvious ones in which to collect data to test hypotheses related to the realist paradigm. The plausibility of this conclusion can be seen by examining how each area was relevant to the realist paradigm.

National attributes, the first area, was highly relevant because Morgenthau and the other power politics theorists had maintained that knowledge of national power was a particularly revealing aspect of the conduct of international relations. Furthermore, Morgenthau (1960, 1973: ch. 9) had attempted to demonstrate in detail that the elements (or indicators) of national power were what in the 1960s would have been called national attributes. Given the paradigm, data on national attributes would not only be of intrinsic value but would also provide a series of key independent variables.

The second and third areas, foreign policy behavior and war, were relevant to the paradigm because they provided the major dependent variables. They were the topics that the paradigm wanted to explain. If the proposition being examined in this chapter is accurate, then it would be expected that data collected in these two areas would reflect

---

[2] For specific criticisms of Wright, which include an attack on the idealist emphasis on legality and the realist emphasis on the importance of wars, see Richardson (1960b: 5).

the characterizations of foreign policy behavior and wars made by the paradigm; that, is, foreign policy behavior would be viewed in terms of a struggle for power and peace (in other words, conflict and cooperation among nations), and war would be viewed as something occurring among nations and related to the balance of power. Since it was demonstrated in chapter 3 that these three areas were of central concern to the realist paradigm, it is only necessary to show that data were collected in these areas.

The initial data published and made available to scholars in the 1960s were products more of comparative politics than international relations (see J. D. Singer 1968: 11–12).[3] The collections consisted basically of attribute data on nations, and although not collected specifically with theories of international relations in mind, they provided a set of relevant variables on what Morgenthau had called the elements of national power. The major collections were *A Cross Polity Survey* (1963) by Banks and Textor and the *World Handbook of Political and Social Indicators* (1964) by Russett, Alker, Deutsch, and Lasswell of Yale.[4] These two projects were initiated not only to collect data for specific research projects but to provide general data sets that could be used by scholars working on a variety of projects. Consequently, not only was the data published, it also was made available on computer tapes stored at the Inter-University Consortium for Political Research, which has become the data library for the entire field of political science. *A Cross Polity Survey* provided data from widely scattered sources on demographic, economic, cultural, and social characteristics of 115 nations. In addition, the authors provided new data on political characteristics through the use of content analysis. The *World Handbook* also provided data on the demographic, economic, cultural, social, and political characteristics of nations; however, none of the data was derived by coding. The *World Handbook* differed from the *A Cross Polity Survey* in that it provided more variables (75 versus 57), but most of these were not as a "political" as the coded data of Banks and Textor.

By the end of the decade, both these projects had produced more data. Banks provided similar attribute data going back as far as 1815 (Banks 1971, 1973). These data permitted hypotheses to be tested

[3] Also see the introductions to Arthur Banks and R. B. Textor, *A Cross Polity Survey* (1963), and Bruce Russett et al., *World Handbook of Political and Social Indicators* (1964).

[4] The book by Banks and Textor did not contain the actual data but did provide a list of the variables available from the Inter-University Consortium for Political Research.

longitudinally. Charles Lewis Taylor and Michael Hudson published a second edition of the *World Handbook* (1972) containing a great amount of new data. In addition to including longitudinal data on attribute variables similar to the ones in the first edition, data on political institutions, internal conflict, interventions, and 57,268 daily coded events were provided. Both these projects, however, were initiated to collect data for testing comparative politics hypotheses dealing with the prerequisites of democracy, modernization, social change, and internal conflict (e.g., Hudson 1977: 405–411).

The earliest data-making project that was directly concerned with international relations was the Dimensionality of Nations (DON) project begun in 1962 by Harold Guetzkow, Jack Sawyer, and R. J. Rummel (see Rummel 1976: 19–21). Rummel has been the guiding force in the project and its director since 1963 (see Hilton 1973: 13). As with the two preceding projects, a large number of variables (over 200) on national attributes were collected for various times in the 1950s and 1960s.[5] Data on internal and external conflict were also collected. The DON project, in addition to providing much more data on what Morgenthau had called the elements of national power, also provided the first extensive data on a dependent variable of interest to the realist paradigm: conflict and cooperation among nations.

The concern in the 1960s with collecting data on more of the dependent variables of interest to the field led to data projects on foreign policy behavior. One of the most readily available sources of data on the foreign policies of nations was their votes in the United Nations.[6] UN votes were first collected early in the 1960s, and this project remained one of the ongoing activities of the Inter-University Consortium for Political Research throughout the 1960s and 1970s. Votes, however, were not really the kind of behavior that followers of the realist paradigm saw as most important; they were more interested in inter-state interactions.

One of the most imaginative and perhaps most influential projects to collect data on inter-state interactions was the World Event Interaction Survey (WEIS) initiated by Charles McClelland (1967, 1976). This project coded the interactions of nations reported daily in sentences in the *New York Times* into sixty-three categories of behavior.

[5] There was not much duplication among Banks and Textor (1963), Russett et al. (1964), and DON, because different measures were employed.

[6] These were really a substitute for more desirable data, which were not readily available; see Russett (1967: 59–60).

These categories could be collapsed into two types – cooperation and conflict. The actual distribution in the categories, however, suggested that perhaps three types might be more appropriate – cooperation, conflict, and participation (McClelland and Hoggard 1969: 714).[7] The excitement generated by the WEIS project is indicated by the fact that it led to an event data movement that resulted in several similar projects and one of the most extensive and lengthy discussions in the field on data making.[8]

War was the third major area in which data were collected in the sixties. The most extensive project in this area and the successor to the efforts of Richardson and Wright was the Correlates of War project of J. David Singer and Melvin Small (1972). They collected data on wars and alliances among states from 1816 to 1965. Unlike Richardson, they concentrated only on wars that had at least one nation involved; unlike Wright, they did not reflect the emphasis on legalism (Singer and Small 1972: 18, 30–35). Instead, they took Wright's and Richardson's lists of wars plus any other wars they found record of, and then removed those wars whose participants' political status did not meet their membership criteria or who failed to meet their minimum threshold of battle-connected casualties (J. D. Singer and Small 1972: 18–19). The first criterion stems directly from the concerns of the realist paradigm, since political status is determined by the extent to which a participant is a sovereign nation, and nations in turn are divided into two categories ("total system" and "central system") depending on their power (see J. D. Singer and Small 1972: 19–24).

In addition to collecting data on war, the Correlates of War project

---

[7] For other attempts to find underlying dimensions in WEIS data see S. A. Salmore (1972); Kegley (1973); S. A. Salmore and Munton (1974); and Wilkenfeld, Hopple, and Rossa (1979: 127–130).

[8] The two main topics of discussion were the validity of sources (whether a single source, like the *New York Times*, would bias data either through selection of events or through the journalists' interpretation of the events and whether multiple sources might solve this problem); and how to code behavior (whether cooperation and conflict should be scaled or classified into discrete categories). Both these questions were addressed through empirical research. On source validity, see the studies of Azar (1970); Gamson and Modigliani (1971: Appendix C); Sigler (1972a, 1972b); Doran, Pendley, and Antunes (1973); Hoggard (1974); Burrowes (1974); McGowan (1974); Bobrow, Chan, and Kringen (1977). On the question of scaling see Moses et al. (1967); McClelland and Hoggard (1969); C. F. Hermann (1971); Brody (1972); Kegley (1973); Kegley, Salmore, and Rosen (1974); S. Salmore and Munton (1974); Azar (1970); Azar and Havener (1976). For general reviews of the event data movement see Burgess and Lawton (1972); Peterson (1975); and Azar and Ben-Dak (1975).

collected data on several important independent variables. The first effort was focused on alliance data, which clearly reflects the realist concern with the balance of power and with the polarity debate (see J. D. Singer and Small 1966a, 1968). The alliance data were collected first for the period 1815–1940 (J. D. Singer and Small 1966b) and then updated to 1965 (Small and Singer 1969). The second major area of data making for the project was on diplomatic ties from 1815 on (J. D. Singer and Small 1966b; see also Small and Singer 1973). These data initially served as a way of determining membership in the central system (see J. D. Singer and Small 1968) and were used by the end of the 1960s to test propositions on status inconsistency (Wallace 1970, 1971). Data were also collected on the number of intergovernmental organizations in the system from 1815 to 1964 (J. D. Singer and Wallace 1970). Each of these data sets was updated periodically, Finally, data on national capability began to be collected in the mid-sixties (J. D. Singer 1976: 27; J. D. Singer, Bremer, and Stuckey 1972; Ray and Singer 1979; Bremer 1980).

The selection of these three independent variables and the order in which they received priority reflect the strong influence of the realist paradigm and its priorities. Alliances and national capability were thought by the early power politics theorists to be the two most important determinants of peace and war. The status-ordering data were taken as an indirect indicator of power, and the data on IGO's were employed to test realist propositions (see J. D. Singer and Wallace 1970; Wallace 1972).

The other major data set on wars was that collected for the 1914 studies on the outbreak of World War I. Unlike the other data sets, this one was not placed on file with the consortium for general use. Nevertheless, it played an important role in data making because it was the first data set produced in the field by content analyzing previously secret government documents from various states in order to delineate decision makers' perceptions just prior to the outbreak of a major war.

Each of these data sets is large and comprehensive enough in its own area so that it can be used by many scholars to test a variety of hypotheses of interest to the realist paradigm, but they were all collected with specific propositions in mind. A brief overview of the initial use of the data by their collectors will underline the association between data making in the field and the realist paradigm.

As was seen in chapter 4, the Dimensionality of Nations project mathematically elaborated and then tested verbal suggestions made by Morgenthau and other power politics theorists about the relationship between national power and states' foreign policy behavior and interaction (see Rummel 1963, 1972a, 1979). UN voting data were used to test hypotheses about bloc allegiances, the struggle for power between blocs, and national power (see Ball 1951; Alker and Russett 1965; Rowe 1969). The initial purpose of WEIS was to map inter-state interactions in two arenas of the Cold War: the Berlin and Taiwan Straits crises (McClelland 1968, 1972a). The Correlates of War data were initially employed to test hypotheses on the balance of power, polarity, and war (J. D. Singer and Small 1968). Finally, the 1914 studies related decision makers' perceptions and the outbreak of war (O. R. Holsti, North, and Brody 1968).[9]

Each of the major data sets, then, reflects the realist paradigm's fundamental assumptions that nations are the most important actors and research should be focused on the struggle for power and peace. In addition, each data set was used to test specific hypotheses relevant to the realist paradigm. Consequently, it is not surprising that most of the data consist of national attributes and inter-state conflict and cooperation. The proposition being examined in this chapter maintains that such a result is not an accident but the product of the power of the realist paradigm to guide and direct scholarly activity within the field. Now that the proposition has been elaborated and its plausibility demonstrated, it is necessary to specify how it will be empirically tested.

Research design

Operationalization and measurement

In order to test the proposition that the realist paradigm guided data making in the field of international relations in the 1950s and 1960s, it is necessary to operationalize *data making* and the *realist paradigm*. Since data making is the transformation of facts into variables for the purpose of hypothesis testing, data making can be operationalized as *variables available to international relations scholars in a form that permits hypothesis testing*. According to this definition, whether an activity is

---

[9] All the claims in this paragraph have been substantiated at length and with extensive citation from the literature in Vasquez (1983: 47–126).

data making is determined by its product, that is, whether it produces variables. In addition, these variables must be in a form suitable for testing and available to international relations scholars. The first criterion means that the variables must be on computer tape or cards, in recognition of the fact that one of the major costs in data making is transforming published data into computerized data. The second criterion allows data that may have been collected by scholars outside the field (e.g., by people in the United Nations or in comparative politics) to be included if the data are available to international relations scholars.

The term *realist paradigm* was operationalized in chapter 3. The coding scheme assumes that if the actors and topics labeled as realist in the coding scheme are indicators of the assumptions of the realist paradigm, variables employing those actors and topics can be used as indicators of realist concepts.

The problem with this measure is that a variable is not necessarily an indicator of only one concept. For example, the variable GNP may be taken as an indicator of wealth, industrialization, and/or national power. In the coding scheme, GNP would be coded as an indicator of national power. A scholar in comparative politics or economics, however, might not view it as such an indicator, and to classify such a variable as reflecting the assumptions of the realist paradigm might be viewed as highly invalid. Since variables do not inherently serve as indicators of a single concept, it is perfectly legitimate to code them as indicators of one concept if that variable is one of the common ways a group of scholars operationalize the concept.[10] This is a valid procedure because within the field, GNP is widely taken and can be used as an indicator of national economic power (see East and Hermann 1974: 284). Although the same measures may be taken as indicators of other concepts outside the field, this is not relevant to the analysis. The validity of the coding scheme rests on a consensus within the field about the use of indicators and cannot be validly applied outside the field of international relations.

The only way systematic measurement error could occur would be if the competing paradigms in the field used indicators that were labeled realist in the coding scheme to measure nonrealist concepts. This type of error cannot occur because the major alternative para-

---

[10] Meaning is not inherent in a word or variable; it is determined by use (see Austin [1962]).

digms – transnational relations, issue politics, and Marxism – do not employ the nation-state as the sole actor, and they emphasize different topics of inquiry.

This use of the coding scheme assumes that if most of the variables for which data have been collected have actors and topics of inquiry that are labeled realist in the coding scheme, this finding would not be an accident. Rather, it would indicate that the realist paradigm has guided data making in the field. This seems to be a reasonable assumption to make. Given these validity arguments and the fact that reliability was established at 0.90, it can be concluded that the dominance of the realist paradigm has been adequately measured for the purpose of this test.[11]

Deriving hypotheses

Two hypotheses can be derived from the proposition to test its adequacy:

2a. Variables available for use by international relations scholars will tend to provide information on nation-states and topics of inquiry that are labeled realist in the coding scheme.

2b. More variables will be available for use by international relations scholars on the two most central concepts in the realist paradigm – national power and inter-nation conflict-cooperation – than on other concepts.[12]

Hypothesis 2a is the most obvious way to test the proposition. It makes the assumption that if data making was guided by the realist paradigm in the 1950s and 1960s, then it is reasonable to expect that, out of all the variables produced, a statistically significant number should provide information on nation states and on topics of inquiry that were deemed important by the realist paradigm; that is, the distribution should not be random. If this were not the case, then it would make no sense to say that the realist paradigm had guided data making, and the hypothesis would be justifiably falsified.

Hypothesis 2b makes a more specific prediction. It not only assumes the accuracy of hypothesis 2a but goes on to say that of all

---

[11] For the reliability formula, see chapter 3, note 6.
[12] These hypotheses are numbered 2a and 2b because they test the second proposition in this book.

the concepts for which data could be collected, more data will be collected on the two most central concepts of the realist paradigm: national power and inter-nation conflict-cooperation. Since the realist paradigm focused on national power as the chief independent variable and on inter-nation conflict-cooperation as the chief dependent variable, it is reasonable to expect that more data would be collected on these two concepts.

The sample

Given the above analysis, it is clear that an important criterion in selecting a sample is to insure that it include only data that are either produced or generally available within the field. A second criterion is that these data be within the time span of the proposition. The major problem in selecting a sample is to find a list of variables produced or available in the field.

Since the Inter-University Consortium for Political Research classifies and lists variables it has on file, the consortium's list of all the variables in its international relations archive was taken as the sample.[13] This provides a nonbiased sample of data available in the field. It also includes the universe of data readily and routinely available to all scholars by the end of the 1960s. It does not, however, include the universe of data produced in the field, since all data may not have been placed on file by that date, either because they were not complete or because the scholars who collected the data may have wanted to analyze it first. While the present analysis might have been more complete if these other cases were included, sufficiently accurate information about them did not exist to make their inclusion feasible.[14] The selection of this sample, however, has the advantage of making the present analysis easily replicable in the future.

This sample provided a list of 1,650 variables, a number more than sufficient for statistical analysis. These variables are presented in the consortium's *Variable Index* as the product of 31 data sets. Since some of the projects produced more than one data set, however, only 20 projects account for all the data on file. With the exception of

---

[13] See Inter-University Consortium for Political Research, *Variable Index for Studies Available from the International Relations Archive* (May 1971).

[14] For a review of some of the major data projects not on file by 1971, see Burgess and Lawton (1972).

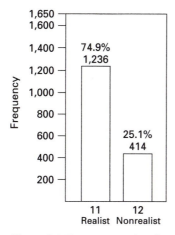

Figure 5.1 Percentage of realist indicators in the field (hypothesis 2a)

Richardson's *Statistics of Deadly Quarrels*, all of the data sets were completed in the 1960s, and even Richardson's data were not made available in computerized form until Rummel transferred the information to tape in the 1960s.[15]

The findings

Hypothesis 2a predicted that variables produced and available in the field would tend to provide information on nation-states and on topics of inquiry that were labeled realist in the coding scheme. In order to test this hypothesis, the 1,650 variables were classified into two categories – realist indicators or nonrealist indicators. In order to be classified as a realist indicator, a variable had to have the nation as its actor and a realist topic; any mixed cases (nation as actor with a nonrealist topic or vice versa) were classified as nonrealist. If the hypothesis were true, it would be expected that a large proportion of the variables would be usable as realist indicators. The findings are presented in figure 5.1. The figure clearly shows that just about three-fourths (74.9 percent) of the variables can be used as realist indicators. This would hardly appear to be a random distribution, and the calculation of a binomial distribution ($p<.01$) for interpretive purposes

[15] Richardson's data, of course, do not support the proposition.

supports this assumption.[16] On the basis of the finding, it can be concluded that hypothesis 2a has failed to be falsified.

Hypothesis 2b predicted that variables produced and available in the field would tend to provide more indicators of national power and inter-nation conflict-cooperation than of any other concept. Table 5.1 tests this hypothesis by rank-ordering the concepts. It can be seen from this table that the concepts of national power and inter-nation conflict-cooperation compose 66.4 percent of the total variables produced (49.9 percent and 16.5 percent respectively). In addition, none of the other concepts constitutes more than 9.1 percent of the data available. On the basis of these findings, it can be concluded that hypothesis 2b has failed to be falsified. These findings, provide considerable support for the proposition. The next section will examine data making in the 1970s to see the extent to which it has continued to be guided by the realist paradigm.

Data making in the 1970s

The major data-making projects of the 1970s can be divided into three categories: national attributes, event data, and, for lack of a better term, reconstructed historical interaction data. The data on national attributes reflect the efforts of two groups to collect independent variables. Both are noteworthy for advancements in measurement rather than for new collecting procedures or new types of data. The first group is that associated with attempts to test Rosenau's pre-theory. Various indicators of size, wealth, and polity were collected by Burgess and Harf (1975) as part of the Inter-University Comparative Foreign Policy project (see also Burgess 1970). Additional data on these concepts were collected as part of the CREON project, with new indicators of regime constraint, capacity to act, and decision makers' personal characteristics and perceptions of the situation (see B. G. Salmore and S. A. Salmore 1975; East 1975; M. G. Hermann 1974; M. G. Hermann, C. F. Hermann, and Dixon 1979; and Brady 1975). With the exception of the perceptual variables of decision makers, these data are all undoubtedly indicators of a reformulated concept of national power.

Even more explicitly tied to the national power concept has been the effort of the Correlates of War project to collect indicators of

---

[16] For a discussion of the use of the binomial distribution, see chapter 6, note 7.

Table 5.1. *Rank order of indicators according to amount of data (hypothesis 2b)*

Actor	Topic	Frequency (number of variables)	Percentage	Rank
NATION	NATIONAL POWER[a]	824	49.9	1
NATION	CONFLICT-COOPERATION[a]	273	16.5	2
Nations and other actors	Conflict-cooperation	150	9.1	3
Nation	Transactions	85	5.2	4
NATION	SUPRANATIONALISM[a]	56	3.4	5
NATION	ALLIANCES[a]	46	2.8	6
NATION	ISOLATIONISM[a]	39	2.4	7
Nation	Issues	37	2.2	8
Nations and other actors	Sociological characteristics	35	2.1	9
Subnational	Conflict-cooperation	16	1.0	10
IGO	Supranationalism	15	0.9	11
IGO	Conflict-cooperation	14	0.8	12.5
Nation	Miscellaneous	14	0.8	12.5
IGO	Issues	11	0.7	14
Nations and other actors	National power	9	0.5	15
IGO	Miscellaneous	5	0.3	16.5
Nations and other actors	Miscellaneous	5	0.3	16.5
Nations and other actors	Alliances	3	0.2	18
Subnational	Issues	2	0.1	21
Subnational	Alliances	2	0.1	21
None	Miscellaneous	2	0.1	21
Nations and other actors	Integration	2	0.1	21
Nations and other actors	Propaganda	2	0.1	21
NGO	Miscellaneous	1	0.1	25
Non-national	Conflict-cooperation	1	0.1	25
Nations and other actors	Transactions	1	0.1	25
		1,650	99.9	

Note: [a] Realist concept.

national capability from 1815 to 1965. Researchers in this project defined capability as containing demographic, industrial, and military dimensions (see J. D. Singer, Bremer, and Stuckey 1972). The primary contribution of this effort, which involves at least two indicators for each dimension, is the care that has been taken to obtain reliable indicators from historical sources. Of even greater significance than the collection of the raw indicators has been the attempt to develop sophisticated measures of national capability by combining the three dimensions (see especially Ray and Singer 1973 and Ray 1980).

Attempts to improve measures have also taken place on data collected earlier on alliances (Wallace 1973b; Bueno de Mesquita 1975) and on intergovernmental organizations (Wallace 1975). The collection of data on national capability marks a transition of the Correlates of War project from testing propositions related to alliances to testing propositions on the distribution of power (see Singer, Bremer, and Stuckey 1972; Bremer 1980; Gochman 1980). The connection between these data and the power politics tradition should be obvious, but, as if to eliminate any doubt, Singer (1980) gave the following subtitle to the second volume of the Correlates of War – *Testing Some Realpolitik Models*.

While the Correlates of War project tested some central realist propositions during the 1960s (see Singer 1976: 26), data collection toward the end of the 1970s indicated that it was moving toward a more general study of violence that might challenge the second assumption of the realist paradigm. This tendency is best evidenced by the publication of data on civil wars from 1816 through 1980 (see Small and Singer 1982). Whether this will give rise to a body of work that challenges the realist paradigm, as some of the work on status inconsistency did, remains to be seen. Nevertheless, the collection of civil war data is certainly something that would not be expected given the first two assumptions of the realist paradigm.

While the efforts to collect more national attribute data are important, particularly in terms of measurement, the real explosion in data making in the 1970s was with event data. The two major event data projects, the heirs to WEIS, have been CREON (Comparative Research on the Events of Nations) and COPDAB (Conflict and Peace Data Bank). The CREON data set has foreign policy data for thirty-six nations for randomly selected periods between 1959 and 1968. The specific nations were selected for theoretical reasons and can be thought of as a representative sample to test propositions related to the Rosenau pre-theory on political accountability and on size (see C. F. Hermann et al. 1973: 23). The project has made two major contributions, one methodological and the other theoretical. Methodologically, CREON reflects several advances over WEIS, the two most important being the conceptualization of a foreign policy event (C. F Hermann 1971; C. F. Hermannn et al. 1973) to include an indirect target, and the development of a coding scheme that could tap a variety of behavior, not just cooperation and conflict. The last development is intimately related to CREON's major theoretical contribution, which is to reconceptualize the notion of foreign policy behavior inherited from Rosenau. Based on the empirical work of S. A. Salmore (1972), CREON attempted to collect data on several different aspects of foreign policy behavior, with major attention being devoted to foreign policy position change, independence/interdependence of action, commitment, affect intensity and direction, acceptance/rejection ratios, external consequentiality, the number and salience of substantive problem (issue) areas receiving attention, and the instrumentalities (resources) employed (see Brady 1975; M. G. Hermann, C. F. Hermann, and Dixon 1979; East, Salmore, and Hermann 1978). As with other data efforts in the 1970s, the CREON group has made important contributions to measurement (see Callahan et al. 1982).

The main criticism of CREON has been that it has only one data source, *Deadline Data*. This has raised serious questions among a few scholars about the data's validity. The response of the members of the project is that they have employed not the summaries but the uncollapsed set of *Deadline Data* obtained from the publishers; they argue that, while this base is not sufficient as a complete record of behavior, it is sufficient for the specific propositions they wish to test (C. F. Hermann et al. 1973: 17–21).

Data that rely on a single source can never be as good as data derived from multiple sources, but the tone and character of some of this criticism, especially that given verbally at professional meetings (but see also Bobrow, Chan, and Kringen 1977), suggests a misunderstanding of the nature of the scientific enterprise. Science does not progress with the sudden birth of perfect research designs, data collections, and statistical analyses. Every design and measure is flawed to a certain extent. The scientist's task is not to replicate reality in the laboratory but to establish a set of conditions under which hypotheses are tested; as long as these conditions are not biased in favor of a particular hypothesis, certain inferences can tentatively be made, keeping in mind any potential validity problems. As others, employing different research designs and data, test the same propositions, more evidence can be brought to bear to determine the utility of any specific proposition. To be too perfectionistic at early stages of inquiry will reduce what little real evidence there is.[17] This is an important point, because collecting data on foreign policy behavior has been the major area of difficulty in the field, and event data provide one of the few hopes for establishing a reliable base for testing hypotheses on inter-state behavior.

The most ambitious event–data set is Azar's COPDAB. Initially a multiple source data set that attempted to collect regional event data on all the Middle Eastern nations and the major powers from 1945 through 1969 (Azar 1970: 13), it has expanded to global coverage of about 135 nations, based on over 70 data sources, for the period from 1948 through 1980 (Azar 1980: 146). Clearly, this is a conscious attempt to fulfill the dream of the WEIS project to become the main data bank for the field for inter-state interactions. The data itself are highly reliable and its source validity should be unquestioned, at least in terms of public sources. In this regard, COPDAB has overcome the major problem of WEIS and CREON. COPDAB's main problems are that there are too few dependent variables, and that the way they are measured, particularly the thirteen-point cooperation-conflict scale, may be too limiting for the data set to serve as the major data bank for inter-state interactions. Nevertheless, a significant number of propositions could and no doubt will be tested with the existing variables. In addition, the mere abstraction of the raw events could prove invaluable to researchers, who could then code their own variables.

While COPDAB has attempted to provide a data set for the entire field, most event–data sets in the 1970s had more limited ambitions. It was the problems with the global WEIS set that initially led Azar (1970) to collect multiple-source regional data on the Middle East. This effort to collect regional data was supplemented by Patrick

---

[17] It is interesting to note that Bobrow, Chan, and Kringen (1979) (see also Chan, Kringen, and Bobrow 1979), after criticizing CREON, have severe problems of their own in collecting event data. This is because instead of going directly to the *People's Daily* of China, they use a data set derived from that source by Katz (1972) and Katz, Lent, and Novotny (1973) for the US army. By their own admission, this data set is incomplete (December 1972 is missing), and the validity of some of the topics in the coding schemes is questionable (see Chan, Kringen, and Bobrow 1979: 277).

McGowan's AFRICA project on sub-Saharan foreign policy interactions (see McGowan and Johnson 1979). McGowan collected event data on participation and cooperation-conflict. This was then supplemented by a variety of national attributes, including data on leadership style, dependence, and penetration, as well as more conventional indicators. Additional African data have been provided by William Copson (1973), who collected event data focusing primarily on conflict. Comparable regional data for Latin America and Asia were not forthcoming, although Doran, Pendley, and Antunes (1973) did explore regional Latin American sources. The hope that global data sets might be supplemented by more in-depth regional sets was eventually fulfilled at the end of the decade by the expansion of Azar's (1980) COPDAB, which includes the best multiple sources for each region.

The most influential effect of the event data movement, which accounts for the myriad of data-making efforts, was the use of event data by individual researchers to test specific hypotheses. Among the best work in this area was Gamson and Modigliani's (1971) highly imaginative use of the front page of the *New York Times*, including interesting scaling techniques for determining salience and weighting measures to reduce bias, to test alternative explanations of the Cold War. Bobrow, Chan, and Kringen (1979) used event data to produce the first major quantitative analysis of the People's Republic of China's foreign policy (see also Chan 1978, 1979). A final example is that of Michael Sullivan (1972, 1979) who coded American presidential speeches to determine how they correlated with escalation in the Vietnam War.

A number of event–data sets were also collected to study inter-state interactions in the Middle East. The most extensive data sets were those of Wilkenfeld, who borrowed from Rummel's DON coding scheme (see Wilkenfeld 1975). Burrowes (1974; Burrowes and Spector 1973) collected data from several sources to test the hypotheses that internal conflict leads to external conflict. Blechman (1972) used event data to provide a detailed account of Israeli reprisals toward the Arabs. Milstein (1972) looked at the role of big-power intervention through the use of event data.

While these studies are only illustrative, it should be clear that the overwhelming focus of event data has been the major dependent variable stipulated by the realist paradigm – cooperation and conflict. In addition, many of these studies employed national attributes to predict the patterns of inter-state interactions; this was certainly the case with some of the CREON tests (see East 1975; B. G. Salmore and S. A. Salmore 1975). Even those who moved to the periphery of the paradigm by looking at decision makers' perceptions or personalities still focused largely on nation-state conflict-cooperation (see M. G. Hermann 1974; Brady 1975; M. G. Hermann et al. 1979; see also Brewer 1973).

By the mid-1970s, however, some of those who were calling for a new paradigm tried to collect data, usually event data, to support their case. O'Leary (1976) recoded WEIS data to show the difference controlling for issues made in analyzing event data and to attempt to test aspects of the PRINCE simulation model. Mansbach, Ferguson, and Lampert (1976) collected data on non-state actors to delineate empirically the role that such actors play in world politics. Mansbach and Vasquez (1981a) attempted to bring these two trends together by delineating the distortions that could result from analyzing event data without including non-state actors and controlling for issues. Analyzing the same data, Henehan (1981) began to test specific issue area typologies to see which would be the most potent. Since both CREON and COPDAB contain an issue-area variable, more work in this last area may be expected.

Towards the end of the 1970s, a new type of data, attempting to overcome some of the problems inherent in event data, began to be collected in several quarters. These various efforts constitute the third area of data making in the 1970s, and in many ways are the most exciting. They differ from event data primarily in that specific cases are preselected and the data about them are usually collected from a variety of sources, not just newspapers. Since this often involves reconstructing a case, these data might be called *reconstructed historical interaction data*.

Although not completed, the most important data set in this area will probably be the collection of serious disputes by the Correlates of War project (see Wallace 1979; J. D. Singer 1979b; Gochman 1980). The effort began with an attempt to locate all serious disputes between 1815 and 1965 in which one or more major power threatened or used military force (see Gochman 1980; A. Levy 1977). Including intervention in a civil war, Gochman found 171 serious disputes (1980: 92–93). Various data were then collected around or about these disputes. J. D. Singer (1979a), with an updated version of the data (1815–1975; 225 disputes), attempted to analyze what makes a dispute escalate to war with data about the disputants' geographical contiguity, alliance pattern, military capability, and defense expenditures. Singer's preliminary analyses were very encouraging.

A more limited analysis of the relationship between serious disputes and the presence of arms races was made by Wallace (1979, 1981). Methodologically related to this effort is the work of Russell Leng (Leng and Goodsell 1974; Leng 1980; Leng and Wheeler 1979) on the relationship between bargaining tactics and the escalation of a crisis to war. He analyzed this set of propositions by comparing crises that preceded war with crises that did not lead to war. This effort on serious disputes, no doubt, will be greatly aided by the work of the Stockholm International Peace Research Institute (SIPRI), which has been systematically collecting data on international conflicts (see SIPRI 1968/1969 and Thompson, Duval, and Dia 1979).

Some attempts to collect data on specific cases predated the datamaking work in the Correlates of War project. Two works – those of Barringer (1972) and Butterworth (1976) – are of particular interest. Trying to answer some of the same questions about war, escalation, and conflict resolution that are of concern to the researchers in the Correlates of War project, both these scholars, working independently of each other and of the project, collected similar data. Richard Barringer (1972) took eighteen disputes and collected data on 300 variables associated with the cases. He then analyzed the data inductively to determine what variables are associated with conflict patterns. Robert Butterworth (1976, 1978; see also E. B. Haas, Butterworth, and Nye 1972) collected data on 310 instances of conflict management from 1945 to 1974 in an attempt to discern the elements that promote successful conflict management and resolution. Although less successful than Barringer (1972) or the Correlates of War studies in producing strong findings, the published summaries of each instance and the variables associated with them provide valuable sources for future studies. More comprehensive and theoretical than these two efforts is the planned project of Michael Brecher (1977) to collect a variety of data on numerous crises. Once completed, this will be an important addition to the comparative study of crises.

The final major effort that can be included in this group is a very large data set collected for the US Defense Department on instances of crisis management (defined very broadly as any instance requiring a rapid response from the Pentagon which will affect the national interest; see Hazlewood, Hayes, and Brownell [1977: 79]). These data were collected by CACI, Inc., under contract from ARPA (Advanced Research Projects Agency of the Department of Defense), and include 289 instances of domestic and international "crises" from 1945 to 1975 (see CACI 1975). These data have been supplemented with more detailed information on 101 global crises from 1956 to 1976 from data supplied by Blechman and Kaplan (1979), and by Mahoney (1976) (see Abolfathi, Hayes, and Hayes 1979). Forty-one of the crises were investigated further, being coded for 70 different management problems that might arise (Hazlewood, Hayes, and Brownell 1977: 90). More recently, data on perceptions of the US Department of State, the CIA, and the Department of Defense for 36 crises from 1966 to 1975 were analyzed by Phillips and Rimkunas (1979). This project is related to Chinese perceptions during crises (Chan 1978; Bobrow, Chan, and Kringen 1979) and Soviet perceptions of crises (Mahoney and Clayberg 1980), the latter containing data on 386 "crises" from 1946 to 1975.[18]

Clearly, the work on reconstructed historical interaction data has produced much material that can be used to test propositions important to the realist paradigm generally and to power politics explanations specifically. The work on serious disputes, although it may ultimately support social psychological models (see Wallace 1979), has tested a number of explicit realist propositions (see Leng 1980). The studies of Barringer (1982) and Brecher (1977) focus on nation-states or their official decision makers and on inter-nation conflict-cooperation. Finally, Butterworth's (1976) data seem to have been gathered to test propositions on the periphery of the paradigm, that is, on the success of IGOs. Thus, while much of the data can and will be used to test realist hypotheses, preliminary use suggests that they may also give rise to findings that may undercut some of the paradigm's fundamental assumptions.

While three major efforts – national attributes, event data, and reconstructed data – reflect the type of data making that has predominated in the 1970s, they have been supplemented by data making on two other topics: arms races and economic dependency. Like some of the work on national attributes, most of this data making involves employing statistics gathered by other agencies; the main contribution

---

[18] Less relevant theoretically or methodologically, but of political interest, is CACI's related project on the attitudes of the American public toward military spending from 1930 to 1978 (see Abolfathi 1980).

100

tends to be measurement, rather than data making per se. Nevertheless, the collection of new data by those outside the field can have a significant impact on research within the field. No other research program better exemplifies this than the arms race studies. Somewhat data-poor at the beginning of the decade, the work on arms races by the end of the 1970s had gathered such a large amount of data that much went unanalyzed, leading two reviewers to claim that there was now a "surfeit of data" (Moll and Luebbert 1980: 178).

The major data sources have been the annual publications of the Stockholm International Peace Research Institute (SIPRI) and the US Arms Control and Disarmament Agency (ACDA) on defense expenditures and armaments. These data have then been used to make very sophisticated measures and models of arms building. In terms of this chapter, it is these measures that can be seen as the data contribution, since the actual data is already available. This point is less true of the more historical data on arms expenditures that have been retrieved by the Correlates of War project, since these were not made available by outside sources.

Although most of the efforts of the 1970s have produced additional or new indicators for the realist paradigm, by the end of the decade data relevant to several Marxist propositions began to be collected. The earliest came from comparative politics with the Kaufman, Chernotsky, and Geller (1975) test of some dependency propositions (see also Ray and Webster 1978). In addition, McGowan collected economic dependency data for Africa in an effort to replicate the Kaufman et al. (1975) study (see McGowan and Smith 1978). Economic data of this type have also been employed by Gochman and Ray (1979) to delineate structural disparities in Latin America and Eastern Europe from 1950 to 1970. Clearly, since most of this economic data have been collected by outside agencies, the data-making contribution is primarily in measurement, particularly measurement of Marxist concepts.

Not all measures of economic data related to dependency took their lead from Marxist concepts. A number relied on power politics concepts related to coercion and influence. This was particularly the case after the 1973–1974 Arab oil embargo. Interesting measures of dependence and interdependence have been developed by Caporaso (1978) and Caporaso and Ward (1979). From a broader comparative foreign policy perspective, Wilkenfeld, Hopple, and Rossa (1979) have developed a set of measures to tap energy, food, and trade dependency. In contrast to the more Marxist measures, these measures attempt to tap aspects of what used to be regarded as national power. The development of alternate measures will make for interesting future comparisons between realist and Marxist concepts of power, dependency, interdependence, imperialism, and dominance.

This review of the major data-making efforts in the 1970s suggests that, although the realist paradigm was not as total in its dominance as it was in the 1960s, it still provided the focus for most of the data making in the field. Only by the end of the decade were seriously funded projects on nonrealist indicators beginning to emerge. Since in many ways control of data projects determines future research, it can be expected that research in the 1980s will revolve largely around evaluating aspects of the realist research program and be more concerned with assessing elements of the Marxist, issue politics, and transnational paradigm research programs. In addition, if this latter research remains within the field, serious and conscious attempts will be made to compare the explanations and performances of the alternative paradigms.

Conclusion

The findings of this chapter provide considerable evidence to support the proposition that data making in international relations was guided by the realist paradigm in the 1950s and 1960s. A review of the major data projects conducted during this time period shows that they have collected data primarily on nations and realist topics of inquiry. It has also been found that the initial use of these data has been to test realist hypotheses. Conversely, it was found that data collected outside the field (Richardson) or inside the field prior to the 1950s (Wright) were not guided by the realist paradigm.

The quantitative tests reported in the second section of the chapter also support the proposition. Of the data on file in the International Relations Archive of the Inter-University Consortium for Political Research, 74.9 percent consisted of realist indicators. The two concepts for which most data were collected – national power and inter-nation conflict-cooperation – were also the most central concepts in the realist paradigm. On the basis of the above findings, it can be concluded that the realist paradigm guided data making in the field during the 1950s and 1960s.

Finally, the review of data making in the 1970s suggests that the proposition still held for most of the projects, but that elements in the field were beginning to investigate new measures for tapping Marxist concepts and to collect data on issue politics and non-state actors. If these efforts continue in the 1980s, authentic paradigm debates (as opposed to debates over competing conceptual frameworks) could be expected to emerge. This prediction specifies a future event which, if it did not occur, could be taken as evidence that would falsify the proposition.

The collection of a large number of realist indicators in the 1960s only demonstrates that a large amount of data have been collected that can be used to test realist hypotheses. It is logically possible, however, that scholars would concentrate their attention on the few nonrealist indicators, or use the realist indicators to test nonrealist hypotheses. To investigate this possibility, chapter 6 will examine the hypotheses that have actually been tested in the field in the 1950s and 1960s.

6   Research as a paradigm-directed activity

The proposition

Kuhn maintains that the chief characteristics of normal science are that research is guided by the dominant paradigm and that research is seen as a puzzle-solving activity (Kuhn 1970a: ch. 4). In normal science, the scientist's primary role is to develop hypotheses to explain puzzles that the paradigm has focused upon. One of the significant characteristics of this research, according to Kuhn (1970a: 146–148), is that the paradigm's failure to resolve puzzles does not lead to the falsification of the entire paradigm, but to incremental changes known as paradigm articulation. Persistent failure to resolve puzzles is not seen as a flaw in the paradigm but as a flaw in the individual scientist (Kuhn 1970a: 35–36). Thus, while Karl Popper's (1959) notion of falsification may be applied to individual hypotheses and even to theories, it is never applied to the most fundamental assumptions of the field, that is, the paradigm (Kuhn 1970a: 146–148). Hypothesis testing in normal science tends to be a process of testing competing hypotheses "derived" from the same paradigm rather than testing hypotheses derived from competing paradigms (Kuhn 1970a: 24). The latter, if it occurs at all in science, occurs during periods of scientific revolution and is then viewed as more of a change of world view than of testing hypotheses from competing paradigms. (Kuhn 1970a: ch. 10). The notion of a crucial experiment is only established with the aid of historical hindsight and is an indicator that the new paradigm has gained dominance in the field (Kuhn 1970a: ch. 11).

Normal science research, then, is quite narrow. It consists of three types of research, which correspond to Kuhn's three classes of facts (1970a: 25–26). The first consists of descriptive research, which attempts to describe and often measure phenomena in terms of those concepts and variables that the paradigm has seen as particularly revealing of the nature of things and hence of intrinsic value (Kuhn 1970a: 30–31). This type of research does not test hypotheses, but assumes their validity (Kuhn 1970a: 25–26). The second type of research is explanatory in nature and involves testing hypotheses that are not central to the paradigm or of intrinsic importance but do allow for the testing of specific predictions of the paradigm (Kuhn 1970a: 26–27). The third type of research differs from the second only in that the hypotheses being tested are viewed as being of intrinsic import- ance and central to the paradigm either initially or through the process of paradigm articulation (Kuhn 1970a: 27–29).

In order to apply Kuhn's analysis to the field of international relations, it is necessary to have some criteria by which to demarcate research activity from theory construction and data making. As was seen in chapter 2, the behavioral revolt resulted in two distinct notions of what constitutes adequate research in the field. Because the proposition that "behavioral" research has been guided by the realist paradigm is more controversial than the proposition that traditional research has been guided by the realist paradigm, and because behavioral research is more similar to the type of scientific research Kuhn analyzes, only behavioral research, that is, research defined as descriptive, or correlational/explanatory analysis that employs data, will be examined in this chapter.

Research design

Operationalization and measurement

The two key terms in the proposition that must be operationalized are *research* and *realist paradigm*. Since the proposition will be limited to behavioral research, which has been defined as descriptive or corre- lation/explanatory analysis that employs data, then *research* can be operationalized in terms of the use of measured variables to describe or predict phenomena.[1] The operational definition of the realist paradigm has been adequately discussed in chapters 3 and 5 and will be defined as realist actors and topics of inquiry employed in variables and hypotheses. Reliability for the data in this chapter was calculated

---

[1] This criterion is similar to that of Jones and Singer (1972: 3–6).

at 0.87 for the first sample and 0.90 for the second sample.[2] As in the previous tests, this measure's validity rests on the assumption (which appears reasonable) that research guided by the realist paradigm would tend to employ in its variables, actors and topics that are viewed as important by the realist paradigm.

Deriving hypotheses

Seven hypotheses can be derived from the proposition to test its adequacy:[3]

    3a   Variables used in descriptive research will tend to have actors and topics of inquiry that are labeled realist in the coding scheme.

    3b   Independent variables used in correlational/explanatory research will tend to have actors and topics of inquiry that are labeled realist in the coding scheme.

    3c   Dependent variables used in correlational/explanatory research will tend to have actors and topics of inquiry that are labeled realist in the coding scheme.

    3d   Correlational/explanatory hypotheses tested will tend to relate independent and dependent variables whose actors and topics of inquiry are labeled realist in the coding scheme.

    3e   National power will tend to be the most frequently used independent variable.

    3f   Inter-nation conflict-cooperation will tend to be the most frequently used dependent variable.

    3g   The most frequently tested proposition will be the one that employs national power to predict or explain inter-nation conflict-cooperation.

Hypothesis 3a tests the aspect of the proposition that relates to descriptive research. If Kuhn is correct in stating that descriptive research will focus on those facts that the paradigm suggests are the most revealing of the nature of things, it is reasonable to assume that variables used in descriptive research will emphasize realist actors and topics. If this were not the case, that is, if the distribution were

---

[2] See chapter 3, note 6 for the method used to check reliability. The two samples are discussed on pp. 107–112.

[3] These hypotheses are numbered 3a, etc., because they test the third proposition presented in this analysis.

random, then it would not be accurate to claim that the realist paradigm guided descriptive research.

Hypotheses 3b and 3c attempt to test the aspect of the proposition that refers to correlational/explanatory research. If Kuhn's analysis is correct, it is reasonable to expect that the independent and dependent variables employed in correlational/explanatory research will be realist.

Hypothesis 3d is the most important of the seven hypotheses being tested. It examines the way independent and dependent variables are related to form hypotheses. It is important to examine hypotheses and not just variables, because individual variables can be related in numerous ways.[4] Hypothesis 3d therefore serves as a validity check on hypotheses 3b and 3c.

Hypotheses 3e, 3f, and 3g test another aspect of the proposition. It was seen in chapter 3 that, while the realist paradigm employed several topics of inquiry, it emphasized national power as the independent variable and inter-nation conflict-cooperation as the dependent variable. If the realist paradigm guided research in the field, it would be reasonable to expect that, while not all independent and dependent variables would be limited to these two topics, they would probably be the modal categories. Likewise, it would be expected that the most frequently tested proposition would be the one that employed national power to explain inter-nation conflict-cooperation.

The samples

The primary problem in choosing a sample is to determine what is international relations research as opposed to comparative politics or social psychological research, and to obtain a list of that research. Such a definition must, of course, be based on the perceptions of scholars in the field. In order to avoid possible bias it would be best, as in chapter 5, if someone other than the author provided the definition and the list of research. Fortunately, this is the case. In

---

[4] In the coding scheme, a realist hypothesis is defined as a hypothesis in which every variable is a realist indicator. If a hypothesis consists of four variables and only one is nonrealist, then the entire hypothesis would be coded as nonrealist. Hypotheses 3b and 3c, however, provide a much less stringent test, since they would find three realist variables and only one nonrealist variable. To insure that mixed cases falsify rather than support the proposition, hypothesis 3d has been included.

Beyond Conjecture in International Politics: Abstracts of Data-Based Research, Susan Jones and J. David Singer (1972) provide a definition as well as a list, which they claim represents the universe of data-based research published as articles prior to 1970 (Jones and Singer 1972: 4–12). They define international politics research as "the political interaction of national, sub-national, and extra-national units in the context of the international system" (Jones and Singer 1972: 8). On the basis of this definition, they delete articles that deal solely with the distribution of public opinions within nations (Jones and Singer 1972: 8–9).

The question arises whether such a list would provide an adequate sample for this analysis. First, since the Jones–Singer definition of research is similar to the operational definition employed in this chapter, that aspect poses no problem. Likewise, their definition of international relations research in terms of international politics appears broad enough to include research employing non-state actors, but limited enough to reflect the perceptions of most scholars in the field. Third, their exclusion of books and nonpublished research makes the list less than complete. However, since many books give rise to at least one related article, the omission of books is not as serious as it would first appear. What is important is that these omissions are not likely to bias the sample; that is, any measurement error in the analysis conducted here resulting from the omission of books or unpublished articles can be regarded as random. This can also be said of any published articles Jones and Singer may have missed.[5] Finally, Jones and Singer's classification of articles into descriptive and correlational/explanatory research, and their listing of variables employed in that research, make it easy to test the hypotheses derived in this chapter. Therefore, the abstracts provided in Jones and Singer were selected as one sample.

These abstracts were converted into data by the following procedure. In each abstract a list of variables employed in the article is provided. In addition, information on the purpose of the research, the spatial–temporal domain of the variables, the data sources and operations, and how the data were manipulated and analyzed were provided in the abstract. This information was used along with

[5] A random sample of journals showed that no articles were missed. However, this author knows of at least one anthology article that was missed: Coplin (1968). See Alger (1970) for other possible omissions.

special instructions for the use of the coding scheme to determine the actor and topic of inquiry of each variable, thereby providing the data base for this chapter (see Vasquez 1974a: app. I).

Although the Jones and Singer volume has many virtues for use as a sample in this study, it has one major flaw that led to a decision to use a second sample – not all hypotheses tested in correlational/explanatory articles are fully reported. Instead, only the major findings are reported. While this device is certainly appropriate for the purpose of providing abstracts, it is less than adequate for testing hypothesis 3d, which is the most important hypothesis being tested in this chapter. It was therefore decided to return to the original articles that Jones and Singer classified as correlational/explanatory and collect a list of hypotheses. A total of 7,827 hypotheses that related one or more independent variables with a dependent variable to determine statistical significance and/ or strength of association were collected from 51 of the original 76 articles classified as correlational/explanatory by Jones and Singer.[6] The variables in these hypotheses were then coded into actor and topic categories. On the basis of this coding, each hypothesis was coded as realist only if every variable employed in it had both a realist actor and a realist topic code. This coded data provided the second sample for the study. The descriptive and correlational/ explanatory articles included in the samples are listed in tables 6.1 and 6.2, respectively.

[6] Hypotheses from the other 25 articles were not included because neither inductive statistics nor measures of association were employed in the data analysis. This criterion was adopted essentially to reduce the high costs involved in data making. Since support for the project was based on the use of the data in chapter 7 to examine statistical significance and strength of association, collection of data outside that realm could not be justified. Exclusion of these articles does not appear to affect the study in any significant manner. First, these articles are included in tests based on the first sample. Second, a comparison of tests using the two samples reveals that the second sample gives much greater support to the proposition than the first sample; that is, scholars relate realist variables to each other much more often than they relate nonrealist variables with each other or with realist variables. Three of the excluded articles were randomly selected to see if this tendency held among them, and it did. Thus any measurement error resulting from the exclusion would falsify the proposition rather than support it. Third, most of these articles test relatively few hypotheses, compared to those that use measures of association, often with large correlation matrices.

Table 6.1. *Descriptive research included in sample 1 (Jones and Singer's classifications)*

ATTRIBUTES OF THE SYSTEM

Alger and Brams (1967)	Lijphart (1963)
Alker and Puchala (1968)	Lijphart (1964)
Angell (1965)	Naroll (1968)
Barrera and E. Haas (1969)	Rieselbach (1960b)
Bernstein and Weldon (1968)	Russett (1966)
Brams (1966a)	Russett (1968a)
Brams (1966b)	Russett (1968c)
Brams (1968)	Russett (1968d)
Brams (1969a)	Russett and Lamb (1969)
Brams (1969b)	Schmitter (1969)
Caplow and Finsterbusch (1968)	Small and Singer (1969)
Feldstein (1967)	Smoker (1965a)
Fisher (1969)	Taggepera (1968)
Lamb and Russett (1969)	Teune and Synnestvedt (1965)

ATTRIBUTES OF NATIONS

Brecher, Steinberg, and Stein (1969)	Lerner and Kramer (1963)
Choucri (1969a)	Namenwirth and Brewer (1966)
Cimbala (1969)	Rosenau (1962)
Coddington (1965)	Sawyer (1967)
B. Cohen (1967)	Sigler (1969)
Deutsch (1966)	J. D. Singer (1964)
Deutsch and Eckstein (1961)	Singer and Small (1966b)
Eckhardt (1965)	Weissberg (1969)
W. Fleming (1969)	White (1949)
Galtung and Ruge (1965a)	Wright and Nelson (1939)
Graber (1969)	Zaninovich (1962)
Jensen (1969)	Zinnes, North, and Koch (1961)
Laulicht (1965b)	

NATIONAL BEHAVIOR

Alcock and Lowe (1969)	Klingberg (1952)
Alger (1965)	McClelland (1968)
Angell (1967)	McClelland and Hoggard (1969)
Ball (1951)	Manno (1966)
Choucri (1969b)	Meyers (1966)
Denton (1966)	Rowe (1964)
Denton and Phillips (1968)	Rowe (1969)
E. B. Haas (1962)	Rummel (1963)
O. Holsti and Sullivan (1969)	Rummel (1966b)
Horvath (1968)	Rummel (1967a)
Horvath and Foster (1963)	Rummel (1967b)
Jacobsen (1969)	Rummel (1969)
Jensen (1968)	Voevodsky (1969)
Kay (1969)	Weiss (1963)
Keohane (1969)	

Table 6.2. *Correlational/explanatory research included in sample 1 (Jones and Singer's classifications)*

ATTRIBUTES OF THE SYSTEM
None found

ATTRIBUTES OF NATIONS

Amor et al. (1967)	Moskos and Bell (1964)
Bell (1960)	[a] North and Choucri (1968)
Brickman, Shaver, and Archibald (1968)	Ohlstrom (1966)
Campbell and Cain (1965)	[a] Rieselbach (1960a)
[a] Cobb (1969)	Rieselbach (1964)
[a] Deutsch (1956)	Ruge (1964)
[a] Galtung and Ruge (1965b)	[a] Russett (1962a)
Gregg (1965)	[a] Russett (1964)
F. Hoffman (1967)	[a] M. Singer and Sensenig (1963)
[a] O. R. Holsti (1967)	[a] R. Smith (1969)
Jensen (1966)	[a] Vincent (1968)
[a] Kato (1968)	[a] Vincent (1969)
[a] Laulicht (1965a)	[a] Weigert and Riggs (1969)

NATIONAL BEHAVIOR

[a] Alger (1966)	[a] McGowan (1968)
[a] Alger (1968)	[a] McGowan (1969)
[a] Alker (1964)	[a] Midlarsky and Tanter (1967)
[a] Alker (1965b)	[a] Milstein and Mitchell (1968)
[a] Chadwick (1969)	Milstein and Mitchell (1969)
[a] Choucri and North (1969)	[a] O'Leary (1969)
[a] East and P. Gregg (1967)	Reinton (1967)
[a] Ellis and Salzberg (1965)	[a] Rummel (1964)
[a] Fink (1965)	[a] Rummel (1966a)
[a] Galtung (1964b)	[a] Rummel (1968)
Galtung (1966)	Russett (1963b)
Gamson and Modigliani (1968)	[a] J. D. Singer and Small (1966a)
Gleditsch (1967)	[a] J. D. Singer and Small (1968)
[a] Gleditsche (1969)	Smoker (1963)
[a] M. Haas (1965)	[a] Smoker (1964a)
[a] M. Haas (1968)	Smoker (1964b)
[a] M. Haas (1969)	[a] Smoker (1965b)
K. Holsti (1966)	[a] Smoker (1966)
[a] O. R. Holsti (1965)	[a] Smoker (1967)
O. R. Holsti (1966)	Smoker (1969)
[a] O. R. Holsti, Brody, and North (1965)	[a] Tanter (1966)
[a] O. R. Holsti, North, and Brody (1968)	[a] Wilkenfeld (1968)
[a] Hopmann (1967)	Wright (1965b)
Jensen (1965)	[a] Zinnes (1966)
Klingberg (1966)	[a] Zinnes (1968)

[a] These articles constitute sample 2.

The findings

Hypothesis 3a predicted that variables used in descriptive research would tend to employ the nation-state as the actor and have a realist topic of inquiry. In order to test this hypothesis, the variables listed in the 82 descriptive articles abstracted in Jones and Singer (sample 1) were examined. These articles employed 377 variables. Of these, 74.3 percent (280) were found to be realist indicators according to the coding scheme, and 25.7 percent (97) were found to be nonrealist indicators. This finding is remarkably similar to the finding in chapter 5 (hypothesis 2a) that 74.9 percent of the data produced consisted of realist indicators. This distribution would hardly appear to be random, and the calculation of a binomial distribution (p<.01) for interpretive purposes supports this assumption.[7] On the basis of this test, it can be concluded that hypothesis 3a has failed to be falsified.

Hypothesis 3b predicted that independent variables used in correlational/explanatory research would tend to employ the nation-state as the actor and have a realist topic of inquiry. In order to test this hypothesis, the two samples were employed. Sample 1 consisted of the independent variables listed in the 76 articles abstracted in Jones and Singer. These articles employed 385 independent variables. Of these, 68.1 percent (262) were found to be realist indicators according to the coding scheme, and 31.9 percent (123) were found to be nonrealist indicators. The calculation of a binomial distribution (p<.01) shows that this is not a random distribution. The test on this sample, then, fails to falsify hypothesis 3b.

The second sample used to test hypothesis 3b consisted of the independent variables actually employed in hypotheses in the 51 articles that employed inductive statistics or measures of association. In this sample, rather than analyzing each independent variable separately, all the independent variables employed in one hypothesis were coded as a unit. Therefore, if a multivariate relationship were being tested with five independent variables, all five variables would receive one code – realist or nonrealist. A realist code was given only

---

[7] The calculation of the binomial distribution is only reported to offer a guideline for interpretation, not as evidence, since its use is mathematically inappropriate when the universe rather than a sample is employed. See Blalock (1960: ch. 10) for the application of the binomial distribution in social science. A table for significance can be found in Harvard University Computation Laboratory, *Tables of the Cumulative Binomial Probability Distribution* (1955).

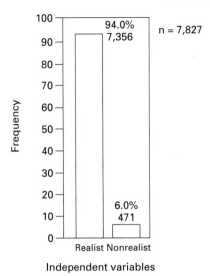

Figure 6.1 Percentage of realist independent variables employed in hypotheses (hypothesis 3b)

if every independent variable in the hypothesis had a realist actor and topic code. A total of 7,827 independent variable units were found in the articles included in the sample. Figure 6.1 reports the findings. From figure 6.1 it can be seen that 94.0 percent, or 7,356 independent variable units, were realist indicators and only 6.0 percent (471) were nonrealist. This figure supports the conclusion that, although on occasion nonrealist independent variables may be produced and employed in research, the emphasis in hypothesis testing in the field is on realist independent variables. On the basis of these two tests, it can be concluded that hypothesis 3b has failed to be falsified.

Hypothesis 3c predicted that dependent variables used in correlational/explanatory research would tend to employ the nation-state as the sole actor and have a realist topic of inquiry. This hypothesis is slightly more important than the previous two, because one of the major functions of a paradigm is to establish a research agenda on what phenomena are to be explained. Samples 1 and 2 were used in this test. The abstracts employed in sample 1 listed 233 dependent variables. Of these 78.9 percent (184) were found by the coding scheme to be realist indicators and only 21.4 percent (49) were found to be nonrealist indicators. This would not appear to be a random

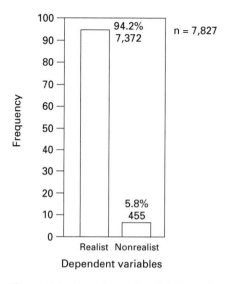

Figure 6.2 Percentage of realist dependent variables employed in hypotheses (hypothesis 3c)

distribution, and the calculation of a binomial distribution ($p<.01$) supports this assumption.

The second sample used to test hypothesis 3c consisted of the actual dependent variables employed in the 7,827 hypotheses collected from the original articles. Figure 6.2 reports these findings. From the figure it can be seen that 94.2 percent (7,372) of the dependent variables are realist indicators and only 5.8 percent (455) are nonrealist. This finding supports the conclusion of the previous test that, although nonrealist variables may occasionally be produced and employed in research, the emphasis in hypothesis testing is on realist indicators. On the basis of these two tests it can be concluded that hypothesis 3c has failed to be falsified.

Hypothesis 3d predicted that hypotheses actually tested in research would tend to relate independent and dependent variables that were realist indicators. This hypothesis is the most important for testing the proposition's adequacy. If the actual hypotheses tested are not realist then it cannot be said that the realist paradigm has guided research. Sample 2 was employed to test hypothesis 3d. In order for a hypothesis in the sample to be coded as realist, every variable in that hypothesis had to have a realist actor and topic code. Given these

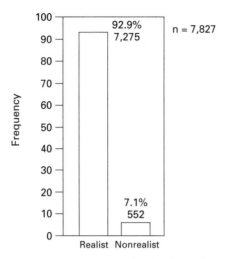

Figure 6.3 Percentage of realist hypotheses tested in the field (hypothesis 3d)

strict requirements, the findings reported in figure 6.3 are quite remarkable. This figure shows that 92.9 percent (7,275) of the hypotheses tested in the field were realist and only 7.1 percent (552) were nonrealist. On the basis of this test, it can be concluded that the critical hypothesis 3d has failed to be falsified.

Hypothesis 3e predicted that national power would be the most frequently employed independent variable in correlational/explanatory research. The independent variable units of sample 2 were employed to test this hypothesis. Independent variable units were given a topic code only if all the variables in the unit had the same topic; otherwise, they were classified as having a mixed topic. The findings are reported in table 6.3, which was produced by cross-tabulating the actor and topic codes of the variables and then rank ordering the independent variables. It can be seen from the table that national power is the modal or most frequently used independent variable unit, constituting 59.4 percent (4,650) of the independent variables. The second ranked independent variable unit, inter-nation alliances, only constituted 13.4 percent (1,050) of the independent variables.[8] On the

[8] It is significant that inter-nation alliances, which rank second, is also the second most important independent variable in *Politics Among Nations*, as noted in chapter 3.

Table 6.3. *Independent variable units employed in research (hypothesis 3e)*

Independent variables	Frequency/percentage		Rank
National power[a]	4,650	(59.4)	1
Inter-nation alliances[a]	1,050	(13.4)	2
Inter-nation conflict-cooperation[a]	604	(7.7)	3
Nation (mixed topic)	544	(6.9)	4
Nations and supranationalism[a]	247	(3.2)	5
National isolationism[a]	209	(2.7)	6
Nation and sociological characteristics	123	(1.6)	7
Nations and other actors and power	116	(1.5)	8
Inter-nation integration[a]	59	(0.8)	9
Nations and other actors and decision makers	56	(0.7)	10
Subnational actors and sociological characteristics	42	(0.5)	11
Nations and other actors and sociological characteristics	32	(0.4)	12
Subnational conflict-cooperation	25	(0.3)	13
Nations and other actors conflict-cooperation	24	(0.3)	14.5
Nations and other actors issues	24	(0.3)	14.5
Nations and other actors (miscellaneous topic)	8	(0.1)	16
Subnational alignments	6	(0.1)	17
Nations and other actors alliances	4	(0.1)	18
Nation (miscellaneous topic)	3	(0.0)	19
IGO and NGO conflict-cooperation	1	(0.0)	20
	7,827	100.0	

[a] Realist independent variables.

basis of this test, it can be concluded that hypothesis 3e has failed to be falsified.

Hypothesis 3f predicted that inter-nation conflict-cooperation would tend to be the most frequently used dependent variable in correlational/explanatory research. Sample 2 was also used in this test. From the findings reported in table 6.4, it can be seen that inter-

Table 6.4. *Dependent variables employed in research (hypothesis 3f)*

Dependent variables	Frequency/percentage		Rank
Inter-nation conflict-cooperation[a]	4,734	(60.5)	1
National power[a]	1,193	(15.2)	2
Nations and supranationalism[a]	970	(12.4)	3
Inter-nation integration[a]	281	(3.6)	4
Nations and other actors and conflict-cooperation	260	(3.3)	5
National isolationism[a]	99	(1.3)	6
Inter-nation alliances[a]	95	(1.2)	7
Nations and issues	70	(0.9)	8
Subnational conflict-cooperation	55	(0.7)	9
Nations and (miscellaneous topic)	34	(0.4)	10
Subnational supranationalism	21	(0.3)	11
Nation and sociological characteristics	10	(0.1)	12
Nations and other actors and supranationalism	5	(0.1)	13
	7,827	100.0	

[a] Realist dependent variables.

nation conflict-cooperation is the modal, or most frequently employed, dependent variable, constituting 60.5 percent (4,734) of the dependent variables. The second ranked dependent variable; national power, included only 15.2 percent (1,193) of the dependent variables. On the basis of this test, it can be concluded that hypothesis 3f has failed to be falsified.

Hypothesis 3g predicted that the most frequently tested proposition in the field would be the one that used national power to predict or explain inter-nation conflict-cooperation. Sample 2 was used to test this hypothesis. Each proposition was rank-ordered in table 6.5 on the basis of the number of hypotheses that tested it. It can be seen that national power related to inter-nation conflict-cooperation was the most frequently tested proposition in the field, having been tested by 3,018 hypotheses (41.7 percent of 7,241 hypotheses). The second-ranked proposition used inter-nation alliances to predict inter-nation conflict-cooperation, which was tested by only 651 hypotheses (9.0

Table 6.5. *Rank order of propositions tested in the field (hypothesis 3g)*

Proposition[a]	Number of hypotheses	Percentage	Rank
316–310	3,018	41.7	1
313–310	651	9.0	2
316–316	626	8.6	3
316–321	539	7.4	4
310–310	433	6.0	5
313–321	347	4.8	6
316–314	281	3.9	7
317–310	208	2.9	8
310–316	162	2.2	9
321–316	153	2.1	10
716–710	116	1.6	11
316–317	93	1.3	12
314–310	57	0.8	14
711–710	56	0.8	14
321–321	55	0.8	14
710–710	49	0.7	16
719–710	48	0.7	17
319–310	47	0.6	18
313–312	40	0.6	19
321–310	39	0.5	20
316–313	33	0.5	21
316–312	30	0.4	22
319–321	29	0.4	23
319–318	28	0.4	24
719–721	26	0.4	25
712–710	24	0.3	26
319–319	10	0.1	27
718–710	8	0.1	28.5
713–710	8	0.1	28.5
316–710	6	0.1	30
319–317	5	0.1	31
310–318	4	0.1	32
313–316	3	0.0	33
310–313	2	0.0	34
313–313	1	0.0	38
313–317	1	0.0	38

Proposition[a]	Number of hypotheses	Percentage	Rank
316–318	1	0.0	38
317–316	1	0.0	38
318–310	1	0.0	38
318–318	1	0.0	38
710–316	1	0.0	38
	7,241	100.0	
Missing cases[b]	586		
	7,827		

[a] Proposition codes to the left of the dash refer to independent variables and codes to the right of the dash refer to dependent variables. The first digit of each three-digit code refers to the actor type and the second two digits refer to the topic of inquiry. The codebook can be found in table 3.1.

[b] Of the 586 missing cases, 544 consist of independent variables that employed mixed topics of inquiry (see table 6.3). The 42 other missing cases consist of hypotheses that were tested by measures of association that did not range from 0.00 to 1.00. Unlike later tests, however (see chapter 7), this test includes 107 hypotheses that are tested by only significance tests or passed a test by accepting the null hypothesis.

percent of 7,241 hypotheses).[9] On the basis of this test, it is clear that hypothesis 3g has failed to be falsified.

Conclusion

The findings of the nine tests conducted in this chapter provide considerable evidence to support the proposition. Employing the Jones and Singer (1972) abstracts, it was found that: (1) about three-fourths (74.3 percent) of the variables employed in descriptive research were realist; and (2) 68.1 percent of the independent variables and 78.9 percent of the dependent variables employed in correlational/explanatory research articles were realist. An examination of how these variables were combined to form hypotheses, using the second sample, revealed that the realist variables are used much more frequently than is suggested by the abstracts in Jones and Singer. It

[9] It is noteworthy that the second-ranked proposition, inter-nation alliances predicts inter-nation conflict-cooperation, is also the second most important proposition in *Politics Among Nations*, as shown in chapter 3.

was found, for example, that 94.0 percent of the independent variable units and 94.2 percent of the dependent variables employed in actual hypotheses were realist. A review of how these independent and dependent variables were combined showed that 92.9 percent of the 7,827 hypotheses tested in the field were realist.

In addition to these tests, a number of predictions were made about the specific variables and propositions used in research. Employing the second sample, it was found that the chief independent variable of the realist paradigm, national power, was the most frequently employed independent variable in research (59.4 percent of all independent variables). It was also found that the chief dependent variable of the realist paradigm, inter-nation conflict-cooperation, was the most frequently employed dependent variable in research (60.5 percent of all dependent variables). Finally, it was found that the central proposition of the realist paradigm, relating national power to inter-nation conflict-cooperation, was the most frequently tested proposition in the field (41.7 percent of the 7,241 tested hypotheses). On the basis of these findings, it can be concluded that research in the field has been guided by the realist paradigm.

The findings of this chapter, when combined with the findings of the two preceding chapters, demonstrate that international relations inquiry has had an underlying coherence since the early 1950s. The realist paradigm has been used by scholars to focus on certain phenomena and develop concepts and propositions about them. This theory construction, or paradigm articulation, has directed scholars to collect data on realist indicators. It has been shown in this chapter that the data collected in the field have been used primarily to test realist hypotheses. The tests of the three propositions on theory construction, data making, and research in the field have all been supported. Therefore, the claim that the realist paradigm has dominated international relations inquiry in the 1950s and 1960s has been given credence.

7 Evaluation: the adequacy of the realist paradigm

This book opened with the claims that the realist paradigm has dominated the field since the early 1950s and that the realist paradigm has not been very effective in explaining behavior. Through a review of the literature and the use of quantitative techniques, it has been found that the realist paradigm has indeed been the major guiding force directing scholarly inquiry in each of the three major scientific activities of theory construction, data making, and research. These findings support the first claim and the interpretation of the field provided in chapter 2. The findings also lend credence to the general interpretation of all scientific work provided by Thomas Kuhn (1970a). However, the findings do not indicate whether the power of the realist paradigm to dominate the field has been beneficial for attaining the purpose of the field – the creation of knowledge. The second claim maintains that up to this time the realist paradigm has not been very beneficial, because it has failed to demonstrate any significant ability to pass tests. The present chapter will attempt to establish the validity of this claim.

The chapter is divided into five sections. The first specifies three criteria – accuracy, centrality, and scientific importance – that can be used to evaluate the adequacy of any paradigm. The second, third, and fourth sections operationally define each of the criteria respectively and apply them in an empirical "test" to determine the adequacy of the realist paradigm. The final section presents the conclusion and examines whether the claim that the realist paradigm has not been very effective in accurately explaining behavior has been supported.

How to evaluate paradigms

The criteria

In order to evaluate anything, it is necessary to specify the criteria that will be employed, justify their use, and indicate how they can be applied.[1] The major criterion that will be employed to evaluate paradigms is their ability to produce knowledge. This criterion is viewed as a *necessary condition* for an adequate paradigm. Its selection is justified on the basis that the primary purpose of science is to produce knowledge. Other purposes of science, such as the improvement of human life, are seen as side benefits stemming from the acquisition of knowledge.

Once the production of knowledge has been selected as the major criterion, the next problem is to specify a set of criteria that can be used to determine whether or not a paradigm has produced any knowledge. It was seen in chapter 1 that whether a paradigm produced knowledge could be determined by examining the empirical content of its theories, that is, the number of hypotheses that have failed to be falsified. This criterion will be called the *criterion of accuracy*, since it reflects the ability of the paradigm to predict behavior accurately.

It was also seen in chapter 1 that the ability of a theory to produce hypotheses that fail to be falsified is only a minimum requirement. More important, a theory must fail to falsify hypotheses that are intended to test its central propositions, where centrality is defined as the level of generality, the scope, and the uniqueness of the proposition (see Stinchcombe 1968: 17–22). The reason for this rule is that the central propositions form the heart of the theory, and if they are falsified, then any incidental propositions that fail to be falsified can be easily incorporated into a rival theory (if they are not already part of that rival theory). Applying this same logic to paradigms, it can be said that a paradigm's central propositions must fail to be falsified when tested. The latter principle will be called the *criterion of centrality*.

The criteria of accuracy and centrality provide two rules for determining whether a paradigm produces knowledge. Production of knowledge, however, is only a necessary condition for paradigm adequacy. The knowledge must also be of some value. A number of

[1] On the necessity of these three tasks see J. O. Urmson (1969: chs. 8–10).

secondary criteria could be provided to assess the value of the produced knowledge, but there is not much consensus in the field over what those criteria might be. One major criterion that scholars agree on is that the knowledge should not be trivial. Recognizing that other secondary criteria can be employed, this analysis will only employ one, that the knowledge should be nonobvious to a large segment of scholars in the field. This criterion will be called the *criterion of scientific importance.*

A framework for evaluating paradigms

In order to determine the extent to which the realist paradigm has satisfied the three criteria of paradigm adequacy, the following propositions will be tested:

4. The realist paradigm should tend to produce hypotheses that fail to be falsified.
5. The central propositions of the realist paradigm should tend to produce hypotheses that fail to be falsified.
6. Realist hypotheses that fail to be falsified should be of scientific importance.[2]

If the above propositions fail to be falsified, then it can be concluded that the realist paradigm has been an adequate guide to scientific international relations inquiry. If the above propositions are falsified, then the claim that the realist paradigm was not very accurate in explaining behavior will be given credence. Before these propositions can be tested, it is necessary to specify what evidence will count as falsifying each of them. For example, proposition 4 states that the realist paradigm should produce hypotheses that fail to be falsified. As it stands, no decision-rule has been provided for determining how

---

[2] These propositions are numbered 4, 5, and 6 because they are the fourth, fifth, and sixth propositions tested in this analysis. A strong argument can be made that these three propositions provide a fair test for determining the adequacy of the realist paradigm. Proposition 4 applies the criterion of accuracy by maintaining that if realist hypotheses were consistently falsified it would make little sense to say that the paradigm was producing knowledge. Proposition 5 applies the criterion of centrality and provides a way to determine empirically if the most important part of the realist paradigm is accurate. Proposition 6 applies the criterion of scientific importance and provides a way to determine whether the knowledge produced by the paradigm is of any value.

many hypotheses must be falsified before a paradigm can be declared to have inadequately satisfied the criterion of accuracy. If a "large" number of hypotheses were falsified, would this be a sufficient number to conclude that the realist paradigm had not satisfied the criterion of accuracy? Without a clearly established decision-rule to interpret the evidence, there is no way to answer this question.

The decision-rule that first comes to mind would be to employ a statistical significance level (such as 0.05). To insist that a paradigm in international relations produce a statistically significant number of "accurate" hypotheses, however, would be quite unfair, given the youthfulness of the discipline and the exploratory nature of much research. A fairer requirement might be one suggested by Lakatos (1970). He states that a theory's adequacy can be evaluated by comparing the empirical content of one theory with the empirical content of a rival theory (Lakatos 1970: 116). Applying the same logic to paradigms, a decision-rule that would permit the three propositions to be tested would be to insist that the realist paradigm produce proportionally more knowledge than its rival paradigms. The problem with applying this rule is that research in rival paradigms such as Marxism, transnational relations, or issue politics has not been conducted in the field. The only alternative is to compare the perform-ance of the realist paradigm with the nonrealist hypotheses that have been tested in the field (about 7 percent of all the hypotheses [see figure 6.3]). These nonrealist hypotheses share the common character-istic of "not being realist," but they do not share a well-defined rival paradigm. To expect such a "nonparadigm," which has so few tests, to produce proportionally more accurate findings than the realist paradigm is giving the latter more than the benefit of the doubt. Nevertheless, if the realist paradigm failed to pass this test, it would demonstrate that the realist paradigm was not adequate and suggest that even a simple rejection of one or more of the realist assumptions might provide a better guide to research. For these reasons, the decision-rule that proportionally more realist than nonrealist hypothe-ses should fail to be falsified or be of scientific importance will be employed.

The preceding decision-rule for testing the three propositions permits an empirical determination of the adequacy of the realist paradigm. However, all conclusions made on the basis of these tests must be tentative. The reason for this is that a number of ad hoc explanations could be offered to give a different interpretation to the test results. Therefore, after testing the three propositions, various ad hoc explanations will be reviewed in the concluding section.[3]

The data

The sample consists of all correlational/explanatory articles listed in Jones and Singer, *Beyond Conjecture in International Politics*, that employ inductive statistics or measures of association to test hypotheses. A content analysis of the original articles produced a sample of 7,827 hypotheses. The following information was collected on these hypotheses: number of hypotheses tested in article; number of independent variables; actor, topic of inquiry, and paradigm of independent and dependent variables; name of independent and dependent variables; paradigm of hypothesis; statistics employed; significance level; strength of association. Reliability of the coded part of the data was established as 0.90. Since questions of data validity were discussed in chapter 6, there is no need to repeat the arguments here.

The criterion of accuracy

Operationalization and measurement

The criterion of accuracy maintains that in order to produce knowledge, a paradigm must produce hypotheses that fail to be falsified when tested. Two basic statistical approaches can be employed to determine when a hypothesis has failed to be falsified: significance tests (inductive statistics), and measures of association and related descriptive statistics (e.g., correlational analysis). However, when significance tests and measures of association are not used together, there is a problem in interpreting the results. First, significance tests show only that there is a nonrandom relationship between variables; they do not describe the strength of the relationship. Without a measure of association, the scholar has no way of knowing how good the hypothesis would be as a guide to guessing the value of the dependent variable. Conversely, a measure of association without a significance test does not tell how generalizable a given hypothesis is

---

[3] Of course there is a limit to the number of ad hoc explanations that can be introduced; otherwise a proposition becomes nonfalsifiable, since what counts as falsifying evidence is never specified. See Lakatos (1970: 116–132); Hempel (1966: 29).

to the population or to another sample. Without a significance test, the scholar only knows how good a guess can be made about one particular sample. It should be clear that the most information is provided by employing both types of analyses. When this is done, a hypothesis might be falsified either because it failed to be statistically significant or because it had a weak measure of association. Because of the latter requirement, falsification would not mean statistical falsification, that is accepting the null hypothesis, but philosophical falsification, that is, rejecting a hypothesis as an adequate guide to knowledge. Since the use of these statistics provides the clearest rules for determining whether a hypothesis is falsified (philosophically), these rules will be employed to operationally define the criterion of accuracy. The accuracy of a paradigm, therefore, can be operationally stipulated as *the extent to which a paradigm produces hypotheses which, when tested by the use of inductive statistics and measures of association, are found to be statistically significant and have strong measures of association.*

Such an operational definition is valid for two reasons. First, inductive and descriptive statistics for testing hypotheses are widely used in the physical and social sciences; the practice is firmly grounded in mathematical theory. The requirement that both significance and strength of association, should be examined is the traditional procedure accepted in social science.[4] Second, the operational definition could only be said to be invalid if it were maintained that hypotheses that were not tested by statistics were by definition inaccurate: This is not the case. The definition refers to only one of the ways hypotheses can be tested, and it can be interpreted as applying to only a sample of all tests. Furthermore, there appears to be no a priori reason to expect that such a sample should bias the results of the evaluation.

Now that the criterion of accuracy has been operationally defined, it is necessary to measure it. Measuring statistical significance it quite easy, since its use is based on the theory of probability (see Blalock 1960: chs. 8 and 9). Within political science, the 0.05 level is usually taken as the dividing point between statistical significance and nonsignificance. Statistical significance can be measured by the following classification: greater than 0.05 is nonsignificant; 0.05 or less is statistically significant.

---

[4] Blalock (1960: chs. 8 and 15, esp. pp. 225–228) provides a good discussion on this rule.

Measuring strength of association is more difficult for two reasons. First, unlike statistical significance, there is no firmly agreed upon rule on the cutoff point between strong and weak association. Second, it is difficult to compare different statistical measures. Both these problems can be solved by examining the purpose of statistical analysis and its nonmathematical rationale. Correlational analysis can be interpreted as a means of measuring how successful a person would be in guessing the value of one variable by knowing the value of another.[5] All measures of association use a scale, usually from 0.00 to |1.00|. A zero means that there is no association between the variables and attempts to guess the value of one variable on the basis of another would be very unsuccessful. A one, on the other hand, means that the association is perfect, and the attempt to guess the value of one variable on the basis of the value of another variable would almost always be successful. Between these two extremes, a measure of association provides an indicator of how successful guessing will be in a particular circumstance. The philosophical question that is of importance is how high a measure of association must be in order to accept a hypothesis as an adequate guide to knowledge, or how many unsuccessful guesses will be permitted before a hypothesis is rejected. No mathematical rule can make this decision. The individual scholar or community of scholars must establish a rule, indicate in what contexts it will be applied, and provide a rationale for acceptance of the rule.

The rules that have achieved the most consensus have been those used in the analysis of variance. In analysis of variance, the object of correlational analysis is to explain as much variance as possible, with the ultimate goal of explaining 100 percent. Since this is the object of research, a hypothesis is as useful as the percentage of variance it explains. This percentage of variance is usually spoken of in terms of deciles or quartiles. For example, scholars speak of a hypothesis explaining less than 25 percent, 50 percent, or 75 percent of the variance. In each case, the lower part of the scale indicates that a hypothesis has not done very well; a hypothesis that explains 10 percent of the variance leaves 90 percent of it unexplained. This sort of hypothesis does not provide a very good guide to knowledge, and for this reason is often declared falsified. The cutoff point for falsification, however, is a matter of convention and could be raised or lowered

---

[5] This guessing rationale is taken from Linton Freeman (1965: 142ff.).

depending on the state of research. In international relations research, 10 percent and 25 percent are often taken as cutoff points (e.g., Rummel 1968: 202–213; Alger 1968: 65). This rule, however, can only be applied to statistics that are interpretable in terms of variance (e.g., Pearson's r). What about other measures of association?

A similar argument can be made for all other measures of association that range from 0.00 to |1.00|. Measures of this type, such as Kendall's tau and Yule's Q, do not explain variance, but they do describe the strength of association. As such, they provide an estimate of how many successful and unsuccessful guesses a scholar can expect to make by using a particular hypothesis as a guide to prediction (see Freeman 1965: 68–142). The stronger the measure of association, the fewer the unsuccessful guesses, and consequently the better the hypothesis. Thus, as with analysis of variance, the purpose of this type of statistical analysis is to produce hypotheses whose measures of association get as close to |1.00| as is possible; that is, to minimize the number of incorrect guesses. The question that remains unanswered is how many incorrect guesses will be permitted before a hypothesis is considered useless and is falsified. Again, there is no firm rule. It is clear, however, that a |0.33| or a |0.45| is weak and that a |0.71| is much better. In this analysis, whatever magnitude is declared to be weak for a Pearson's r will also be declared weak for all other measures of association that range from 0.00 to |1.00|.

Although the problem of how to determine a cutoff point between strong and weak association has been resolved, the question of how to compare different statistical measures of association remains. The problem here is that a Pearson's r of 0.02 and a Kendall's tau of 0.02 are not mathematically equivalent. The problem is resolvable because, as indicated earlier, the decision to falsify or accept a hypothesis as an adequate guide to knowledge is not a mathematical decision. It is a philosophical decision based on a mathematical analysis of the data. On the nonmathematical level, a Pearson's r and a Kendall's tau of 0.02 are highly comparable. They are both "weak" associations. In terms of Freeman's (1965) guessing rationale they both indicate how successful a hypothesis has been in eliminating incorrect guesses. In this hypothetical case, neither one would be very successful. Thus, although the Pearson's r and Kendall's tau provide different mathematical information, the philosophical information they provide on the adequacy of a hypothesis as a guide to knowledge is the same – weak or not very good. Consequently, it would be perfectly legitimate to declare a hypothesis that had a Pearson's r or a Kendall's tau of 0.02 to be falsified.

On the basis of the preceding analysis, two indices – Predictive Power Index (PPI) A and B – were constructed to measure the accuracy of a hypothesis. These are reported in tables 7.1 and 7.2. In PPI (A) all statistically nonsignificant findings, no matter how high their measures of association, are placed in category 10 (i.e., very weak). Only those measures of association that were greater than |0.33| and significant at the 0.05 level, or were greater than |0.33| and were reported without a significance test are placed in the stronger categories of PPI (A). PPI (B) differs from PPI (A) only in that there are four categories in the scale. In this case nonsignificant findings are placed in category 25.

Whether Predictive Power Indices A and B provide a good or valid measure depends on the purpose for which they were created. In this analysis, the indices are being employed to interpret how accurate an explanation the hypothesis provides. To say simply that a hypothesis has been "supported" or "not supported," as has been done in other analyses that review a large number of findings (see C. F. Hermann 1972a: appendix), is to lose a tremendous amount of information and often not even provide a reliable measure, since the rules employed for determining "supported" are not specified. To repeat the actual findings, however, would not provide much interpretation and would be an exhausting process. Predictive Power Indices A and B try to strike a balance between providing too much or too little information, while at the same time providing a reliable measure.

Because of the scale's logic, it can only be applied to measures of association ranging from 0.00 to |1.00|. Measures that did not have this range were removed from the analysis.[6] Since these statistics consist of only 42 cases out of 7,827, it can be concluded that their removal does not substantially affect the findings reported in this study.[7]

---

[6] Hypotheses tested by Pearson's product moment correlation r, Spearman's rho, Partial Correlation r, Path coefficients, R^2 (path analysis), R^2 (regression), and standardized Regression Coefficients (Causal Modeling), account for over 90 percent of the cases in the sample. Hypotheses tested by Kendall's tau, Factor analysis loadings, Chi Square, Mann–Whitney U Test, Yule's Q, and the Z test were included in the sample. Hypotheses tested by the Contingency coefficient C or the Phi coefficient were not included in the tests in this chapter.

[7] In addition, 100 cases that were tested solely by significance tests, and all tests that sought to accept the null hypothesis (seven cases) were dropped.

Table 7.1. *Predictive Power Index A   PPI (A)*

Description	Category	Significance	Range of measures
Very weak (inadequate hypothesis)	10	Not significant or not reported	0.00 to |0.32|
	20	0.05 or not reported	|0.33| to |0.45|
	30	0.05 or not reported	|0.46| to |0.55|
	40	0.05 or not reported	|0.56| to |0.63|
	50	0.05 or not reported	|0.64| to |0.71|
	60	0.05 or not reported	|0.72| to |0.77|
	70	0.05 or not reported	|0.78| to |0.84|
Very strong (adequate hypothesis)	71 +	0.05 or not reported	|0.85| to |1.00|

Table 7.2. *Predictive Power Index B   PPI (B)*

Description	Category	Significance	Range of measures
Very weak (inadequate hypothesis)	25	Not significant or not reported	0.00 to |0.50|
	50	0.05 or not reported	|0.51| to |0.71|
	75	0.05 or not reported	|0.72| to |0.87|
Very strong (adequate hypothesis)	100	0.05 or not reported	|0.88| to |1.00|

Test design

Proposition 4 maintained that if the realist paradigm were accurate, it would produce hypotheses that fail to be falsified. One of the best ways to test this proposition would be to employ Predictive Power Indices A and B to see whether realist or nonrealist hypotheses failed to be falsified more frequently. The test of such a hypothesis would provide evidence to determine how well the realist paradigm satisfied the criterion of accuracy in comparison to a nonrealist paradigm. Thus the hypothesis that can be used to test proposition 4 is:

4. Realist hypotheses should fail to be falsified more frequently than nonrealist hypotheses.

In order to test proposition 4, the 7,827 hypotheses that compose the test sample were coded as either realist or nonrealist according to the coding scheme outlined in chapter 3. The statistical significance and strength of association reported on each of the hypotheses were measured on the two Predictive Power Indices. Since the two Predictive Power Indices did not produce substantially different findings, only the findings from PPI (B) will be reported in the main body of the analysis; the findings from PPI (A), which is a more refined measure, are briefly mentioned in the notes.

The findings

The findings of the test of hypothesis 4 are reported in figure 7.1. It can be seen from this figure that 93.1 percent of the realist hypotheses were falsified, compared to 83.1 percent of the nonrealist hypotheses. This means that 93.1 percent of the realist hypotheses and 83.1 percent of the nonrealist hypotheses fell into the weak category of PPI (B); that is, they were statistically insignificant or had a measure of association of |0.50| or less.[8] Turning to the stronger categories in PPI (B), it can be seen that only 2.2 percent of the realist hypotheses have a measure of association higher than |0.71| (categories 75 and 100) compared to 4.6 percent of the nonrealist hypotheses.

The test results of hypothesis 4 indicate that the realist paradigm has not been very successful in passing empirical texts. Although early success would not be expected, one would not expect about 90 percent of over 7,000 realist hypotheses to be falsified. Also, the fact that nonrealist hypotheses, which consist of simply rejecting the fundamental assumptions of realism, can more successfully pass empirical tests than the realist paradigm, which has been the object of much work, raises serious questions about the accuracy of the realist paradigm. In light of these findings, it can be said that proposition 4 has not been supported, and it can be tentatively concluded that the realist paradigm has not, up to this time, satisfied the criterion of accuracy.

---

[8] The findings on PPI (A) indicate that 80.2 percent of the realist hypotheses compared to 65.6 percent of the nonrealist hypotheses are statistically insignificant or have a measure of association of less than |0.33| (category 10); 90.7 percent of the realist hypotheses compared to 78.1 percent of the nonrealist hypotheses have a measure of association of less than |0.46| (categories 10 and 20).

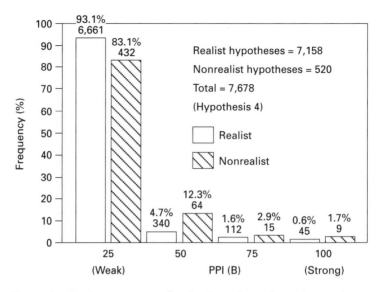

Figure 7.1 Predictive power of realist hypotheses (hypothesis 4a)

The criterion of centrality

The criterion of centrality is based on the recognition that certain propositions in a paradigm are more important than others. They are more important either because the adherents of the paradigm claim that these propositions have greater theoretical explanatory power or because they are what distinguishes the paradigm from rival paradigms. Because these propositions form, in a sense, the heart of the paradigm, it is important that hypotheses testing these propositions should fail to be falsified. Unlike the criterion of accuracy, the criterion of centrality introduces a qualitative element in assessing paradigm adequacy. It does not treat every hypothesis as equal in importance, but establishes a category of hypotheses that are given more weight.

In this light, the criterion of centrality provides a test of the adequacy of the realist paradigm that is different from the test provided by the criterion of accuracy. Even though the tests applying the criterion of accuracy resulted in the tentative conclusion that the realist paradigm did not produce many accurate hypotheses, it could be argued on the basis of the criterion of centrality that it is not important if the noncentral realist propositions are found to be inaccurate if the central realist propositions are accurate. If the results of the tests of proposition 4 were due to a large number of noncentral realist hypotheses being falsified, this finding would not, given the criterion of centrality, be a sufficient basis for concluding that the realist paradigm is inadequate. That conclusion could only be made if the central propositions were found to be inaccurate. The tests of the criterion of centrality examine whether this is the case and thereby serve as a control on the validity of the test on the criterion of accuracy.

Operationization and measurement

Early in this chapter, *centrality* was defined as the level of generality, scope, and uniqueness of a proposition. The more universal the proposition, the greater its generality. For example, a proposition intended to hold for all nations during the last two hundred years is more general than a proposition intended to hold only for Latin American nations in the last twenty years. *Scope* refers to the variety of phenomena or behavior the proposition intends to explain. The greater the variety of phenomena a proposition intends to explain, the greater its scope. For example, a proposition that attempts to explain all kinds of inter-nation conflict-cooperation is obviously greater in scope than a proposition that attempts to explain only economic conflict-cooperation among nations. *Uniqueness* refers to whether rival theories contain the same proposition. Uniqueness is included because it is the criterion by which one theory or paradigm is distinguished from another. Unique propositions, no matter what their generality or scope, provide the reasons for selecting one theory or paradigm over a rival. These three definitions can be employed to operationally define the criterion of centrality as the failure to falsify hypotheses that: hold over long periods of time and a great deal of space; explain a variety of phenomena or behavior; and offer predictions that are not made by a rival paradigm(s).

One way of determining the importance or centrality of a hypothesis for a realist paradigm is to examine the relationships postulated among the most frequently used concepts in *Politics Among Nations* – balance of power, national power, and war.[9] Applying the operational criteria, albeit in a somewhat judgmental manner, it was found that propositions relating these concepts tended to be highly general, great

---

[9] See chapter 3, pp. 53–54.

in scope, and unique. They were general to the extent that they applied to all nations in the modern state system (i.e., since the Peace of Westphalia) (see Morgenthau 1960, 1973: 8–10). They were great in scope in that the balance of power and national power were intended to explain not only war but all types of conflict-cooperation in the system (see Morgenthau 1960, 1973: 27–28, and chs. 4 and 11). They were unique in that competing paradigms such as idealism, Marxism, transnational relations, and the issue politics paradigms did not offer them as explanations. In addition, these propositions are central to the paradigm in that, as was shown with the textual analysis presented in chapter 3, the relationship between national power and conflict-cooperation forms the key theoretical focus of *Politics Among Nations*. The notion of a balance of power can also be regarded as central because it sharpens the national power focus by describing the power relationship between two or more nations.

On the basis of this examination, it was decided that it would be valid to declare that the national power variables and alliance variables that were related to conflict-cooperation variables were indicators of central hypotheses in the realist paradigm. All other variable relationships were coded as noncentral. This nominal classification was used in the analysis as the first measure of the nation of centrality.

Two other measures of centrality were developed by assuming that any proposition that employed national power or inter-nation alliances as a predictor, or any proposition that tried to explain inter-nation conflict-cooperation, would be a central proposition in the realist paradigm. The rationale for this procedure was that, since these three concepts are the most frequently discussed and used concepts in the realist paradigm, any proposition using them in their respective roles as chief independent or dependent variables was more important to the paradigm than propositions not using them.

It should be evident that, despite any problems of measurement validity, the reliability of the measure provides some confidence in the results of the tests on centrality, because they are subject to additional and future tests.

Test design

Proposition 5 maintained that if the realist paradigm satisfied the criterion of centrality, then its central propositions should produce hypotheses that fail to be falsified. The most obvious way to test this proposition would be to employ the measures of centrality and the Predictive Power Indices to see how many central realist hypotheses fail to be falsified in comparison to all other hypotheses, that is, noncentral realist hypotheses and nonrealist hypotheses. Since the central realist hypotheses were defined by the first measure of centrality as those hypotheses that relate national power or inter-nation alliances with inter-nation conflict-cooperation, the following hypothesis can be derived from proposition 5:

5a. Realist hypotheses that relate national power or inter-nation alliances with inter-nation conflict-cooperation should fail to be falsified more frequently than all other hypotheses – noncentral realist or nonrealist.

Two additional ways to test the criterion of centrality would be to examine whether the concepts the realist paradigm declares as theoretically powerful for explaining behavior do in fact successfully explain behavior, and whether the realist paradigm has successfully explained those topics it set out to explain. It was established in chapter 3 that the concepts that play the largest role as predictors or independent variables in the realist paradigm were national power and inter-nation alliances. It was also established that the chief purpose of the realist paradigm was to explain inter-nation conflict-cooperation. Using the second and third measures of centrality, the following hypotheses can be derived from proposition 5:

5b. Hypotheses that employ national power or inter-nation alliances as independent variables should fail to be falsified more frequently than hypotheses that employ different independent variables.

5c. Hypotheses that employ inter-nation conflict-cooperation as a dependent variable should fail to be falsified more frequently than hypotheses that employ different dependent variables.

The three hypotheses that will be employed to determine how well the realist paradigm has satisfied the criterion of centrality provide a good test of the adequacy of the realist paradigm. These tests allow the realist paradigm to produce a large number of inaccurate hypotheses so long as its most central hypotheses fail to be falsified. Hypotheses 5a–5c provide evidence about how adequate the strategy of explaining inter-nation conflict-cooperation by national power or inter-nation alliances has been; how powerful national power and inter-nation alliances have been as predictors; and how successful the realist paradigm has been in achieving its own purpose – the explanation of inter-nation conflict-cooperation. These tests permit the power politics core of the realist paradigm to be examined.

The findings

Hypothesis 5a predicted that realist hypotheses that related national power or inter-nation alliances with inter-nation conflict-cooperation should tend to fail to be falsified. Four hypotheses can be formed from relating these three concepts:

HY 1 National power *with* inter-nation conflict-cooperation
HY 2 Inter-nation conflict-cooperation *with* national power
HY 3 Inter-nation alliances *with* inter-nation conflict-cooperation
HY 4 Inter-nation conflict-cooperation *with* inter-nation alliances

In order to test hypothesis 5a, the preceding four hypotheses were selected from the data and compared to all the other hypotheses in the data.

The findings are reported in table 7.3, which employs PPI (A). From the table, it can be seen that HY 1, 2, and 3 account for 49.5 percent of all the hypotheses in the data, with HY 1, which was declared the most central in the realist paradigm, accounting for 39.0 percent of all the hypotheses tested.[10] It can be seen that HY1 does very poorly, with 91.7 percent of its tests being statistically nonsignificant or having a measure of association of less than $|0.33|$. If categories 10 and 20 are combined, then 98.2 percent of the hypotheses relating national power and inter-nation conflict-cooperation are falsified. Relating the concepts in the opposite manner (HY 2) does not help either, since 95.1 percent of these hypotheses are statistically nonsignificant or have a measure of association of less than $|0.46|$. Relating inter-nation alliances with inter-nation conflict-cooperation (HY 3) does somewhat better in that only 71.8 percent of these hypotheses fall into category 10 and 86.5 percent in categories 10 and 20 combined. However, at the other end of the scale, none of HY 3's findings fall in the "strong" category of 70 and 71+. HY 2 produces one finding out of 162 in these categories, and HY 1 produces four out of 2,994.

---

[10] No cases of HY 4 were found in the data. The main tests of this hypothesis come after 1970 (see Holsti, Hopmann, and Sullivan 1973).

Table 7.3. *Performance of central realist propositions (hypothesis 5a) PPI (A)*

	10	20	30	40	50	60	70	71+	Row total Total percentage	
Noncentral hypotheses	2,722	511	258	126	89	63	41	67	3,877	(count)
	70.2	13.2	6.7	3.2	2.3	1.6	1.1	1.7	50.5	(row percent)
HY 1 (nat. pow. with inter-nat. confl.-coop.)	2,746	194	43	3	4	0	1	3	2,994	
	91.7	6.5	1.4	0.1	0.1	0.0	0.0	0.1	39.0	
HY 2 (inter-nat. confl.-coop. with nat. pow.)	138	16	4	0	3	0	1	0	162	
	85.2	9.9	2.5	0.0	1.9	0.0	0.6	0.0	2.1	
HY 3 (inter-nat. alliances with inter-nat. confl.-coop.)	463	95	50	21	11	5	0	0	645	
	71.8	14.7	7.8	3.3	1.7	0.8	0.0	0.0	8.4	
Column total	6,069	816	355	150	107	68	43	70	7,678	
Total percentage	79.0	10.6	4.6	2.0	1.4	0.9	0.6	0.9	100.0	

Note: the number of cases differs from that in table 6.5 because independent variables with mixed topics of inquiry have been kept in the sample and cases employing statistical tests incompatible with PPI (A) have been dropped.

Table 7.4. *Rank order of realist and nonrealist independent variables, percentage of weak findings (hypothesis 5b) N = 7,189*

Concept	Rank	PPI (B) Category 25 %	Classification	Rank PPI (A) 10 and 20
Nation (miscellaneous topics)[a]	1	100.0	Nr	1 (weak)
National isolationism	2	99.5	R	2
Nations and other actors power	3	95.7	Nr	4
NATIONAL POWER[t]	4	94.1	R	3
INTER-NATION ALLIANCES[t]	5	93.2	R	5
Nations and others decision makers perceptions	6	92.9	Nr	11
Inter-nation conflict-cooperation	7	88.6	R	8
Nation and supranationalism	8	87.9	R	10
Nation and others non-war issues	9.5	87.5	Nr	6.5
Nation and others (miscellaneous topics)[b]	9.5	87.5	Nr	6.5
Nation and sociological characteristics	11	86.1	Nr	9
Nation and others sociological characteristics	12	71.6	Nr	12
Nation and others conflict-cooperation	13	70.0	Nr	13
Inter-nation integration	14	57.9	R	14
Nation and others alliances[c]	15	25.0	Nr	15 (strong)

Notes: R = Realist   [a]N = 2   [c]N = 4
Nr = Nonrealist   [b]N = 8   [t] = central concepts

These results are hardly encouraging for the realist paradigm. A comparison with the "other" hypotheses tested in the field shows that the three most central hypotheses of the realist paradigm do less well than the combined noncentral and nonrealist hypotheses. On the basis of this test, it can be tentatively concluded that hypothesis 5a has been falsified and that the realist paradigm has not been very successful in getting its central propositions to pass empirical tests.

Hypothesis 5b predicted that hypotheses that employ national power or inter-nation alliances as independent variables should fail to be falsified more frequently than hypotheses that employ different independent variables. This hypothesis examines how well specific concepts predict behavior, particularly how well the central realist (and power politics) concepts predict behavior. Hypothesis 5b was tested by ranking the various independent variables used in research according to their predictive power. Table 7.4 ranks the concepts according to the number of hypotheses that they produce in category 25 of PPI (B). It can be seen from table 7.4 that 94.1 percent of the hypotheses that employ national power and 93.2 percent of the hypotheses that employ inter-nation alliance as independent variables have been falsified. This means that hypotheses using these two variables tend to be statistically nonsignificant or have a measure of association less than |0.50|. Only three concepts are weaker predictors. Six other concepts, four nonrealist and two realist, have over 85 percent of their hypotheses falling into the weak category. Of the remaining four concepts, all have less than 72 percent falling into the weak category. Of these concepts, three are nonrealist and one is realist. The findings from table 7.4 support two conclusions: (1) the central realist (and power politics) concepts of national power and inter-nation alliances are poor predictors; and (2) the realist concept of inter-nation integration is one of the best predictors of all the concepts.[11]

Table 7.5 ranks the concepts according to their ability to produce strong measures of association (i.e., greater than |0.71|). When the data are analyzed this way, some interesting results appear. First, seven concepts, six of them nonrealist, fail to produce any findings. The realist concepts of inter-nation alliances and national power still rank low (seventh and sixth from the top), with less than 2 percent of their findings in the strong categories of PPI (B). The nonrealist, sociological characteristics do rather well (3.0 percent and 14.9 percent, respectively). The nonrealist concept of conflict-cooperation also does well (12.0 percent). But by far the most powerful predictor is the realist concept of integration (28.1 percent).

---

[11] For a detailed assessment of specific topics and indicators within such broad topics as national power see Vasquez (1976b). When this is done, "military power and political status" have only 81.57 percent in category 25. These deal primarily with arms races and war; see below pp. 146–147. From a perspective of trying to discover what has been learned, that article elaborates on the many topics not treated here.

Table 7.5. *Rank order of realist and nonrealist independent variables, percentage of strong findings (hypothesis 5b) N = 7,189*

Concept	Rank	PPI (B) categories 75 and 100 %	Classifi- cation	Rank PPI (A) 10 and 20	Rank PPI (B) 25
Nation (miscellaneous topics)[a]	12	0	Nr	15	15 (weak)
Nations and other actors power	12	0	Nr	12	13
Nation and others non-war issues	12	0	Nr	9.5	6.5
Nation and others (miscellaneous topics)[b]	12	0	Nr	9.5	6.5
Nation and supranationalism	12	0	R	6	8
Nations and others decision makers perceptions	12	0	Nr	5	10
Nation and others alliances[c]	12	0	Nr	1	1
National isolationism	8	0.5	R	15	14
INTER-NATION ALLIANCES[t]	7	0.9	R	11	11
NATIONAL POWER[t]	6	1.8	R	13	12
Nation and sociological characteristics	5	3.0	Nr	7	5
Inter-nation conflict-cooperation	4	5.6	R	8	9
Nation and others conflict-cooperation	3	12.0	Nr	3	3
Nation and others sociological characteristics	2	14.9	Nr	4	4
Inter-nation integration	1	28.1	R	2	2 (strong)

Notes: R = Realist   [a]N = 2   [c]N = 4

.   Nr = Nonrealist   [b]N = 8   [t] = central concepts

In light of the preceding tests of hypothesis 5b, the following conclusions can be tentatively made: (1) the central power politics concepts of the realist paradigm, national power and inter-nation alliances, are among the poorest predictors of behavior; (2) the strongest predictor is the realist concept of inter-nation integration, followed by the nonrealist concepts of sociological characteristics and

Table 7.6. *Rank order of realist and nonrealist dependent variables, percentage of weak findings (hypothesis 5c) N = 7,691*

Concept	Rank	PPI (B) category 25 %	Classification	Rank PPI (A) 10 and 20
Nation and sociological characteristics[a]	1	100.0	Nr	1 (weak)
Nation and supranationalism	2	96.2	R	2
INTER-NATION CONFLICT-COOPERATION[t]	3	95.4	R	4
Nation (miscellaneous topics)	4	94.3	Nr	3
Inter-nation integration	5	86.8	R	9
National isolationism	6	86.7	R	6
Inter-nation alliances	7	84.9	R	5
Nation and others conflict-cooperation	8.5	83.3	Nr	8
National power	8.5	83.3	R	7
National nonwar issues	10	78.9	Nr	11
Nation and others supranationalism[b]	11	76.9	Nr	10 (strong)

Note: R = Realist   [a]N = 1   [t] = central concepts
Nr = Nonrealist   [b]N = 26

conflict-cooperation; (3) a large number of realist and nonrealist concepts are poor predictors. Therefore, in terms of the criterion of centrality, hypothesis 5b has been falsified.

Hypothesis 5c predicted that hypotheses employing inter-nation conflict-cooperation as a dependent variable should fail to be falsified more frequently than hypotheses employing other dependent variables. This hypothesis examines how successful the realist paradigm has been in achieving its own purpose – the explanation of inter-nation conflict-cooperation. Hypothesis 5c was tested by ranking the various dependent variables used in research according to their predictive power.

Table 7.6 ranks the dependent variables from weak to strong by employing category 25 of PPI (B). It can be seen from this table that 95.4 percent of the hypotheses that attempt to explain inter-nation conflict-cooperation are falsified; that is, they either are statistically nonsignificant or have a measure of association of less than $|0.50|$.

Table 7.7. *Rank order of realist and nonrealist dependent variables, percent-age of strong findings (hypothesis 5c) N = 7,691*

Concept	Rank	PPI (B) categories 75 and 100 %	Classifi-cation	Rank PPI (A) 10 and 20	Rank PPI (B) 25
Nation and sociological characteristics[a]	10.5	0.0	Nr	1	1 (weak)
Nation (miscellaneous topics)	10.5	0.0	Nr	3	4
Nation and supranationalism	9	0.9	R	2	2
National nonwar issues	8	1.4	Nr	11	10
INTER-NATION CONFLICT COOPERATION[t]	7	1.6	R	4	3
Inter-nation integration	6	2.1	R	9	5
National power	5	5.2	R	7	8
Inter-nation alliances	4	5.4	R	5	7
Nation and others conflict-cooperation	3	5.5	Nr	8	8
National isolationism	2	7.1	R	6	6
Nation and others supranationalism[b]	1	11.5	Nr	10	11 (strong)

Note: R = Realist   [a]N = 1   [t] = central concepts
       Nr = Nonrealist   [b]N = 26

Only two out of the ten other dependent variables are less successful. It is also evident that four nonrealist dependent variables and four realist dependent variables do better than inter-nation conflict-coop-eration. Finally, on the basis of category 25 of PPI (B), it is clear that research has been most successful in predicting the nonrealist topic of issues and the nonrealist approach to supranationalism.

Table 7.7 ranks the concepts according to how many hypotheses they have produced in categories 75 and 100 of PPI (B) (i.e., having a measure of association above |0.71|). The realist dependent variables do significantly better than they did in table 7.6. The strongest concept, however, is the nonrealist concept of supranationalism; 11.5 percent of its hypotheses had a measure of association greater than |0.71|. However, despite the generally better performance of the realist concepts, inter-nation conflict-cooperation – the central realist dependent variable – does not do very well; only 1.6 percent of its hypotheses have a measure of association greater than |0.71|.

In light of the preceding tests of hypothesis 5c, the following conclusions can be tentatively made. First, most research has not been very successful in explaining behavior. Second, although most research efforts have tried to explain the central topic in the realist paradigm – inter-nation conflict-cooperation – this effort has produced proportionally fewer findings than other efforts. This suggests that the realist paradigm has failed to conceptualize adequately the main dependent variable of the field. Third, the tests of hypothesis 5c showed that the most successful tests have been on attempts to predict the realist topics of national power, inter-nation alliances (the two main realist independent variables), national isolationism, and the nonrealist topics of conflict-cooperation and supranationalism. On the whole, then, the tests of hypothesis 5c have shown that although some realist concepts have been productive, the central realist concepts have not been very productive. Therefore, in terms of the criterion of centrality, hypothesis 5c has been falsified.

The three tests of proposition 5 are hardly encouraging for the realist paradigm. It has been found that the central realist hypotheses that relate national power or inter-nation alliances with inter-nation conflict-cooperation employ national power or inter-nation alliances as predictors, or try to predict inter-nation conflict-cooperation have been consistently falsified. These findings indicate that the area of the realist paradigm that promised to be the most theoretically powerful, the central power politics framework, have been among the poorest performers in actually predicting behavior. It has been found that noncentral realist hypotheses and nonrealist hypotheses provide more adequate predictions of behavior, even though these hypotheses have not been as extensively elaborated and tested as the central realist hypotheses. In light of these findings, it can be said that proposition 5 has not been supported. Therefore, it can be tentatively concluded that the realist paradigm has not satisfied the criterion of centrality.

The criterion of scientific importance

The tests of propositions 4 and 5 have attempted to examine how well the realist paradigm has satisfied the criteria of accuracy and cen-

143

trality. These two criteria must be satisfied in order to declare a paradigm an adequate guide to knowledge. It was stated at the beginning of this chapter that if a paradigm satisfied these two necessary conditions, a number of secondary criteria could be applied to determine how valuable the knowledge was that the paradigm produced. It was also stated that only one secondary criterion would be employed in this analysis – the criterion of scientific importance. This criterion maintains that knowledge produced by the paradigm should not be trivial; that is, the produced knowledge should not be considered obvious or trivial to most scholars in the field. It might be thought that since the realist paradigm did so poorly in satisfying the criteria of accuracy and centrality, an attempt to apply the criterion of scientific importance is irrelevant. There is some validity to this argument, but the failure to apply this third criterion would result in not assessing the value of the few hypotheses in the field that have failed to be falsified. Therefore, it will be applied in this section.

Operationalization and measurement

Because triviality is more subject to personal interpretation than other matters, the criterion of scientific importance is very difficult to operationalize and measure. Perhaps the best way to measure it would be to survey scholars and allow them to use their own criteria of triviality to code each hypothesis. Hypotheses that failed to be declared nontrivial by a large segment of the scholarly community could then be declared as "scientifically important." Such an effort would be expensive and would not deter readers from making their own "definitive" evaluation. Therefore, the author has simply coded the major findings as either trivial or nontrivial according to his own assessment of "importance." In order to provide the reader with some basis for determining how "biased" this "test" might be, the raw and coded data have been published in Vasquez 1974a: appendix III.

Three types of trivial hypotheses were found in the data. The first type is a hypothesis that, even though it may be perceived as significant by the scholar testing it, is in fact highly descriptive and/or a familiar generalization made in newspapers or history texts. An example of this type is a hypothesis tested in an article by Chadwick Alger (1968) on the United Nations that finds that the percentage of the total UN budget a nation contributes is predicted by its GNP.

The second type is that which tends to correlate measures of the

144

same concept, which hardly qualifies as scientifically important explanation. An example of this type are some of the hypotheses tested by Richard Chadwick (1969) in an article about the Inter-Nation Simulation. Although a number of scientifically important hypotheses are tested in that article, a large proportion of the ones that fail to be falsified really correlate different measures of the same concept. For example, Chadwick correlates threats with accusations and basic economic capability with quality of consumer goods in a nation.

A third type of trivial hypothesis is that which is highly idiographic and therefore of little importance in terms of building a general theory of international relations. Examples of this type are many of the hypotheses tested by Nils Gleditsch (1969) in an article about integration and airline networks. Typical of the hypotheses that failed to be falsified in the article was the hypothesis that correlated national population size with number of airline flights. While this finding may have policy implications, it does not seem to have much importance for building a general theory of international relations.

As indicated earlier, the notion of "failed to be falsified" is measured by using categories 75 and 100 of Predictive Power Index B, which means that any hypothesis not reported as statistically nonsignificant and having a measure of association of $|0.72|$ or higher has failed to be falsified. It should be evident that, given the problems of operationalizing the criterion of scientific importance, the findings on this criterion are the most tentative of all those presented here. This situation is somewhat ameliorated by the fact that the findings on scientific importance are the least important for evaluating the adequacy of the realist paradigm.

Test design

Proposition 6 maintained that if the realist paradigm satisfied the criterion of scientific importance, the hypotheses it produced that failed to be falsified should be important. Given the measurement problem with this criterion, the only hypothesis that will be tested is:

6. More realist than nonrealist hypotheses that fail to be falsified should be scientifically important.

In order to test hypothesis 6, it is necessary to employ a sample of hypotheses that have failed to be falsified in the field. The data used in the tests of propositions 3 and 4 consisted of all hypotheses that were tested in correlational/explanatory articles published from 1956 to 1970. Of these 7,827 hypotheses, only 7,691 could be used in all of the previous tests. Of these 7,691 hypotheses, only 181 have failed to be falsified (i.e., fell into categories 75 and 100 of PPI [B]). Of these, 157 were realist (2.2 percent of the 7,158 realist hypotheses tested), and 24 were nonrealist (4.6 percent of the 520 nonrealist hypotheses tested). In order to provide a data sample for the test of hypothesis 3, the 181 hypotheses were coded as either trivial or nontrivial. Because of the small number of cases for nonrealist hypotheses, the findings must be interpreted with caution.

The findings

The performance of realist and nonrealist hypotheses, as evaluated by the criterion of scientific importance, is reported in figure 7.2. It can be seen from this figure that about two-thirds (69.5 percent) of the realist hypotheses were declared trivial, compared to about half (54.2 percent) of the nonrealist hypotheses. On the basis of this distribution it appears that the nonrealist hypotheses have performed slightly better. This finding suggests that accepting rather than rejecting realist assumptions does not result in comparatively more scientifically important findings. However, before reaching this conclusion a more detailed review of the nontrivial findings is warranted.

Less than one-third (30.5 percent) of the 157 realist hypotheses that failed to be falsified were declared nontrivial. Most of these hypotheses attempted to explain three types of behavior – military expenditures, conflict, and UN voting.

The major findings on military expenditures are in an article on World War I by Robert North and Nazli Choucri (1968) and in the work of Paul Smoker (1964a, 1965b, 1966). North and Choucri (1968) fail to falsify seventeen of their hypotheses that attempt to explain in a nontrivial fashion the military budgets of the major powers in World War I. Smoker's work is concerned with testing and elaborating Lewis Richardson's model of arms races. He has been very successful in obtaining high correlations, but in order to do this it has been necessary, on occasion, for him to eliminate deviant cases.

The major findings on inter-nation conflict-cooperation come from four articles. The first is an article by Choucri and North (1969) on World War I. They use national attributes and levels of competition to predict the outbreak of violence. Of the many hypotheses they test,

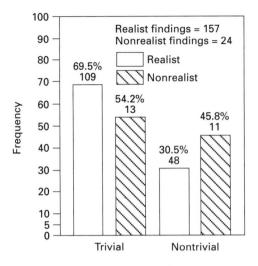

Figure 7.2 The scientific importance of realist findings (hypothesis 6)

nine fail to be falsified. Additional major findings are two hypotheses that fail to be falsified in the J. D. Singer and Small (1966a) article on alliances. Singer and Small find a correlation between the number of times a nation was allied before a war and the number of battle deaths.

Another finding on conflict-cooperation is reported in an article by Maurice East and Philip Gregg (1967). By employing six independent variables, they can explain 81 percent of the variance for cooperation. However, when they use the same variables to try to explain conflict, they account for only 35 percent of the variance. The finding, then, is somewhat mixed, and the accuracy of the proposition from which it was drawn must be interpreted with caution. A third set of findings on conflict-cooperation deals with treaties between nations. Richard Chadwick (1969) uses economic variables to predict the number of economic, cultural, and military agreements a nation will sign.

Finally, an article by Midlarsky and Tanter (1967) on US economic presence and internal conflict in Latin America contains two hypotheses that fail to be falsified. Both deal with the outbreak of revolution in nondemocratic Latin American nations. Midlarsky and Tanter find a correlation of 0.85 between the per capita GNP of a nation and the number of revolutions it has, and a correlation of 0.73 between US economic presence and the number of revolutions in a nation. As with the other research, a large number of their other hypotheses are falsified.

The third major area of significant findings for the realist paradigm is the attempt to explain UN votes. This research consists of two types. The first is concerned with uncovering what national attributes lead a nation to vote a particular way on a specific issue. Alker's (1964) research has been successful in producing findings in this area. He finds that various indicators of East–West alignment will predict voting patterns on East–West issues in the United Nations. He also discovers that communist nations do not support "supranationalism" votes in the UN. The work of Ellis and Salzberg (1965) reflects the second type of successful research in this area – the attempt to predict alignment patterns. Using a variety of indicators of dependence on the major Western powers – the United States, United Kingdom, France – as well as demographic and trade data, they are able to successfully predict African bloc adherence in the UN.

Although the findings of Alker and of Ellis and Salzberg have been declared nontrivial, they are really borderline cases. The studies have confirmed and made more precise some well-known "facts" familiar to any serious traditionalist scholar of the United Nations. Nevertheless, before their research, the hypotheses were never systematically tested.

It can be seen from figure 7.2 that almost half (45.8 percent) of the twenty-four nonrealist hypotheses that failed to be falsified were declared nontrivial. These hypotheses generally deal with individuals' attitudes toward international relations. Three of the findings come from O. R. Holsti's (1967) case study of John Foster Dulles. Holsti is somewhat successful in predicting the conditions under which Dulles would perceive Soviet policy as hostile. Six of the findings come from a study by Jerome Laulicht (1965a) on foreign policy attitudes of Canadian subnational groups and the general public. He is able to predict the attitudes of business, labor, and political elites as well as the voting public on coexistence-disarmament and internationalism. Another finding in this area is an extremely interesting one produced by Bruce Russett (1962a). He finds a correlation of 0.86 between a US state involved in Anglo-American trade and the responsiveness of the state's congressmen to the United Kingdom on foreign policy questions. The final nonrealist hypothesis declared nontrivial deals with UN voting. Produced by Alker (1964), it predicts UN votes on self-determination issues on the basis of membership in the "Old Europeans" group.[12]

The question is whether, in light of these findings, hypothesis 6 has been falsified. This is difficult to answer, because, on the one hand, some nontrivial knowledge has been gained about military expenditures, violence, and UN voting. On the other hand, it is quite sobering that of 7,827 hypotheses tested in the field, of which over 90 percent are realist, only 157 realist hypotheses failed to be falsified, and, of these, over two-thirds were trivial. This means that since 1956, only 48 realist hypotheses have produced findings of any major scientific importance. When the percentage of nontrivial findings for realist and nonrealist hypotheses are compared (see figure 7.2), it is clear that the nonrealist hypotheses have done proportionally better in satisfying the criterion of scientific importance. In other words, it cannot be claimed that, despite the poor performance of the realist paradigm on the first two criteria, its assumptions might be able to produce more important findings than a paradigm that rejected them. It can be tentatively concluded that proposition 6 has been falsified.

Conclusion and implications

The three propositions in this chapter provide evidence for determining the adequacy of the realist paradigm. The tests of proposition 4 showed that on the whole the realist paradigm has not produced much knowledge. It also demonstrated that rejecting one or more of the realist assumptions produces proportionally more hypotheses that failed to be falsified. On the basis of the tests of proposition 4, it could be concluded that the realist paradigm has not satisfied the criterion of accuracy.

The tests of proposition 5 demonstrated that the central propositions of the realist paradigm were not as powerful in predicting behavior as they were theoretically expected to be. It was found that the central proposition of explaining inter-nation conflict-cooperation by using the concept of either national power or inter-nation alliances was consistently falsified. Likewise, the central independent and dependent variables in the realist paradigm tended to rank among the

---

[12] A propositional inventory of all the strong findings (and all the null findings) is provided in Vasquez (1976b: 200–206).

lowest in their power to successfully predict behavior. Finally, it was shown that certain noncentral realist and certain nonrealist concepts were more successful in predicting behavior than were the central realist concepts. Since the central realist propositions do not tend to produce hypotheses that fail to be falsified, it could be concluded that the realist paradigm has not satisfied the criterion of centrality.

The tests of proposition 6 demonstrated that the realist paradigm has not produced very many scientifically important findings. Although the important findings it has produced are interesting, it is quite striking to think that so much effort and time has produced so little. What is even more amazing is that research that rejected one or more realist assumptions produced proportionally more scientifically important findings. On the basis of the tests of proposition 6, it could be tentatively concluded that the realist paradigm has not satisfied the criterion of scientific importance.

The tests of the three propositions lead one to conclude that the realist paradigm has not been a very adequate guide to knowledge. The use of quantitative analysis to test aspects of the realist paradigm, which began in 1956 and was well underway by the mid-1960s, did not produce much knowledge by the 1970s, although it commanded a great deal of effort. The field did not, as had been expected, move "beyond conjecture." The question that must be answered is why this is the case. This book suggests that the reason for this dismal performance is that the view of the world provided by the realist paradigm is incorrect. This explanation is certainly consistent with the evidence. However, a number of competing explanations, which on the surface also seem consistent with the evidence, can be offered. Before a final conclusion can be made, these ad hoc explanations must be scrutinized.

Six ad hoc explanations can be offered to account for the findings of the previous tests: (1) the findings are to be expected because of the youthfulness of the field; (2) the findings are due to the bivariate character of many of the hypotheses being tested, and as more complex relationships are tested the success rate of the realist paradigm will go up; (3) the findings might be due to the inaccuracy of one large article included in the sample;[13] (4) the findings are due to

---

[13] For example, one article by Rummel (1968) tested over 2,500 hypotheses. Since this analysis was repeated without the article and the results were substantially the same, the ad hoc explanation is not correct.

Table 7.8. *Analysis of ad hoc explanations*

1.	"Youth of the field;; Correlation between year and PPI (B) Kendall's tau$_c$ = 0.019 Result: inconclusive
2.	"Bivariate character of hypotheses" Correlation between number of independent variables and PPI (B) Kendall's tau$_c$ = 0.041 Result: falsified
3.	"Size of article" Correlation between article size and PPI (B) Kendall's tau$_c$ = -0.051 Result: falsified
4.	"Statistics employed" Correlation between statistic employed and PPI (B) Kendall's tau$_c$ = 0.034 Result: falsified
5.	"Quantitative analysis inadequate" Untestable
6.	"Measurement error" Untestable

the particular statistics employed in the articles; (5) the findings show that quantitative analysis is inadequate, not that the realist paradigm is inadequate; (6) the findings are due to measurement error in the articles providing the sample.

Table 7.8 summarizes how these ad hoc explanations are assessed. Three, those that attributed the findings to the effects of the bivariate character of hypotheses, article size, and statistics employed, were tested and falsified. The ad hoc explanation that attributed the findings to the youthfulness of the field was also falsified, but because it could be argued that the entire pre-1970 period was youthful, the test was declared inconclusive. Two of the ad hoc explanations, the fifth and sixth, are untestable and must be assessed on the basis of their face validity.

The fifth ad hoc explanation suggests that the findings presented in this chapter do not show that the realist paradigm is inadequate but that quantitative analysis cannot be applied as a methodology for the study of the more interesting and important empirical questions in international relations. This is the position of the traditionalists and of

Morgenthau himself.[14] The problems with this position are that it fails to explain why a "defective" method was more successful with nonrealist than realist hypotheses; it fails to account for the discovery of some nontrivial findings; and it sidesteps all the epistemological arguments made against the traditional method during the last decade and a half. This ad hoc explanation is therefore rejected.

The final ad hoc explanation maintains that the absence of major findings in the field is due to measurement error in the original articles that reported the findings. This implies that as more accurate measures are developed more important findings will be produced. The problem with this explanation is that in conducting any quantitative research, a scholar does not know whether the findings are a result of the measurements and test design or because that is the way "reality" is structured. A valid test of this explanation would be logically impossible. The best that could be done would be to examine the measures and test designs employed in each article and make some assessment of their validity and reliability. The data to conduct such a test are not available and the adequacy of this explanation must therefore be left open to future analysis.

The above review of ad hoc explanations has eliminated four of them – the argument on the bivariate character of the hypotheses, the argument on the effect of articles, the argument on the effect of particular statistics, and the traditionalist argument on the inapplicability of quantitative analysis. The adequacy of two of the explanations, however, is still open to further analysis. The question that must now be addressed is: What can be concluded about the adequacy of the realist paradigm in light of the tests of propositions 4 through 6 and the two untested ad hoc explanations?

The findings presented in this chapter demonstrate that international relations inquiry had produced little knowledge. The findings in chapters 4 through 6 demonstrated that the realist paradigm has dominated the field since the early 1950s. This book maintains that there is a connection between the dominance of the realist paradigm in the field and the failure of the field to produce much knowledge. The evidence presented in this chapter does not falsify this claim, but lends it greater credence than the two ad hoc explanations, since it has passed a set of rigorous tests, but the ad hoc explanations have not.

---

[14] Personal communication from Hans J. Morgenthau, March 13, 1973. See also Bull (1966).

It can therefore be concluded that while the present data analysis has not demonstrated beyond doubt that the realist paradigm is inadequate, it has raised the following questions about its adequacy. If the view of the world presented by the realist paradigm is correct or useful as a guide to understanding, why have so many hypotheses guided by this view been consistently falsified? If the view of the realist paradigm is correct, why have hypotheses that have rejected the view been falsified proportionally less often? If the view of the realist paradigm is correct, why have the central realist propositions, which have been extensively elaborated and tested, been consistently falsified? If the view of the realist paradigm is correct, why has the realist paradigm produced only 48 scientifically important findings out of 7,158 realist hypotheses that were tested from 1956 to 1970?

These questions must be answered. In Kuhn's terms, these questions pose an anomaly for the field. How the field deals with the anomaly depends on what individual scholars believe has caused the anomaly. The present chapter has gone about as far as possible in terms of delineating a "cause." Until there is more evidence, a definitive assessment of the adequacy of the realist paradigm cannot be made. The present analysis has served to raise as a serious question the possibility that the most fundamental assumptions of the field are incorrect.

The next chapter will try to answer these questions by taking a less synoptic view and a more in-depth approach toward research. This will provide another perspective on the question of measurement error, since a judgment on the validity of particular studies can be made. It will also provide additional evidence to examine the "youthfulness" explanation, by reviewing systematically the important research in the two subfields that have received the most attention in the past decade – foreign policy and the causes of war. When this is done, the conclusions reached in this chapter are given even further support.

8 Theory and research in the 1970s: the emerging anomalies

Introduction

The synoptic analysis presented in chapter 7 is not intended to supplant traditional literature reviews and assessments of research but to supplement them by providing a test design that will make claims about the adequacy of theory and paradigms subject to the principle of falsifiability. There are limitations to such an approach, however. As the two ad hoc explanations on measurement error and youthfulness of the field make clear, any body of evidence is subject to interpretation, even if only on the question of how much emphasis to put on the evidence. Rather than treating each finding equally, as the predictive power indices do, it might be argued that it would be more proper to place a different weight on research depending on the validity of its research design and the theoretical significance of its findings. After all, it might be argued that even in the physical sciences one or two important experiments, like the Michelson–Morley experiment or the investigations leading to the decoding of DNA, are much more important than the vast multitude of work published in a field. Although most of the flaws with which this potential criticism is concerned would be eliminated by the test on the criterion of scientific importance, there is merit in systematically reviewing research to see if it is consistent with findings from a data-based and more synoptic approach. The present chapter will draw on the most important recent research on foreign policy and causes of war to assess the adequacy of the three fundamental assumptions of the realist paradigm.

Most of this research has already been reviewed in chapter 4 so in this chapter it is only necessary to integrate the relevant theories and findings required to assess the validity of the paradigm's fundamental assumptions. By reviewing research of the last ten years in terms of each assumption, it will be possible not only to assess potentially weak areas in each assumption but also to suggest how a new paradigm or different assumptions might correct these problems. The procedure for this review will be to treat the first and third assumptions in considerable detail. Since there is little work directly relevant to the second assumption, however, it will be assessed in light of the other two.

Once the research of the 1970s is reviewed, the most obvious conclusion to be drawn is that the ad hoc explanation on the youthfulness of the field has a great deal of merit. On the whole, the empirical research in the 1970s has not only been more extensive, thorough, and sophisticated but has produced a number of important findings in the major subfields. These findings, once fully understood, belie some of the negative reviews of quantitative analysis that have grown in popularity in recent years (e.g., Waltz 1975: 5–15). The explosion in quantitative research in the 1970s, which uncovered some important nontrivial and nonobvious findings, suggests that the traditional argument against quantitative analysis was incorrect.

The ad hoc explanation on measurement error was probably only partially correct. More refined measures and sophisticated analysis of previously collected data did produce stronger findings (compare J. D. Singer and Small [1968] with Wallace [1973b] and Bueno de Mesquita [1978]). On the other hand, any measurement error produced by the data collection procedures was not so great as to require new data. Advancement has been attained by improving the analysis of existing data.

The existence of a body of strong findings does not change the assessment given in the last chapter on the adequacy of the realist paradigm; rather, it reinforces it, because now there are findings that would not be expected if the power politics explanations were accurate and the assumptions of the paradigm were valid. Of course, at this preliminary stage the research does not demonstrate conclusively the invalidity of the three assumptions, if indeed that were logically possible (since there can always be ad hoc explanations or theories to save the paradigm). The findings do, however, raise even more serious questions about the paradigm than the null findings in the 1960s, and have already given rise to theories that deviate from the paradigm's assumptions.

The first assumption

The first major assumption of the realist paradigm is that nation-states or their official decision makers are the most important actors in international politics. At the core of the realist paradigm, the power politics explanation makes the additional assumptions that nation-state behavior can be explained and predicted on the basis of a rational-actor model. The accuracy and validity of this model has been seriously questioned by the findings of recent research in several of the subfields.

As might be expected, among the work that has undercut this model the most has been that associated with social and cognitive psychology. Experimental studies in this area have been employed to develop propositions on global political behavior in foreign policy making, deterrence and bargaining, and the causes of war. In each case, the belief that the nation-state can be understood as a rational actor or treated as a single collectivity for the purpose of analysis is called into serious question. The remainder of this section will examine the extent to which these two separate criticisms, rationality and treating states as a collectivity, are valid.

The work on foreign policy making relevant to this question can be divided into three areas: information processing; general decision making; and crisis decision making. The rational-actor model as employed by power politics theorists assumes that decision makers will behave in a similar fashion and will be affected not by personal or other idiosyncratic factors but only by the nature of the situation and the structure of the global environment (see Wolfers 1959). They then go on to argue that foreign policy can be deduced by seeing how any decision maker would pursue a nation's interest by acting on the basis of its selfish interest (see Morgenthau 1951).

Even though the rational-actor model employed by the power politics theorists is a more sophisticated and less stringent version of the rational decision-making model discussed in public administration,[1] it has been undercut by recent research in psychology. The first argument against the model is that individuals and groups generally do not make decisions in a rational manner, because they process

---

[1] When assessing the rational-actor model, it is important that the specific version of this model used in power politics be analyzed. Otherwise there is a danger of criticizing a model that is an ideal type that no one really accepts as an accurate description or explanation of behavior.

156

information not on the basis of logical rules but on the basis of a set of psychological principles which do not necessarily correspond with logical reasoning (see Jervis 1976; Janis and Mann 1977). Generalizing from numerous studies in psychology and examining their plausibility to explain a number of diplomatic and historical events, Jervis (1976) argues that decision makers process information in terms of images they have developed of other actors and of the environment. These images are a product of past interactions and particularly of intense learning during traumatic experiences. These lessons of the past are often overgeneralized, producing inappropriate analogies (Jervis 1976: ch. 6; see also May 1973). New information that conforms to existing images tends to be emphasized, and information that is dissonant with the images is often not seen, ignored, or explained away (Jervis 1976: chs. 5 and 7). Especially during crisis situations, overreliance on images and analogies to what worked in the past plays an important role in decision making (Jervis 1976: ch. 6; C. F. Hermann 1972b).

These are strong tendencies, but this model does not mean that good decisions cannot be made or that the tendencies cannot be controlled. Jervis (1976: 3–10, 165–172) relies on the example of scientific reasoning to show that such tendencies do not necessarily result in disastrous information processing. Nevertheless, it is clear that models of action, particularly foreign policy action, based on the assumption of selfish interest and/or calculation of costs and benefits, are too simplistic as either descriptions or predictions of behavior, and certainly as explanations. While the work of Jervis (1976) clearly undercuts the first assumption, it only raises serious questions and is not definitive because he provides mostly anecdotal and not replicable evidence for the countermodel. His most convincing evidence comes from experiments in another field (see also Janis and Mann 1977).

The second argument against the power politics version of the rational-actor model is that, since certain types of individuals and specific kinds of groups behave differently, it is incorrect to assume that they would all behave rationally. This means that a state's foreign policy cannot be deduced on the basis of a rational national-interest calculus, because personal and/or idiosyncratic factors affect individual behavior, and internal structural characteristics affect group decision making. There is some scientific evidence within the field relevant to this problem, consisting mostly of some experiments conducted with the Inter-Nation Simulation.

The findings from INS strongly support the claim that different individuals make different kinds of foreign policy. They show that persons who have a simple cognitive structure tend to be more aggressive (Driver 1965); persons who are more nationalistic or militaristic tend to escalate more quickly (Crow and Noel 1965: 8, 20); and persons who are rigid tend to view the world in terms of good and evil (M. J. Shapiro 1966) (all cited in Guetzkow 1968: 211–225; see also Guetzkow and Valadez 1981).

The major reason this research has not received more attention within the discipline is the belief that real decision makers facing real situations would not behave in this manner. This objection has been handled in part by Margaret Hermann (1974), who compared personality and other individual characteristics of heads of state with the foreign policy of their nation-state. Although her sample was quite small, her evidence is very consistent with the claim that decision makers do not all behave the same way. She found that when heads of state are very nationalistic, have a simple cognitive structure, and do not have confidence in their ability to control events, their nation tends to be conflict-prone, to act unilaterally, and not to commit many resources (M. G. Hermann 1974: 220–223). Evidence consistent with the finding that personal characteristics can have an impact on foreign policy is also provided by Etheredge (1978).

It might be argued that such tendencies would be reduced in a group situation. Even though such a claim does not adequately account for M. G. Hermann's analysis, the research on this question suggests that this potential claim lacks merit and that the group structure itself introduces factors that make decision making deviate from directions that would be necessary for the power politics model to hold. One of the more popular propositions along these lines was the "groupthink" hypothesis offered by Janis (1972), which claimed that a group accentuates nonrational tendencies in the way it processes information (see also J. Thompson 1968; and Janis and Mann 1977). In a theoretical article, Charles Hermann (1978) stipulated the structural characteristics of a group that will encourage certain kinds of information processing and foreign policy behavior. A preliminary empirical test (M. G. Hermann, C. F. Hermann, and Dixon 1979) shows that there is an interaction effect between the structure of the group and the personal characteristics of decision makers and the foreign policy behavior of nation-states.

It must be emphasized that all these findings are preliminary and suggestive. They can all be criticized on methodological grounds, but as research continues the methodological objections are being answered. To the extent the findings remain consistent in light of this further research, the more difficult it is to reject the findings for methodological reasons.

Studies of this kind have led some to try to explain or at least describe and predict foreign policy behavior by reconstructing the particular cognitive processes that specific decision makers might use in interpreting information and making a decision. The major work associated with this effort is the operational code approach of Alexander George (1969) and Ole Hoslti (1970, 1976); the work on cognitive maps by Robert Axelrod (1976a, 1976b); the attempt of Bonham and Shapiro (1973, 1976) to simulate these cognitive processes with foreign policy data; and the cybernetic decision-making model of Steinbruner (1974), which attempts to combine some of the cognitive models with the bureaucratic models of Allison and Halperin (1972). Each of these related approaches suggests that foreign policy behavior can be described adequately and to a certain extent even predicted (see Bonham and Shapiro 1976) by using a cognitive approach. The more serious problem is how to convert this description into a theoretically significant explanation (O. R. Holsti 1976).

One way to do this is to ask new questions. For Holsti (1976: 40–41), research topics on the decision maker as believer, perceiver, information processor, strategist, and learner now become pressing areas of inquiry. All this suggests that nation-labeling shorthands (like "England") that were adopted in the field can no longer be legitimately accepted. Instead, it appears necessary to start from the beginning. Fortunately, an extensive body of research in a sister discipline, psychology, provides a wealth of information and models that now have new relevance.

If these concerns were thought to affect decision making generally, their impact was seen as even greater under conditions of crisis. It was in the study of crises that the concerns with cognitive processes and group dynamics were first raised (Snyder and Paige 1958; Robinson and Snyder 1965; Pruitt 1965; Paige 1968; Hermann 1969a). Because of this initial concern, more research exists on crisis decision making than in any other area of foreign policy making. Holsti and George (1975) have reviewed the major research in this area in order to develop a theory of the effects on stress on decision making. They argued that, on the individual level, stress increases the effects of subjective appraisal, the reliance on cognitive as opposed to logical processes, and the impact of personality (Holsti and George 1975: 302). The usual result is to produce a reduced attention span, greater cognitive rigidity, and a reduced time perspective (more concern with short-term than with long-term consequences). These factors tend to reduce receptivity to new information and tolerance for ambiguity, and to increase reliance on past experience and stereotyping (Holsti and George 1975: 284). At the group level, high stress produces a smaller group and greater cohesion. These, in turn, generally restrict diversity of views and produce greater pressure for conformity, including putting the interest of the group before that of any particular member. While the latter may save the group from a deviating member, there is a danger of "groupthink."

At both the individual and group level, high stress tends to produce a decision-making process characterized by a restricted search for information, a reduced analysis and evaluation of alternative consequences, and a reduced choice of alternative policies (Holsti and George 1975: 284, 292). While such processes can increase the efficiency of decision making and reduce the impact of parochial interests (particularly of bureaucracies or of deviating individuals), the way in which information is processed does not conform to the assumption of the power politics explanation, which is that understanding reality is not a major obstacle once the role of power is appreciated. Instead, this research suggests that images arise in order to cope with information processing and that these images are subject to a number of perceptual distortions. Since these images can vary with different types of individuals, the foreign policy of a state cannot be deduced or explained by a rational-actor national interest perspective.

In addition to the work from psychology, the rational-actor model has also been criticized from a bureaucratic and organizational perspective. The bureaucratic view, as pointed out by Allison (1971) and Halpern (1974) (see also Allison and Halperin 1972), suggests that foreign policy is a product not of external politics but of internal political pressures and fights. This, of course, implies that personal, subnational, or organizational/bureaucratic interests, not solely the national interests, govern foreign policy making. In a further elaboration of organizational tendencies, Steinbruner (1974) treated foreign policy decision making as if it were a simple cybernetic system that responds to stimuli in terms of standard (almost programmed) operating procedures that permit little innovation or flexibility. Such a perspective obviously undercuts much of the power politics explanation; but, aside from several case studies (see Halperin and Kanter 1973), it is difficult to find a test that adequately measures the impact of bureaucratic and organizational factors.

The quantitative studies that come closest to fulfilling this requirement are those of Philips and Crain (1974), Tanter (1974), and McCormick (1975). Each found that, except in a crisis situation, the foreign policy actions of states do not correlate as strongly with the actions others take toward them (reciprocity) as they do with their own previous actions. In other words, if one wants to know what the United States will do toward the USSR tomorrow, one should not look at what the USSR has done or is doing to the United States, but at what the United States did to the USSR yesterday. While such behavior could be seen as reflecting a basic rationale, it is also consistent with the view that foreign policy is a function of bureaucratic inertia and unchanging images.[2]

The best evidence that images play a predominant role in foreign policy making comes from the work on mirror images. While there have been a number of theoretical analyses on mirror images (White 1965, 1966; Bronfenbrenner 1961) as well as White's (1970) review of several cases, the best quantitative study is Gamson and Modigliani's (1971) study of the Cold War. They examine alternative belief systems (or explanations) of the Cold War, including the ones accepted by the respective official decision makers, and find that there is very little correspondence between the images each side has of the other and the way the other side behaves. On the other hand, self-images do account for one's own behavior. This means that each side refuses to accept the image that best predicts the other side's behavior. These findings support the mirror-image hypothesis and show that cognitive processes can have an impact not only on individual decisions but on the basic rationale and world view underlying a state's foreign policy.

The preceding evidence suggests that foreign policy is not based on a rational calculation of the national interest. Any alternative paradigm that sought to explain foreign policy would have to develop a set of concepts that would not only provide an accurate prediction of foreign policy output but a description of the role of cognitive and

---

[2] It should be pointed out, as O. R. Holsti and George (1975: 295–300) have, that one of the "beneficial" effects of crisis is to eliminate or reduce this inertia. Unfortunately, stress has other "dysfunctional" effects.

bureaucratic factors. One hopes that an explanation of these factors could be given in a theoretical manner that would reintroduce the effect of the foreign policies of other states. The major deficiency of the cognitive and bureaucratic approaches to date has been their failure to give a parsimonious explanation of when and why certain processes govern decision making. One way to do this would be to supplement a rational cost-benefit calculus with psychological decision-making calculi and then explain under what conditions decision makers or groups are likely to employ each calculus.

If these criticisms of the power politics explanation of foreign policy making are correct, then the errors made at this level of analysis must inevitably affect the predictions realists make about inter-state interactions. Again, the empirical evidence is only preliminary and limited, but there is enough to suggest that rational-actor models cannot account for behavior in the two circumstances in which realist explanations would be expected to be most applicable – crisis interactions and the onset of war. In both cases, serious questions have been raised about the validity of a rational-actor model.

If adherents to the realist paradigm have claimed anything for their paradigm, it has been its ability to explain the struggle for power. The failure to account for this behavior is a serious anomaly requiring explanation. The scientific study of inter-state interactions during crises is just beginning, with the major studies being those of McClelland (1961, 1968, 1972a); O. R. Young (1968); Azar (1972); and G. H. Snyder and Diesing (1977). Of these, only the last is directly relevant to the rational-actor model. An examination of three models – a rational maximizing utility model; a bounded rationality model (similar to Simon's [1957] model); and a bureaucratic model – resulted in Diesing's (Snyder and Diesing 1977: ch. 5) conclusion that the assumptions for the use of a rational cost-benefit analysis are rarely met and, more important, that actors do not exhibit the kinds of bargaining behavior that would be expected if this model were adequate. Glenn Snyder (Snyder and Diesing 1977: 348, 407–408) dissented from this conclusion, arguing that the evidence is not as clear or as damaging as Diesing maintained. Both agreed, however, that the bounded rationality model, which includes elements drawn from cognitive psychology, provided a better fit for decision making. They suggested that this model was an ideal type and that the bureaucratic model supplemented it. They also suggested when and why deviations would be likely to occur (Snyder and Diesing 1977:

405–407). In particular, the combination of bounded rationality and bureaucracy was seen as the best explanation of how inter-state interactions change each state's behavior.

Equally interesting and relevant is their analysis of information processing and decision makers' definitions of the situation. Their examination of cases led both Snyder and Diesing to reject rational utility models employed in a game-theoretic analysis of crisis bargaining in favor of a model that took into account differing perceptions and misunderstandings. Unlike a power politics perspective, their model did not assume that the power structure will be accurately perceived and/or make behavior conform to certain patterns. Of critical importance for Snyder and Diesing were decision makers' images and whether they were "hard-liners" or "soft-liners." This dichotomy, although somewhat simple, makes the analysis much more theoretical and less descriptive than the work on operational codes and cognitive maps in the foreign policy subfield. Snyder and Diesing's analysis fits in nicely with the work on mirror images, brings in important political variables, and gives a role to the kind of bureaucratic and domestic political in-fighting that Neustadt (1970) discussed. Their analysis suggests that the decision process that produces strategies is not a function of the kinds of power calculations that Morgenthau and other realists talked about.

Even more damaging to the first assumption of the realist paradigm has been the empirical analysis of deterrence theory and coercive bargaining. This has been more damaging because deterrence theory is an elaboration of the realist paradigm and does not rely solely on the power politics framework; for it to fail indicates the need for more radical changes. The comparative case studies of George and Smoke (1974), the earlier analyses of Rapoport (1964) and Russett (1963), as well as the studies of Morgan (1977) and Jack Snyder (1978), all undermined the empirical accuracy of most of the propositions on deterrence and compellence. The primary criticism of the work of Kahn, Schelling, and others was that decision makers (even when advised by the strategic experts) do not think in the rational terms the theory says they should and do not engage in the predicted kinds of behavior. In addition, the behavior they do engage in has consequences that are not anticipated by the theory (see George and Smoke 1974; Russett 1963). If this theory cannot account for American behavior, one cannot help but doubt its relevance for decision makers who have a different culture, history, language, and ideology.

The evidence on deterrence theory is building slowly, and it all suggests the same conclusion – that images and perceptions are much more critical than rational calculations. Snyder and Diesing showed that this is the case with game theory in particular, demonstrating that utility-maximizing approaches to game theory simply do not account for crisis behavior as well as other models do. They found that contending actors often had different perceptions of the situation, and they used this insight to expand and enrich the conventional typology of games (zero-sum, Prisoner's Dilemma, Chicken) into such games as Bully, Big Bully, Protector, Deadlock, Called Bluff, Hero, Leader, and Critical Risk (Snyder and Diesing 1977: ch. 2). Again, while the evidence is not complete, the direction of the findings is consistent with what was found in the last chapter. As the assumptions of rationality are abandoned, explanations of behavior are bound to be more accurate. In addition, this research suggests the kinds of variables and research topics that might be necessary to develop a more complete and adequate paradigm.

Some of the research on the causes of war also undercuts the rationality assumptions. For power politics theorists, war should not be a product of misperception, and yet there is now some strong evidence from the 1914 studies and from the theoretical work of Ralph White (1966, 1970; see also Stoessinger 1961, 1971; Heradstveit 1979) to suggest that misperception plays an important role in the onset of war. War is not the rational or Machiavellian calculation and test of strength that many realists implied. Many wars start by reaching a point of no return beyond which all are helpless (Russett 1962b). Elements of anger, frustration, and hostility (Holsti, North, and Brody 1968; O. R. Holsti 1972), perhaps fueled by status inconsistency (Wallace 1973a) create a hostile spiral that results in war (see J. D. Singer 1958). Wars like this become wars that everyone wants and at the same time nobody wants.

The cognitive and psychological aspects of the onset of war have clearly been underemphasized by the realist paradigm generally and by power politics explanations specifically. To claim, however, that all wars are avoidable if cooler heads prevail, or if decision makers perceive their true interests and each other's motives accurately, is to go to the opposite extreme and make the same kind of idealist errors that led to the realist reaction in the first place. The recent research on war and misperception, when combined with earlier realist insights on the importance of conflict of interest, suggests that hard-line and soft-line views are both too simplistic. On a more theoretical level, any alternative paradigm will need at minimum a typology of wars that can adequately distinguish wars that result from misperception from those that do not, and a theory that can explain why each type is different and the conditions under which each is likely to occur. The research on misperception and war points to a deficiency in the realist paradigm and in the rational-actor model, but it fails to deal with the realist critique of soft-line foreign policy. Any successful competitor of the realist paradigm must fill that gap and develop a theory of war broader than the one on misperception.

After the criticism of the rational-actor model, the two other major areas of the first assumption of the realist paradigm that have been criticized are the notion that nation-states are unitary actors and the idea that non-state actors are relatively unimportant. The idea of the nation-state as a unitary actor is sometimes referred to as the *billiard ball model, or black-boxing internal politics* (Burton et al. 1974: 6). Clearly, the research of G. H. Snyder and Diesing (1977) and of Jervis (1976), as well as the theoretical work of Allison (1971) and Halperin (1974), raises serious questions about treating decision making in a state as if the state were a single collectivity. Nation-states may not have a single interest or a single coherent policy developed by a cohesive group; instead, the foreign policy of a state may very well reflect internal political outcomes. In light of the research mentioned here, it cannot be automatically assumed that the state is a unitary actor; rather, this must be investigated empirically to determine which states can be treated in a billiard ball fashion and whether they can be treated that way in all issue areas.

The problem with treating the nation-state as a unitary actor is primarily conceptual. Is it, for example, better to treat Chile as a single nation-state with a government and foreign policy, or as a set of competing and conflicting groups fighting over who should control the economic resources and the governmental apparatus of the state? In the latter conception, the nation-state is not even seen as an entity, but as the territorial location of the battle and as a set of political institutions which, if controlled by one of the groups, gives that group additional resources and weapons. In such a conceptualization, the real groups or entities in politics might be seen as classes (see Wallerstein 1974) or transnational coalitions among groups (see Galtung 1971; Kaiser 1971). In this perspective, the concepts of penetration and imperialism would be used to determine the real coalitions in the world. To a certain extent, the realist proscription against inter-ference in the internal politics of another nation-state has made it tardy in recognizing the extent to which penetration and transnational coalitions have played an important role in world politics.

Questions such as these have led to a greater focus on the non-state actors that were playing an important political role. The role of multinational corporations, either as mechanisms of technology trans-fer or as agents of neocolonialism, was investigated by a number of scholars, all of whom agreed that these entities could not be seen as handmaidens of nation-states (although there was less agreement about whether they were handmaidens of a particular class). The role of corporations in controlling oil and in the production of food on the global level and the role of the International Monetary Fund and the International Bank for Reconstruction and Development in controlling states' economies has also pointed out the limited view presented by a so-called state-centric perspective. Finally, the de-emphasis on inter-governmental organizations in the realist paradigm has been seen as hiding their current and potential role in creating global regulations (Keohane and Nye 1974, 1977).

Unfortunately, most of this work has either been conceptual or has consisted of case studies. A better way of testing each perspective is needed. To a certain extent, this is provided by Mansbach, Ferguson, and Lampert (1976), whose quantitative examination of the role of non-state actors permits the evidence to falsify their claims. They find that non-state actors play an important role in understanding conflict and that their influence varies according to the region and issue area. In addition, their data suggest that the unitary model of behavior may not be as useful a model as looking at specific intragovernmental actors (see Mansbach et al. 1976: ch. 11).

The work on transnational relations, non-state actors, and neo-colonialism has made a strong case against the conceptualization of the world along state-centric lines. How devastating this is for the realist paradigm is an open question. It is clear that a truly transna-tional society has not emerged and does not seem likely to do so in the near future. Since this is the case, it is then a relatively simple matter for adherents of the realist paradigm to include those non-state actors that are important without changing very much in their analysis. Since the realist paradigm never totally ignored non-state actors, the criticism posed by a transnational perspective can be interpreted as one of emphasis. Indeed, one could argue that the realist concern with sovereignty is simply an idealist, legalistic vestige and that a true analysis of power would certainly look at penetration. In all these ways, the transnational criticism is considerably less radical than is often implied.

The review of the first assumption suggests that it is an inadequate guide to inquiry because the behavior of nation-states cannot be explained solely by the power realities of world politics. This is because individual decision makers will differ, and the ability of governments to act in a unitary fashion will vary. Recent research has delineated the pitfalls of trying to deduce the foreign policy of a state by using a rational-actor model. In addition, the bureaucratic politics perspective has caused questions to be raised about the potency of external factors on the foreign policy of a state in noncrisis situations. Finally, the presence of non-state actors and the role they play in penetration has raised questions about the fundamental conception provided by the paradigm's state-centric emphasis.

The third assumption

The third assumption of the realist paradigm maintains that international politics is a struggle for power and peace. This is a picture of the world, and as such it is very difficult to determine whether this picture, as opposed to some other picture, is a useful guide to inquiry. The analysis in the previous chapter raised serious questions about the picture by examining its research output; this section will examine it more directly by asking whether this picture of the world has produced explanations that provide a complete and accurate understanding of global behavior.

The major claim that can be made against the third assumption, particularly in its classic power politics format, is that *realpolitik* explanations do not provide a theory of world politics, but merely an image that decision makers can have of the world. Power politics is not so much an explanation as a description of one type of behavior found in the global political system. If this is correct, then power politics behavior itself must be explained; it does not explain.

As an image of the world employed by policy makers, power politics promotes certain kinds of behavior and often leads to self-fulfilling prophecies. An adequate theory of world politics would seek to discover when policy makers adopt a power politics image of the world, what kinds of behavior this image fosters, and when such behavior results in war. If this approach is correct, then it should be possible to find non-power politics behavior and to develop a theory of what conditions promote power politics and non-power politics behavior, and how a system or issue area characterized by one mode of behavior might be transformed to the other. Such an approach would provide an authentic alternative to the realist paradigm because it would not only explain everything the realist paradigm purported to explain but would also discover and explain a vast area of behavior that the realist paradigm purportedly ignored.

How does one tell if this second approach is more adequate? There are two possible tests. The first is to see if power politics behavior is just one kind of behavior in the world, and the second is to see if the realist paradigm's explanations of power politics behavior are adequate. The first test can be reduced to the claim that power politics behavior is historically contingent and confined to certain issue areas, and that an examination of other historical periods or issue areas will not reveal any power politics behavior. Power politics behavior can be defined as perceptions of insecurity (the security dilemma); struggles for power; the use of Machiavellian strategems; the presence of coercion; attempts to balance power; and the use of war to settle disputes. In certain historical eras, particularly during the twentieth-century periods associated with World War I, World War II, and the Cold War, this kind of behavior proliferated. In other periods, 1816–1870 and most of the Middle Ages, for example, this sort of behavior did not predominate. Even in times when it did, power politics tended to be characteristic mainly of big-power diplomacy on certain issues. For other aspects of world politics, like the spread of imperialism, the anticolonial struggles, and the emergence of neocolonialism, power politics did not provide an appropriate explanation or image. From this perspective, the realists' main error has been to confuse certain periods of history with all of history, and certain issues with the entire population of issues. As Jervis (1976: ch. 6) would claim, the traumatic lessons learned from the past were overgeneralized.

While there has been little historical research on this question (see Luard 1976 for an exception), there has been an increasing realization that the coming of détente and the ending of the Cold War inaugurated a period of superpower relations that may not be fully apprehended through a power politics prism (see McClelland 1977). When this phenomenon is coupled with some of the major economic transformations occurring along North–South lines, many scholars have seen national security issues and their power politics prone behavior being replaced by other issues (see Morse 1976; and Keohane and Nye 1977).

The analysis of issue areas suggests to some that power politics behavior is confined to territorial and military issues and does not reflect behavior in other issue areas (particularly economic questions, but also other transnational areas that need regulation – e.g., food, the sea, the environment, air travel, etc.). Handelman et al. (1973), Coplin (1974: ch. 13), Kihl (1971), Hopkins and Puchala (1978), and Vasquez (1974b) have given credence to this view, and a data-based study of issue areas by O'Leary (1976) shows that behavior does vary by issue area. This suggests that a period that appears power politics prone is probably dominated by certain kinds of issues or some other issue characteristic (see Dean and Vasquez 1976: 18–28). An issue politics paradigm could provide a very attractive alternative to the realist paradigm in that it provides a broader perspective that explains both power politics and non-power politics behavior and the relationship between the two. Before such a paradigm can be taken seriously, however, it requires a real theory (not just a framework) and some supporting evidence. By the end of the 1970s, unfortunately, neither was forthcoming.[3] Nevertheless, these criticisms of the realist paradigm raise problems that the paradigm's adherents must address and that may with further work provide important anomalies.

Since research on issues and on non-power politics behavior is still limited, greater reliance must be put on a second test: Does power politics explain what it purports to explain best? A review of the research of the 1970s is more satisfying than the review of the research of the 1960s; now that there are stronger findings, a better assessment of this question can be made. The answer seems to be that the realist paradigm has produced some findings, but that on the whole it has failed to account for a great deal of behavior it would have been expected to predict. Furthermore, the areas in which it has successfully generated predictions have been better predicted by non-power politics propositions.

[3] This author has over the years attempted to develop elements of an issue theory of politics (see Vasquez 1974b; Dean and Vasquez 1976; Vasquez 1976a). A theory of world politics that is based on an issue politics paradigm and that is as complete and as policy relevant as the power politics explanations of the realist paradigm is now in the process of being completed; see Mansbach and Vasquez (1981b).

The assessment will focus on the area that has been the major concern of the realist paradigm – the analysis of conflict struggles and of the onset of war. In both these areas, the failures and successes of the realist paradigm, particularly the central part of it, power politics, will be reviewed. Next, findings from non-power politics explanations, which might serve as possible anomalies for the paradigm, will be reviewed.

As mentioned earlier, the power politics approach has prided itself on its ability to explain and guide the struggle for power. Several of the strategies it prescribes have been tested by Russell Leng (1980) to see if following those strategies produces the predicted consequences. He then tested a counter-realist model. His analysis produced mixed results. On the one hand, he found, as realists would predict, that threats are somewhat more successful than promises in getting adversaries to do what one wants, and that, as negative inducements increase, the probability of compliance increases. He also found, however, as the counter-realist model he tested predicted, that when controlling for the power of the contending parties, defiance, not compliance, was the consequence of threats, and at times this defiance in the face of threats can lead to a cycle of interaction that produces war. These latter findings, although only preliminary because of the sample size, suggest that a power politics strategy will not work with actors that are relatively equal in power, and that to take a consistently hard line often results in war.

Similar kinds of lock-in, no-escape spirals were found by G. H. Snyder and Diesing (1977: ch. 2). They found that pure hard-line strategies are not always successful and do not always avoid war. Their empirical investigation of successful strategies shows that there is a need to combine coercion, persuasion, and accommodation with trust and face-saving techniques (Snyder and Diesing, 1977: ch. 3). Other empirical studies have produced findings consistent with these (see George, Hall, and Simons 1971; O. R. Young 1968: ch. 9; McClelland 1972a).

A related weakness within the realist paradigm is its relative inability to offer detailed strategic guidance when compared to the more social psychological orientation reflected in Morton Deutsch (1973) or in Rubin and Brown (1975). Whereas social psychological models have been developed and tested and can explain and apprehend different stages of the bargaining process, realism seems to flounder and rely on insight and the "art" of diplomacy. In this sense, the realist paradigm has failed to provide much understanding of the dynamics of bargaining, even though specific findings may sometimes be consistent with its propositions.

The inability to understand the dynamics of interaction is best reflected in the inability of power politics explanations to account for why and when the struggle for power approaches or degenerates into a state of war. J. D. Singer (1980: xxiv–xxvi) and his associates in the Correlates of War project stipulate the following temporal stages in a conflict system: (1) a rivalry between states in which each party is salient to the other and they both have an above average conflict pattern; (2) a "disputatiousness" stage in which behavior is designed to thwart or punish the other side; (3) the escalation of one serious dispute to war. The realist paradigm relies on several power explanations to explain the transition from each stage, and recent research in the field raises questions about the validity of these explanations and whether they are more useful than other approaches.

Among the strongest findings associated with the realist paradigm are those on the magnitude and severity of war. Michael Haas (1970; 1974: ch. 10) found that different types of systems (bipolarity, multipolarity) have different kinds of wars. Wallace (1973b) found that several wars are most apt to occur when there is very high polarity (many actors and few alliances) and very low polarity (few actors and many alliances). He interprets this finding to mean that when there are no alliances the weak fall victim to the strong, and when there are many alliances, intense rivalry and preparation for war develop. Similarly, Bueno de Mesquita (1978) found that, for the twentieth century, increasing tightness (more alliance bonds) is associated with longer wars.

Less clear-cut are the relationships between alliances and the presence or absence of war. J. D. Singer and Small (1968) did not find any relationship between the number of wars and the number of alliance bonds in the system. Reanalyzing this data, Ostrom and Hoole (1978) found that within the first three years after alliances are made, there is a significant positive relationship with the onset of war; four to twelve years after they are made there is a negative relationship; and after twelve years there is no relationship. This very descriptive statistical analysis suggests that alliances do not prevent war but are indicators of preparation for war. Bueno de Mesquita (1978) found little relationship between the type of alliance system and the occurrence of war; but he did find that increasing systemic tightness in the twentieth century does lead to war, whereas declining tightness (fewer alliance bonds) does not. All these suggest that the balance of power and alliance aggregation generally do not prevent war, but are preparations for war. This conclusion is given further support by an examination of the balance of power during its heyday, 1870–1881 by Rosecrance et al. (1974), who found that there was no relationship between the balance of power and conflict.

The studies on polarity and on the balance of power pose anomalies for the realist paradigm, or at least that aspect of it that places emphasis on alliances as a way toward peace. In the mid-1960s, many scholars debated whether a bipolar or multipolar system would produce peace. If the realist paradigm were an adequate guide to inquiry, at least one side would have been expected to be correct. Instead, both were wrong. The only major difference is whether one will pay the Grim Reaper all at once with a few severe wars, or on the installment plan with many wars.

It is now clear that alliances do not produce peace but lead to war. Alliance making is an indicator that there is a danger of war in the near future (less than four years). This means that the attempt to balance power is itself part of the very behavior that leads to war. This conclusion supports the earlier claim that power politics is an image of the world that encourages behavior that helps bring about war. Since it is now known that alliances, no matter what their form, do not being about peace, the theoretically interesting question is what causes actors to seek alliances. This question begins to push beyond the parameters of the third assumption.

Although the findings on alliances are not very promising for the realist paradigm, some will point out that many realists, for example Morgenthau (1960, 1973: ch. 14), were among the first to delineate the problems in using the balance of power as a peace mechanism. For them, not alliances but the actual distribution of power is critical. Here, as J. D. Singer, Bremer, and Stuckey (1972) make clear, there are two contradictory propositions in the realist tradition. One maintains that power parity prevents war, because no side will initiate a war unless it is sure of winning. The other maintains that preponderance of power prevents war, because no side will initiate war unless it has a chance of winning. The findings produced in this study are among the most impressive for the realist paradigm and power politics. Singer, Bremer, and Stuckey found a strong relationship between parity of power and peace for the nineteenth century, but a moderate relationship between preponderance and peace in the twentieth century. This is an important finding, indicating that power politics explanations can produce strong correlations, but at the same time it poses something of an anomaly, because there is no theoretical reason (and the one offered by Singer et al. appears very weak) for why one relationship should hold in one century and the opposite should hold in the next.

In related studies, Bremer (1980) and Ferris (1973) added evidence that power politics behavior itself leads to war. Bremer (1980: 68–82) found that the more powerful states are, the more involved they become in wars. He concluded that this does not lend much credence to the often expressed view that strength is the best insurance against war. Ferris (1973: 115–116) found that changes in the distribution of power in the system are related to the amount of war in the system. This means that changes in power are apt to set off a security dilemma and inter-state rivalry. This interpretation is supported by Ferris's second and third findings, which maintain that the greater the disparity of power between states, or the greater the change in capability, the greater the probability that states will become involved in intense conflicts. While aspects of these findings lend some credence to power politics explanations, they also provide descriptions of power politics behavior that, if put in a broader theoretical perspective, could support an alternative to the realist paradigm.

The broader perspective, for which there is evidence, is the status explanation of conflict and war. Following Galtung (1964), Michael Wallace (1972) has elaborated a status-inconsistency model that can incorporate many of the findings that support the realist paradigm into a nonrealist model with greater explanatory power. Before constructing this model, Wallace (1970, 1973a) attempted a direct comparison between status inconsistency explanations and distribution of power explanations and found the former more able to pass empirical tests. He then developed a path model which remains the most complete model of the onset of war to date. Wallace (1972) found that changes in the capability of states lead to status inconsistency. A system that is high in status inconsistency tends to promote alliance aggregation, which in turn tends to encourage arms races, which have a very strong correlation with war. This path to war, then, exemplifies a power politics syndrome and supports the claim that such behavior ends in war. Its opposite, the path to peace, occurs when status inconsistency in the system is low. This is positively correlated with the number (and presumably the effectiveness) of IGOs, which are negatively correlated with arms races. The last path provides evidence that can be used to suggest that war is a way of making decisions, and that if certain images associated with power politics can be avoided, then alternative modes of decision making may work. Such an interpretation would place global decision making and the resolution of issues at the heart of analysis and see the struggle for power as a means to an end rather than the end itself.

Wallace's model is consistent with the findings of Choucri and North (1975), who maintained that war occurs because an increase in population, a need for resources, and technology encourage nations to expand abroad. This leads to an intersection of interests, which leads to a conflict of interests. With these come perceptions of threats, which are dealt with by increased military expenditures, alliances, and arms races. Under these conditions, crises tend to proliferate, and, because of the likelihood of misperception and a hostile spiral, one crisis is apt to be unsuccessfully managed and to result in war. In the period after 1870, that crisis occurred in 1914. Choucri and North's model is different from Wallace's in that it specifies more clearly the sources of status inconsistency, and in doing so relies on aspects of a Marxist analysis.

The findings on the causes of war, which is what the realist paradigm purported to explain and understand so much better than the idealist paradigm, appear in light of the preceding findings to pose an anomaly for the realist paradigm. Concepts such as the balance of power and national power have not resulted in propositions that have passed empirical tests in an unambiguous manner. In addition, other models, especially those associated with status, have provided better empirical results and a broader theoretical explanation, which supports the claim made here that power politics is a type of behavior that precedes war and is not an explanation of it. Further evidence for this view is provided by a status model of foreign policy behavior developed by Rummel (1972a).

Rummel (1972a) has produced two pieces of evidence that undercut the third assumption of the realist paradigm. The first is that status field theory can produce very high correlations, indeed some of the strongest published in the 1970s, when used to predict general foreign policy behavior. The second is that as long as foreign policy behavior is treated as a unidimensional struggle characterized by conflict-cooperation, efforts to predict behavior will not be very successful.

This is because conflict and cooperation are separate and uncorrelated dimensions, which means that the same variables cannot predict both. In a factor analysis of American foreign policy behavior, Rummel (1972a) found that it could be classified in six patterns: deterrence. Cold War, negative sanctions, foreign aid, Western European (type) cooperation, and Anglo-American (type) cooperation. Most of these patterns were predicted by looking at the attribute distances between the United States and the target state. Rummel's theory suggests that status-related explanations could provide a basis for explaining not only war but more general foreign policy behavior. It also provides critical evidence to show that inter-nation interactions should not be characterized along a simple conflict-cooperation dimension. This supports the contention that different issue areas encourage different behavior.

Toward a new paradigm

What is significant about the preceding findings is not any single definitive finding (each individual piece of research could be challenged or explained away), but the consistent pattern that appears to be emerging from the research. As the field truly begins to progress, propositions based on realist assumptions do not do as well as those that reject realist assumptions. This conclusion holds for both the first assumption and the third, and for studies dealing with both foreign policy and the causes of war. Specific research findings have been produced that would not have been expected if power politics explanations were accurate, and realist assumptions seem to ignore certain phenomena or ways of perceiving these phenomena that have later led to important theoretical explanations and accurate predictions. While there is no need at this point to decide whether the realist paradigm should be rejected, it can be concluded that the research of the 1970s has called that paradigm into question, that the paradigm has still failed to satisfy the criteria of accuracy and centrality, and that it has satisfied the criterion of scientific importance less well than status, social psychological, or cognitive psychological explanations of global behavior.

In light of this conclusion, a few words can be said about the realist paradigm's second assumption. The studies based on status and psychological models challenge this assumption by showing that a theory based at the individual or group level can account for behavior at the global level. This finding is emerging in a number of the social sciences, which suggests that there will not be a single theory of economics, politics, sociology, psychology, and world politics, but a single theory for each topic that cuts across these fields. Thus, one might expect a single theory of perception, of information processing, of decision making, of interaction of conflict, and of violence. Each of these theories could then be adapted to fit the peculiar circumstances of a specific discipline, much as theories of mechanics are adapted to take cognizance of climatic and atmospheric conditions. This suggests that international relations inquiry should become more interdisciplinary than it has been and that it should incorporate more general political science theory and research. In particular, it should take a more general definition of politics, perhaps David Easton's (1965: 50) "authoritative allocation of values," and help develop a general theory of how collectivities allocate values authoritatively under different conditions – with legitimate governments, with no government, etc. Now that the possibility has arisen that international politics is not necessarily a struggle for power and peace, a more general definition of politics may lead to a more correct view of the world that international relations scholars are trying to study.

If the analysis presented in this chapter and chapter 7 is correct, the most pressing task for the field is to develop an alternative paradigm. When the findings on status explanations are coupled with social psychological models, the elements of a potentially powerful nonrealist paradigm begin to take shape. While a detailed exposition of those elements is beyond the scope of this book, the general outlines can be suggested, and the major problems that a new paradigm must deal with can be delineated.

Attempting to create a new paradigm is no mean task, and the best way to begin is with a new definition of politics. A juxtaposition of Easton's (1965: 50) authoritative allocation of values with Morgenthau's (1948) struggle for power would probably lead to a number of insights. In particular, it would have the effect of putting issues at the center of any inquiry, thereby making power politics behavior and the kinds of issues associated with it but one aspect, albeit a very important one, of a general theory of world politics.

The next task would be to reconceptualize the major dependent variables in the field. Rummel (1972a) has already demonstrated empirically that the concept of conflict-cooperation does not provide a useful guide for predicting foreign policy behavior because these are

176

two separate dimensions. This means that different models of each must be developed, and it suggests that the dynamics of conflict may be different from the dynamics of cooperation. Since this suggestion is not entirely incongruent with certain social psychological models (see M. Deutsch 1973), the latter might be helpful. In a similar vein, some of the findings on war, for example those on misperception and war, suggest that more attention to developing a theoretically based typology of wars might help produce stronger findings. Finally, much of the behavioral work in foreign policy has been confined to explaining conflict-cooperation or participation and has gone far astray from analyzing the substantive content that is usually referred to when speaking of the foreign policy of a nation. There is a pressing need to return to that original topic of inquiry.

The issue politics paradigm advocated by Coplin and O'Leary (1971; see also Coplin, O'Leary, and Mills 1972; Handelman et al. 1973) provides an alternative picture of the world that could aid in reconceptualizing each of the major dependent variables. For them, politics consists of raising and resolving issues. This means that the purpose of politics is to get a desired authoritative allocation of values for the issues that are considered the most salient. With this assumption, the struggle for power is only one aspect of behavior and a means to a greater end. If scholars took this assumption, the first thing they would want to explain about foreign policy is an actor's issue position on each issue on the global agenda. Next, they would want to explain the interactions actors take to get their issue position accepted. Interaction can involve conflict and cooperation, which might be distinguished along three lines: (1) differences (or agreement) in issue position; (2) the exchange of positive or negative acts as a way of changing the other side's issue position; and (3) the development of attitudes of friendship or hostility. Finally, scholars would want to know how an issue would be resolved, and how the values represented by that issue would be authoritatively allocated. There would be a need to develop a typology of allocation mechanisms, of which war would be one type.[4]

It should be clear from the literature review in this chapter and in chapter 4 that the explanation of each of the preceding topics will have to incorporate the findings on perception and information

---

[4] Mid-range theories for each of these topics have been developed in Mansbach and Vasquez (1981b).

processing from cognitive and social psychology with the findings on the effect of status differences and inconsistency on foreign policy interactions and the onset of war. The development of such models and theories will be an immense task, but with more and more evidence emerging from empirical studies, as well as existing findings in related disciplines, the effort could take on the classic characteristics of a puzzle-solving activity. Before this can be done, a more adequate conceptual framework and set of assumptions about the world must be developed.

The future of the scientific study of international relations

The findings presented in this chapter and in chapter 7 present an anomaly for the field. The anomaly is that the extensive hypothesis testing that has been going on in the field has not produced many strong findings supporting the realist paradigm. This book claims that the reason there have been so few findings is that the realist paradigm is an inadequate guide to inquiry. Others, of course, will not be so quick to accept this conclusion. Nor should they be, since evidence is still coming in. Those who would reject the conclusion would turn to the two untested ad hoc explanations to support their position – youthfulness of the field and measurement error. Each of these explanations implies a different research strategy that scholars might use to deal with the anomaly. A review of these strategies will provide some guidance as to how scholarship in the field might proceed until the evidence on the realist paradigm becomes definitive.

The ad hoc explanations that account for the absence of much produced knowledge in the field by attributing it to either the youthfulness of the field or measurement error imply that the anomaly is only temporary. These two explanations suggest that as more research is conducted, measurement will improve and the amount of produced knowledge will increase. The explanations imply that there is nothing seriously wrong with the realist paradigm. The strategy these explanations recommend to scholars is the continuation of research on realist hypotheses and the development of more sophisticated measures of realist concepts. Adopting this strategy has the advantage of allowing scholars to build on the extensive work already done. But the strategy has the disadvantage of not really permitting the two explanations to be falsified. For example, if continued research produces results, then it could be concluded that the explanations were correct. If continued research does not produce any results, however, it could always be argued that better measures or more time are needed. At some point the possibility must be faced that the paradigm, not the research, is inaccurate. Adherents to this position, therefore, must explain the emergence of new anomalies in the research conducted in the 1970s.

This book attributes the absence of many findings in the field to the dominance of an inadequate paradigm – that is, the realist paradigm. It assumes that although there may be some measurement error in research, the primary problem lies not in the research methodology of the field but in the incorrectness of the hypotheses that are being tested. Until a paradigm is found that shows promise of adequately explaining behavior, there will be no major progress in research. This implies that the realist paradigm must be rejected as the dominant paradigm in the field. Since the realist paradigm is not likely to be rejected in the absence of a better paradigm, the strategy that this explanation suggests is to have more paradigm diversity in the field.

Given these various explanations, what would be a good strategy for scholars in the field to adopt in order to increase the amount of knowledge produced in the field? One way of deciding on a strategy would be to adopt a procedure offered by Braybrooke and Lindblom (1963). They suggest that when knowledge of "causes" is limited, as they are in this case, decisions should be incremental (Braybrooke and Lindblom 1963: 61–79). If this rule were used here, there would be no need to choose between the prescriptions offered by the various explanations. Aspects of both prescriptions could be followed and their consequences observed to see if they were aiding the field in producing knowledge.

What would such an incrementalist strategy look like? First, under this strategy the realist paradigm would not be rejected, nor would research on it cease. A number of large data projects in the field are producing new realist indicators. The rest of this decade will probably be needed to analyze this data fully. It would be foolish not to conduct this research given the tremendous amount of time and money already devoted to the projects. An evaluation of this research will provide further evidence on the adequacy of the realist paradigm. If at the end of this research not many findings are produced, then the realist paradigm could be rejected.

Second, given the absence of many findings to date, no new projects guided by the realist paradigm should be permitted to occupy a large amount of the intellectual energy and financial resources of the field. Rather, more attention should be devoted to developing new paradigms; articulating and elaborating already existing paradigms, such as Marxism, issue politics and transnational relations; and collecting data and conducting research on hypotheses derived from these new paradigms. This has already begun as the field enters the 1980s, which is good, because until such work is conducted, the adequacy of rival paradigms cannot be evaluated. Unless such work is encouraged and financed, adherents of the realist paradigm can always claim that, despite its poor performance, there is no rival available to replace the realist paradigm.

This incrementalist strategy has two advantages. First, if followed it would provide data to test the various explanations of the anomaly. Following the strategy would, in a sense, be a quasi-experiment. Further evidence would be provided on the fruitfulness of additional research on the realist paradigm and the adequacy of rival paradigms. Second, given the limited knowledge of the "causes" of the anomaly, the strategy would minimize costs by not acting on the basis of one explanation. If one explanation – for example, the argument on the youthfulness of the field – were accepted and turned out to be incorrect, then tremendous resources would have been wasted. By acting on the basis of both explanations, high risks are avoided.

It should be clear from the above strategy that periodic and systematic evaluation of research in the field is needed. Without evaluation it cannot be known how useful various research approaches are. The present analysis has attempted to demonstrate how quantitative analysis can be used to conduct such evaluations. In a field with few findings, there will always be questions about the utility of various paradigms. If the framework developed in this analysis allows these questions to be asked systematically and answered on the basis of evidence, it will have served its purpose.

Part II

Neorealism and Neotraditionalism: International Relations Theory at the Millennium

9 Retrospective: neorealism and the power of power politics

Looking back at this book, which I began over twenty years ago, I am heartened to see that so much of it has stood the test of time. Although the book did not weaken the hold of the realist paradigm as much as I would have liked, it did help make certain contributions to the way we view international relations theory. I will begin this chapter with a brief review of these, but most of the chapter will deal with whether the work in international relations theory in the 1980s and 1990s has led me to reassess the two major tenets of the analysis – that the realist paradigm has dominated the field and that it has failed to provide an adequate guide to knowledge. The straightforward answer is – no. Indeed, if anything, the work of the past fifteen to twenty years has convinced me more than ever of the tenacity of the paradigm's grip on scholars, especially in the United States, and of the need to abandon it as a guide to both theory and practice. In short, this chapter will update why I think the claims I made about the realist paradigm in the original text are still valid. In this chapter, I will focus on neorealism, primarily Waltz, but also with some attention to Gilpin.

In the remaining chapters, I will focus on selected major intellectual currents within the discipline. In chapter 10, I examine the implications of post-modernism and post-positivism for the analysis herein. On the one hand, post-modernism represents a clear paradigmatic shift, and there is much in it from which the field can learn. On the other hand, post-modernism and its sister, post-positivism, raise fundamental questions about the epistemological foundation of the kind of paradigm evaluation conducted in the original text and in Part II. In order for that earlier work to stand and for the second to go forward, a defense of the very project of theory and paradigm appraisal must be made. Chapter 10 provides that epistemological defense and lays out a set of criteria for evaluating contemporary neotraditional discourse and research guided by the realist paradigm.

The next three chapters apply these criteria to some of the most important questions in international relations that have been the focus of concern by neotraditionalists since the publication of Waltz (1979). Chapter 11 applies Lakatos' (1970: 118–119) criterion that a series of scientific theories should be *progressive* in their problemshifts to demonstrate that the realist paradigm is producing a *degenerating* research program in the core area of neorealism (and a time-honored topic of inquiry of the realist paradigm) – the investigation and elaboration of Waltz's articulation of balancing power. Chapter 12 looks at the second major area of neorealism that has been a focus of neotraditional inquiry – the application of Waltz's analysis of bipolarity and multipolarity to understand the future. Here, the focus is on Mearsheimer's work, including his attack on one of the major alternatives to realism – liberal institutionalism. The criteria of *empirical accuracy* and *empirical soundness* are applied. Chapter 13 questions the *explanatory power* and *policy relevance* of the realist paradigm by looking at the recent debate over the end of the Cold War. This debate is important because it raises questions about the future ability of the realist paradigm to continue to satisfy the two criteria on which it has traditionally scored high. In the closing chapter, I draw together the threads of each of these case studies to make an overall appraisal of the realist paradigm in light of the work of the past twenty years or so. I also discuss where I think the field needs to go from here and elaborate why my criticisms of the realist paradigm should not be taken as an endorsement of liberalism, a paradigm that I also find fundamentally flawed. As with the concluding chapter to the original text, I try to make a case for both the importance of theory appraisal, as well as the need for more imagination in constructing new theories about the world we study.

The contribution of *The Power of Power Politics*

When I started writing this book, I wanted to write and test a Kuhnian intellectual history of the field. That effort I think has been fairly successful and various parts of it have become incorporated into the standard ways of telling the story of contemporary international relations inquiry (see Banks 1985a; Smith 1987, 1995: 13–17; Ferguson and Mansbach 1988: 97–102; Olson and Groom 1991; George 1994; Schmidt 1994: 351, 357). My purpose in using Kuhn, however, was not simply to write an intellectual history, but to use Kuhn to write a *theoretical* intellectual history with a point. The point was to show that there were not many different contending theories in international relations in the 1950s and 1960s (see Dougherty and Pfaltzgraff 1971; Knorr and Rosenau 1969b), but a single dominant (yet fundamentally flawed) theoretical point of view that was acting as a paradigm. These claims, at the time, were doubly controversial, in terms of the idea that there was a single dominant paradigm and, what was even worse, that it was fundamentally flawed.

The first claim has now, I think, been generally accepted in the field constituting one of the major contributions of the book. At the time, however, the claim was fiercely resisted.[1] One of the major reasons for this was that the field often used the word *theory* in a very loose fashion and had little sense of what paradigms were and whether they existed in international relations. *Theory* was used to apply to any conceptual framework, so that one had decision making theory, systems theory, game theory, communications theory (cybernetics), and so forth, without any regard for whether these "theories" actually embodied propositions (that linked variables) or provided competing explanations (e.g. Dougherty and Pfaltzgraff 1971; Charlesworth 1967). Because they offered different conceptual perspectives (and sometimes techniques), they were seen as competing theories, and realism (narrowly defined as the work centered around Morgenthau, Kennan, and Niebuhr) was seen as just one of several approaches, albeit one that many thought the most useful.

After reading Kuhn, I saw realism, and specifically Morgenthau's (1948) work, as not just another approach, but as an exemplar that established a paradigm. The other conceptual frameworks, in this light, were rarely competing explanations, but perspectives that were being incorporated in order to articulate the basic assumptions of the paradigm and resolve puzzles posed by the exemplar. If this interpretation was correct, then the field was much more coherent and research much more cumulative (in procedure, but not results) than had been previously thought.

---

[1] I knew that that would be the case, which is why I took such pains to try to test the Kuhnian explanation with data and not simply try to write a rhetorically forceful interpretation.

This interpretation, or what today would be called a reading, of the field ran against the prevailing view that the field was at best cacophony (if not babel). Most scholars did not have a clear idea of how a paradigm could organize, unconsciously, the disparate work of scholars. Kuhn did not help by saying he did not think his work would apply to social science. Likewise, many dismissed Kuhn's work entirely in a skeptic's frenzy by seizing upon Masterman's (1970) analysis that the word was used in a variety of senses – as if this problem could not be solved by simply stipulating the most important meaning, which Kuhn (1970a: Postscript) proceeded to do, as did I (see pages 22–25).

` When Kuhn's work was applied, it was applied in a manner that further hid the influence of realism. Many saw the field as in a pre-paradigmatic phase (e.g., Ashley 1976) and not in normal science as I was to argue. This conclusion was reached by many in the early years of the comparative study of foreign policy movement apparently because they saw normal science as producing knowledge, and since the field had none (because scientific inquiry was just starting), there could be no normal science. It did not occur to them that a scientifically untested theory could serve as a paradigm, even though Kuhn said that a paradigm need not provide answers, but only the promise of answers. What they failed to look at was whether there was a consensus on how to view the world in order to gain knowledge, i.e., on whether there was agreement on certain fundamental assumptions about how the world (of international relations) works.

The other common application of Kuhn's work was to see behavioralism as a paradigm and to compare it to traditionalism (Lijphart 1974; Alker 1971), a position following Wolin's (1968) work in political science. This also hid the role of realism by denying the theoretical and substantive content of a paradigm. To me this last position made little sense, because Kuhn's explanation presupposed the scientific method. If the scientific method was the paradigm, then astronomy and physics would never have had the kinds of paradigm shifts Kuhn discussed. Methods of analysis and special techniques could be part of a paradigm, but a paradigm also needed theoretical content. Game theory, formal theory, systems theory make some assumptions about how the world works, but without a theoretical content, they cannot explain the world at hand. That is why these techniques and conceptual approaches can move from field to field, but to provide a contribution within a field they must be given a content. That content comes from the dominant paradigm in the field. In international relations it came from realism.

The Power of Power Politics corrected what, from my point of view, were a number of errors. First, it showed that there was a paradigm in the field, that it had supplanted an earlier paradigm – idealism – and that it was now guiding theory and research. Second, it maintained that behavioralism was not a paradigm, but a research technique being used to test and articulate the realist paradigm. Third, it defined the realist paradigm as consisting of three fundamental assumptions – that nation-states are the most important actors, that domestic politics is fundamentally different from international politics, and that international relations is defined as a struggle for power and peace. Fourth, it made clear that it was this paradigm, and not what some were calling the state-centric paradigm, that was really guiding the field. Over the years I have been gratified that these positions have been accepted by a number of scholars. Now it is common to speak of the realist paradigm when it was not before (compare Keohane and Nye 1972 with Keohane 1983 [1989: 44]).[2]

The most general philosophical concern after publication was, as one might expect, with the use of Kuhn's concept of paradigm and its use to write a history of the discipline. Of these criticisms, one of the most important was that of Nicholson (1992) (see also Nicholson 1996a). He argues that the inter-paradigm debate spurred by Banks (1985a) and Vasquez (1983) is mislabeled because the debate among realism, pluralism, and (Marxist-oriented) structuralism is a debate among "schools of thought" and not paradigms per se. For Nicholson (1992: 15), paradigms are fundamentally *incommensurable* and "cannot be compared and therefore cannot compete." "[T]wo paradigms literally cannot be held simultaneously" (Nicholson 1992: 6). For Nicholson, since realism, pluralism, and structuralism clearly are competing and can be compared by establishing testable differences, they are not paradigms, by definition. For him, empirical research will permit a "rational" choice among these conflicting "schools of thought."

Nicholson (1992: 16) is concerned that since paradigms are defined as incommensurable there is no rational basis for choosing among

<hr />

[2] See also the recent debate on the ending of the Cold War (Lebow 1994; Koslowski and Kratochwil 1994). On scholars' use of my various analyses of the field, see Banks (1985a, 1985b); Smith (1987); Hollis and Smith (1991: 31, 35); Kugler and Organski (1989: 172–173); Olson and Groom (1991: 275–276); George (1994: 82, 101–102).

them. My disagreement with Nicholson is not so much with the latter concern, which I equally share, but with his interpretation of Kuhn that paradigms must by definition be seen as fundamentally incommensurable. Here, I have been much more influenced by Scheffler (1967), who argues that paradigms are commensurable on some basis and thus subject to comparison. Since I do not accept incommensurability as the key indicator for distinguishing paradigms, I have no disagreement with his substantive points about the inter-paradigm debate – namely, that some of the disagreements among the paradigms can be empirically resolved (for example, the disagreement between pluralism and realism over the importance of various actors). Likewise, in principle, there is no reason why certain elements in these three competing views could not be synthesized, since at some points they are not mutually exclusive.

Nevertheless, I use the term paradigm to characterize realism, Marxism, and the world society-issue politics frames[3] because Kuhn's concept of paradigm and empirical theory of scientific inquiry provide important and relevant insights into the intellectual history of the field. The key reason for using Kuhn and his concept, despite various criticisms by Nicholson and others, is that it permits us to see things about the field we did not see before and to discuss the very kinds of epistemological questions that Lakatos (1970) and Nicholson raise. In that sense, *paradigm* is a theoretical term that is part of a sophisticated historical analysis about the nature of scientific inquiry, whereas terms like "schools of thought" and its functional equivalents are not. Despite some of the controversy stirred up by Kuhn, on the whole, the use of his theoretical terms tells us more about the intellectual history of the field and permits us to frame the key

---

[3] I have never felt that the alternative paradigm (issue politics) that Mansbach and Vasquez (1981b) offered really was best characterized as pluralism. The same, I think, is true of the world society paradigm of Burton et al. (1974). Pluralism connotes an objection to the state-centric bias of realism. It also suggests that power may vary by issue area. Both of these are shifts away from realism and form part of the world society–issue politics paradigm. However, the real disagreement with realism is over the third assumption of that paradigm – the idea that international politics should be portrayed as a struggle for power. It is the rejection of this portrayal of the world that makes the world society–issue politics paradigm see politics as fundamentally broader than power politics and capable of radical change. Differences between the world society–issue politics paradigm and the Liberal Kantian paradigm are discussed in chapter 14.

188

questions about how we should study international relations than more common sense terms.

Although my purpose was to use Kuhn so as not to write "merely" an intellectual history of the field since its formal establishment in 1919, this does not mean I have not taken care "to describe the evolution of conceptual forms the discipline has taken" (Schmidt 1994: 365). Indeed, the original text is one of the few attempts at writing a history which actually subjects its tenets to empirical testing. My characterization of the field as having gone through three stages – the idealist phase, the realist tradition, and the behavioral revolt – was based on a close examination of what scholars said at the time. I have sought to provide a "historical" narrative of the debates that actually occurred since 1919 and to relate the views of the major participants in those debates. Kuhn tells us that history is rewritten by each new dominant paradigm, emphasizing what is progressive and which lessons are to be learned from previous "errors." Realism, of course, did this with a vengeance. Likewise, the behavioral revolt excoriated traditionalists for failing to apply scientific procedures. Nor could anyone argue seriously that such points, at the time, were not seen by most of the field's scholars as occupying the central place on the field's agenda. To borrow Schmidt's (1994: 363) phrasing, this part of the original text was intended as "faithfully reconstructing past ideas, practices, and conversations."

This can be seen even in the analysis of one of the more original points that was made; namely, that the behavioral revolt accepted the fundamental assumptions of the realist paradigm and sought to reconstruct and test realist theory according to scientific principles. They did not seek to supplant the realist paradigm or develop non-realist explanations. This, of course, does not mean that Morgenthau (1960) or Bull (1966) agreed with the behavioralists, as Schmidt (1994: 357) implies they would have to when he says "one cannot read [them] and not be struck by the thoroughly damning indictment they gave to those involved with the behavioural project." That is true, but the issues were primarily epistemological, not narrowly "methodological" and not substantively theoretical in terms of whether states followed the "objective laws" of "power politics" that Morgenthau (1960: 4) had outlined. Both sides saw this as a debate over what it meant to be scientific and how far that could be taken. Schmidt's (1994: 357) characterization that the issue under debate "concerned the very ontological claims about the nature of social reality" is really to rewrite the debate in anachronistic presentist post-modernist terms that were not at the center of the field's agenda at the time.

Schmidt's (1994) deeper point is that disciplinary histories are often very political. Kuhn makes a similar point, as have Foucault (1972), Lakatos (1970: 175–180), and, of course, Marx. The point, however is most telling against those who maintain that there is a realist tradition going back to Thucydides. This is, at best, an "analytical" narrative that imposes a construct or "myth" to reconstruct the past for a presentist purpose and not the kind of "historical" narrative Schmidt (1994) feels needs to be written. The original text (Part I of this volume) begins its analysis with the first chair of international relations precisely to avoid reading a tradition into the field that is primarily "analytical" rather than "historical." This is not to say that analytical narratives are unimportant to a discussion of the merits of intellectual issues, but simply that they must be consciously separated from a historical narrative of the actual concepts and debates that occurred in a discipline's past. In this regard, Schmidt (1994) has provided a valuable service, and his call for a more careful detailed reconstruction of the pre-1919 history of international relations inquiry is to be welcomed.

The continuing validity of its tenets: cause for celebration and despair

I had hoped when I completed the original text in the spring of 1980 that it would help provoke a debate about the realist paradigm that would loosen its grip on the field. Indeed, for a while it seemed that a variety of attacks on the dominant approach might, in fact, overthrow realism (Smith 1987: 196; Buzan, Jones and Little 1993: 2; Little 1996: 67; Olson and Groom 1991: ch. 8, especially p. 176). That did not happen. Instead, the realist paradigm got a new lease on life (neorealism) by the publication of two major works – Waltz's (1979) *Theory of International Politics* and Gilpin's (1981) *War and Change in World Politics*. These works support, incontrovertibly, the first thesis of this book – the power of the realist paradigm to dominate inquiry. If there had been any doubt about that thesis then, and there was in several quarters, the past twenty years should have put that to rest.

Neorealism emerged as the dominant form of theory in the 1980s and 1990s, and it did so precisely in the manner that I argued paradigm articulations would occur (see chapter 4 above). Both Waltz and Gilpin, in different ways, borrowed conceptual approaches that had been successful in other fields and applied them to deal with problems within the realist paradigm. In part because it was published first and, in part, because it was more sweeping in scope, Waltz (1979) had more of an immediate impact on the field. For that reason, it will be dealt with first and more extensively here. Gilpin's (1981) work will be discussed toward the end of the chapter in the section on war.

Waltz's main contribution to the field was to bring in structuralism.[4] *Theory of International Politics* can be seen as basically a systematization of Morgenthau's thought cast in a logically rigorous and parsimonious frame that subordinates all other levels of analysis. In doing this, Waltz raises in importance three factors that played a more marginal role in Morgenthau's theory of power politics. First, anarchy is now given a pre-eminent role in the realist paradigm, a role that it did not have in *Politics Among Nations*.[5] This emphasis later played an important role in the debates between neorealism and neoliberalism. Second, the balance of power becomes a key law (behavioral regularity) in international relations that theory must explain. Morgenthau never saw the balance of power as automatic (see Claude's [1962: 25–37] analysis) but as a foreign policy that leaders had to follow in order for it to be implemented. Furthermore, Morgenthau (1960: ch. 14) was skeptical about the merits of the balance of power as a foreign policy.[6] Third, the number of actors in the "great power" system (bipolar or multipolar) was seen as critical, something which Morgenthau again did not see as salient for explaining international politics. More important than these specific original contributions, however, was the elegance and deductive rigor with which Waltz rewrote classical realism to create a structural realism. Even his critics cannot deny the intellectual achievement of melding structuralism with realism. This, when coupled with language from economics, at a time when political economy was grabbing the attention of the field, accounts for much of the influence Waltz has commanded during the last two decades.

Part of the way influence is exerted is through generating criticism, and structural realism has generated criticism right down to the

---

[4] Wallerstein (1974) did this earlier and effectively for political economy.

[5] Anarchy does not even have an index entry in Morgenthau (1960: 631).

[6] It is unfortunate that this important chapter was eliminated in the abridged text edition prepared by Thompson (Morgenthau and Thompson 1993).

present. Putting neorealism into perspective, in terms of its place in the intellectual history of the field, then, requires keeping two things distinct. The first is that neorealism is important because it articulates the realist paradigm through the use of structuralism, which was a widespread movement within the social sciences at the time. In this sense, Waltz follows a well-worn path in "cumulating" knowledge by "seeing things from a new perspective"; i.e., with a new set of conceptual lenses (see above, pages 71–72). The individual achievement is finding and grinding the new lenses to correct the specific visual defects of the discipline.

The second thing to keep in mind is that once structuralism (or any conceptual innovation, such as decision making or bureaucratic politics) is introduced, then the field attempts to evaluate its adequacy through criticism. This can be done through a variety of ways depending on the intellectual maturity of a discipline. Scholars can see if an innovation produces accurate explanations, is historically accurate, heuristically useful, etc.[7] I shall not dwell on the many (and well-known) criticisms of Waltz's structural realism or neorealism in general, but only note the main areas of concern that I and others have had. In doing so, neorealism's dominance of the field and why I think it is inadequate should become evident.

The unchanging structure

One of the earliest criticisms was that of Ruggie (1983), who argues that Waltz assumed an unchanging structure and an eternal regularity in behavior in international politics, an assumption that came straight out of Morgenthau (1960: 4). For Ruggie (1983: 273–276) this claim obfuscates real differences (of a structural nature) between the modern period and the medieval feudal period. More significantly, it uncovers the main lacuna in structural realism – the lack of a theory of change.[8]

---

[7] Immature disciplines tend to spend most of their time criticizing concepts and moving from one conceptual framework to another without ever doing any real research. Debates are settled through argumentation rather than through research and scientific testing. Unfortunately, this has been a tendency within the neotraditionalist international relations mainstream; see, for example, the debate on relative and absolute gains (Baldwin 1993).

[8] Gilpin, likewise, assumes a basically unchanging reality, despite his focus on change within that reality (see Gilpin's [1989] analysis). A denial of the fundamental behavioral difference between modern and feudal world politics is the focus of Fischer (1992); see Hall and Kratochwil (1993) for a rebuttal. A criticism of neorealism

The other major early criticism of neorealism that has been of lasting note is that of Keohane (1983, 1984), who, while admiring a great deal of its research program and doing much to spread its influence (see Keohane 1986), feels that it ignores and drastically underestimates the influence of institutions on behavior. Norms for Keohane help shape the nature of system structure, and therefore must be included in any systemic analysis. This position foreshadows the neorealist–neoliberal debate (Baldwin 1993; Kegley 1995), as well as criticisms from an international law perspective (see Kocs 1994).

Criticism from a post-structuralist perspective has come from Ashley (1984). In an article that was not fully appreciated and understood at the time, Ashley (1984: 228) made some very telling criticisms of neorealism (both Waltz and Gilpin) as a structuralism that treats "the given order as the natural order" and blasts neorealism for its economism and scientism (see also Ashley 1983a, 1983b, 1987), something which he maintains was not present in Morgenthau's analysis (see Ashley 1981). This criticism comes, as Ashley (1984: 225) notes, directly out of the criticism of structural marxism by E. P. Thompson (1978) and others. Likewise, Cox (1981, 1986) uses critical theory to uncover the status quo orientation of neorealism and its ideological bias.

Structuralism, outside of political science, gave rise to a number of debates, particularly in sociology and in Marxism, so it is no surprise that these should find their way into international relations (see for example, Wendt 1987; Dessler 1989; Hollis and Smith 1991, 1992). Of these, the most significant would be those of the post-structuralists, especially Foucault (1977, 1979, 1980), whom Ashley (1987, 1988) in particular turned with great force on the assumptions and tenets of neorealism (see also George 1993: 207–10). The thrust of these various points is that the depiction of the current structure of world politics by neorealists is inaccurate because it denies the historical character of the present and treats it instead as eternal, when in fact it is constructed. Within this larger point there is disagreement over the accuracy of the specific picture of the structure painted by Waltz and whether it indeed works as postulated.

---

similar to that of Ruggie's but from a more Marxist perspective is Rosenberg (1994), who argues that history is not just a repeating pattern, but a real history that evolves new things, including new structures and new forms of behavior. Schroeder (1994a: 148) makes a similar observation from a diplomatic historian's perspective.

Domestic politics and levels of analysis

A second set of critics deals with the inability of a system-level account of international politics to provide a completely accurate explanation. Since Waltz emphasized what he labeled the third image (Waltz 1959) as the most explanatory, it should come as no surprise that many critics, from the earliest on (see Ruggie 1983: 273), have sought to correct Waltz by bringing in other levels of analysis. Snyder and Jervis (1993) argue that in the attempt to be parsimonious ,Waltz has produced a theory too incomplete to account for the complexities of the international system. They assemble a group of studies that demonstrate the need to look at factors other than anarchy and the distribution of power to explain international behavior. In particular, they see the need to examine the role of internal politics. From a stance sympathetic to Waltz, Posen (1984) attempts to do this early on by deriving a theory of foreign policy from Waltz (see also Elman 1997, and the reply from Waltz 1997b). Most analysts have been more critical, and since the publication of Putnam's (1988) analysis on two-level games, there has been an emerging consensus that domestic politics cannot be ignored as they play an essential role in explaining outcomes (Snyder 1991; Evans, Jacobson, and Putnam 1993; but see also Zakaria 1992). Rosecrance and Stein (1993) have demonstrated in their collection of studies that it is extremely difficult to explain the grand strategies of states without paying detailed attention to the role of domestic factors. These, of course, are criticisms that echo the point that the realist assumption – that states can be treated as a unitary rational actor – will simply not provide an adequate guide to research.

One of the major problems with Waltz's (1959) three images and the way the level of analysis problem has been generally conceptualized (Singer 1961) is that they leave out what is turning out to be the most important level – i.e. the interaction level (Coplin 1974) or what Burton et al. (1974) called more humanistically the study of *relationships*. This missing fourth image (or 2.5 image if one were to interpolate it within Waltz's [1959] numbering), has been shown to be much more successful in guiding quantitative research than other levels – looking at the foreign policy of a single state or looking at the system. Working at the dyadic level, i.e., examining the *relations* between pairs of states – what they actually do to each other – has been much more productive in terms of producing stronger correlations in the analysis of foreign policy behavior and in retrodicting the onset of war (see Rummel 1972; Kegley and Skinner 1976: 308–311; Vasquez and Mansbach 1984: 415; Singer 1982: 37–38; Bueno de Mesquita and Lalman 1988; Bremer 1992: 310; Vasquez 1993: 43–45). Theoretically, Wendt (1992) has argued that what states do to each other will determine the kind of relationship they build and even the kind of system that is constructed. In other words, interaction constructs the system and not vice versa, as Waltz maintained. Whether this is the case, of course, must be decided empirically and not theoretically. Nevertheless, the point is that both empirically and theoretically focusing on *relationships* is something that the realist paradigm has not done, because for it, every relationship is the same – one of power politics. Even Buzan et al. (1993: 66–67) who recognize the need to emend Waltz by introducing "the missing level" of interactions strip this insight of its paradigm-shifting potential by framing interactions in terms of relative power rather than the nature of the relationship.

This criticism clearly spills over into a criticism of the third assumption that international relations be defined as a struggle for power. For those who have worked outside the realist paradigm (e.g., Burton et al. 1974; Mansbach and Vasquez 1981b; Banks 1985a) or those who have taken a conflict resolution approach (M. Deutsch 1973; Pruitt and Rubin 1986), not all interstate relationships are the same, nor do states need to be dominated by a power politics relationship. Post-structuralists and critical theorists, like Ashley (1987), Der Derian and Shapiro (1989), Campbell (1992), Walker (1993), George (1994), and Klein (1994), go a step further and argue that everything neorealists see as structural and eternal is really a social construction (see also Wendt 1987, 1992; Onuf 1989). This means that history is much more open and radically indeterminate than is being supposed.

In many ways, the work of the 1980s and 1990s has extended and deepened the criticisms made of the first and third assumptions in the original text (see ch. 8, above). The work of Putnam (1988) and of Rosecrance and Stein (1993), among many others, demonstrates the need to open up the black box, this time by bringing in the effect of domestic politics. Likewise, recent quantitative work, for instance Bueno de Mesquita and Lalman (1992), has shown that domestic politics is critical in explaining the onset of war and has more of a direct impact than other levels. The findings that democracies do not fight each other (Russett 1993; Ray 1995), as will be discussed more extensively below, have been particularly damaging for the systemic perspective and for the realist paradigm generally, because they are so unexpected and anomalous for the paradigm. Also, recent work on World War II has shown that one of the main factors leading to war was a shift in foreign policy toward territorial expansion that was brought about by regime changes in Germany and Japan (see Vasquez 1996a, 1998), a conclusion consistent with current findings in the comparative study of foreign policy (Hagan 1993, 1994) that domestic leadership changes can bring about major changes in international relations (see also Stein 1994). Even those sympathetic to neorealism have seen the need to bring in second-image variables, as does Snyder (1991), in his account of overexpansion, and as Van Evera (1984, forthcoming) does by looking at the cult of the offensive and the role of offensive and defensive weapons (see also Jervis 1978; Snyder 1984).[9]

From the perspective of those working in the world society-issue politics paradigm (Burton et al. 1974; Mansbach and Vasquez 1981b) or in conflict resolution, what is significant about these findings is that they confirm that the most potent factors for shaping behavior come from how interactions form relationships. The Mansbach and Vasquez (1981b) "fourth image" theory attempts to explain all that the realist paradigm does (e.g. conflict and war) while simultaneously identifying an entire body of behavior whose prevalence the realist paradigm minimizes (e.g., cooperation).

A nonrealist perspective, for instance, makes it clear that interactions can change structure (Wendt 1992) by building up new system norms (Kegley and Raymond 1990, 1994; Axelrod 1984), which can give rise to regimes (Young 1980) that can fundamentally construct a new reality (Ashley 1987; Wallensteen 1984; Vasquez 1994; Schroeder 1994b). Such observations and conclusions are much easier to make when it is assumed that ongoing relationships can be consciously changed by the parties themselves (or by third parties) from a zero sum (lose-lose) relationship to a positive sum (win-win) relationship (see Kriesberg 1995; Pruitt 1995), rather than when behavior is seen in

---

[9] While structural realism has great difficulty co-opting these criticisms because of its emphasis on a single level, the broader realist paradigm does not. Snyder's (1991) and Van Evera's (forthcoming) work, as well as a host of others (e.g., Glaser 1994/95), have made this move as a way of saving the paradigm, but as will be argued in chapter 11, such moves, as exemplified by the neotraditional work on the balance of power, rather than saving the paradigm, really indicate the degenerating nature of the realist research program.

terms of an atomistic set of acts trapped in a primordial and un-changing egoistic struggle.

Ultimately, the world society–issue politics paradigm does not focus on just one level of analysis, but shows how relationships affect and are affected by the other levels (the internal [domestic] context and systemic structure). Burton (1984) alluded to the need for such an approach early on, and explicit models of the process were presented by Mansbach and Vasquez (1981b). Vasquez (1993: 43–45, 198, 263–64, 309–23) offers a detailed exposition of how the different levels of analysis can be integrated to give a coherent explanation of the onset and expansion of war. Post-structuralists, like Ashley (1987) and constructivists, like Onuf (1989) and Wendt (1987, 1992), have also made the resolution of the level of analysis problem a clear emphasis in their work, although they have tended to look at it in terms of the agent-structure problem.

Anarchy

Given these intellectual currents, it is not surprising that a third criticism of neorealism is of Waltz's concept of anarchy. For Ashley (1988), anarchy is not something that is given in nature, but a social conception that constructs reality. Wendt (1992) extends this line of reasoning by analyzing how anarchy is constructed and how power politics arises. Power politics and the self-help system that Waltz identifies are not caused by the structure of anarchy (i.e. the absence of hierarchical government). For Wendt (1992: 394) there is no logical reason why power politics and self-help grow out of anarchy. Wendt maintains that power politics and self-help are not automatic system effects, but grow out of how actors treat each other,[10] in other words, the pattern of their interactions. If actors are predatory and threatening, then you get power politics. Power politics is a function not of structure, but of a process (of learning) (Wendt 1992: 391) that gives rise to identity and interests (of oneself and of others). This set of meanings (whether one is an enemy or friend) determines whether the structure of anarchy will be associated with power politics, indifference, or cooperative security. Behavior in anarchy is not

---

[10] For Hobbes and classical realism, the origins of power politics are not a problem since each assumes that power politics is inherent in a predatory human nature.

predetermined; "anarchy is what states make of it" (Wendt 1992: 394–395).

While Wendt (1992: 391) is concerned with undercutting the impact of structure and emphasizing the role of process in constructing reality, others have sought to deny the "reality" of global anarchy. Even before Waltz published his *magnum opus* in 1979, Hedley Bull (1966, 1977) denied on the basis of the historical record the most important premises (or "presumptions," as Alker [1996] aptly puts it) Waltz was to make about global anarchy. For Bull, the absence of world government does not mean that there is a Hobbesian state of nature present (something that Waltz had argued in 1959 and would argue again in 1979).[11] Bull maintains there is a great deal of order in global politics, so much so that he sees it not as a state of nature but as a society of states:

> A *society of states* (or international society) exists when a group of states, conscious of certain common interests and common values, form a society in the sense that they conceive themselves to be bound by a common set of rules in their relations with one another, and share in the working of common institutions. (Bull 1977: 13)

Contrary to Waltz, and consistent with Wendt, both of whom were yet to write, Bull (1977) argues that the system of sovereign states can provide a viable path to world order.[12] He spends a great deal of time pointing out how various practices within international politics, like the balance of power, war, diplomacy, and international law, create an order. This order has often been overlooked, of course, because the realist paradigm's view of the world has dismissed the Grotian perspective.

Sometimes, even the most basic and fundamental constructs of order have not been seen by neorealists. Thus, while neorealists are absorbed with Waltz's anarchy, David Campbell (1989: 104) points out that the defining characteristic of the modern global system (since the sixteenth century) has not been anarchy, but capitalism! Capitalism requires a certain level of order for it to flourish, as Hobbes (1651)

---

[11] It should be noted that Bull is not particularly attacking Waltz, whose main neorealist treatise was to come after he wrote.

[12] Buzan et al. (1993) have criticized this "English School" conception of international relations, but have also used it to reformulate Waltz's idea of anarchy, while remaining within the realist paradigm. On the debate over whether international relations is better seen as a "system," an "international society," or a "world society," see Little (1995), Buzan (1993), and Shaw (1992).

recognized, and it tends to produce more order as it takes root, as Kant (1795) hypothesized.[13] Can it be an accident that international trade moves so smoothly and differently today than in the time of Marco Polo? Does it make sense to refer to his time and ours, as both occupying the same anarchic structure? Yet, despite the work of Wallerstein (1974) and the rise of international political economy within international relations, this most obvious of social "facts" – the world capitalist order – has been hidden by the realist paradigm.

Likewise, the theoretical significance and implications of the presence of the norm and practice of sovereignty for the assumption of anarchy has been completely missed by realists. The system of sovereign states, which Morgenthau and Waltz used to make the distinction between domestic and international politics, lies in fundamental contradiction to the idea of a Hobbesian state of nature. Indeed, as Wendt (1992: 415) asseverates, the very practice of sovereignty and its legal institutionalization is a construct that reduces competition over territory and replaces a Hobbesian world with a Lockean world of property rights (cf. Ashley 1988).

The reason the contradiction is missed is that Waltz (1979: 88–89, 114) formally defines anarchy as the absence of hierarchical government and sees it entailing (logically) the violence and chaos of a Hobbesian state of nature. The latter, of course, are often taken as part of the definition of anarchy, although Waltz (1979: 114) explicitly excludes this in his stipulative definition. Nevertheless, he takes pains to show that while economic markets and international politics are similar, the latter is "more nearly a realm in which anything goes," and in which it is plausible to assume that "states seek to ensure their survival," even though they may engage in a variety of behaviors (Waltz 1979: 91). War, then, is, as Waltz maintained in 1959, permitted, and indeed occurs, because there is nothing to stop it. This realist case appears persuasive in light of the survival assumption (or Morgenthau's view of human nature) because it takes two distinct

---

[13] In "The Condition of Warre," Hobbes (1651 [Everyman edn 1950: 104]) argues: ". . . there is no place for Industry; because the fruit thereof is uncertain: and consequently . . . no Navigation, nor use of the commodities that may be imported by Sea . . ." (part I, ch. 13). Kant (1795 [1991: 114]) goes on to say that commerce will diminish war: "For the *spirit of commerce* sooner or later takes hold of every people, and it cannot exist side by side with war . . . Thus states find themselves compelled to promote the noble cause of peace . . ." (italics in the original).

referents of the word *anarchy* – lack of government and a violent state of nature – and collapses them into a cause–effect relationship.

Whether the absence of government produces the violent chaos Hobbes supposed needs to be determined by empirical research and not by the meaning of words or "anthropological" thought experiments. The history of the modern state system does not seem to reflect the constant state of war Hobbes envisioned. Many states have been at peace for very long periods, and even states that have been involved in war have not been involved in all the wars they logically could have been, given the extent of their military reach. Empirically, Wallensteen (1984) has shown that there are clear periods of peace among major states, and Small and Singer (1982: 59–60) show that war is much rarer than is commonly thought, once a precise definition of war is used as a basis of measurement. In fact, more civil wars and revolutions occur in many periods than do interstate wars (see Small and Singer 1982: 233). The mere presence of hierarchical government cannot insure the absence of violence, nor does the absence of government insure the presence of violence. At the basic empirical level, Waltz (1959, 1979) may simply be wrong about war and anarchy.

Even at the philosophical level, however, questions need to be raised. As Hedley Bull (1977: ch. 8) points out, the practice of war in the modern global system (1495 to the present) requires a great deal more order than Waltz is prepared to admit. War is not the same as ubiquitous violence (Bull 1977: 185), but a human institution governed by rules and norms (see also Vasquez 1993: 31). International society determines for what purposes war can be fought and it usually stipulates the *casus belli* and legitimate reasons for war (Bull 1977: 188). The presence of war cannot be taken, *ipso facto* as evidence of the lack of order; "rather the strength of order in a global society is reflected in how it makes war" (Vasquez 1993: 31).

While Waltz (1979: 114) is prepared to deny the world can be "reliably peaceful," he does not say that there is no order whatsoever. In fact, one of his queries is to try to explain how an order can emerge "without an orderer" (Waltz 1979: 89). For the answer, he turns to microeconomic theory, and ends up making the balance of power a law that brings order out of potentially pervasive chaos. Because such great emphasis is placed on power, as would be expected in any preeminent theory produced by the realist paradigm, other possible sources of order, specifically rules, norms, and institutions, are seen as impotent (almost by definition). What is significant about Waltz, then, is not that he will deny that order can emerge, but that the order he sees is so narrow, and the possibilities for more and/or different kinds of order so limited. If one kind of order can emerge from this anarchy, why cannot another (Vasquez 1995: 133)?

One of the reasons Waltz underestimates the amount of order in the system – from the role of capitalism to the nature of sovereignty – is that he wants to treat anarchy/government as a dichotomy and not as a continuum (Vasquez 1992: 854).[14] Anarchy (chaos)/order or anarchy/government (hierarchy) are better seen as matters of degree than either/or phenomena. There are a variety of practices and informal institutions that bring about a degree of order to global politics. Likewise, the absence of a hierarchical world government does not mean that there is no governance going on in the system (see Rosenau and Czempiel 1992). As Milner (1991 [1993: 152]) maintains, even though there is no centralized global government, there are still a number of governing institutions and a body of international law that exist (on the latter see Johnson 1995). The precise degree to which authority is concentrated in the international system will vary depending on the issue area and the historical period (Milner 1991: 76).

Yet, Waltz (1979: 114) explicitly rejects the idea of a continuum. First, he does this by saying that those who advocate a continuum really see anarchy–order as the concept, and this he says confuses structure with process (Waltz 1979: 114). Nevertheless, so much of Waltz's rhetorical force turns precisely on linking his stipulative definition with Hobbes's conception of the state of nature that this is not a fully persuasive argument. Second, he says to add several types might make the classification more descriptively accurate because "some societies are neither anarchic nor hierarchical," but that this temptation should be resisted unless it can be shown that these "societies are ordered according to a third principle" (Waltz 1979: 115). A continuum, however, does not require a unit to be defined by a third principle, because it is not a nominal classification system. All that is necessary is to show that units (in this case, societies) vary by the *degree* to which they are anarchic–hierarchical or chaotic–orderly. Furthermore, one would be hard-pressed to argue that using a comparative concept rather than a classificatory one would make an explanation any less

---

[14] Milner (1991: 76, 78) also makes this point, but I derived it independently, becoming aware of her article only subsequently. I have added several points of hers below to my previous discussion of anarchy (Vasquez 1992: 854; 1993: 268).

parsimonious or elegant. Indeed, in terms of elegance, the opposite is probably the case, since comparative concepts are more precise and less procrustean than classification schemes.

These aesthetic concerns pale, however, in the face of the more serious question as to actual empirical nature of the structure modern global system. To see the modern global system as "anarchic" is to hide the historical fact that an arbitrary system of organization (i.e. a sovereign nation-state system within a capitalist world economy) evolved at a particular moment of history. This system has been guided by clear principles (which discourse has identified and refined) that make this system much more like a society than a state of nature. To call it an anarchy rather than a society has been fundamentally misleading and hides a number of governing practices and institutions that make the system much more ordered than many a domestic government.[15]

What then does the neorealist conception of anarchy supply, if not an accurate description or explanation of the system? Let me venture to say, realist discourse has made global anarchy a constructed condition that institutionalizes how actors (in a jungle) *should* treat each other in their relationships (in order to survive) (Vasquez 1993: 282). Reflecting on one set of experiences, namely those associated with the most devastating wars within the war-torn Eurocentric context, it has generalized one set of traumatic experiences to all experience. Realist discourse thereby helps construct a normative reality to which states are then prodded and advised to conform by realist intellectuals from Machiavelli to Kissinger. Since those prescriptions are not always followed and fail to guide in certain realms, realist theory often falls short as a description and predictor of actual practice. It hangs on, however, in part because of its familiarity and its institutionalization in certain critical governmental and academic circles, and in part because certain of its practices are followed, even though they do not always work out the way they were intended.

---

[15] It also, as Milner (1991 [1993: 68]) points out, makes international politics seem radically different from other kinds of politics. International politics is still politics, and Waltz's emphasis on anarchy obscures that insight, tending to reduce politics too much to the use of force and overlooking the rather complex and rich nature of authority, obligation, and institutionalized practices (Milner 1991: 72–73; cf. Claude 1962: 256–265).

Neorealism and the central concern of the field – war

The final criticism that will be made of neorealism is that it has failed to produce an adequate explanation of war, one of the central topics of inquiry of the realist paradigm. Here I will treat not only Waltz's work, but also that of Gilpin (1981) who speaks more explicitly about war in propositional format. These works are both theoretically deficient in their explanation of war, i.e., the explanation they provide fails in principle to provide a theoretically adequate explanation, and to the extent that they have empirical implications, they seem to be historically inaccurate.

Strange as it may seem, Waltz (1959, 1979), like Morgenthau before him, does not really provide a full explanation of war. Even when he treats this question, specifically, ten years after the publication of *Theory of International Politics* in Waltz (1989) he does not add much to what he had said about war in Waltz (1959). His basic explanation is that the anarchic system structure permits war to happen because it cannot, in any effective manner, regulate the use of armed force. As a result, any state must be prepared to meet force with force, if it is to survive. Waltz (1959: 232–234) refers to this as a "permissive cause," but it is susceptible to the same criticism that Waltz makes of the human nature (first image) explanation of war; namely, since system structure (for Waltz) is constant, it cannot explain a variable, i.e., war/ peace.[16]

Ironically, if Waltz had treated anarchy as a continuum, then this logical problem would have been avoided. In addition, the explanation would have had more plausibility, since it could be hypothesized that in a rich global institutional context, more channels are available for the political (and nonviolent) resolution of issues, whereas in an anarchy only unilateral practices, such as force, are available (see Vasquez 1993: 281–282). But once one starts talking about institutions and "rules of the game" that create a context in which politics can be played and act as substitute for the war game, one is getting pretty far afield from neorealism and the realist paradigm.

Even with a move toward a world society-issue politics paradigm, a structural explanation is not going to provide a complete explanation of war for the simple reason that within the system there are likely to

---

[16] Suganami (1996: 24–25) also makes a similar point. See Suganami (1996: chs. 1–2) for several trenchant criticisms of Waltz's (1959) classic.

be many actors that are not involved in war and dyads that are at peace. Again, a structure that has only one value over several years will have difficulty explaining variation in behavior. At best, what a structure does establish is a context (see Goertz 1994) in which war becomes more probable and peace more difficult. Thus, interstate war might be more frequent in some structures than in others.

Waltz, however, cannot even say this. He can either predict constant warfare (which he does not do presumably because he knows it is untrue), or he can do what he does – say that an anarchic system permits war, but fail to tell us how or why it comes about in any one specific instance. It is the latter that constitutes the great failure of Waltz's work, albeit a failure of omission. For a paradigm and theory whose main concern has been security and survival in the face of the threat of war, it still does not have any precise idea as to what makes war come about! In more technical language, Waltz's permissive cause, by definition, leaves unspecified either the sufficient or neces-sary conditions of war.

By leaving them unspecified, Waltz suggests by default that the sufficient conditions (and perhaps the necessary conditions) lie outside the system structure, which means they will be found in something other than the third image. Since Waltz (1959) has already shown that these sources of war cannot lie within the first or second image, we are left with something of a mystery. The solution to the mystery lies in the missing "fourth image." War is caused not because of human nature, nor because of evil governments or societies, but because of how actors *treat each other* in their contention over certain kinds of issues. Looking at relationships and how and why they evolve toward war is the key to putting together the war puzzle, as I have tried to show elsewhere (Vasquez 1993).

Only with a shift in paradigms was it possible to find the missing clues Waltz overlooked. These clues include looking at certain kinds of issues to see whether they are more war prone than others, studying relationships to see how states learn to go to war, looking at how external interactions affect the domestic political context (and vice versa), and seeing how the global institutional context makes war more or less frequent depending on the extent to which it provides functional equivalents to war for making political decisions. In *The War Puzzle*, I attempted to construct a nonrealist scientific explanation of interstate war based on insights from the world society–issue politics paradigm. Even if all of this explanation does not survive empirical testing, at this point it has provided a plausible account of the onset of war that presents an explanation of the factors that actually bring about specific wars, something Waltz and Morgenthau are unable to do.

Gilpin's (1981) analysis comes closer than Waltz's to providing an explanation of war. He argues that major state wars occur because a rising challenger finds the system established by the hegemon contrary to its interests. This disequilibrium in power is resolved by war (Gilpin 1981: 197). Although Gilpin (1987: 55) is not sure that such a disequilibrium always has to result in war, especially in the nuclear era, he does maintain that the historical record to date suggests that every transition to a new hegemon has been accompanied by a hegemonic war (Gilpin 1987: 351). The original formulation is indefinite with regard to whether the rise of a challenger is a sufficient or necessary condition of hegemonic war. A similar problem exists with Organski's (1958) power transition, which is a more precisely specified and an earlier explanation along the same lines, minus the hegemonic language (see also Organski and Kugler 1980). In a later formulation, Gilpin (1989: 17) corrects this underspecification and maintains that the disequilibrium is a necessary condition.[17]

This is an important emendation, because to assume that a disequilibrium is a sufficient condition produces a major anomaly for the explanation in that the United States replaces Britain as the hegemon without their fighting a war with each other; instead they become close allies (see Wallensteen 1981: 80–84 for a host of anomalies). Nevertheless, to make the explanation one that presents only a necessary condition of war means that the sufficient conditions of war are not specified. This is an advance over Waltz in that now we have moved from knowing that an anarchic structure always permits war to knowing that only an anarchic structure in disequilibrium permits *hegemonic* war. Yet we still do not know what factors make war occur, and this is important because without these factors war will not come about. The failure to specify sufficient conditions means that the major neorealist theory of war is still woefully incomplete, if not otiose.

It is also incomplete in another sense – it provides an explanation for only the small set of hegemonic wars that have occurred, and leaves unexplained the multitude of other interstate and imperial

---

[17] Kugler and Organski (1989: 179) make the same emendation for their power transition hypothesis.

wars that have occurred in history – again, not a very good record for a paradigm whose main focus is on war and the struggle for power.

While the explanation is incomplete, many would argue that it is a theoretical advance over Waltz, and this is true in the short run. In the long run, however, it can only be seen as an advance in knowledge if it turns out to be true, i.e., if it is historically accurate that a rising challenger to a hegemon is present prior to hegemonic wars. Because they are much more precise than Gilpin, Organski and Kugler's (1980) version of this claim has been subjected to far more systematic testing, so this evidence will be examined first. A careful review of the tests shows that the power transition is neither a necessary nor sufficient condition for hegemonic-type wars (see Vasquez 1996c; Siverson and Miller 1996). The major tests by Kim (1992, 1996) and Kim and Morrow (1992) show that other variables are more important. Even when there appear to be associations, these are insufficiently strong to conclude that the power transition is a necessary condition for war. Likewise, specific tests of Gilpin, by Spiezio (1990), Boswell and Sweat (1991), and Väyrynen (1983) find that hegemonic-type wars can occur at several different points in a hegemonic cycle. All this suggests that even the incomplete theory is inaccurate, although research is still ongoing.

The one significant finding in favor of Gilpin and of Organski and Kugler that clearly emerges from this research is that overwhelming hegemonic power or preponderance of power is associated with the absence of hegemonic wars. In part, this finding may be a statistical artifact, merely indicating that after major wars: (1) a hegemon has overwhelming power, (2) no major wars are fought (mostly because one has just been concluded), and (3) no one poses a challenge (because no one is able to pose a challenge). In a truly unipolar system, how is it logically possible to have a hegmonic war?

This finding, however, may also indicate that a hegemon has not been challenged, not because no one is able to do so, but because the global political system established by the hegemon is working to satisfy the demands of other major states and resolving existing political issues, at least to the extent that major war is avoided. In the end, Organski and Kugler and Gilpin provide much more accurate insights about the conditions of peace than they do about the mechanics of the onset of war. In doing so, however, each moves away from a focus on power and toward an emphasis on satisfaction and creating a political system that can resolve issues (see also, Doran 1971). In power transition theory, satisfaction has loomed as a key variable (see Werner and Kugler 1996). In other words, as they move away from the core concepts of the realist paradigm and toward the core of the world society-issue politics paradigm, the more success they have.

At both the theoretical and empirical levels, neorealist work on war has been profoundly disappointing. It has failed to provide a complete explanation, and the major explanation it has provided appears to be historically inaccurate. It is often stated that until an alternative explanation emerges, nothing can be done, but to continue to investigate along realist lines (see Wohlforth 1994/95: 93; Elman and Elman 1995: 192). One of the major reasons I wrote *The War Puzzle* was to meet this objection. There now exists at least one nonrealist explanation of war. At the theoretical level, it provides a complete explanation of wars between equal states, as well as world wars, in that it specifies factors that increase the probability of war and posits a theoretical model of the dynamics that lead to war. Whether this will prove to be an accurate explanation will have to await the outcome of its testing. For the time being, however, it demonstrates that a nonrealist paradigm can provide new insights and explanations that the realist paradigm has been unable to provide.

Given these theoretical lacunae and empirical deficiencies, things do not seem too promising for the realist paradigm, at least in terms of its scholarship on war. One last possible defense of Morgenthau, Gilpin, and Waltz (although the latter does not hold this position) is to argue that realism predicts constant war, and constant warfare is what we have in international politics. It could be said that realism postulates that war is generally constant because of human nature (Morgenthau), the rise and fall of hegemons (Gilpin), and the anarchic structure (Waltz) are all fairly constant. No further explanation of war is required because it is such a natural outcome of the struggle for power. From this point of view, what is misleading about nonrealist analyses is the illusion that permanent peace is possible. This position is best illustrated by the famous Morgenthau (1960: 38) quote:

> All history shows that nations active in international politics are continuously preparing for, actively involved in, or recovering from organized violence in the form of war.

Despite the tautological tendencies inherent in this statement, it provides an accurate view of the paradigm's perspective.[18] It also

---

[18] This statement is tautological in the sense that Morgenthau takes a fairly frequent

provides the basis for a set of empirical tests. Has war been fairly constant except for respites due to war recovery and war preparation, as one would expect given Morgenthau's view of the world? Sometimes the world appears that way. Certainly, during Morgenthau's time (during the 1930s and previously during World War I). Likewise, during the time of Thucydides, of Machiavelli, of Hobbes, and of Clausewitz, the world seemed this way. "Their worlds were *realpolitik* worlds and the lessons they derived from their experiences captured a historical reality, but not all history, not all worlds" (Vasquez 1993: 88).

In order to have a test of these conflicting claims, it is necessary to have some operational indicator of what would constitute a time of war and a time of peace. Using the standard Correlates of War operational definition of 1,000 battle deaths, Peter Wallensteen (1984) found that among major states in the post-Napoleonic era, there have been definite periods of peace when not even a single war between major states has been fought and militarized confrontations are reduced by half. These periods are: the Concert of Europe (1816–1848), Bismarck's order (1871–1895), the League of Nations (1919–1932), and Détente (1963–1976 [where his study ends]). To this last period we could add the post–Cold War era. Although other wars occurred in the world, what is important about these periods is that wars between major states are non-existent. Nor is it just a coincidence that each of these periods reflects a concerted effort by major states to manage their rivalries and work out a system (i.e., a set of rules of the game) whereby they could resolve the issues that separated them (see also Kegley and Raymond 1990).[19]

Some might object that this is not a real peace, because other wars were ongoing. Looking at all wars, Small and Singer (1982: 59–60) find that there are only 67 interstate wars and 51 other wars from 1816 to 1980 involving at least one nation-state (these are mostly colonial or

activity, like war, and then looks at the logical possibilities that can occur around it, i.e., something can occur before a war, during a war, or after it. A Marxist paradigm, or a gourmand for that matter, might see all history as showing that humanity is continuously preparing to eat, actively involved in eating, or recovering from eating. Likewise, one could say that all history shows that humanity is continuously preparing for sleep, actively involved in sleep, or recovering from sleep. A strict Freudian could make the same point about sex, but I shall leave it to the reader to actually derive the necessary proof through quotation for that perspective on the world.

[19] For an extended discussion of the validity of these studies and their consistency with other empirical studies, see Vasquez (1993: 269–281).

imperial wars, or wars of national liberation). Is this constant warfare? Small and Singer argue that these findings indicate that war is relatively rare. By this they mean that it is statistically rare given the number of possible dyads (and hence wars) in the system at any given moment. If one were to reduce this large number of possible dyads to the number of contiguous dyads, this number of wars would still be well below the number of possible fighting pairs. Even as it stands, there are only 67 interstate wars (and a total of 118 wars involving nation-states) in 165 years. This is considerably less than one a year, since these wars are clustered in time and space (Houweling and Siccama 1985). Because there has not been an agreement beforehand as to an operational definition of "constant" warfare, there could be a tendency for a discussion of these numbers to reduce to "the glass is half full/half empty" debate.

Such an important matter, however, cannot be resolved by resorting to a cliché. The idea of constant warfare due to a struggle for power leaves unexplained why most states do not experience wars for very long stretches of time. Sweden, Switzerland, Venezuela, Cuba, Uruguay, Indonesia, and most sub-Saharan African states have had no interstate wars in the post-Napoleonic era (see Small and Singer 1982: 166–174, 179, esp. table 10.1, and Bremer et al., 1992: 390–392, table 15–2 for a complete list of states without interstate wars). Most states, in fact, have fewer than three interstate wars in the post-Napoleonic era (Small and Singer 1982: table 10.1; Bremer et al., 1992: table 15–2).

Conversely, a few states have a large number of wars. If one were to eliminate interstate *and* extrasystemic wars involving major states or regional powers, like Israel and India, there would be only a few wars left on the Correlates of War list. This means that not all states are equally involved in war, the opposite of what one would expect if structural factors were primarily responsible for war or if war were the product of human nature or some inherent struggle for power.

Bremer (1980) finds that the more powerful states are, the greater the number of wars in which they are involved. While this supports the realist idea that power and war are connected, it does not support the idea of constant warfare. States of moderate means, as well as weak states, are much less frequently involved in wars and not the victims of predation that a Hobbesian state of nature would lead one to expect. Nor does it seem that weak states escape predation by being protected by strong allies – alliances between major and minor states tend to be prone to war contagion (Siverson and King 1980; see also

Siverson and Starr 1991). Instead, contrary to realist thought, predation seems to be avoided by simply not playing the power politics
game (see Vasquez 1993: 161–162 for some indirect evidence).

The disagreement over whether warfare is constant could get even
more intractable if a Hobbesian position were taken that insisted that
"War consisteth not in actual fighting, but in the known disposition
thereto, during all the time there is no assurance to the contrary"
(Hobbes 1651: part 1, ch. 13). This position is quite compatible with
the Morgenthau quote and very consistent with Waltz's logic, which
stresses the negative effect of the possibility that survival could be
seriously threatened at any time. To insist that anything short of
complete security should be taken as a state of war, however, is quite a
broad definition of war, one that would eliminate a number of the
long peaces identified by Gaddis (1986) and others. It seems like a
very easy test for the realist paradigm to pass and a very hard test for
any other position. At the same time, however, if one were to find
evidence of this kind of peace, that would be a rather serious anomaly
for the realist paradigm.

Using Deutsch's definition of peace as a security community "in
which there is real assurance that the members of that community will
not fight each other physically, but will settle their disputes in some
other way" (Deutsch et al. 1957: 5; see also Rock 1989), there are three
pieces of evidence that seem to seriously undercut the realist paradigm. Of these, the most important has been the finding that democracies do not fight each other. Such a finding, which seems to have
been sustained by a variety of tests (see Russett 1993, 1995; Ray 1995)
poses a major problem for the realist paradigm in general and
structural realism in particular. This is because it is unclear why a
class of dyads (based on a state characteristic no less) should be
immune from a system-wide effect. Likewise, it is not clear why a
class of dyads should not be subject to the struggle for power.[20] These
findings are both unexpected and anomalous. They are not easily

---

[20] Nor does the argument that this effect is a product of a greater external threat by non-
democratic states appear plausible, because at best this should only result in a
temporary alliance of expediency, like the Hitler-Stalin Pact or the Big Three (Britain,
US, USSR) in World War II and not the more Deutschian security community that
appears to be present. At any rate, this kind of ad hoc explanation should soon be
easily tested since it predicts with the ending of the Cold War that democratic states
will turn on each other (see Mearsheimer 1990: 46–48).

explained away, and what is worse, they were predicted long ago by a rival liberal paradigm (Kant 1795; see also Doyle 1986).

While the findings on democracies not fighting each other are the most well known that identify zones of peace, other such zones have been identified. Some of these are prominent regional systems that lack war. The Scandinavian system is one (see Choucri 1972), North America after 1848 is another. These regional systems seem not to be subject to the kind of interstate relations that realists talk about. Lastly, Western Europe since 1945 has been almost a paragon of Deutsch's peaceful security community, posing a major anomaly for the realist paradigm, especially since the Schuman Plan and the ECSC was consciously created as a way of solving the problem of war in Western Europe on the basis of a nonrealist understanding of world politics (Kegley 1991, 1993; Wayman and Diehl 1994: 17).

Likewise, the Western Hemisphere as a whole, while hardly free from war, seems to have experienced considerably fewer wars and less severe wars than other regions, particularly Europe. Discovering the reason for this might lead to a broader understanding of the conditions of peace and the causes of war. One plausible explanation put forth by the world society–issue politics paradigm is that neighbors who have settled their borders are much less likely to go to war than other states (Vasquez 1993: ch. 4).

From this perspective, the Western Hemisphere has fewer wars for several reasons. First, it has fewer states, therefore fewer possibilities for border wars. This is particularly true in North America, because of American continental expansion. Imagine the number of wars there might have been if instead of three states, North America had as many states as Europe. Second, the presence of powerful third parties (Britain, France, and the United States) have facilitated (through their intervention) a number of states' resolving their border disputes (the best example being the creation of Uruguay as a buffer state between Brazil and Argentina). Third, once neighbors settle their borders, this explanation predicts that states will be at peace, even if other salient disagreements arise. One of the zones of peace to watch then is that among neighbors who no longer fight over territory (see Kacowicz 1995). Such a zone of peace is not predicted by the realist paradigm. Neither Morgenthau's view of human nature nor Waltz's structure of anarchy would permit it. If further research should confirm the identification of a territorial zone of peace, then that would further undercut the paradigm.

Conclusion

This review has shown that despite neorealism's ability to articulate the realist paradigm in new directions, it has still failed to produce accurate explanations of international politics that are able to pass empirical tests. In addition, at the center of the paradigm's concern, neorealism, like classical realism before it, has failed to provide a theoretically complete explanation of war.

Waltz's (1979) analysis, which in many ways has served as an exemplar for a third generation of realists, illustrates these deficiencies in several ways. His conception that the international structure is given, and is an eternal verité, does not appear to be true. As a result, he has no explanation of change in the international system (Ruggie 1983). Likewise, he lacks an explanation of identity and preference formation, and how these might change between structures and within them (Wendt 1992, 1994; see also Keohane 1983 [1989: 48, 54]; Nye 1988: 238).

Also, the structure of the international system does not seem to work the way Waltz claims it does. It does not appear that the logic of anarchy compels actors to behave in a power politics and self-help manner (Wendt 1992). The latter is an outcome of how states treat each other; it is a product of interactions. Structure rather than being given is actually socially (or historically) constructed (Ashley 1984; 1987; Wendt 1992; Cox 1981).

More importantly, the structure of the system does not exist as he depicts it. It is not as anarchic as his stipulative definition of anarchy makes it out to be. In modern times, it has certainly not been the kind of Hobbesian state of nature that has characterized realist discussions of the system (see Bull 1977; Alker 1996). Its level of governance and order varies, both over time and by issue area (Milner 1991). Anarchy/hierarchical government or anarchy(chaos)/order are much better conceived as a continuum than as a dichotomy (Milner 1991; Vasquez 1992: 854; 1993: 268). The paradigm's conception of the system as anarchic has hidden two of the real fundamentals of the system that have profoundly shaped its order and nature; namely, that it has been an international capitalist system and that it has been an international legal system constructed around the rule of state sovereignty. Focusing on the anarchy of the system has hidden these other structural characteristics that are probably more important.

In addition, focusing on structure to the exclusion of other levels of analysis has proven to be too simple to account for the complexities of world politics (Snyder and Jervis 1993). The role of domestic politics cannot be left out (Putnam 1988; Rosecrance and Stein 1993; Hagan 1994); neither of course can the foreign policy interactions of states (Posen 1984; Vasquez 1993). Parsimony and elegance are not a substitute for empirical accuracy. Theories need not include all possible variables (Vasquez 192: 230–231), but they should not exclude critical variables just because they may operate at a different level of analysis, especially if these have been shown to have an important impact on the behavior in question.

Lastly, neorealism's analysis of the processes and behavior that are supposed to be produced by the system's structure are woefully inadequate. Neither Waltz nor Gilpin has succeeded in producing a theoretically satisfying explanation of war. The findings on the democratic peace and other possible zones of peace were unanticipated and profoundly anomalous both for neorealism and the paradigm as a whole.

As with earlier work in the 1950s, 1960s, and 1970s, the work in the 1980s and 1990s has shown that the realist paradigm can guide inquiry into areas that appear theoretically fruitful and provide new insights, but these, on closer inspection, turn out to be inaccurate or theoretically flawed explanations. Theoretical productivity cannot be seen as progressive if the new insights and emendations never pass empirical tests, but continue to spew out an endless series of puzzles and anomalies that must be fixed and/or explained away. Such theoretical development (sic) is not an advancement of knowledge, but a kind of intellectual spinning of wheels that leads nowhere. Chapter 11 will try to make the case that this is precisely the effect that neorealism and the realist paradigm have had on the field in the 1980s and 1990s by looking at the dengenerating tendency of its major neotraditional research program. Before doing so, however, it is necessary to address one of the other main intellectual movements since the publication of the original text – post-modernism and post-positivism – and the implications of them for the kind of paradigm evaluation done in this analysis.

10 The promise and potential pitfalls of post-modernism: the need for theory appraisal

Kuhn's analysis of the history of science helped sustain within philosophy of science a series of attacks on positivism and its view of science. This eventually emerged in a full-fledged "post-positivism" that sought to undercut the logical foundation of the attempt to apply the scientific method to the study of human behavior. This movement made a number of criticisms of social *science* including: the impossibility of a value-free, neutral, and objective science (Taylor 1985: ch. 2), the lack of an Archimedean point to build knowledge (Lapid 1989), and the absence of an independent database to test theories (Hawkesworth 1992). Post-positivism was superseded by an even more epistemologically radical post-modernism that sought to undercut not simply positivism and science, but all aspects of modern thinking, aspiration, practices, and institutions.

Both movements would raise philosophical questions about the paradigm evaluation conducted in the original text. Post-positivists would raise fundamental questions about the logical status of any attempt to appraise theories, let alone paradigms (see Lapid 1989). Post-modernists would see such appraisals as basically power plays, intended to silence and kill off dissident thinking. Yet, if criticism of the realist paradigm is to be taken seriously, it is necessary to have some sort of theory and paradigm appraisal. Post-modernism's claims can be so broad, however – involving a rejection of the entire Enlightenment – that a defense of theory appraisal entails a reconstruction of the very foundation of scientific inquiry. This chapter begins that reconstruction by elucidating the essential points that a reconstruction must accept from post-modernism and post-positivism and then goes on to show the need and justification for theory/paradigm appraisal and rejection.

More of an attitude than a position, post-modernism means different things in different fields. Within international relations, it has not fully arrived and may be abandoned in favor of a more critically reasoned post-structuralism before it has even gotten much of a foothold. Although there are many technical differences between post-structuralism and post-modernism, for the purpose of this essay, the main difference that will be the focus of analysis has to do with the question of relativism. Whereas post-structuralists, particularly those who are inspired by Foucault (1972), flirt with relativism, post-modernists, like Lyotard (1984) and Baudrillard (1990), embrace it. It is important to keep this distinction in mind, particularly in international relations inquiry where many of those who write in the post-structuralist vein are heavily influenced by critical theory and resist the charge of relativism. Despite these nuances, the use of post-modernism and post-structuralism promises to make important contributions to the field and to international relations theory specifically.

The promise of post-modernism

I see five major insights that constitute the promise of post-modernism. All of these in one way or another involve freeing us from our conceptual jails, and for this there is much reason to celebrate (George and Campbell 1990). The so-called Third Debate (Lapid 1989) is not a dead end. Rather than jumping to conclusions and dismissing claims, this is an important time for listening. If that is done, not only will there be a great deal learned, but there may actually be some fresh air to breathe.

Nevertheless, these insights are not without potential pitfalls, so while I present them here as working assumptions, which when applied to existing international relations theory are apt to lead to some important contributions, this does not mean that I do not have reservations about each of the claims – and in some cases, as will be clear in the next section, rather severe reservations. For now, let it be said that one of the major pitfalls is that some of these insights, if followed to their logical outcomes and applied consistently, can easily become overgeneralizations that simply are not true. The claim that reality is a social construction is perhaps the most glaring example. Having made this caveat, I try to present in this section the case post-modernism is making that is most relevant for international relations theory and the scientific study of world politics.

The first contribution of post-modernism and the one that is on the verge of assassinating the Enlightenment deals with:

1. The arbitrary nature of modernity

To the children of the Enlightenment, modernity is the path of progress, perhaps even culminating in the perfection of humanity. To be modern is to be free from superstition, from ignorance, and from a set of institutions and ideas that shape destiny at birth. Even today "modernization," with its concomitant ideas of economic and political development, connote these sentiments. Beneath them is the firm belief that there exists an optimal way, and perhaps only one way, to progress, and that reason, science, and technology will uncover that way.

Post-modernism denies the Enlightenment on two grounds. First, it denies the idea of progress, and in its stead, it places the idea of discontinuities. This is one of Foucault's (1972) major insights. History is not moving forward or backward. It lacks teleology, as well as evolution. Second, post-modernism not only denies the idea of progress, but rejects the notion that the purported end of the Enlightenment, the Modern, is the end of history, the perfection of humanity, or even a worthwhile goal. For the post-modernist, there is no optimal way of doing things. There are many ways, and one is not necessarily better than the other. Likewise, there is no one Truth (with either a capital T or small t) but many truths. Post-modernism rips off capitalism's mask of science and denies the claim of modern economics that there is but one way to solve the problem of food and shelter and that other forms of organizing economies will be less efficient or beneficial, if they "work" at all. At the same time, it denies Marxist claims that certain modes of production are appropriate to certain conditions of history. For the post-modernist, "nothing is written."

What this means is that modernity and its claims need not have been the products of history, although they were the products of Western European history. Modernity is not a model, it is simply an instance. Modernity was not inevitable, nor was it necessary. It is a project. Something else could equally well have occurred. Modernity is arbitrary, and may or may not have served as well as other projects.

More important than these insights themselves are the implications derived from them. Post-modernism not only insists that modernity is an ongoing project, but denies its benevolence. It stands in opposition to the homogenizing role that modernization has played both within and between states. What it fears most is the bureaucratic/all seeing/scientific-investigating/liberal social-engineering/technology-wielding world reformer that will make everyone the same and drown all cultures in one global culture. It stands for the different, the dissenter, the non-conforming (Ashley and Walker 1990). To post-modernism, the ideas of economic and political *development* are just so many modernist conceits in a litany of conceits that have been imposed on the weak and the defeated. Modernity is not progress. It is not optimal. It is not superior. It is culturally and ethically arbitrary.

Once the illusions of the Enlightenment are stripped away, the modern era comes to an end and the post-modern era begins. Post-modernism, then, refers not only to a philosophical position, but to a historical era we have entered. Because of the ambiguity of the term, it is possible for post-structuralists to write about the post-modern without always embracing all of post-modernism (for an example, see the preface to Der Derian and Shapiro [1989]).

The second contribution of post-modernism is the realization that what exists in the world is:

2. Choice posing as Truth

This insight flows naturally from the first; for if it is the case that nothing is necessary (because historicist conditions or positivist causes do not determine things-as-they-are), then it follows that the arrangements that do exist were created by human beings either consciously or unconsciously. Such constructions were in fact choices that were made. How much freedom went into the choices is a matter for historical research, but they were choices in the sense that other arrangements could have been selected by struggles within history.

Human beings, however, have not been satisfied to call these outcomes choices that were contingent on preference, cultural biases, or political fights. Instead they have sought to cloak them as the outcome of metaphysical categories – God, Reason, or History. Rather than seeing things as arbitrary choices coming out of power and interests, the victors have justified their choices in terms of divine law, natural law, or scientific analysis. Even when choice is recognized, these warrants make any other choices sinful, unnatural and un-reasonable, or unscientific. Such claims when seen in the context of Enlightenment beliefs about the inevitability of progress take on an added weight. The post-modernist denies all of this.

The third contribution, which is naturally derived from the second, is:

3. Reality is a social construction

If what exists is at one and the same time arbitrary and the product of human choice (at some level), then it follows that what exists must have been socially constructed by people. Reality is created and constructed by beliefs and behavior. Structures do in fact shape beliefs and behavior the way some positivists thought, but these structures are the product of human action. Reality is not God-given or Nature-given, but human-imposed. And some would add, *this* is an imposition.

Foucault (1972, 1977) is responsible for much of this contribution, but his thinking on this point fitted in nicely with other intellectual currents in hermeneutics, anthropology, and sociology (especially the work of Berger and Luckmann 1966). As a result, something of a wide consensus exists on this point, although thinkers arrive at it from very different starting positions. What can remain of positivist social science, however, if this point is accepted in its entirety?

Exploring how beliefs and social science in particular help construct reality leads to Peter Winch's (1965) idea of social science and the fourth contribution:

4. Language and conceptual frameworks are prone to self-fulfilling prophecies

Whenever ideas spread and people believe and act on them, then that part of the world portrayed by these ideas actually comes into being. In this way realities are constructed. As certain rules and norms are obeyed, institutionalized, and enforced through a variety of social control mechanisms, then a reality comes into existence. Since people often conform to such cultures, it is possible to have a science, like economics, that appears to predict and explain patterns accurately.

Because of this effect, social science cannot be entirely value free or neutral. Of course, it must be pointed out that when positivists argue in favor of a value-free, neutral, and objective science, they do not necessarily mean that values play no role in motivating research, and they certainly do not mean that science should have no impact on the lives of people. What they mean is something much narrower, and that is simply that a scientist should act as an impartial judge in terms of which specific theories and explanations are accepted, rather than as an advocate.

218

Nevertheless, scientific inquiry is not wholly value free because it helps build structures that support and nourish some lifestyles or forms of life and starve and kill other forms of life. Science is not simply a useful tool, but a practice that creates a mode of life that consciously destroys other ways of thinking and living.

This is even more evident in the social sciences. Modern economics, for example, is very supportive of capitalism in terms both of providing an ideological veneer and solving and researching real problems. The contemporary emphasis on rational choice can be read in this light. Rational choice is seen as a modernist conceit that makes choice pose as Truth. The extent to which rational-choice analysis can become a rigorous science will depend very much on the extent to which people or leaders accept its rules to guide their behavior. In doing so, they will not only create a reality but people who are "rationally-calculating individuals." Such a science succeeds in explaining more and more of the variance not because it is able to uncover the "causes" of behavior, but because it produces them.

Post-modernism directs us toward researching how language, conceptual frameworks, and paradigms shape the world. In international relations, one would clearly want to know how power politics and the realist paradigm socially constructed reality (see Vasquez 1993: chs. 1, 3). In democratic polities, one would want to explain how liberal social thought constructed reality. Objectivity, for example, which is generally seen as the absence of a point of view, is seen from the postmodernist perspective very much as a point of view and a pernicious point of view at that. To insist that everything must be seen from two or more sides makes all kinds of assumptions about truth, the way knowledge should be sought, lifestyle, and so on and so forth.

From the ideas of social construction and self-fulfilling prophecy, the fifth contribution of post-modernism follows:

5. The process of identification and the construction of identity is a form of power and an act of violation

Identity is probably one of the more intimate forms of social construction that is imposed on individuals. There can be no doubt from a post-modernist point of view that identity is a social construction. Why one identity rather than another? Who decides and with what consequences? Since identity is often associated with wars and/or persecution, not to mention privilege/victimization, what one's identity is can have profound influences. Who controls identity obviously has profound influence over the destiny and life of an individual, group, or society. Because of this, it is an act of power. Because identity is typically not chosen (at best it can be rejected with pain and agony) – it is a violation of human freedom.

These five contributions of post-modernism cut across all inquiry, and their implications have had dramatic and sometimes long-lasting effects in certain disciplines, particularly literary criticism. In international relations and comparative politics, their implications have not been fully explored. Their potential impact on social thought is profound, particularly on the question of modernization and the creation of a new homogenizing world order. Already within international relations theory, the impact of the small band of scholars writing under the post-structuralist label has been significant. Scholars like Ashley (1987), Michael Shapiro (1981), Der Derian (1987), R. B. J. Walker (1993), David Campbell (1992), Jim George (1994), and Bradley Klein (1994), as well as feminist theorists like V. Spike Peterson (1992), Christine Sylvester (1994) and Ann Tickner (1992) have influenced how we think about international relations theory and have changed the terms we use to describe and conceptualize its project, as well as our understanding of international relations theory's past and its future (see also Der Derian and Shapiro 1989). These contributions provide the heart of what post-modernism has to offer international relations theory. As these insights are applied to specific areas, I would argue, contrary to Keohane (1988: 392), that a very rich research program can be expected.

The pitfalls

Post-modernism places scientific inquiry across the social sciences in a crisis. There is a looming pitfall that Lapid (1989) and Pauline Rosenau (1992), among others, have pointed out, and this is the question of relativism. Within the philosophical writings of Jean-Francois Lyotard (1984) and Jean Baudrillard (1990) it is clearly evinced. For Lyotard (1984), the grand narratives shaped by the Enlightenment, including universalistic claims about freedom, rationality, and human rights, are just so many attempts to master and suppress differences. For Lyotard, specific communities supply their own meaning and truth for themselves, and any evaluation across communities is an act of power seeking to destroy differences. With

Baudrillard (1990), the idea of representing the world is entirely overturned and replaced with the notion that only simulation is possible, because there is no reality or truth to be represented; indeed the distinction between truth and falsity is blurred.

It should not be assumed, however, that the position of Lyotard and Baudrillard is necessarily embraced by international relations scholars working with post-modernism. While several have dealt with the question of relativism explicitly (see Campbell 1992: 5, 13–14; George and Campbell 1990; and Walker 1993: 74–76, 81ff.), it is fair to say that their position on the underlying epistemological issues is still in the process of being elaborated. Nevertheless, two points of consensus among post-modernists and post-structuralists in international relations exist. First is that the very question (or "problem") of relativism only makes sense from a positivist, scientific, or objectivist perspective (Campbell 1992: 1; see also Ashley 1988). Second is that universal claims tend to smother differences and are hegemonic power plays (Campbell 1992: 5; Walker 1993: 74–79). These universal claims are profoundly arrogant and seek to silence, precisely at a time when what is most needed is an opening up inquiry.

Both of these points have a certain reasonableness, and clearly in the short term post-modernists must be permitted some presumptions to allow their inquiry to go forward. The concern here is with the logical outcomes of consistently applying the principles underlying this consensus. Thus, while the critique of positivism moves the scientific study of politics off center, it seems unfair to dismiss the questions of relativism and theory appraisal by stating that this is only a problem within the old framework. Of course, by definition, the problem of theory appraisal is a question raised by the scientific frame, but that does not mean that somehow this question is illegitimate or unworthy of discussion simply because it is tied to that framework.

Put another way, post-modernism seeks to open up inquiry and create a space for itself, but there is a danger (more potential and logical than actual given the structure of the discipline) that it could do so by silencing and dismissing other methodological approaches, particularly "positivist" ones.[1] Likewise, the charge that modernity consists of "universalist conceits" certainly reflects a reading with

---

[1] To a certain extent it is inevitable that post-modernism would dismiss approaches based on Enlightenment traditions because it dissolves their philosophical foundation.

which many would agree, especially as it deals with issues of the way in which life should be organized and with questions of ethics. This reading, however, like the five contributions listed in the previous section, consists of broad brushstrokes which, when applied across the board, seems to raise problems.

In this analysis, I will seek to address primarily the challenge and pitfalls posed by post-modernism to the questions of theory appraisal and scientific inquiry within international relations. The area of ethics and of meaning will be treated separately and only in outline form, if for no other reason than that of space, although I will note that my position on these questions is much closer to that of the post-modernists than those, like Habermas (1984, 1987), who have tried to resurrect the Enlightenment tradition.

The very attempt to separate aspects of empirical from normative inquiry, however, will raise post-positivist objections. Although one could argue that at the most fundamental level, the justification of science or any empirical inquiry will not be logically different from that of ethical inquiry (see Toulmin 1950), this does not mean that the specific criteria for accepting an empirical or ethical claim will be the same. The distinction between inquiry that seeks to explain why and how something occurs and inquiry that seeks to prescribe or commend action is useful for both logical and practical reasons.

At a logical level, since these two inquiries have different immediate purposes, they will use different criteria to accept or reject statements. Thus, normative inquiry will want to have some definition of the good, whereas empirical inquiry need not have this discussion in the same way. Since normative analysis involves several values in defining "good" and scientific analysis assumes that truth is the highest value, the criteria of practical/normative theory accept a variety of positions, approaches, and lifestyles as fairly adequate; whereas scientific criteria only accept the true. There is nothing necessarily wrong with this. In the areas of meaning, interpretation, and lifestyle, variety may be seen as an intrinsic good – a diversity many post-modernists celebrate. Nevertheless, at the normative level, criteria provide some basis for a reasonable discussion among alternatives.

In empirical matters, the commitment to truth applies more stringent criteria, especially that of accuracy, which makes rejection of theories more possible. Although the criteria make truth more of a process than an end product, the very idea of truth implies ultimately a single accurate explanation rather than a plethora of equally true theories. The question of erroneous beliefs appears more amenable to settlement on the basis of an agreement on criteria that justify belief. Why it rains, why people get sick and die, or why they kill each other are questions whose answers must be evaluated by criteria that are different from criteria that address questions such as whether there is too much rain, whether people deserve to get sick and die, and why it is wrong for people to kill each other.

Two additional comments need to be made about separating empirical and normative analysis. First, the position given here – that the distinction between empirical and normative analysis is still useful because of the different criteria used to appraise statements – is very different from the position of early logical positivists, who argued that normative statements could not be verified and therefore were meaningless. Obviously *meaning* is not the same as the criteria used to accept a statement, and therefore the verificationist position was not valid on the grounds it was offered. Second, just because science may be motivated by value concerns and have normative effects, as noted earlier in the discussion of the fourth contribution of post-modernism, that does not mean that procedurally science cannot be objective in terms of how it treats evidence. Objectivity in this sense is a procedural norm maintaining that preferences about the truth or falsity of a proposition should not affect judgments about evidence or procedures in handling the evidence. Rules developed to support objectivity in this narrow sense enable science to avoid being ideological in the sense of supporting a theory because of political or economic interests.[2] Science, however, cannot avoid the pitfalls of being used for normative purposes, including class-based interests.

Reconstructing scientific inquiry after Enlightenment's fall

It is the questioning of the possibility of a single accurate explanation and the abandonment of its desirability that makes post-modernism

---

[2] In international relations inquiry, much of the concern of critical theorists over the issue of political bias of quantitatively oriented scholars is misplaced, for it is not the case in the West that those who take a scientific (i.e., data-based) approach are the main advisors to foreign policy makers; traditionalists have occupied this role, and their excoriating of evidence has made them more prone to ideological influences.

so controversial and places theory appraisal and scientific inquiry in a crisis. There is no doubt that post-modernism along with a number of other post-postitivist critiques have severely damaged the philosophical position of the scientific study of world politics. If that practice is to continue on some logical foundation, then it is essential that it be reconstructed on a new philosophical basis.

The spectre of relativism stemming from the post-modernist critique, and from constructivism in general, questions the legitimacy of the modernist conception of knowledge. Theory and science are not embodiments of truth from this view, but constructions of reality that are imposed arbitrarily as acts of power (Foucault 1980: 112–114, 131–133). For post-modernists, the role of the theorist should not be to invent and impose meaning, but to deconstruct and expose such impositions. In many ways, this kind of post-modernism is a logical outcome of the hermeneutic approach, which maintains that only the analysis of meaning is possible. The scientific project, which includes Marxism and critical theory as well as positivism, says more is possible, because while meaning may be imposed arbitrarily, there is more to be analyzed than the signification humans attribute to their experience. Indeed, such signification may not be the most important aspect shaping behavior and human life (see Bhaskar [1989: 2] and the discussion of structure in Buzan et al. [1993: 7–8]).

It is not an accident that post-modernism has had its most profound impact on literary theory. Literary theorists, after all, deal with fiction, so for them empirical truth is never really a concern; for them there is only metaphysical Truth or constructions of meaning (i.e., texts). There are no pre-given texts. There is no nature; there is no animal inheritance; there is no biology; there is no chemistry, no genetics. There are no human brains, but only creations of human minds and imagination. For them, humanity and its world are plastic – authorless – where every reader can make his/her own meaning.

This fundamental assumption, which underlies all constructivism, is post-modernism's one essentialist sin; it provides a universalistic understanding of human nature and acts as a grand narrative of history. This produces a fundamental self-contradiction that is post-modernism's logical refutation. For if everything is a social construction and nothing is permanently true, then how can post-modernism's view of the world and history as a set of constructions be anything but a social construction? And if it is a social construction, then in what sense can it be true? Indeed, if the post-modernist conception of humanity is accurate, how could post-modernism's analysis conceivably be correct? And why would a post-modernist try to give an explanation of history and human cognition and behavior that was invariant across time? Let me suggest that the very foundation upon which post-modernism makes its appeal is in fact parasitic on an alternative epistemology and view of the world. The very charge of essentialism, which is post-modernism's warrant to dismiss philosophically any statement, is in fact an empirical question that is best answered through empirical research and not philosophical analysis. This opening provides a way of reconstructing scientific inquiry and addressing some of the post-positivist criticisms that have made positivist science so vulnerable.

The most basic question that needs to be addressed in any attempt to reconstruct the scientific project is whether one conception or framework is as good as any other, or put another way, whether there is any non-arbitrary way of distinguishing among concepts on the basis of (what science calls) their truth or falsity. Empirically, we know enough about the world to conclude that not every imaginative narrative can be imposed on the world. People make mistakes and recognize them as such and not simply as a change in beliefs. Utopian efforts are unable to be put into practice, even when the utopians have immense power. Schizophrenics live in a very real and meaningful world of their own making, but they are dysfunctional. Many theories fail to work in natural science and in the social world. *The word "reality" refers to this resistance of the world to conform to every imaginable conception humans think up.* We can imagine unicorns, even develop very coherent and meaningful texts about them. In a sense they are real in our lives, but they do not exist in the world, only in our imaginations. Likewise, we can develop worlds of witches, devils, angels, ghosts, and goblins, and these can be very real and dangerous, but as far as we know they do not exist in the world either. Humans are constantly creating social worlds, but only some can survive careful and rigorous scrutiny.

The *differences* between accuracy and error, reality and fiction, truth and falsity are in fact constructed by concepts. Concepts and words do construct a world around us; yet we need not be prisoners of this world. We are free to reject concepts on some basis other than whim or personal taste. Not all concepts or theories are equal; there are good reasons (and not just those of interest or convenience) for accepting some concepts and theories over others.

Of the various criticisms made by post-positivists,[3] there are two that question the possibility of rejecting concepts or theories on any scientific basis. The first looks at the empirical foundation for testing theories and argues that there are no independent facts, databases, or "reality" to test theories. The second looks at the process of making inferences about the adequacy of theories and argues that science is not based on logic, but on an act of power that imposes its criteria for determining truth on the culture.

The first area where some post-positivists believe science has not been reconstructed is in still holding on to the "naive" belief in "an independent database." Post-positivists rightly argue that facts do not simply exist in the world, but are the products of concepts, which in turn are a function of theories, or at least theoretical assumptions. It is argued, based on the work of Quine (1961) that facts are not independent of theories, and therefore cannot be used to test theories. Since theories create facts, facts can always be found to support theories. These post-positivist philosophical claims in and of themselves are not definitive, but they are often treated that way to dismiss empirical findings.

At first blush, this analysis, because it can be quite sophisticated, appears persuasive, but on further inspection it is at best paradoxical. While it is true that the way one sees the world and what constitutes its facts are a function of the concepts one employs, this does not mean that no observations or puzzles existed before the theory. Theories and concepts often follow observations and are meant to explain or account for a pattern. When this occurs, as it does quite frequently in international relations inquiry, "facts" clearly are independent of theory. In addition, it must be pointed out that even when facts are constituted by the introduction of new concepts that permit us to see these "facts" for the first time, theorists may not be so much interested in "facts" per se as they are in the relationships between "facts" (variables).

Post-positivists argue, however, that because concepts create facts, any operational definition derived from concepts does not create an independent database. All data are theory laden. Any good social scientist would agree with this, but the word "independent" means different things to each side in this situation. For the post-positivist

---

[3] See Hollis and Smith (1991) and Smith (1996) for an overview of criticisms by post-positivists and Nicholson (1983, 1996b) for a defense of empiricism.

critic, it seems to mean that any data set will always be biased in favor of the theory that informed its collection. The implication here is that datasets will always produce confirmation rather than falsification of an explanation or theory. As Hawkesworth (1992: 16–17) puts it:

> . . . if what is taken to be the "world", what is understood in terms of "brute data" is itself theoretically constituted (indeed, constituted by the same theory that is undergoing the test), then no conclusive disproof of a theory is likely. For the independent evidence upon which falsification depends does not exist; the available evidence is preconstituted by the same theoretical presuppositions as the scientific theory under scrutiny . . .

This view is widely accepted by political philosophers, and I venture to say that one reason for this, is that they have never really tried to test a hypothesis that was incorrect. If in fact this presumption were true, we should have thousands of strong findings in international relations. Instead we have comparatively few! Data are not independent in the sense that they have no connection with concepts, but they are independent in the sense that they do not assure confirmation of theories. Databases can be considered independent if two competing explanations of the same behavior (i.e. set of observations) have the same chance of being rejected. We know this is often the case, because, in international relations (with the exception of a few areas of inquiry), the most frequent finding is the null finding (see above, ch. 7).

The second area where some post-positivists think scientific inquiry still needs further reconstructing and where their criticisms are much more telling has to do with science's epistemological foundation. The early logical positivists had hoped science and its method could be established on logic, so that its conclusions would be *compelling*. No such epistemology and logical solution has been established. The most recent effort to do so and the focus of much post-positivist criticism has been that of Popper (1959). He attempted to test scientific criteria for acceptance of beliefs on the principle of falsification.

However, as most are prepared to concede, Popper's efforts fall down because the principle of falsification, as well as the other standard criteria for rejecting theories, must be seen as *decision rules*, norms if you will, and not as logical conclusions compelling belief. From this view, science becomes a project for making decisions about belief according to fairly rigorous rules, norms, and definitions.

Establishing a consensus on rules becomes the basis for reconstructing science in a post-modern era.[4]

These rules and norms need not be seen as philosophically arbitrary because they are justified on the basis of good reasons. They also are not arbitrary at the practical level in that the rules they embody are applied to make appraisals in a rigorous manner that limits the intrusion of personal preferences. In this way, science can act as a self-correcting mechanism and is one of the few ways people have to save themselves from self-delusion. Although science is a language game, like all other language games in a culture, it can claim adherence over competing games because of its self-correcting mechanism and its ability to settle differences on empirical questions once its procedures are accepted. Ultimately, while science draws upon aspects of the correspondence and coherence theory of truth, it rests – as a final check – on the pragmatic theory of truth. Putting ideas to test and examining evidence are important strategies that should not be cavalierly discarded by those interested in political inquiry.

This conception of science concedes much to post-positivist criticisms, but it reconstructs the scientific project on firmer philosophical ground. In addition, it makes it clearer exactly what role science can play in society. Science, however, is more than just a tool, although it could be reduced to that. It must be conceded that at the very center of the scientific spirit are values and practices that make it a way of thinking; indeed it can be argued that they constitute a way of life. The commitment to truth and the search for truth as the highest values are more than just preferences – they are fundamental value commitments. Truth is not simply a semantic concept (Tarski 1949), but a value that guides inquiry. To say that truth is the prime value means that theories and beliefs should be accepted or rejected solely on the basis of their ability to be consistent with the evidence and not because their acceptance will have beneficial consequences, promote a particular economic or political interest, be consistent with preconceived revealed doctrine, or provide an enabling function that allows

---

[4] Reconstructing science on this ground is not very different from what Kuhn (1970a: 199) said when he maintained that nothing about his thesis on debates over theory choice implies "that there are no good reasons [for choosing one theory over another] . . . Nor does it even imply that the reasons for choice are different from those usually listed by philosophers of science: accuracy, simplicity, fruitfulness, and the like." This hardly sounds like the radical skeptic that anti-positivists want to make Kuhn out to be (see Spegele 1996: 46).

a society to shape the world by controlling people and resources. These other considerations, one or more of which are often important criteria in ethics, religion or public policy for the acceptance of statements, are in competition with the scientific spirit. Even those who take an instrumental philosophy of science position (and prefer to speak of adequacy or utility rather than truth) still see that what I am calling "truth" is the central value commitment of the scientific project. Science insists that for empirical questions its value commitment to the search for truth must be taken as guiding, and its practices privileged as the best way of attaining knowledge. In non-empirical matters, it is willing to give way; i.e., it recognizes the legitimacy of using additional and sometimes other criteria for accepting or rejecting non-empirical statements.

Science then is an act of power in that it imposes its criteria for determining truth on the entire society. At a particular point in Western history, science emerged as a discourse that competed with other discourses and institutions for the control of language and belief in certain domains, and after a long struggle, which still continues in certain quarters, it won the battle. Although this was a political battle, this does not mean that there are not good reasons (both epistemological and practical) for choosing scientific criteria of truth over others in the questions science has demarked within its domain.

All of this does not mean that post-modernism's insights about the Enlightenment are ill-founded or incorrect. They stand and should make international relations theory more humble, more cautious about human learning and "progress," and more mindful of the corrupting nature of power. Nevertheless, building on the criticisms of logical positivism to establish a new rational foundation for science on the basis of decision rules makes it possible to avoid the abyss of relativism. To do so concedes to the critics that science is a system of conventions for decision making and not an Archimedean fulcrum lifting us to irrefutable knowledge.

Overcoming relativism within scientific inquiry

Efforts to overcome relativism center on the question of establishing criteria for theory appraisal. Within international relations, this has been seen as a crucial area of concern both because of post-positivism and because of the inter-paradigm debate on the adequacy of the realist paradigm (see Lapid 1989; Banks 1985a). While some have celebrated the idea of theoretical pluralism, the idea of building knowledge requires some appraisal of existing beliefs, explanations, theories, and paradigms. Since there are both empirical and normative theories in international relations, and since empirical and normative statements are accepted on the basis of different criteria, each type of theory needs its own set of criteria.

The criteria of adequacy for empirical theory presented here are based on the assumption that a good theory must be true. The criteria are justified on the basis of the argument that following and using them increases the probability that an empirical theory, research program, or paradigm that satisfies the criteria is less likely to be false than one that does. If one prefers not to accept a philosophically realist view of theories (see Nagel 1961: 117–118, 141–152, 196), then in more instrumental terms, a theory that satisfies these criteria can be said to be more promising for achieving and making progress toward the ultimate goal of science, which is the acquisition of knowledge.[5]

There are six criteria (all of them standard in philosophy of science) relevant to international relations inquiry. "Good" empirical theories should be:

1. *accurate*
2. *falsifiable*
3. capable of evincing great *explanatory power*
4. *progressive* as opposed to *degenerating* in terms of their research program(s)
5. *consistent* with what is known in other areas
6. appropriately *parsimonious* and elegant.

I label these, respectively, the criteria of accuracy, falsifiability, explanatory power, progressivity, consistency, and parsimony.

A set of propositions is accepted as satisfying the *criterion of empirical accuracy* if they consistently pass a set of reasonable and valid tests. Although theories are never proven and science is open-ended, theories whose propositions have passed tests can be tentatively accepted as accurate (and true), or at least not inaccurate and false. Conversely, theories that consistently do not pass tests can be

---

[5] I confine this analysis to empirical theories that claim to be scientific, at least in some sense of that word. Since traditional realists, like Morgenthau (1960) and Carr (1939 [1964]) claim that, I do not exclude theories whose adherents have eschewed quantitative analysis from these criteria (nor would they take exception to these criteria).

regard as false or dismissed as no longer being useful guides to research. This is because if the purpose of scientific inquiry is to produce knowledge, then failure to produce strong and statistically significant associations is an indicator of the failure to produce knowledge.

The criterion of empirical accuracy was the main criterion employed in the original text (see above, ch. 7). Some, like Spegele (1996: 42–43), have sought to criticize my application of it in the original text, by arguing that "any richly-textured theory" cannot be refuted "by determining the empirical adequacy of single hypotheses" or "on a proposition-by-proposition basis . . ." Spegele seeks to deny the claim (that if a central proposition of a theory is found to be false, then the theory as it stands cannot be true) without showing that there is anything logically invalid with this inference. Even if one is willing to be more pragmatic than logical, it needs to be pointed out that in the original text, not one or several, but all of the then existing propositions that had been tested statistically were examined. These included numerous tests of propositions at the center of the paradigm. In addition, the few propositions that did pass tests were then evaluated in terms of their scientific importance. What Spegele (1996: 42–43) would prefer is a more holistic application and one that presumably examines evidence other than that produced by statistical analysis. The case studies in this second part of the volume are meant to meet that concern. Nevertheless, I believe it is a mistake, as well as highly risky, to dismiss an entire body of evidence and to continue to adhere to a theory as if that discrepant evidence does not matter. Theory appraisal will never be rigorous by adopting such a strategy.

Because testing is such an important step in determining whether a theory is true, Popper (1959) maintains that, in order for a set of statements to be considered a scientific theory, they must specify in advance (or at least at some point) what evidence will falsify them. If theories (or a set of statements) do not satisfy this *criterion of falsifiability*, then Popper (1959) would reject them as inadequate to begin with. When two theories have passed tests and are vying for the allegiance of the scientific community, the *criterion of explanatory power* maintains that the theory that resolves puzzles and anomalies that could not be explained before, and predicts or explains new phenomena, is superior.

This brief discussion should make it clear that the criteria work most powerfully when seen in relation to each other. They should not be applied in a rigidly isolated manner. To say that one theory is better on one criterion but not on another in comparison with a competing theory is not as useful as comparing how the theories in question do on the entire set of criteria.

This is particularly the case, since some criteria are more important than others. Thus, the first two are essential; if a theory is not accurate or falsifiable (in at least the broad sense of specifying at some point what evidence would lead the theorist to say the theory was inaccurate), it cannot be accepted regardless of how well it satisfies the other criteria. Having great explanatory power is of little use if the explanation turns out to be inaccurate or is non-falsifiable. Likewise, the case for *parsimony* is often given too much weight in international relations. Theories, as Craig Murphy (personal communication 1993) argues, should have an appropriate degree of complexity. They should not include all possible variables without regard for their relative potency; nor should they leave out important factors to keep the explanation simple. What is crucial is that theories be able to pass tests – first in principle and then in fact.[6]

A criterion that is of great relevance to the inter-paradigm debate is that research programs must be progressive rather than degenerative. This is the key criterion used by Lakatos (1970) to overcome some of the problems Kuhn (1970a) identified about paradigms and their alleged incommensurability (on the latter, see Scheffler 1967). Lakatos shows that while it is logically compelling for one valid test to falsify a theory, there is no logical reason to prohibit a reformulation of a theory on the basis of an almost infinite number of auxiliary hypotheses. Thus, while specific theories or explanations may be falsified, it is very difficult to falsify a research program with a single underlying theoretical perspective; i.e., what Kuhn would call a paradigm. Suffice it to say here that research programs that are always developing ad

---

[6] It is for this reason that one must reject Waltz's (1997a: 916) position that "success in explaining, not predicting, is the ultimate criterion of good theory." This cannot be the ultimate criterion for evaluating theories. Waltz (1997a) tries to make this point by defining "predicting" somewhat narrowly, so as to focus only on the future and not to include "retrodiction," but this is not how "positivists" usually define the term when speaking of testing. It makes no sense to explain patterns that do not exist. As will be demonstrated in the next chapter, this is precisely what Waltz (1979) did in claiming that one of the major patterns in international politics is that states balance. Both historical and data-based research seriously question this claim.

hoc propositions and/or having their theories reformulated or emendated because they are not passing empirical tests should be considered as degenerating and not as progressing. Finally, good theories should not contradict what is known in other fields of knowledge. Assumptions about motivation or cognition in international relations should be consistent with what is known (as opposed to theorized) in psychology.

While such criteria will make theory appraisal rigorous, it is important that they not be applied too early in a theory's development so as to close off an avenue of inquiry prematurely. All in all, these criteria must be seen as goals toward which we should strive, with concerns being raised if theorists no longer seem able to move toward the goals with the explanations being developed.

In addition to empirical work, most of the history of international relations theory has had a strong normative component, and one would expect more significant work along these lines as the intellectual climate moves further away from positivist biases. While post-modernism and post-positivism has made space within international relations inquiry for normative analysis, such work has not been very rigorous, and if it is to gain more respect, it too must have criteria for appraisal.

Since the purpose of normative theory in international relations is to guide practice, it can be assessed in terms of the extent to which it provides an enabling function; that is, how well it guides practitioners. Throughout history most international relations theorizing has been devoted to this kind of *practical theory*. Practical theory can be appraised directly in terms of whether the theory actually provides information practitioners need to know and can use. A philosophy and theory of practice can also be tested indirectly by the policies and actions to which it gives rise. Practical theory, therefore, can be appraised both by looking at some of its intrinsic characteristics (e.g., the kinds of information it provides) and by the quality of policy prescriptions it produces. There are seven criteria of adequacy that can be applied to make such an appraisal. A "good" guide to practice must:

1. have a *good* purpose and consequences
2. be able to be implemented in *practice*
3. provide comparatively *complete* and precise advice as to what should be done

4. be *relevant* to the most difficult policy problems of the day
5. have *anticipated costs* (including moral costs) that are worth *anticipated benefits*
6. achieve *success* and avoid *failure*.

I label these, respectively, the criteria of goodness, practicability, completeness, relevance, anticipated utility, and success-failure. To this we can add a seventh, which is that:

7. the latent *empirical* theory of a practical theory must be scientifically *sound*.

I call the latter the criterion of empirical soundness. To the extent to which practical theory has an empirical domain, and almost all do, it can be evaluated by some of the scientific criteria of adequacy, especially accuracy. However, practical theory needs its own criteria to ensure that it is satisfactorily meeting its own purpose, which is different from that of scientific theory despite the narrowing of the philosophical differences between empirical and normative analyses.

The criterion of *goodness* is the most fundamental in that it is a prerequisite for the rest. The key is in defining "good," which can only be determined (or contested) by the larger ethical, religious, professional or organizational goals guiding the group (for example in foreign policy – the state or its competitors). One of the contributions of post-positivism and critical theory is to invite more discourse on this topic. What are and should be the purposes of foreign policy; what are the consequences of policy; and do the consequences live up to certain ethical or other social standards?

Goodness is only a prerequisite; ideas must be put into practice and that is very difficult given the constraints of the world. There is always a slippage between what philosophy and policy look like on paper and what they look like in practice. This gap between theory and practice (George and Smoke 1974: 503) provides a way of evaluating the adequacy of practical theory on the basis of the *criterion of practicability*. The criterion of practicability acknowledges that there are many fine theories but that they lose much when they are implemented; i.e., their most interesting aspects sometimes cannot be implemented.

Being able to implement a policy or practice a way of life is a way of testing a practical theory, but it is very costly. Discourse needs ways of evaluating new ideas before they are put into practice. The *criterion of completeness* admirably satisfies this demand. The more precise and detailed the advice and recommendations offered by a practical theory, obviously the more useful it will be. The criterion of completeness recognizes that some theories, like the realist notion of national interest, provide general rules, but no advice as to how to apply the rule in a specific situation. Realism, for example, provides little guidance as to how to determine which option in a crisis is really in the national interest. Likewise, sometimes the best rational choice (before the fact) is not always clear. Although no general advice can be entirely complete, analysts must have some clear way of deriving guidance in a specific situation, if the theory is to be of any use. Theories that simply postulate "pursue the national interest" or "be rational" without providing a theory that will permit practitioners to determine what is the national interest or what is rational in a given situation are incomplete and flawed. They are too vague and are plagued by ambiguity.

A good practical theory, however, must do more than just provide detailed advice. An adequate practical theory must provide guidance on the most difficult policy dilemmas of the day. A theory that can do that is satisfying an important need and a theory that is unable to do so, is clearly *irrelevant*.

The *criterion of completeness* and the *criterion of relevance* are two ways in which a practical theory can be evaluated before it is put into practice. Another way in which it can be evaluated before it is tried is to examine its *anticipated costs*. Costs should be defined not only in material terms, but also in terms of intangible costs, such as moral costs, costs to the prevailing character and structure of a society, costs to internal and external relationships, as well as the general decision costs in adopting a new practice. These costs must then be compared with anticipated benefits and the probability of success. Many of the techniques of policy evaluation can be fitted into this *criterion of anticipated utility* so long as this is not done in a narrow technocratic manner, but within a broad humanistic perspective.

Nevertheless, there are real limits to the extent to which a practical theory can be evaluated before it is put into practice. Ultimately, practical theories tend to be judged by their *success* or *failure*. Jervis (1976: ch. 6) has shown that approaches to foreign policy are evaluated by whether they appear to succeed or fail. Nothing will discredit a foreign policy (and the practical theory underlying it) faster than a dramatic failure. Appeasement at Munich is the classic example.

Conversely, once a practical theory is in place, only a dramatic failure may lead to its displacement, even if all the other criteria have been flouted.

The critical test for practical theories is their ability to deal with the great political questions of the time. If the prevailing theory is associated with a great catastrophe, then it is replaced by the alternative theory best able to explain the failure and most likely to produce a modicum of success, if it is adopted. The mere association of ideas with a catastrophe, even if this association is coincidental, can bring about a theory's downfall. The result of using the *success–failure criterion*, as Jervis (1976: 281–282) points out, is often to learn the wrong or exaggerated lessons. In order for this powerful criterion to be a more adequate guide to theory appraisal, the standards for success and failure must be defined more precisely and the grounds for inference must be rigorously analyzed.

Finally, since a large component of practical theory is its latent (and sometimes explicit) empirical theory of how the world works, most of the criteria applied to scientific theory can be applied to the empirical aspects of the practical theory. Obviously, a practical theory that is based on a set of empirical assumptions and propositions that are found to be false or questionable is not as good a practical theory as one that is consistent with accepted knowledge. A practical theory that builds upon a weak empirical base is eventually bound to give advice that is *empirically unsound*.

Conclusion

Post-modernism and post-positivism has placed the scientific study of world politics in a serious crisis. Many in the field take glee in this, for they believe it sounds the death knell for a form of analysis they never liked and which they found boring and difficult. They underestimate the extent to which a threat to scientific inquiry may also be a threat to much of what they do. Surely, a critique of all empiricism, let alone the entire Enlightenment, is not without severe implications for a variety of approaches within the field.

The criteria for appraising theory presented in this chapter can be used to place international relations inquiry, especially scientific inquiry, on a new foundation, answering some of the major criticisms of post-positivism and avoiding the potential relativism of post-modernism. This is important because one of the problems posed by relativism is that it does not allow the field to address one of its major questions, a question in which post-structuralists seem keenly interested – namely, the adequacy of the realist paradigm. If the inter-paradigm debate is to be faced, there must be some criteria of adequacy that can be used to appraise theories and explanations, and, indirectly, paradigms.

For me, the real crisis in international relations inquiry is the absence in both empirical and normative analysis of serious, sustained, and rigorous theory appraisal. Post-modernism brings this crisis to a head. In both the scientific and practical realms, the inability to evaluate stultifies cumulation and learning and hampers research progress. The reasons for this lack of appraisal are twofold: first, the dearth of criteria; and second, the lack of discipline in applying what criteria there have been.

In my view, the main reason for the lack of cumulation has been that the set of theoretical approaches the scientific-oriented have been testing – realism – is probably wrong. In fact, one of the messages that scientific research has been persistently giving us is that the dominant realist paradigm is not providing a very fruitful and progressive guide to inquiry (see Part I: The Original Text, above). Part of the lack of rigor in the field is to dismiss all too quickly the method rather than the theory. What makes this a rather serious issue is that the main opponents of data-based work are often those most tied to realism and neorealism.

While some traditionalists were not slow to question the ability of scientific inquiry in international relations to find anything that was not trivial, they have not been able to show why a supposedly flawed method has had more success when it has tested hypotheses that have deviated from the realist research program than when it has tested hypotheses central to realism (see above, pp. 132–143, 151–152). If realists and neorealists are to be taken seriously, they must specify at some point precisely what criteria they will accept for rejecting their theory. The criteria I have offered would replace a casual approach to theory acceptance with a much more rigorous procedure.

Such rigor will be needed if we are to make any headway with the inter-paradigm debate. Lakatos and Kuhn point out that paradigms cannot be falsified by an application of what I have called the criterion of accuracy. This is because any decent theory that a dominant paradigm would have to have had to become dominant in the first place is going to be articulated along a number of lines. Part of the reason realism has been extensively articulated, however, is that it is constantly being reformulated in the face of anomalies and discrepant findings. Realism's penchant for predicting contradictory things (and embodying contradictory propositions [often added to save the paradigm in light of discrepant evidence]) at times violates Popper's (1959) criterion of falsifiability, as well as Lakatos' (1970) concern about innumerable auxiliary propositions that lead to degenerating problemshifts.

Violation of this principle explains why realism lives on despite extensive criticism of its concepts, falsification of many of its hypotheses, and a lack of scientifically important findings. Only by utilizing all the criteria of adequacy in a systematic fashion and by shaping research in light of the theory appraisal's agenda can the interparadigm debate be resolved. The next chapter will begin this process by applying Lakatos' criterion that theory shifts must be progressive and not degenerating.

The debate on post-modernism need not lead to a dividing discipline and an acceptance of a relativism where there are many incommensurable empirical perspectives with no way of comparatively evaluating them for fear of silencing a voice. One can restore normative practical theory to its rightful place within international relations discourse without at the same time introducing empirical relativism under the guise of empirical diversity. Theoretical diversity is a means to an end – knowledge about a given phenomenon – and not an end in itself. While the third debate has placed the scientific study of world politics and international relations inquiry in a position where it must reconstruct its philosophical foundation, this need not necessarily jeopardize the ideal of a cumulation of knowledge. Instead, treating science as a self-contained system, with its own rules and norms based on scholarly conventions and reason rather than irrefutable principles of logic, places the scientific approach on a more adequate epistemology.

Eventually, of course, the post-modernist critique will affect most approaches to international relations and not just quantitative approaches. Nevertheless, the critique has ended much of the myopia associated with logical positivism and created a more congenial space for normative and legal approaches, as well as theory construction and conceptual analysis in general. Post-positivism and post-modernism can have beneficial effects so long as they do not become the new orthodoxy. The danger is that some traditionalists will use post-positivism as a weapon to replay the second debate (on traditionalism vs. science) and to dismiss and ignore quantitative research rather than to engage it on its theoretical and substantive merits. Such an outcome will further divide the discipline and reduce rigor at a time when more comparison of research findings using different methodologies and more rigorous appraisal of theories and paradigms are needed. The next three chapters engage in such an appraisal by applying several of the criteria presented in this chapter to some of the most important non-quantitative neotraditional discourse in the field.

11 The realist paradigm as a degenerating research program: neotraditionalism and Waltz's balancing proposition

> Why, then, is Realism dominant? . . . In Lakatos's reply to Kuhn, all turns finally on a distinction between progressive and degenerating research programmes. In that case, Realism is dominant because, despite anomalies, its selection of aspects of events and identification of trends is more enlightening and fertile than those of its rivals.
>
> (Hollis and Smith 1990: 66)

> The search for a new paradigm will have its supporters, but we believe that such an approach throws the realist baby out with its dirty bathwater. Abandoning realism first assumes that viable alternatives are present. We are aware of no other world view of international relations that is as well developed (despite the ambiguities and imprecision of realism) or that has received as much empirical confirmation (despite the limited support found) as realpolitik.
>
> (Diehl and Wayman 1994: 263)

These quotations demonstrate the power of paradigms in scholarly inquiry. That these scholars, who are among the best, respectively, in international relations theory and quantitative peace research, and for whom I have the highest respect, could still find merit in the realist paradigm in the face of devastating conceptual criticism, historical anomalies, a large number of null findings, and a general dearth of strong empirical findings reflects at one and the same time the conservative nature of the discipline and the poor state of theory appraisal in the field.

Clearly, I had hoped that the readers of the original text would come to a different conclusion. Nevertheless, the larger context within which these quotes appear demonstrates considerably more hesitancy, if not ambivalence. Hollis and Smith (1990: 66) follow with: "But, we are bound to add, its [realism's] intellectual superiority is by no means plain." Diehl and Wayman (1994: 262) preface their remarks with:

> Another approach would be to regard realism as a dead end . . . This view is not entirely without merit. Realism suffers from some serious flaws . . . its empirical record here and elsewhere (Vasquez 1983) is far from awe-inspiring. Furthermore, realpolitik has difficulty meeting the criteria for a good paradigm or theoretical framework that Lakatos (1976), Kuhn (1962), and Popper (1963) suggest. In their crudest forms, realist predictions are sometimes nonfalsifiable and contradictory and have innumerable auxiliary propositions.

The realist paradigm may still be dominant and it still guides inquiry, but the strength of its grip is not what it was when Morgenthau lived, nor even what it was in the immediate heyday after the publication of Waltz (1979). There are doubts now, even among the believers.

No one can fault mainstream scholars for being incremental and cautious in their rejection of a dominant paradigm. Even in the original text, I said at the end that research on the realist paradigm should continue and that: "If at the end of this research not many findings are produced, then the realist paradigm could be rejected" (p. 179, above). This is not far from Diehl and Wayman's (1994: 264) position, who insist that realism must be evaluated empirically. Unlike myself and other nonrealists, however, they believe some variant of realist propositions will actually manage to pass systematic testing.

Ultimately, if any progress is to be made, scholars must have a set of criteria for appraising the empirical component of theories and paradigms. In the original text, I argued that three criteria – accuracy, centrality, and scientific importance – were essential criteria for a paradigm to satisfy. In this chapter, I will apply the main criterion I did not apply in the original text and the one on which Lakatos laid great stress for the evaluation of a series of theories; namely that theories must be progressive as opposed to degenerating in their research programs (see ch. 10 above).

One of the main differences between Lakatos and early positivists is that Lakatos maintains that the rules of theory appraisal are community norms and cannot be seen as logically compelling. The case that any given research program is degenerating (or progressive) cannot be logically proven. Such a stance assumes a foundationalist philosophy of inquiry that has been increasingly under attack in the last two decades (see Hollis and Smith 1990; ch. 10, above). A more reasonable stance is that exemplified by the trade-off between type 1 and type 2 errors in deciding to accept or reject the null hypothesis. Deciding whether a research program is degenerating involves many individual decisions about where people are willing to place their research bets, as well as collective decisions as to which research programs deserve continued funding, publication, etc. Some individuals will be willing to take more risks than others. This analysis seeks to elucidate the philosophical and empirical basis upon which such decisions will be made.

The task of determining whether research programs are progressive or degenerating is of especial importance because a number of analysts (e.g., Hollis and Smith 1990: 66; Wayman and Diehl 1994: 263) argue that, despite anomalies, the realist paradigm is dominant because it is more enlightening and fertile than its rivals. While the ability of the realist paradigm to reformulate its theories in light of conceptual criticism and unexpected events is taken by the above authors as an indicator of its fertility and accounts for its persistence, I argue that the proliferation of emendations is not a healthy sign. Indeed, it exposes the degenerating character of the paradigm. I will demonstrate that, contrary to widespread belief, the theoretical fertility that realism has exhibited in the last twenty years or so is actually an indicator of the degenerating nature of its research program.

The criterion

Imre Lakatos (1970) argued against Popper (1959) and in favor of Kuhn (1962) that no single theory could ever be falsified because auxiliary propositions could be added to account for discrepant evidence. The problem, then, is how to evaluate a *series of theories* that are intellectually related.

A series of theories is exactly what we have posing under the general rubrics of realism and neorealism. All of these theories share certain fundamental assumptions about how the world works. In Kuhn's (1962) language, they constitute a family of theories because they share a *paradigm*. Since a paradigm can easily generate a family of theories, Popper's (1959) falsification strategy was seen as problematic because one theory could simply be replaced by another in incremental fashion without ever rejecting the shared fundamental assumptions. It was because of this problem that Kuhn and his sociological explanation of theoretical change within science was seen as so undermining of the standard view in philosophy of science, and it was against Kuhn that Lakatos developed his criteria for appraising a series of theories (see Lapid 1989). To deal with the problem of appraising a series of theories that might share a common paradigm or set of assumptions, Lakatos stipulated that a research program that comes out of this core must develop in such a way that theoretical emendations are progressive rather than degenerating.

The main problem with this criterion is that, unless it is applied rigorously, with specific indicators as to what constitutes "progressive" or "degenerating" research programs, it will not provide a basis for settling the debate on the adequacy of the realist paradigm. In an early application of this criterion to structural realism, Keohane (1983 [1989: 43–44, 52, 55–56, 59]), for example, goes back and forth talking about the fruitfulness of neorealism, but also its incompleteness and the general inability of any international relations theory to satisfy Lakatos' criteria. Nye (1988: 243) is more conclusive on the negative side, but still reformist.

Once the criterion is defined, it remains to clarify how it fits with other criteria, such as accuracy and falsifiability. Eventually, it would be highly desirable to construct operational indicators of the progressive or degenerating nature of a paradigm's research program. Since these are not available, I will try to make explicit the characteristics that indicate that a research program is degenerating. Lakatos (1970: 116–117) sees a research program as degenerating if its auxiliary propositions increasingly take on the characteristic of ad hoc explanations that do not produce any novel (theoretical) facts and new "corroborated" empirical content. For Lakatos (1970: 116) "no experimental result can ever kill a theory: any theory can be saved from counterinstances either by some auxiliary hypothesis or by a suitable reinterpretation of its terms." Since Lakatos finds this to be the case, he asks, why not "impose certain standards on the theoretical adjustments by which one is allowed to save a theory?" (Lakatos 1970: 117). Adjustments that are acceptable he labels progressive, and those that are not he labels degenerating.

The key for Lakatos is to evaluate not a single theory, but a series of theories that are linked together. Is each theoryshift[1] advancing knowledge or is it simply a "linguistic device" for saving a theoretical approach? A theoryshift or problemshift is considered: (1) theoretically progressive if it theoretically "predicts some novel, hitherto unexpected fact" and (2) empirically progressive if these new predictions are actually corroborated, giving the new theory an excess empirical content (Lakatos 1970: 118). In order to be considered progressive, a problemshift must be *both* theoretically and empirically progressive – anything short of that is defined (by default) as *degenerating* (Lakatos 1970: 118). A degenerating problemshift or research program, then, is characterized by the use of semantic devices that hide the actual content-decreasing nature of the research program through reinterpretation (Lakatos 1970: 119). In this way, the new theory or set of theories is really ad hoc explanations intended to save the theory (Lakatos 1970: 117).

It should be clear from this inspection of Lakatos' criterion that progressive research programs are evaluated ultimately on the basis of a criterion of accuracy in that the new explanations must pass empirical testing. If this is the case, then they must in principle be *falsifiable*. The generation of new insights and the ability to produce a number of research tests, consequently, are not indicators of a progressive research program if *these do not result in new empirical content that has passed empirical tests*.

How can we tell whether a series of theories that comes out of a research program is degenerating? First, the movement from T to T' *may* indicate a degenerating tendency if the revision of T involves primarily the introduction of new concepts or some other reformulation that attempts to explain away discrepant evidence. Second, this would be seen as degenerating if this reformulating never pointed to any novel unexpected facts, by which Lakatos means that T' should tell us something about the world and its regularities other than what was uncovered by the discrepant evidence. Taken together, these two indicators are one type of ad hoc explanation – what Lakatos (1970: 175 note 2) calls ad hoc$_1$ (see Elman and Elman 1997: 923). Third, if T' does not have any of its new propositions successfully tested or lacks

---

[1] Lakatos (1970: 118, note 3) says that by problemshift he really means theoryshift, but has not used that word because it "sounds dreadful." Actually, it is much clearer (see his use of "theoretical shift" on p. 134). On the claim that problemshifts that are degenerating are really just linguistic devices to resolve anomalies in a semantic manner, see Lakatos (1970: 117, 119).

new propositions (other than those offered to explain away discrepant evidence), then it does not have corroborated excess empirical content over T, which can be an indicator of a degenerating tendency in the research program – what Lakatos (1970: 175 note 2) calls an ad hoc_2 explanation (see Elman and Elman 1997: 923).[2] Fourth, if a research program goes through a number of theoryshifts, all of which have one or more of the above characteristics *and* the end result of these theoryshifts is that collectively the family of theories has fielded a set of contradictory hypotheses that greatly increase the probability that at least one of them will pass empirical testing, then a research program can be appraised as degenerating.

This fourth indicator is crucial and deserves greater explication. It implies that while some latitude may be permitted for the development of ad hoc explanations (as Lakatos [1970: 134] suggests), the longer this goes on in the face of discrepant evidence, the greater the likelihood that scientists are engaged in a research program that is constantly repairing one flawed theory after another without any incremental advancement in the empirical content of these theories. What changes is not what is known about the world, but semantic labels to describe discrepant evidence that the original theory(ies) did not anticipate.

How does one determine, however, whether semantic changes are of this sort or the product of a fruitful theoretical development and new insights, what Kuhn calls paradigm articulation (and Lakatos [1970: 135] calls the elaboration of the positive heuristic of a research

---

[2] My thanks to Elman and Elman (1997) for suggesting the inclusion of Lakatos' different types of ad hoc explanations. I do not see the need, however, given the state of neotraditional research, to further specify ad hoc_2 by choosing between two different meanings of research success: (1) whether none of the new content is corroborated, or (2) all of it is refuted (Elman and Elman 1997: 924, citing Zahar 1973: 101, note 1). No doubt, partial satisfaction of either would be persuasive, if central propositions were involved. Lakatos (1970: 116) only insists that *some* of the new content be verified. Lakatos' third type of ad hoc explanation has not been incorporated because it would be too stringent. Ad hoc_3 is an emendation that does not flow from the logic of the positive heuristic or the hard core of a program. Such emendations appear to be attempts to "patch up" in an "arbitrary" even "trial-and-error" fashion (Lakatos 1970: 175), rather than showing how the emendation can be logically derived from the assumptions of the core. Since so few theories in international relations, let alone emendations, are logically or even tightly derived from a set of assumptions, use of this rule might be overly dismissive. Nevertheless, I will point out when reformulations move away from the core, especially if they bring in nonrealist concepts that do not focus on power.

program)? An effect of the repeated semantic changes that are not progressive is that they focus almost entirely on trying to deal with experimental outcomes or the identification of empirical patterns that are contrary to the initial predictions of the theory. One consequence of this kind of scholarly practice is that collectively the paradigm begins to embody contradictory propositions such as (1) war is likely when power is not balanced and one side is preponderant and (2) war is likely when power is relatively equal. The development of two or more propositions that are contradictory increases the probability that at least one of the paradigm's propositions will pass an empirical test. When a series of theories, all of which are derived from the same paradigm (and claim a family resemblance, such as by using the same name – e.g., Freudian, Marxist, or realist), predict one of several contradictory outcomes as providing support for the paradigm, then this would be an example of the fourth indicator. Carried to an extreme, the paradigm could prevent any kind of falsification, because collectively its propositions would in effect be posing the bet, "Heads, I win; tails, you lose." A research program could be considered blatantly degenerative if one or more of the behaviors predicted were only predicted after the fact.

This does not mean that there cannot be disagreements among scholars or a variety of theories within a paradigm (cf. Walt 1997: 933; Elman and Elman 1997: 924). These theories should predict different things, however, and not primarily contradictory things. The fourth indicator is needed because as more contradictory things are predicted, then at some point the paradigm becomes logically non-falsifiable. A variety of theories is going to be least susceptible to degeneration if they are independent theories in their own right (as are Morgenthau 1960 and Waltz 1979) and not just theoryshifts constructed as a direct reaction to discrepant evidence or an anomaly. Yet, even if they are purely theoryshifts of this sort, they are not, in principle, necessarily degenerative, if they can make new predictions.

To be progressive, a theoryshift needs to do more than just explain away the discrepant evidence. It should show how the logic of the original or reformulated theory can account for the discrepant evidence and then show how this theoretic can give rise to new propositions and predictions (or observations) that the original theory did not anticipate. The generation of new predictions is necessary because one cannot logically test a theory on the basis of the discrepant evidence that led to the theoryshift in the first place, since the outcome of the experiment or statistical test is already known (and therefore cannot be objectively predicted before the fact). The stipulation of new hypotheses that pass empirical testing on some basis other than the discrepant evidence is the minimal logical condition for being progressive.[3] Just *how* fruitful or progressive a theoryshift is, beyond the minimal condition, depends very much on how insightful and/or unexpected the novel facts embodied in the auxiliary hypotheses are deemed to be by scholars within the field. Do they tell us things we did not (theoretically) know before? And how important is this for the paradigm as a whole (i.e., for understanding the world the discipline is studying)?

It should be clear from all of the above that the criteria of adequacy involve the application of disciplinary norms as to what constitutes progress. The four indicators outlined above provide reasonable and fairly explicit ways to interpret the evidence. Applying them to a body of research should permit a basis for determining whether a research program appears to be, on the whole, degenerative or progressive.[4]

---

[3] Walt (1997: 932) does not seem to appreciate the logical problems that lead Lakatos (1970: 117) to establish "standards on the theoretical adjustments by which one is allowed to save a theory." He states, "[a]n ad hoc adjustment that resolves an existing anomaly but does not lead to any other new facts is still an advance in our understanding; after all, it does answer a puzzle" (Walt 1997: 932). From my perspective and that of Lakatos, novel facts are needed, otherwise there is no way of determining whether a theoryshift can pass empirical testing.

[4] Such an appraisal, of course, is only worth conducting if scholars accept Lakatos' criterion as useful. Lakatos (1970) has been widely cited by both quantitative and non-quantitative scholars, most of whom seem to accept his criteria as legitimate (see Keohane 1983; Bueno de Mesquita 1989: 151; Organski and Kugler 1989: 171; King, Keohane, and Verba 1994; and Lustick 1997), and he is generally seen as an advancement over the more "naive falsificationist" approach of Popper (1959). In this regard, it comes as a bit of a surprise that Walt (1997: 932) objected to my earlier use of Lakatos (Vasquez 1997) to evaluate his work, referring to Lakatos (1970) as a "now-dated analysis [that] has been largely rejected by contemporary historians and philosophers of science (Diesing, 1992; Laudan 1977; Suppe 1977; Toulmin 1972)." He goes on to ask "(w)hy should social scientists embrace a model of scientific progress that has been widely discredited by experts in that field?" *Discredited* is a very strong term, especially since what is at issue here is not Lakatos' historical description of progress, but his recommendation of how auxiliary propositions, should be treated. Contrary to Walt, I would maintain that Lakatos is very much at the epistemological core of political science. Lustick (1997: 88, notes 1 and 2), for example, sees Lakatos' criteria as the most legitimate to use in his appraisal of a key research program in comparative politics. He also points out the use of Lakatos' criteria in the recent debate over rational choice sparked by the Green and Shapiro (1994) volume and that "[b]etween 1980 and 1995 the *Social Science Citation Index* lists an annual average of 10.5 inches of citations to works by Lakatos."
One suspects that what is really bothering Walt is not Lakatos, but the conclusion I

It will be suggested here that for at least one core research program of the realist paradigm, the evidence in support of degeneracy is sufficiently clear to raise a warning flag. Researchers need to take greater cognizance of the problem of degenerating research programs than they have. This is especially important because a degenerating research program is not something produced by a single individual, but the product of a group of scholars, often working independently, but with the *collective result* that theoryshifts are not progressing toward a cumulation of knowledge, but hiding discrepant evidence. In many ways, this chapter is an exploration of how collectivities try to determine what constitutes "truth."

It will be argued that what some see as an apparent theoretical fertility and development of the realist paradigm is really a proliferation of emendations that prevent it from being falsified. It will be shown that the realist paradigm has exhibited (1) a protean character of theoretical development, which plays into (2) an unwillingness to specify what form(s) of the theory constitutes the true theory that if falsified would lead to a rejection of the paradigm, (3) a continual and persistent adoption of auxiliary propositions to explain away empirical and theoretical flaws that greatly exceeds the ability of researchers to test the propositions, and 4) a general dearth of strong empirical findings. Each of these four characteristics can be seen as "the facts" that need to be established or denied to make a decision about whether a given research program is degenerating.

The research program to be analyzed

Any paradigm worth its salt will have more than one ongoing research program, so it is important in assessing research programs to select those that focus on a core area of the paradigm and not on areas that are of more peripheral concern or can easily be accommodated by a competing paradigm. Also of importance is that the research program be fairly well developed in terms both of the number of different scholars and the amount of time spent on the program.

reach about his work by applying Lakatos. Nevertheless, since Hollis and Smith (1990) have employed Lakatos and commonly speak of neorealism as being progressive, it is perfectly appropriate to employ this criterion even though an individual scholar might object to it – although one cannot help noting that Walt (1997) entitled his response "The *Progressive* Power of Realism" (emphasis added), presumably a reference to Laudan (1977) rather than Lakatos (1970) (see footnote 10 below).

Neorealism can be seen as an articulation of the realist paradigm along at least two distinct lines – the first, by Waltz (1979), dealing with security and the second by Gilpin (1981), dealing with international political economy and historical change. Both of these efforts have developed research programs. Since the main concern here is on security, this chapter will concentrate on the work of scholars who have been influenced by Waltz and have attempted to examine empirically his most important claims. It is generally conceded that Waltz's influence on those who study security questions within international relations in what might be called a neotraditional (i.e., non-quantitative) manner is without equal.

Waltz (1979) centers on two empirical questions – explaining what he considers to be one of the fundamental laws of international politics, the balancing of power, and delineating the differing effects of bipolarity and multipolarity on system stability. While the latter has recently given rise to some vehement debates about the future of the post–Cold War era (see Mearsheimer 1990a; Van Evera 1990/91; Kegley and Raymond 1994), it has not given rise to a sustained non-quantitative research program. In contrast, the first area has. The focus of this appraisal will be not so much on Waltz himself as on the neotraditional research program that has taken his proposition on balancing and investigated it empirically. This work has been fairly extensive and appears to many to be both cumulative and fruitful. It is widely cited within the field and commonly assigned to graduate students. Specifically, I will look at the work of Stephen Walt (1987) and Schweller (1994) on balancing and bandwagoning, at the work of Christensen and Snyder (1990) on "buck-passing" and "chain-ganging," and at historical case studies that have uncovered discrepant evidence to see how these have been treated in the field by proponents of the realist paradigm.

In addition, unlike the work on polarity, that on balancing focuses on a core area for both classical realism and neorealism. It is clearly a central proposition within the paradigm (see pages 132–143) and concerns with it can be traced back to David Hume and from there to the Ancients in the West, India, and China. Because contemporary research on balancing has been focused on a core area of both neorealism and the realist paradigm, and because this research has been sufficiently extensive and has involved a number of scholars, it can be said to constitute the most obvious and best case to test the paradigm's ability to produce a research program that would satisfy

Lakatos' criterion.[5] Given the prominence of the balance of power concept, a research program devoted to investigating Waltz's analysis of the balancing of power that has attracted widespread attention and is generally well-treated in the current literature cannot fail to pass an examination of whether it is degenerating or progressive without reflecting on the paradigm as a whole – either positively or negatively.

Before beginning this appraisal it is also important to keep in mind that the criterion on research programs being progressive is only one of several that can be applied to a paradigm. A full appraisal of a paradigm would involve the application of other criteria, such as accuracy, to all areas of the paradigm, some of which will be applied in the next two chapters.

Likewise, because only one research program, namely that on balancing, is being examined, it can be argued that logically only conclusions about balancing (and not the other aspects of the realist paradigm) can be made. This is a legitimate position to take in that it would clearly be illogical (as well as unfair) to generalize conclusions about one research program of the paradigm to other research programs of the paradigm. Those obviously need to be evaluated separately and appraised on their own merit. They may pass or they may fail an appraisal based on the criterion of progressivity or on the basis of other criteria – e.g., empirical accuracy or falsifiability. Nevertheless, while this is true, it would be just as illogical to assume in the absence of such appraisals that all is well with the other research programs.

---

[5] Note, contrary to Walt's (1997: 932) alarmist reactions, adopting Lakatos' standard on progressivity would not "force us to reject virtually every research tradition in the social sciences." This is because to claim that a research program is degenerating, there must be at least several theoretical reformulations, and these must fail to produce corroborated excess empirical content. This effort, as Elman and Elman (1997: 924) recognize, must take some time (see also Lakatos 1970: 134, 179). The debate over multipolarity initiated by Mearsheimer (1990a), for example, could not be a candidate for appraisal on the progressivity criterion and be rejected as degenerating, because it does not involve a series of reformulations based on research. Rather it is a fairly straightforward disagreement about the effects of multipolarity and the nature of the future.

Conversely, the research program on balancing is a legitimate candidate because it has embodied both theoretical reformulation and empirical investigation. The mere necessity of theoretical reformulation, however, does not of itself indicate degeneracy, as (Walt 1997: 932) would have us believe. Such a conclusion can only be reached if there is persistent emendation because of repeated discrepant evidence and the reformulation provides no new basis (other than the discrepant evidence itself) to test the theory.

Logically, while this analysis can only draw conclusions about the degeneracy (or progressiveness) of the research program on balancing, nevertheless, the implication of failing or passing this appraisal for the paradigm as a whole is not an irrelevant question. This is particularly the case since paradigms are not tested directly, but indirectly through the success of the research programs to which they give rise. Certainly, if a major research program that deals with a central question of a paradigm is shown to be degenerating, this cannot enhance the paradigm; nor can this outcome be seen as simply neutral for the paradigm. If Waltz's neorealism is seen as reflecting well on the theoretical robustness and fertility of the realist paradigm (Hollis and Smith 1990: 66), then the failure of a research program meant to test his theory must have ˈsome negative impact on the paradigm. The question is how negative. The concluding section will return to this question since such matters are more fruitfully discussed in light of specific evidence rather than in the abstract.

The balancing of power – the great new law that turned out not to be so

One of the main purposes of Waltz (1979) was to explain what he saw as a fundamental law of international politics – the balancing of power. Waltz (1979: 5, 6, 9) defines theory as statements that explain laws (i.e., regularities of behavior). For Waltz (1979: 117) "[w]henever agents and agencies are coupled by force and competition rather than authority and law" they exhibit "certain repeated and enduring patterns." These he says have been identified by the tradition of *Realpolitik*. Of these the most central pattern is balance of power, of which he says, "If there is any distinctively political theory of international politics, balance-of-power theory is it" (Waltz 1979: 117). He maintains that a self-help system "stimulates states to behave in ways that tend toward the creation of balances of power" (Waltz 1979: 118) and that these balances "tend to form whether some or all states consciously aim to establish [them] . . ."(Waltz 1979: 119). This law or regularity is what the first six of the nine chapters in *Theory of International Politics* are trying to explain (see, in particular, Waltz 1979: 116–128).

The main problem, of course, was that many scholars, including realists, like Morgenthau (1960: ch. 14), did not see balancing as the given law Waltz took it to be. In many ways, raising the balancing of power to the status of a law dismissed all the very extensive conceptual criticism that had been made of the concept (Haas 1953; Morgenthau 1960: ch. 14; Claude 1962; see Waltz's [1979: 50–59, 117] review). Likewise, it also sidestepped a great deal of the theoretical and empirical work which suggested that the balance of power, specifically, was not associated with the preservation of peace (Organski 1958; Singer et al. 1972; see also the more recent Bueno de Mesquita 1981; the earlier work is discussed in Waltz 1979: 14–15, 119).

Waltz (1979) avoided contradicting this research by arguing, like Gulick (1955), that a balance of power does not always preserve the peace because it often requires wars to be fought to maintain the balance of power. What Waltz is doing here is separating two possible functions of the balance of power – protection of the state in terms of its survival and security versus the avoidance of war or maintenance of the peace. Waltz does not see the first as a legitimate prediction of balance-of-power theory. Waltz sees *balancing* as the law and does not go the extra step and associate balancing with peace. All that he requires is that states attempt to balance, not that balancing prevents war.

From a Kuhnian (1970a: 24, 33–34) perspective, one can see Waltz (1979) as articulating a part of the dominant realist paradigm. Waltz is trying to solve one of the puzzles (as Kuhn 1970a: 36–37 would call them) that Morgenthau left unresolved in *Politics Among Nations*; namely, how and why the balance of power can be expected to work and how major a role this concept should play within the paradigm. Waltz's (1979) book can be seen as a theoryshift that places the balance of power in a much more positive light than does Morgenthau (cf. 1960: ch. 14). His theoryshift tries to resolve the question of whether the balance is associated with peace by saying that it is not. He then, unlike Morgenthau, sees the balance as automatic and not the product of a particular leadership's diplomacy (what will later be called "human agency"), but the product of system structure. The focus on system structure and the identification of "anarchy" as central to all explanations of international politics are two of the original contributions of Waltz (1979). These can be seen as the introduction of new concepts that bring novel facts into the paradigm. The elegance and parsimony with which Waltz uses these concepts to explain international politics and, specifically, balancing and the stability of bipolarity over multipolarity account for much of the influence and praise this work has received.

Potentially, the introduction of these new concepts appears to be a progressive theoryshift, because it focuses scholars' attention on two phenomena – structure and anarchy – which they had not seen as clearly, as they did after Waltz (1979) wrote. Basically, Waltz introduces two novel independent variables and stipulatively defines the dependent variable (balancing) in a non-ambiguous manner to overcome previous criticism of the concept (cf. Haas 1953). Such a shift appears quite progressive, but whether it will be turns on whether the predictions made by the explanation can pass empirical testing.[6]

It should come as no surprise, therefore, that the proposition on balancing, which is eminently testable, should become the focus of much of the research of younger political scientists influenced by Waltz. Stephen Walt (1987), Schweller (1994), Christensen and Snyder (1990), Mastanduno (1997) and the historian Schroeder (1994a) all cite Waltz (1979) and consciously address his theoretical proposition on balancing. They also cite and build upon each other's work; i.e., those who discuss bandwagoning or balance of threat cite Walt (1987) (e.g., Schweller 1994; Levy and Barnett 1991; Larson 1991; and Mastanduno 1997); those who talk about buck-passing cite Christensen and Snyder (1990). More fundamentally they all are interested (with the exception of Schroeder, who is a critic) in working within the realist paradigm and defending it.[7] They differ in terms of how they defend realism.

---

[6] It should be clear from the above why a Kuhnian analysis of international relations theory would put Morgenthau and Waltz within the same paradigm, just as it would put Marx and Lenin in the same paradigm. Waltz (1997a: 913) objects to this because he says he has a structural theory and Morgenthau does not. I have not said there are no differences between the two "theories," but they clearly share a family resemblance and they share the three fundamental assumption of the realist paradigm delineated earlier (see p. 37). In addition, Waltz (1979) builds upon propositions on balancing found in Morgenthau (1960: 167, 187–189). Where he differs is on how he explains why states balance and in his assumption that the goal of states is security (or survival) and not a striving for ever more power (Waltz 1997a: 917). Because the exemplar set the agenda, Waltz can be seen as articulating the larger paradigm. The two theories are not so fundamentally different that they must be seen as constituting two paradigms rather than as two different theories within the same paradigm. If this were not the case, then no one would think of calling Waltz's theory structural *realism*.

[7] This does not mean that they all share the same variant of realism, nor that they are all neorealists. Schweller (1994: 85), for example, puts himself closer to the classical realism of Morgenthau. Christensen (1997: 65) seeks "to marry the major strands of contemporary realist thought: balance-of-power theory and security dilemma theory." Snyder (1991) works within "defensive realism." He maintains that "clear-thinking states" adhere to the tenets of this theory, and "[i]n this sense, my theory in *Myths of Empire* is fully compatible with what I see as the true form of realism" (Snyder 1995:

Several emend Waltz, some reject Waltz and defend the paradigm by going back to the classical realism of Morgenthau (e.g., Schweller). Because they all share certain concepts, are all concerned with balancing, share a view of the world, and share the general purpose of trying to work within and defend the paradigm, they can all be seen as working on the same general research program on balancing. Thus, what they have found and how they have tried to account for their findings provides a good case for appraising the extent to which this particular research program is progressive or degenerating.

Balancing vs. bandwagoning

One of the passing comments Waltz makes in his (1979: 126) theory is that in anarchic systems (unlike domestic systems), balancing not bandwagoning (a term for which he thanks Stephen Van Evera) is the typical behavior.[8] This is one of the few unambiguous empirical predictions in his theory. Waltz (1979: 121) states: "Balance-of-power politics prevail wherever two, and only two, requirements are met: that the order be anarchic and that it be populated by units wishing to survive."

The major test is conducted by Stephen Walt (1987), who looks primarily at the Middle East from 1955 to 1979. He maintains that, "Balancing is more common than bandwagoning" (Walt 1987: 33). Consistent with Waltz, he argues that, in general, states should not be expected to bandwagon except under certain identifiable conditions (Walt 1987: 28). However, contrary to Waltz, he finds that they do not balance power! Instead, he shows that they balance against threat. Walt (1987: 172) concludes:

> The main point should be obvious: balance of threat theory is superior to balance of power theory. Examining the impact of several related but distinct sources of threat can provide a more persuasive

113). However, because not all states are "clear thinking," and perceptions matter, Christensen and Snyder (1990), as will be discussed later, are further removed from the core of the realist paradigm in comparison to a Waltz or a Schweller.

[8] For Waltz (1979: 126), bandwagoning is allying with the strongest power, i.e., the one that is capable of establishing hegemony. Balancing predicts that such an alignment would be dangerous to the survival of states and that instead they should oppose (i.e., try to balance against) such power. Walt (1987: 17, 21–22) defines bandwagoning in the same manner except he introduces the notion of threat: "*Balancing* is defined as allying with others against the prevailing threat; *bandwagoning* refers to alignment with the source of danger" (italics in the original).

account of alliance formation than can focusing solely on the distribution of aggregate capabilities.

He then extends his analysis to East–West relations and shows that if states were really concerned with power, they would not have allied so extensively with the United States, which has a very overwhelming coalition against the Soviet Union and its allies. Such a coalition is a result not of the power of the Soviet Union, but of its perceived threat (Walt 1987: 273–281).

Here, then, is a clear falsification of Waltz – in the naive falsification sense of Popper (Lakatos 1970: 116) – but how does Walt deal with this counterevidence, or counterinstances as Lakatos would term it? He takes a very incrementalist position. He explicitly maintains that balance of threat "should be viewed as a refinement of traditional balance of power theory" (Walt 1987: 263). Yet in what way is this a "refinement" and not an unexpected anomalous finding given Waltz's prediction?[9]

For Morgenthau and Waltz, the greatest source of threat to a state comes from possible power advantages that another state may have over it. In a world that is assumed to be a struggle for power and a self-help system, a state *capable* of making a threat must be guarded against because no one can be assured when it may actualize that potential. Hence, states must balance against power regardless of immediate threat. If, however, power and threat are independent, as they are perceived to be by the states in Walt's sample, then something may be awry in the realist world.[10] The only thing that reduces the anomalous nature of the finding is that it has not been shown to hold

---

[9] In his reply to my earlier analysis (Vasquez 1997), Walt (1997: 933) never answers this question. It makes all the difference in the world whether one sees the failure of states to balance power as a falsification of Waltz.

[10] Even under Laudan's (1977: 115) terms of progress, whom Walt (1997: 932) cites approvingly in contradistinction to Lakatos, Walt's theory is not progressive because it does not resolve the puzzle of why states fail to balance power in terms of the logic of Waltz's or Morgenthau's theory – it merely describes the fact that states generally balance threat and not power. Put another way, for Walt, nation-states rarely balance power unless these states also pose a threat – and sometimes the most powerful state in a system, like the United States, does not. Conversely, for Morgenthau and Waltz, the most powerful state must always be seen as at least a potential threat, because power (regardless of intentions) is what is important to those who are realistic. Interestingly, Kenneth Waltz (1997a: 915–916) applies this hypothesis when he predicts that current US preponderant power will lead China and/or Japan to balance the United States, shifting the system away from unipolarity to multipolarity (see also Waltz 1993: 50, 66, 74–75, 77; Layne 1993; Mastanduno 1997: 54). (Before

for the central system of major states, i.e., modern Europe. If it were there that states balanced threat and not power, then that would be serious, if not devastating, for neorealism and the paradigm.[11]

As it stands, despite the rhetorical veneer, Walt's findings are consistent with the thrust of other empirical research; namely, that the balance of power does not seem to work or produce the patterns that many theorists have expected it to produce. For Walt, it turns out that states balance but not for reasons of power, a rather curious finding for Kenneth Waltz, but one entirely predictable given the results of previous research that did not find the balance of power significantly related to war and peace (see pp. 132–143 above; Bueno de Mesquita 1981).

The degenerating tendency of the research program in this area can be seen in how Walt conceptualizes his findings, and how the field then "refines" them further. "Balance of threat" is a felicitous phrase. The very phraseology makes states' behavior appear much more consistent with the larger paradigm than it actually is. It rhetorically captures all the connotations and emotive force of balance of power while changing it only incrementally. It appears as a refinement – insightful and supportive of the paradigm. In doing so, it strips away the anomalous nature and devastating potential of the findings for Waltz's explanation.[12]

This problemshift, however, is degenerative, and it exhibits all four of the characteristics outlined earlier as indicative of degenerative tendencies within a research program. First, the new concept, "balance of threat," is introduced to explain why states do not balance the way Waltz thought they would. The balance-of-threat concept does not appear in Waltz (1979) nor in the literature before Walt introduced it in conjunction with his findings. Second, the concept does not point to any novel facts other than the discrepant evidence, and therefore (third) this new variant of realism does not have any excess empirical content compared to the original theory, except that it

anyone rushes out to test such a prediction, however, one needs to measure capability to see if we have been in a unipolar system since 1990 – I have my doubts.)

[11] Schroeder (1994a, 1994b) provides this devastating evidence on Europe (see the discussion below; see also Schweller 1994: 89–92).

[12] Walt (1997: 933) argues that I cannot say that balance-of-threat theory is both a "'devastating' challenge to Waltz" and "merely a semantic repackaging of Waltz's theory." I do not say the first. What is "devastating" for Waltz is the *evidence* that states do not balance power, not balance-of-threat *theory*, which by its very phrasing mutes the negative impact of the finding.

now takes the discrepant evidence and says it supports a new variant of realism.[13]

These three degenerating characteristics open up the possibility that, when both the original balance of power proposition and the new balance of threat proposition (T and T' respectively) are taken as versions of realism, either behavior can be seen as evidence supporting realist theory (in some form) and hence the realist paradigm or approach in general. Waltz (1979: 121) allowed a clear test, because bandwagoning was taken to be the opposite of balancing. Now, Walt splits the concept of balancing into two components, either one of which will support the realist paradigm (because the second is but "a refinement" of balance-of-power theory). From outside the realist paradigm, this appears as a move to dismiss discrepant evidence and explain it away by an ad hoc theoryshift. It is a degenerating shift on the basis of the fourth indicator because it reduces the probability that the corpus of realist propositions can be falsified. Before Walt wrote, the set of empirical behavior that states *could* engage in that would be seen as evidence falsifying Waltz's balancing proposition was much broader than it was after he wrote.

The semantic utility of Walt's reformulation in saving realism can be seen by both contrasting and comparing his use of the balancing phraseology with the use by Mastanduno (1997). Like Walt (1987), Mastanduno also finds that, in the security area, balancing of power does not occur the way it is expected to operate. For Mastanduno (1997: 59, 72), the behavior of the United States and other major states does not conform to the predictions of balance-of-power theory; instead, balance-of-threat theory provides an explanation "that is more persuasive than that offered by balance-of-power theory." Unlike Walt, however, Mastanduno (1997: 85) is far more willing to

---

[13] Walt (1997) argues that several of his analyses, including some of his articles not discussed here (Walt, 1988, 1992), do offer novel facts – for example, that states did not balance against the United States in the Cold War and that East European states failed to balance against Germany and the USSR in the 1930s. This is "new information" in the sense that it is evidence brought to bear by Walt that shows that states do not balance power, but meet threats posed against them. With respect to Waltz's balancing proposition, however, this new information is "discrepant evidence" that is then explained (away) by "balance of threat" theory. Any particular fact relating to the failure to balance cannot be a "novel fact" because it is part of the discrepant evidence, by definition. To be progressive, Walt's theory needs to predict and explain something other than the failure of states to balance power because they balance threat (see Lakatos 1970: 124).

recognize the falsifying potential of this evidence for neorealism, calling it "a central puzzle" that the theory must confront. He even goes so far as to say: ". . . the longer unipolarity persists, the more imperative it will become to reconsider the logic of balancing behavior and to reassess the historical evidence that presumably supports that theory" (Mastanduno 1997: 86).

Mastanduno is one of the few realists to accept the implications of this evidence in a straightforward manner, but he is still a realist and clearly wants to work within that paradigm's research program. Thus, he moves on, like Walt, to support balance-of-threat theory as a better explanation of security behavior. Next, he examines the economic behavior of major states in terms of balancing power and balancing threat. Here, he produces an ironic finding – in the economic area, major states in the post–Cold War era seem not to balance threat but to balance power! Mastanduno (1997: 85) recognizes that "critics might counter that, by generating contradictory expectations, realism actually explains nothing." He tries to dismiss this by saying that such a claim misses the point that, "[R]ealism *per se* is not an explanation, but a research program" from which various explanations can be derived, a comment similar to that of Walt (1997: 932). As made clear several times in this book, it is true that the realist paradigm can give rise to different theories; however, this does not mean that there is no danger that these variations may be degenerative and may hinder the falsification of realist theory as a general body of work.

Such a danger is most likely to occur in the interpretation of evidence and its implication for making predictions that adequately test theories. Mastanduno's finding that major state behavior is contradictory in the security and economic issue areas illustrates the way in which semantic phrasing can make falsifying evidence less clear than it may actually be. Having the word "balancing" in both theories implies that balancing in the security realm is of one type and balancing in the economic realm is of another type. The phraseology suggests progress and cumulation through a specification of domain (an issue that will be discussed toward the end of the chapter). But does the phraseology help analysts see new patterns or does it mute a contradiction that would undercut the general theoretical approach and perspective? I would argue it does the latter.

The way in which this is the case can be seen by first asking which of the predictions Mastanduno makes about economic behavior is the one most properly derived from classical realism. As Mastanduno

(1997: 81) recognizes, this is a difficult specification, as is any derivation used to test a theory, whether it be a quantitative or qualitative test. He states that, "[B]alance-of-threat theory predicts that the United States will use its economic relationships and power as instruments of statecraft to reinforce its security strategy toward other major powers" (Mastanduno 1997: 73). I think any realist who is going to explain foreign policy has to make such a claim; my objection to Mastanduno's prediction is that he *confines* such a prediction to balance-of-threat theory and makes a different prediction for balance-of-power theory. What does the evidence indicate about this prediction? The following quote *removes* from the sentence Mastanduno's (1997: 82–83) theoretical interpretation to leave only a descriptive conclusion:

> U.S. economic strategy thus far has reflected, . . . [theoretical phrase deleted], a greater concern for the pursuit of relative economic advantage than for using economic relations to support the preferred national security strategies of reassuring and engaging potential challenges.

Does such evidence support realism? I would argue it does not, and that Mastanduno's analysis provides discrepant evidence for realism in both the security and economic issue areas. Mastanduno does not see it this way, because he sees the pursuit of relative economic advantage as a prediction of "balance-of-power theory" and hence supportive of a different realist theory. Thus, if one reinserts the deleted phrase, one gets: "US economic strategy thus far has reflected, consistent with balance-of-power theory, a greater concern for . . ." The use of balancing phraseology, which Walt (1987) has made possible, takes what could be seen as discrepant evidence and makes it seem considerably less problematic. This is what theoryshifts do, but is this shift and the application here more than just semantic labelling and a rhetorical move?

One can see, given the debate over relative gains (see Mastanduno 1991), why Mastanduno would see the pursuit of relative economic advantage as supporting realism as against a more liberal assumption on absolute gains. The issue here, however, is broader than just the debate over relative and absolute gains. The question is whether a prediction of pursuing relative economic advantage without much regard for security strategy (Mastanduno 1997: 81) is a proper specification of realist balance-of-power theory or simply a label that has been placed on behavior that could be easily and perhaps more fruitfully labeled as something else.

From outside the realist paradigm, the evidence Mastanduno (1997) marshals would be interpreted differently. First, the evidence against balancing would be taken, as he interprets it, as falsifying Waltz's proposition. It would also be seen as more important for Waltz (and one might add Morgenthau) that balancing of power be exhibited in the security area than in the economic area. Second, pursuing of economic advantage, even though it might be for relative gains, would not be seen as more important for any variant of realism than the prediction (or belief) "that economic relations are subordinate to political relations" (Mastanduno 1997: 81). Third, not only does this go against the overall logic of the core of the paradigm, but a prediction of pursuing economic advantage (including the very kind of behavior Mastanduno presents) is consistent with three other theoretical approaches: (1) a Marxist explanation that would see the state controlled by business interests, (2) a mercantilist explanation, and (3) a general capitalist explanation that sees behavior shaped more by economic forces and interests than by political, philosophical, or normative motives. The availability of Walt's phrasing mutes the more radical implications of these questions and may even prevent one from clearly seeing these as pressing issues. At any rate, it should be clear that having two forms of the balancing proposition is a great advantage to the paradigm in terms of protecting it from falsification.

This protection, however, comes at a price – the further stretching of the balancing concept. In what sense is pursuing economic advantage "balancing"? Certainly, this does not capture Waltz's and Morgenthau's notion of checking a state, or even economically checking a state, as say Britain did against Nazi Germany in Romania just before World War II (Bell 1986: 156–157). The end result is that Mastanduno's (1997) case evidence on economic behavior stretches *balancing* to include any pursuit of economic self-interest whether it balances or not.

Theoryshifts that degenerate, however, rarely stop at just one or even two shifts. Part of how we can tell if they are truly degenerative is that they persist in reformulating themselves. The danger posed by degenerative theoryshifts can be seen by conducting a mental experiment. Would the following theoretical emendation be regarded as a new progressive shift for the realist paradigm or a degenerative shift? Let us suppose that the concept of bandwagoning, which first gained attention because of Waltz's (1979: 126) use of the term, but which came into prominence only with Walt, now becomes the focus of empirical research in its own right. Both Waltz (1979: 126) and Walt (1987: 33) make it clear that they believe balancing is much more frequent than bandwagoning.[14] If someone finds bandwagoning to be more frequent, should such a finding be seen as an anomaly for Waltz's T, Walt's T', and the realist paradigm or simply as the foundation on which to erect yet another version of realism (T")? I would argue that if the latter occurred, it would demonstrate yet a further degeneration of the paradigm's research program and an unwillingness of these researchers to see anything as anomalous for the paradigm as a whole.

By raising the salience of the concept of bandwagoning and giving an explanation of it, Walt leaves the door open to the possibility that situations similar to the thought experiment might occur within the research program. Through this door walks Schweller (1994), who argues, contradicting Walt, that bandwagoning is more common than balancing. From this he weaves "an alternative theory of alliances" that he labels "balance of interests," another felicitous phrase, made even more picturesque by his habit of referring to states as jackals, wolves, lambs, and lions. Schweller (1994: 86) argues that his theory is even more realist than Waltz's, because he bases his analysis on the assumption of the classical realists that states strive for greater power and expansion, and not security as Waltz (1979: 126) assumes. Waltz is misled according to Schweller (1994: 85–88) because of his status-quo bias. If he looked at things from the perspective of a revisionist state, he would see why they bandwagon – they bandwagon to gain rewards (and presumably power).

Schweller (1994: 89–92), in a cursory review of European history, questions the extent to which states have balanced and argues instead that they frequently bandwagon. To establish this claim, he redefines bandwagoning more broadly than Walt, so that it is no longer the opposite of balancing (i.e., siding with the actor that poses the greatest threat or has the most power) but simply any attempt to side with the stronger, especially for opportunistic gain. Because the stronger state often does not also pose a direct threat to every weak state, this kind of behavior is much more common and distinct from what Walt meant.

Three things about Schweller are important for our appraisal of this

---

[14] Waltz (1979: 126) firmly states, "balancing, not bandwagoning, is the behavior induced by the system."

research program. First is that, despite the vehemence of Schweller's (1994) attack on the balancing proposition, this is nowhere seen as a deficiency of the realist paradigm, but rather as Waltz's distortion of classical realism (however, see Morgenthau 1960: 187 for the degree of similiarity with Waltz on this point). The latter is technically true in that Waltz raises the idea of balancing to the status of a law, but one would think that the absence of balancing in world politics, especially in European history, would have some negative impact on the realist view of the world. Certainly, Schweller's (1994: 93; 1997: 929) "finding" that bandwagoning is more prevalent than Waltz or Walt suggest is something classical realists, like Morgenthau (1948), Dehio (1961), or Kissinger (1994: 20–21, 67–68, 166–167) would find very disturbing.[15] They would not expect this to be a common behavior of states, and, if it did occur, they would see it as a failure to follow a rational foreign policy and/or to pursue a prudent realist course (see Morgenthau 1960: 7–8).

Second is that Schweller, by his theoryshift (T''), has made bandwagoning a "confirming" piece of evidence for the realist paradigm. So if he turns out to be correct, his theory, which he says is even more realist than Waltz's, will be confirmed. However, if he is incorrect, then Waltz's version of realism will be confirmed. Under what circumstances will the realist paradigm be considered as having failed to pass an empirical test? We are now in a position (in this research program) where any one of the following can be taken as evidence supporting the realist paradigm: .balancing of power, balancing of threat, and bandwagoning. At the same time, the paradigm as a whole has failed to specify what evidence will be accepted as falsifying it – a clear violation of Popper's (1959) principle of falsifiability. From my perspective, findings revealing the absence of balancing of power and the presence of balancing of threat or bandwagoning are taken by these researchers as supporting the realist paradigm, when instead these outcomes should be taken as anomalies. All their new concepts do is try to hide the anomaly through semantic labeling (see Lakatos 1970: 117, 119). Hiding anomalies, even inadvertently, is a particular

---

[15] Schweller (1997: 929) states that although his review of the European evidence shows that bandwagoning is more common than expected, he did not claim that he had falsified the "balancing predominates" proposition. Nevertheless, his review of the failure of major states to balance in the periods of Louis XIV, the Napoleonic wars, and in the 1930s does not leave many cases in support of the idea that states balance against hegemonic bids in Europe (cf Schweller 1997: 928; and Waltz 1997a: 915).

problem for neotraditional research because it relies so much on interpretation of case material as its evidence rather than on data whose indicators have been tested for their reliability. This is even evinced in Schweller's own attempt to specify the domain of his proposition.

Third, Schweller (1994, 1997: 928–929) is not entirely successful in explaining away why balancing should not occur by establishing the domain of when bandwagoning can be expected. For Schweller (1997: 928), bandwagoning rather than balancing will occur among "[u]nthreatened revisionist states" who are great powers. He then goes on to cite examples of these that fit his claim, like Italy and Japan in World War II, but other important cases he cites do not fit – namely Prussia, Austria, Russia, and Spain in the Napoleonic wars and the Soviet Union (and perhaps Vichy France) in World War II. These states do not fit the domain because they were not *un*threatened states. Their bandwagoning must count against Waltz and cannot be explained away by Schweller's analysis.

The theoretical discussion on balancing and bandwagoning has been commonly seen as one of the more fruitful theoretical innovations of the last ten years. Each of the major contributors, including Waltz, has been seen as having new insights and developing new explanations. But the emendations cannot be taken as progressive, because the main effect of each is to explain away major anomalies for the paradigm as a whole. To show that the concept of the balance of power lacks empirical significance must be devastating for the paradigm because it is a central concept. Each emendation tries to salvage something, but does so by moving further and further away from the original conception of balance of power. Thus, Waltz moves from the idea of a balance of power to simply balancing power, even if it does not prevent war. Walt finds that states do not balance power, but oppose threats to themselves. Schweller argues that states do not always balance against the stronger, but frequently bandwagon with it to take advantage of opportunities to gain rewards.

Walt and Schweller recognize discrepant evidence and explain it away by using a balance phraseology, but such attempts are degenerating because, while the concepts may be new and catchy, they are simply semantic changes that hide the fact the observed behavior is fundamentally different from the behavior that was expected by the original theory. We hardly need realism to tell us that states will oppose threats to themselves (if they can) or that revisionist states will seize opportunities to gain rewards (especially if the risks are low). In addition, these new concepts do not point us to any novel theoretical facts; they are not used to describe or predict any pattern or behavior other than the discrepant patterns that undercut the original theory.

Ultimately, under the fourth indicator, such theoryshifts are also degenerating because they increase the probability that the realist paradigm will pass some test, since now three kinds of behavior can be seen as confirmatory. While any one version of realism (balance of power, balancing power, balance of threats, balance of interests) may be falsified, the paradigm itself will live on, and indeed be seen as theoretically robust. In fact, however, the protean character of realism is preventing the paradigm from being falsified because as soon as one theoretical variant is falsified, another variant pops up to replace it as the "true realism" or the "new realism."

The point here is not that Walt or others are engaged in "bad" scholarship or have made mistakes; indeed just the opposite is the case – they are practicing the discipline the way the dominant paradigm leads them to practice it. They are theoretically articulating the paradigm in a normal science fashion, solving puzzles, engaging the historical record, and coming up with new insights – all derived from neorealism's exemplar and the paradigm from which it is derived. In doing so, however, these individual decisions reflect a collective degeneration.

Even as it is, other research on bandwagoning (narrowly defined) has opened up further anomalies for the realist paradigm by suggesting that one of the main reasons for bandwagoning (and indeed for alliance making in general) may not be the structure of the international system or the dynamics of the struggle for power, but domestic political considerations. Larson (1991: 86–87) argues antithetically to realism that states in a similar position in the international system and with similar relative capabilities behave differently with regard to bandwagoning; therefore, there must be some intervening variable to explain the difference. On the basis of a comparison of cases, she identifies weak domestic institutions as the key intervening variable. Specifically, she argues that some elites bandwagon to preserve their domestic rule (see also, Strauss 1991: 245, who sees domestic considerations and cultural conceptions of world politics as critical intervening variables). Similarly, Levy and Barnett (1991, 1992) present evidence on Egypt and Third World states that shows that internal needs and domestic political concerns are often more important in alliance-making than external threats. This research suggests that realist assumptions that the primacy of the international struggle for power and the unitary rational nature of the state will lead elites to formulate foreign policy strictly in accordance with the national interest defined in terms of power are flawed. Theories need to take greater cognizance of the role domestic politics and concerns play in shaping foreign policy objectives. To the extent bandwagoning (narrowly defined) is a "novel" fact (even if not a predominant pattern), it points us away from the dominant paradigm, not back to its classical formulation.

Buck-passing and chain-ganging

The bandwagoning research program is not the only way in which the protean character of realism has been revealed. Another and perhaps even more powerful example is the way in which Christensen and Snyder (1990) have dealt with the failure of states to balance. They begin by criticizing Waltz for being too parsimonious and making indeterminate predictions about balancing under multipolarity. They then seek to correct this defect within realism by specifying that states will engage in chain-ganging or buck-passing depending on the perceived balance between offense and defense. *Chain-ganging* is when states, especially strong states, commit "themselves unconditionally to reckless allies whose survival is seen to be indispensable to the maintenance of the balance"; whereas *buck-passing* is a failure to balance and "counting on third parties to bear the costs of stopping a rising hegemon" (Christensen and Snyder 1990: 138). The alliance pattern that led to World War I is given as an example of chain-ganging, and Europe in the 1930s is given as an example of buck-passing. The chain-ganging/buck-passing proposition is applied only to multipolarity because in bipolarity balancing is seen as unproblematic.

This article is another example of how the realist paradigm (since Waltz) has been articulated in a normal science fashion. The authors find a gap in Waltz's explanation and try to correct it by bringing in the offense/defense variable from Jervis (1978) (see also Van Evera 1984, as well as the earlier work of Quester 1977). They are concerned with why alliance behavior prior to 1914 is different from that of the 1930s, despite the fact that both periods are multipolar (see Christensen and Snyder 1997: 919). This gives the impression of cumulation and progress through further specification, especially since they have come up with a fancy title for labelling what Waltz identified as possible sources of instability in multipolarity.

On closer inspection, there are two major problems that reveal the degenerating character of this emendation. First, and most importantly, the argument that states will engage in either buck-passing or chain-ganging under multipolarity is an admission that in important instances, like in the 1930s, states fail to balance the way Waltz (1979) says they must because of the system's structure. Recall Waltz's (1979: 121) clear prediction that "Balance-of-power politics prevail wherever two, and only two, requirements are met: anarchy and units wishing to survive." Surely, these requirements were met in the pre-World War II period, and therefore failure to balance should be taken as falsifying evidence.

Christensen and Snyder (1990) need to recognize that more directly. Instead, they seem to want to explain away the pre-World War II period, in which they argue there was a great deal of buck-passing going on. Waltz (1979: 164–165, 167), however, never says that states will not conform (overall) to the law of balancing in multipolarity, but only that there are more "difficulties" in doing so. If Christensen and Snyder see the pre-World War II period as a failure to balance properly, then this is an anomaly that adherents to Waltz would need to explain away. The buck-passing/chain-ganging concept does that in a rhetorical flourish that grabs attention and seems persuasive. However, it "rescues" the theory not simply from indeterminate predictions, as Christensen and Snyder (1990: 146) put it, but explains away a crucial case that the theory should have accurately predicted.

This seems to be especially important because, contrary to what Waltz and Christensen and Snyder postulate, balancing through alliance-making should be more feasible under multipolarity than bipolarity, because under the latter there simply are not any other major states with whom to align. Waltz (1979: 168) says that under bipolarity *internal* balancing is more predominant and precise than external balancing. Thus, if under bipolarity we have, according to Waltz, a tendency to balance internally (i.e., through military build-ups), and under multipolarity we have, according to Christensen and Snyder, a tendency to pass the buck or chain-gang, then when exactly do we get the kind of alliance balancing that we think of when we think of the traditional balance of power Waltz has decreed as a law?[16] What we have in Christensen and Snyder is a proteanshift in realism that permits the paradigm (which by definition includes all forms of realist theory) to be confirmed if states balance (internally or externally), chain-gang or buck-pass (as well as bandwagon, see Schweller 1994). This is degenerating under the fourth indicator because it produces a situation where the probability of falsification decreases to a very low level. It seems to increase greatly the probability that empirical tests will be passed by some form of realism.

Of course, one could argue that Christensen and Snyder's (1990) proposition on offense/defense is falsifiable in principle, and that is true, but this brings us to the second problem with their analysis: namely, the offense/defense concept is very troubling because, as Levy (1984) has shown, this concept is extremely difficult to operationalize. Levy is unable to distinguish in specific historical periods whether offense or defense has the advantage. Obviously, neither are contemporary military experts always able to determine whether the period they are living in favors the offense or the defense, otherwise they would have understood that, in 1914, defense not offense had the advantage. Even Jervis (1978: 211) recognizes that the offensive/defensive advantage is not always distinguishable and has a category for such instances. Snyder (1984) knows this all too well (as does Christensen 1997: 65–66, 78–79, 92), so what is really being introduced here is not some realist "hard-core" power-related variable (offense), but *perceived* offense/defense – a "belief" variable that takes us away from realism and toward a more psychological-cognitive paradigm.

Nevertheless, once perceived offense/defense becomes the variable,

---

[16] Christensen and Snyder (1997: 920) never address this question in their response to my earlier analysis. They restate that "balancing occurs less smoothly in multipolar worlds than bipolar ones," but I do not see how using alliances to balance can proceed more smoothly in bipolar periods, when there are no countries who, by Waltz's definition of bipolarity, can shift the balance of power in a bipolar system – if there were, then the system would be multipolar. All that Waltz can mean by this is that internal balancing (a terrible expression for military build-ups) is more smoothly implemented, but why is it necessarily any more smoothly implemented in bipolar than multipolar systems? What he is also implying is that arming is easier than alliance making, but as Morrow (1993) shows, this really depends on the interaction of the domestic and international political environment and not on the external structure per se.

it becomes difficult to precisely measure the perceptions that count, leaving open the possibility for ad hoc interpretations. For example, some domestic political actors may perceive the offensive as having the advantage, while others may not. In the 1930s, Christensen and Snyder (1990) argue that states saw the defensive as having the advantage and therefore passed the buck. Yet as Morrow (1993: 228) reports, the French general staff feared in 1938 that its air force "would be wiped out in a few days," as General Vuillemin put it. Neville Chamberlain also felt that German air power was very threatening and an offensive weapon for which there was not much defense. Even Christensen (1997: 85) has recognized, in his recent article, British fear of a "knockout blow from Germany against the home islands," which means that a defensive advantage on the Continent would be irrelevant to Britain. The Germans, of course, believed in *Blitzkrieg*. So, it is not clear whether perceptions of the defensive having the advantage was uniform in the 1930s or even dominant. More importantly, the fact that one can differentiate offensive and defensive advantages depending on the theatre of operation and for different weapon systems shows how slippery this concept can be and how fruitful it is for an endless series of ad hoc explanations.[17]

Imprecise measurement leaving open the possibility for ad hoc interpretation is also a problem with identifying buck-passing and chain-ganging. Are Britain, France, and the Soviet Union passing the buck or just slow to balance? (The USSR is willing to sign an alliance earlier, but has no takers.) Or are Britain and France really pursuing an entirely different strategy, i.e., appeasement, because of the lessons they derived from World War I?[18] If it is the latter, which seems more plausible, then buck-passing is not involved at all, and the factor

---

[17] One way to ease this measurement impasse is to look at whether leaders expect the next war to be short or a war of attrition, as Christensen and Snyder (1997: 920) suggest, rather than looking at perceptions of the offensive/defensive advantage. A study of perceptions of the length of the coming war, however, may take research even further away from the hard-core realist variable of power, since perceptions of a war's length might be subject to psychological overconfidence (White 1966) or to lessons derived from the previous war (Jervis 1976: 266–269), rather than cold "objective" calculations of capability.

[18] From a realist perspective, adopting appeasement in the face of such an increase in power and in threat should not occur because it will only "whet the appetite of the aggressor" as realists later claimed *ad nauseam*. The use of appeasement, therefore, must be considered as something that realists see as both unexpected and imprudent (compare Christensen and Snyder 1997: 921).

explaining alliance behavior is not multipolarity, but an entirely different variable.[19] What is even more troubling is that while Christensen and Snyder (1990) see pre-1939 as buck-passing and pre-1914 as chain-ganging, it seems that Britain was much more hesitant to enter the war in 1914 than in 1939, contrary to what one would expect given the logic of Christensen and Snyder's historical analysis.[20] After Hitler took Prague in March 1939, domestic public and elite opinion moved toward a commitment to war (Rosecrance and Steiner 1993: 140), but in 1914 that commitment never came before the outbreak of hostilities (see Levy 1990/91). The cabinet was split, and only the violation of Belgium's neutrality tipped the balance. Thus, the introduction of the new refinement is far from a clear or unproblematic solution to the anomaly even on its own terms.[21]

In addition, identifying chain-ganging and buck-passing (as well as perceptions of the offensive/defensive advantage) is subject to teleological effects. In other words, because historians know that a major event (like the French Revolution or World War II) is coming, this can affect how they see and interpret the events they write about. There is a danger that they will read the outcome into the events they are studying. Identifying buck-passing after the fact may be subject to such a tendency, as is identifying the failure of decision makers to accurately perceive the offensive/defensive advantage. This is not

---

[19] Rosecrance and Steiner (1993) argue that domestic sources are more important than international factors in shaping British policy toward Hitler. This contradicts Waltz and Morgenthau, who see external threat as the key factor in shaping the assessment of national interest. Instead, what happens in Britain, according to Rosecrance and Steiner (1993: 127), is that the weakened economy and military conditions should have (from a strict realist cost–benefit analysis of relative capability) led it to avoid defending Poland, but persistent provocation by Hitler created a "hard-line" constituency that forced Chamberlain to declare war at a point when Britain's military power and economic capability did not warrant it.

[20] Christensen and Snyder (1990: 156) recognize British buck-passing in 1914, but they say Britain was an outlier and "did not entirely pass the buck" (see also Christensen 1997: 83).

[21] Christensen and Snyder (1997: 920) counter by saying that Britain was slower to respond with troops in 1939 than in 1914, because it saw the defensive as having the advantage. I am not concerned here with troop deployment. My point is that the *political* commitment and *decision to go to war* in the event of a German attack was much slower in 1914 than in 1939. The lack of a clear British commitment in 1914 to fight affected German calculations and in the view of some analysts was an important factor in failing to "deter" Germany (Levy 1990/91). If this is the case, then 1914 is an instance when major states fail to balance power and threat when they are supposed to, resulting in revisionist states taking risks they otherwise might have avoided.

to say that Christensen and Snyder have done this, but that in the absence of precise measurement, teleological effects make some concepts more susceptible to ad hoc theorizing than others.

It also must be pointed out that Christensen and Snyder's (1990) analysis is only illustrated by two cases and not systematically tested. Morrow (1993: 211–213) argues that offense was perceived as having the advantage in the 1860s, yet in 1866 and again in 1870 threatened states did not chain-gang as Christensen and Snyder's explanation predicts. Systematic testing of more cases will be needed before their proposition is accepted as empirically accurate. The point here is not to prejudge that research (see Christensen's [1997: 70–81] discussion of Morrow), but to emphasize that in order for their theoryshift to be progressive, it cannot just *"explain* when chain-gaining occurs and when buck-passing occurs" (Christensen and Snyder 1997: 920, emphasis added); their explanation must pass *empirical* testing as well (Lakatos 1970: 116).

That research may not get off the ground, however, because Christensen (1997: 66) has reformulated his and Snyder's "original thesis," which placed great weight on perceptions of the offense/ defense, into a very refined calculation of perceived power and offensive/defensive advantage by the various actors. In terms of the analysis of this chapter, two important points must be kept in mind about Christensen (1997). First, he admits "de facto" that not only Waltz's proposition on balancing, but even the more refined Christensen and Snyder (1990) proposition, must be further refined to account for cases. It is far from clear after reading Christensen (1997) that this "new formulation" is one that "can explain a large number of new observations" and is not one where "additional observations demand ad hoc adjustments to the theory," as Christensen and Snyder (1997: 920) put it. Second, the need to examine calculations of perceptions shows why anarchy provides no invisible hand that automatically institutes Waltz's balancing, and it makes it clear why Morgenthau's prescription that balancing be brought about by prudent leaders is difficult to implement in a manner that conforms to objective conditions. Christensen's (1997) analysis demonstrates further the weakness of focusing on realist power variables, while his introduction of perceptions to save these variable drives analysts away from both the core of the paradigm and from nomothetic explanation.

My objection to Christensen and to Snyder is not with their

270

criticisms of neorealism, but their apparent unwillingness to admit the extent to which the evidence they present poses such a damning portrayal of Waltz's balancing proposition. I can agree that balancing often does not occur because of misperception (generally), because of uncertainty (i.e., low information), because of the role of domestic politics, but for those outside the realist paradigm all this is another way of saying that balancing never occurs in the systematic fashion that Waltz believes, and "power" is not the core of what shapes world politics.[22]

The refinements of Waltz produced by the literature on bandwagoning and buck-passing are degenerating because they hide, rather than deal directly with, the seriousness of the anomalies they are trying to handle. A theory, the main purpose of which is to explain balancing, cannot stand if balancing is not the law it says it is. Such an anomaly also reflects negatively on the paradigm as a whole. Even though Morgenthau (1960: ch. 14) did not think the balance of power was very workable, power variables are part of the central core of his work, and he does say that the balance of power is "a natural and inevitable outgrowth of the struggle of power . . . [and] . . . a protective device of an alliance of nations, anxious for their independence, against another nation's designs for world domination . . ." (Morgenthau 1960: 187, and see also 167, 188–189). Waltz's (1979) theory, which has been characterized as a systematization of classical realism (Keohane 1985: 15) and widely seen as such, cannot fail on one of its few concrete predictions without reflecting badly (in some sense) on the larger paradigm in which it is embedded.

One might ask hypothetically, what would have been a progressive problemshift. In principle, one could have tried to explain when states balance or fail to balance by introducing new concepts. Focusing on multipolarity and introducing the ideas of offense/defense and buck-passing/chain-ganging are moves in that direction, but these concepts do not *confirm* when states balance and when they do not, because they do not present systematic evidence of balancing occurring (across numerous cases) in the domain it is suppose to occur. Likewise, they do not explain (if balancing is for Waltz [1979: 104–123, 163–165] primarily a function of anarchy), why the logic of this (anarchic)

---

[22] In Lakatos' (1970: 175) terms, Christensen and Snyder come close to an ad hoc₃ explanation here, not so much that this emendation is based on trial and error, but because it so undercuts the rationality of the power politics of Morgenthau's realism and Waltz's anarchic system (i.e., their respective positive heuristics).

structure makes it more difficult for balancing to occur under multi-polarity than under bipolarity. Lastly, the concepts of offensive/defensive perception, chain-ganging, and buck-passing are difficult to operationalize and may be subject to teleological effects making them prone to the development of ad hoc auxiliary hypotheses.

It should be pointed out that because Waltz (1979) is very much a structural theory, it is difficult to amend it by introducing third variables, since to protect his theory one would ideally want to introduce only structural variables. One possibility might be that system norms might explain when attempts to balance would occur and when they might not, but this would introduce a non-power politics variable into the scheme. For Morgenthau, the diplomatic wisdom of a state's leadership or the intrusion of domestic politics (and irrational concerns) might explain when the balance of power would work or fail. In both instances, however, one would have to document that balancing is a *pattern* of behavior and not just a random occurrence. Unlike Waltz, Morgenthau (1960: 187–189) says a balance is likely primarily when states face the threat of world domination. Others (e.g., Dehio 1961; Snyder 1991: 6–7) have also seen this as the defining condition for balancing to occur. When pushed, even Waltz (1997a: 915) says this (see also Walt 1997: 933, note 7). Yet even here with this very limited condition (as opposed to the broad condition of Waltz), the historical evidence seems to contradict the proposition.

Historical case studies

Unlike the above explicitly sympathetic work, there have been several historical case studies that have focused on the balancing hypothesis and which have given rise to more severe criticism of realist theory. Rosecrance and Stein (1993: 7) see the balancing proposition as the key prediction of structural realism. In a series of case studies, they challenge the idea that balancing power actually occurs or explains very much of the grand strategy of twentieth-century major states they examine; to explain grand strategy for them requires examining domestic politics (Rosecrance and Stein 1993: 10, 17–21). In contradiction to structural realism, they find that balance-of-power concerns do not take "precedence over domestic factors or restraints" (Rosecrance and Stein 1993: 17). Britain in 1938, the United States in 1940, and even the Soviet Union facing Reagan in 1985 fail to meet powerful external challenges, in part because of domestic political factors (Rosecrance and Stein 1993: 18; see also the related case studies in chs. 5–7). States sometimes under- or over-balance. As Rosecrance (1995: 145) maintains, states rarely get it right – they either commit too much or too little, or they become so concerned with the periphery they overlook what is happening to the core (see Kupchan 1994; Thompson and Zuk 1986). And of course they do this because they are not the unitary rational actors the realist paradigm holds them to be. Contrary to Waltz, and even Morgenthau, states engage in much more variegated behavior than the realist paradigm suggests.

This last point is demonstrated forcibly by the historian Paul Schroeder (1994a, 1994b). He shows that the fundamental generalizations of Waltz – that anarchy leads states to balancing and a self-help system, and that anarchy leads states to act on the basis of their power position – are not principles that tell the actual story of what happened from 1648 to 1945. He demonstrates that states do not balance in a law-like manner, but deal with threat in a variety of ways – among others, they hide, they join the stronger side, they try to "transcend" the problem, or they balance. In a brief but systematic review of the major wars in the modern period, he shows that in the Napoleonic wars, the Crimean War, and the two World Wars, there was no real balancing of an alleged hegemonic threat – so much for the claim that this kind of balancing is a fundamental law of international politics. When states do resist, as they did with Napoleon, it is because they have been attacked and have no choice – "they resisted because France kept on attacking them" (Schroeder 1994a: 135; see also Schweller 1994: 92). A similar point could also be made about French, British, Soviet, and American resistance to Hitler and Japan.

Basically, Schroeder shows that the historical record in Europe does not conform to neorealists' theoretical expectations about balancing power. Their main generalizations are simply wrong. For instance, balancing does not occur for Schroeder against Napoleon, where if anywhere in European history it should have (see also Rosecrance and Lo 1996). Many states leave the First Coalition against Revolutionary France after 1793 when they should not have, given France's new power potential. Periodically, states would bandwagon with France, especially after victories, as in late 1799 when the Second Coalition collapsed. Hiding or bandwagoning, not balancing, was, according to Schroeder (1994a: 120–21), the main response to the Napoleonic hegemonic threat, the exact opposite of what not only

273

Waltz would predict, but such long-time classical realists like Dehio (1961) have asserted. For World War I, Schroeder (1994a: 122–123) argues that the balancing versus bidding for hegemony conceptualization simply does not make much sense of what each side was doing in trying to deal with their security problems. With World War II, Schroeder (1994a: 123–124) sees a failure of Britain and France to balance and sees many states trying to hide or bandwagon.[23]

For Schroeder (1994a: 115, 116), neorealist theory is a misleading guide to inquiry:

> [T]he more one examines Waltz's historical generalizations about the conduct of international politics throughout history with the aid of the historian's knowledge of the actual course of history, the more doubtful – in fact, strange – these generalizations become . . . I cannot construct a history of the European states system from 1648 to 1945 based on the generalization that most unit actors within that system responded to crucial threats to their security and independence by resorting to self-help, as defined above. In the majority of instances this just did not happen.

All of this suggests that the balancing of power was never the law Waltz thought it was. In effect, he offered an explanation of a behavioral regularity that never existed, except within the logic of the theory. As Schroeder (1994a: 147) concludes:

> [My point has been] to show how a normal, standard understanding of neo-realist theory, applied precisely to the historical era where it should fit best, gets the motives, the process, the patterns, and the broad outcomes of international history wrong . . . it prescribes and predicts a determinate order for history without having adequately checked this against the historical evidence.

Shirking the evidence and proving the point

How has that part of the field sympathetic to realism responded to Schroeder? They have sought to deny everything and done so precisely in the degenerating manner that Lakatos (1970: 116–119)

---

[23] Numerous other deviant cases are discussed or listed in Schroeder (1994a: 118–122, 126–129, see also 133–147), particularly his discussion of the failure of states to attempt to balance British hegemony in the nineteenth century. For Schroeder's own detailed nonrealist reading of the 1763–1848 period in Europe, see his mammoth narrative (Schroeder 1994b). Issue number 4 of the 1994 *International Review of History* is devoted to examining this work; Levy's (1994b) essay in that special issue is relevant to the discussion here.

predicted. The reaction by Elman and Elman (1995) to Schroeder in the correspondence section of *International Security* illustrates best the extent to which the past ten years of realist research has cumulated in degenerating problemshifts. Elman and Elman (1995) make three main points against Schroeder (1994a). First, although his evidence may challenge Waltz's particular theory, it still leaves the larger neorealist approach unscathed. Second, Waltz recognizes balancing failures so that not every instance of these necessarily disconfirms his theory. Third, even if Schroeder's evidence on balancing poses a problem for Waltz, "[o]nly better theories can displace theories . . . Thus, Waltz's theory should not be discarded until something better comes along to replace it" (Elman and Elman 1995: 192).

The first point – that Schroeder's evidence leaves the larger neorealist approach unscathed – somewhat misses the mark, since so much of neorealism is associated with Waltz. There remains mostly Gilpin (1981) and Krasner (1978). It is primarily Gilpin[24] whom Elman and Elman have in mind when they argue that Schroeder's "omission of entire neo-realist literatures" leads him to fail to understand that "balancing is not the only strategy which is logically compatible with neo-realist assumptions of anarchy and self-help" (Elman and Elman 1995: 185, 186; see also Schweller 1992: 267, whom they cite). They argue that for Gilpin (1981) and power transition theory "balancing is not considered a prevalent strategy, nor are balances predicted to occur repeatedly" (Elman and Elman 1995: 186). The problem with using Gilpin and the more quantitatively oriented power-transition thesis of Organski and Kugler (1980) is that the two main pillars of neorealism predict contradictory things. Thus, between Waltz and Gilpin, threat can be handled by either balancing or not balancing. It certainly is not a very strong defense of neorealism to say that opposite behaviors are both logically compatible with the assumptions of anarchy.

The Elmans are technically correct that evidence against balancing

---

[24] By saying that Schroeder leaves much of the neorealist approach unscathed, Elman and Elman (1995) seem to fall into the trap of assuming that Gilpin (1981) is empirically accurate unless proven otherwise, when normally in science we do not assume a theory is empirically acceptable until it has passed a number of tests. In fact, Gilpin (1981), as it relates to security questions, has not been extensively tested – (this is one indicator, by the way, that Waltz is more central to neorealism and neotraditionalism than Elman and Elman seem willing to admit). Further, what tests do exist are not very encouraging for his theory (see Spiezio 1990, as well as Boswell and Sweat 1991, and the discussion in Vasquez 1993: 93–98; and ch. 9: 205–207, above).

does not speak against all of the larger realist paradigm in that neorealism also embodies Gilpin. But it is this very correctness that proves the larger point being made here and illustrates what so worried Lakatos about degenerating research programs. At the beginning of this chapter, four indicators of a degenerating research program were presented. Elman and Elman (1995) serves as evidence that all of these are very much in play within the field. On the basis of their defense of neorealism and the review of the literature above, it will be shown that the protean nature of realism, promulgated by the proliferation of auxiliary hypotheses to explain away discrepant evidence, has produced an unwillingness to specify what evidence would in principle lead to a rejection of the paradigm. The end result has been a continual theoretical articulation but in the context of a persistent dearth of strong empirical findings.

Using Gilpin and power transition in the manner they do is degenerating because permitting the paradigm to be supported by instances of either "balancing" or "not balancing" reduces greatly the probability of finding any discrepant evidence.[25] As if this were not enough to cover all sides of the bet, Elman and Elman (1995: 187–188) maintain that within the neorealist assumption of self-help, threat can be handled by bandwagoning, expansion, preventive war, balancing, hiding, and even what Schroeder has labelled "transcending."[26] In other words, there is always some behavior (in dealing with threat) that will prove that realism is correct, even though most versions will be shown to be incorrect, and even though they admit that neorealists, "often consider balancing to be the most successful strategy for most states most of the time" (Elman and Elman 1995: 187). But if this caveat is the case, then why do states not regularly engage in this behavior? Elman and Elman rightly capture the theoretical robustness of the realist paradigm – showing that Waltz, Gilpin, and others are part of the paradigm – but they fail to realize the damning protean portrayal they have given of its research program, and how this very

[25] The proper way to assess Gilpin (1981) is to see whether the rise of challengers to a hegemon is a necessary condition of major-state wars (i.e., wars involving most of the major states in the system fighting each other) and to see whether it makes sense to interpret the sweep of global history in terms of a succession of hegemonic bids. Historians, like Schroeder (1994a, 1994b), question this. See David Kaiser (1990) for a systematic undermining of this sort of realist and neorealist historiography. See Kim (1992, 1996) for empirical evidence that would raise questions about this thesis.

[26] Transcending is seen by Schroeder (1994a) as particularly discrepant for realism, but Elman and Elman (1995: 188) see this as part of the realist approach.

theoretical development makes it very difficult for the paradigm to satisfy the criterion of falsifiability.

Instead, they conclude of Schroeder's (1994a) historical evidence that "No evidence could be more compatible with a neo-realist reading of international relations" (Elman and Elman 1995: 184; contrast this with Mastanduno 1997: 86 note 115). They conclude this because each of these strategies (bandwagoning, etc.) does not challenge the realist conception of a rational actor behaving in a situation of competition and opportunity. For them, so long as states choose strategies that are "consistent with their position in the global power structure and pursue policies that are likely to provide them with greater benefits than costs" (Elman and Elman 1995: 184), then this is seen as evidence supporting the broad realist approach. Only Wendt's (1992) claim that states could be "other-regarding" as opposed to "self-regarding" is seen as discrepant evidence (see also Elman 1997: 50–51). Basically, these are "sucker bets" of the "I win, you lose" variety. Let me hasten to add that these are not bets that Elman and Elman are proposing; they are merely reporting what, in effect, the entire realist research program described in the first part of this analysis has been doing from Walt to Christensen and Snyder, to Schweller, and so forth. Collectively, the realist mainstream has set up a situation that provides a very narrow empirical base on which to falsify the paradigm.

What kinds of political actors would, for example, consciously pursue policies that are "likely to provide" them with greater costs than benefits? To see only "other-regarding" behavior as falsifying leaves a rather vast and variegated stream of behaviors as supportive of the paradigm. Schroeder (1995: 194) has a legitimate complaint when he says in reply, "The Elman argument . . . appropriates every possible tenable position in IR theory and history for the neo-realist camp." He concludes, ". . . their whole case that history fits the neo-realist paradigm falls to the ground because they fail to see that it is their neo-realist assumptions, as they understand and use them, which simply put all state action in the state system into a neo-realist mold and neo-realist boxes, *by definition*" (emphasis in the original, Schroeder 1995: 194).[27]

Instead of defending the paradigm, Elman and Elman (1995) expose the degenerating nature of its research program and the field's

---

[27] In this regard, see the very revealing Diagram 1 in Elman (1997: 50–51) that lists most international relations theories with the exception of Wendt as some form of realism.

collective shirking of the evidence through proteanshifts. Many neo-traditionalists, as will be seen of Mearshemier (1990a) in the next chapter, have eschewed the quantitative evidence that has challenged the adequacy of the realist paradigm; if realists will now refuse to accept historical evidence as well, what kind of evidence will they accept as falsifying their theories? Only "other-regarding" behavior? That simply will not do.

The cause of this problem is the lack of rigor in the field in appraising theories. The nature of this problem can be seen in Elman and Elman's (1995) second point against Schroeder. Drawing upon Christensen and Snyder (1990), they note that balancing under multipolarity, for Waltz, is more difficult than balancing under bipolarity: "Thus Schroeder's finding that states failed to balance prior to World War I (pp. 122–123) and World War II (pp. 123–124) does not disconfirm Waltz argument . . . In short, a failure to balance is not a failure of balance of power theory if systemic conditions are likely to generate this sort of outcome in the first place" (Elman and Elman 1995: 190–191). This sets up a situation where any failure to balance under multipolarity can be taken as confirmatory evidence because, according to Elman and Elman (1995: 90), ". . . Waltz's theory also predicts balancing *failures*" (emphasis in the original). This again poses an "I win, you lose" bet. If the periods before World War I and World War II are not legitimate tests of Waltz's prediction of balancing, then what would be? The implication is that balancing can occur only under bipolarity, when external balancing is structurally impossible by definition. If this is the case, how is balancing a "law," or the main outcome of anarchy? This is especially problematic because there is a tendency in Waltz to see only the post-1945 period as a true bipolarity (see Nye 1988: 244), which means the rest of history is multipolar and subject to balancing failures. In the end, Elman and Elman (1995: 192) concede that Waltz does believe that "on aggregate" states should balance, so that: "Schroeder's evidence that states rarely balance does indeed pose a problem for Waltz's theory."

This is a much better reaction to Schroeder than what Waltz (1997a), Walt (1997) and even Christensen and Snyder (1997) say. Waltz (1997a: 914) says, "What Vasquez takes to be Schroeder's 'devastating evidence' turns out to be a melange of irrelevant diplomatic lore." From the scholar who became renowned for dismissing all quantitative evidence as "correlational labors" (Waltz 1979: 12), we now find that serious discussion of the historical record is simply "diplomatic lore." Will any evidence ever be sufficient to test his proposition?

In Waltz (1997a: 915), he seems to provide the basis of a test when he goes on to say:

> Faced by unbalanced power, states try to increase their own strength or they ally with others to bring the international distribution of power into balance. The reactions of other states to the drive for dominance of Charles I of Spain, of Louis XIV and Napoleon Bonaparte of France, of Wilhelm II and Adolph Hitler of Germany, illustrate the point.

Yet Schroeder (1994a, 1994b), and even Schweller (1994), question this one-line history (see also Kaiser 1990; Rosecrance and Lo 1996). The major states, as a group, did not balance against Napoleon and Hitler. They often reacted only to invasion or attack, as did the Soviet Union and the United States in 1941. Likewise, Britain did not clearly commit against Germany in the summer of 1914 and so failed to provide a possible "deterrent effect." Morgenthau's (1960: 187) original claim that states balance against attempts of "world domination," and which Waltz presents here as one representative of his broader balancing generalization, must mean something more theoretically useful than simply the truism that those states which are invaded will eventually get into the war.

Put another way, simple evidence that states arm or ally when faced with a "drive for dominance" is too weak a test of his proposition. It provides too broad a set of behavior to "confirm" the balancing proposition. Likewise, to claim eventual involvement in a war as evidence of balancing without looking at how these states got involved in the war is too weak a test to "confirm" the proposition. For this reason one cannot accept the following Christensen and Snyder (1997: 921) argument:

> By underreacting to the threat posed by Hitler, the British, French, and Soviet leaders did not maximize the security of the future alliance. But to suggest that they did not balance at all is simply wrong. The most obvious fact in this regard is that Germany was defeated. If no one balanced, then how did this happen?

Appeasing while building up one's military (but hoping appeasement will work, as in Britain in 1938), surrendering (France, 1940), bandwagoning (the Soviet Union, 1939), and remaining isolated but supportive (the United States) cannot be taken as evidence of a law-like pattern of balancing permeating history just because these countries found themselves, at one time or another, at war with Hitler. If the theoretical import of balance of power is to be reduced to this and Waltz's descriptive truism, then we have wasted centuries of time on the trivial. Waltz's (1997a: 915) claim on Napoleon and Hitler, Christensen and Snyder's (1997: 921) claim on the defeat of Hitler, and Walt's (1997: 933, n.7) claim that ". . . realism provides cogent explanations for (1) the failure of *all* modern efforts to gain hegemony over the state system; (2) the nearly *universal* tendency for great powers to be extremely sensitive to shifts in the balance of power . . ." (emphases added) must mean more than just that states arm and seek allies when threatened by revisionist countries and fight wars when physically attacked.

It must mean that they follow a balancing strategy in preference to other strategies or have such behavior induced by the system as opposed to other behavior; i.e., that, at minimum, these states *actually move* diplomatically to check the power (or threat) of a challenging state with their own power (usually in the hope that this will limit that power or threat). If states fail to do that, then this is one instance where the balancing proposition is not supported. If adherents to the balancing proposition cannot accept such a test (or some reasonable emendation of it), then the entire debate will have moved from the purview of scientific inquiry to the purview of scholasticism. Schroeder's evidence cannot be shirked, unless it can be shown that its details are incorrect.

The Elmans are more respectful of such details and are prepared to admit that the historical record does pose a problem for the balancing proposition. They conclude, however, by citing Lakatos that only better theories can displace theories, and that therefore Waltz's theory should not be discarded until something better comes along (see also Kapstein 1995: 751–753, 773–774) – their third and final point against Schroeder. They then proceed to outline a general strategy for improving the theory, namely, adding variables, identifying the domain to which it is applicable, and broadening definitions (especially of threat). Some of these, however, have been precisely the tactics that have produced the degenerating situation the field now faces. Thus, they say by broadening the definition of threat to include internal threats from domestic rivals, decision makers could still be seen as balancing, and bandwagoning "would not necessarily disconfirm the prediction that balancing is more common" (Elman and Elman 1995: 192). This would take the discrepant evidence of Levy and Barnett (1991, 1992) and of Larson (1991) and make it confirmatory. This is precisely the kind of strategy that Lakatos (1970: 117–119) declaimed.

Specifying the domain of a proposition is a typical procedure by which to advance research while incorporating discrepant evidence. Waltz (1979: 121), of course, did not specify any domain to his proposition other than the anarchic system – thus it is expected to apply not just to hegemonic threats but to the general pattern of behavior of major and minor states. The problem is how to distinguish a legitimate specification of the domain of a proposition from a degenerating trend. This can be difficult and complex, but there are some obvious rules.

Let us suppose that research shows that 50 percent of the cases support the proposition and 50 percent do not, clearly a random relationship. A reformulation that was degenerative would simply group the cases that supported the proposition, give them a label (e.g., balancing states or prudent states) and say that this is the domain of proposition; whereas the other group could be given another name (e.g., impaired states) and it could be "hypothesized" that in this domain the proposition did not hold. If the labels lack any ability to predict (before examining the evidence) which states will be prudent and which impaired, then the reformulation is just semantic relabelling. Likewise, if the labels are merely hunches that borrow the paradigm's phraseology, but lack a clear theoretical explication distinguishing what the cases have in common that makes them behave in two different ways, then the reformulation is degenerative. Lastly, if the theoretical explication of why one set of cases behaves one way and the other set the opposite way can only explain the outcome of this experiment, then its explanatory power is *ex post facto* (and it fails to provide any novel facts). Likewise, if it can explain other patterns or predict novel facts, but these new explanations and predictions do not survive testing, then the reformulation lacks excess corroborated empirical content and is degenerative.

One cannot, therefore, simply assume that a specification of a domain will be progressive as Elman and Elman (1995: 193) do without examining how that specification is made (see also, Schweller 1997: 929; Christensen and Snyder 1997: 919). Elman and Elman (1997) argue that what I have seen as degenerating shifts are simply the changes Lakatos (1970: 133–138) would expect to occur in the positive heuristic of the research program (i.e., the logic that guides the construction of auxiliary hypotheses intended to protect its core). They imply that none of these changes challenges the hard core (or negative heuristic); hence they are what is to be expected. Yes, they are to be expected, but do they successfully protect the core or do they fail to deal with discrepant evidence? How well they are protecting is the question the criterion of progressivity is intended to address. If the emendations cannot explain the discrepant evidence away and predict and corroborate novel facts, then they are degenerating, especially if the attempts to explain away are themselves problematic. Repeated failures at protecting the core are indicators that the hard core may be a problematic way of looking at the world. If the theory and its research program are successful, then research corroborates the main proposition(s) of the original theory and the anomalies are minor. Changes and reformulations fill in the details; they are not focused on anomalies.[28] Findings and "discoveries" proliferate. Domains are clearly established. Changes that are progressive produce these kinds of effects.

This has not been the case with neotraditional research on Waltz's balancing proposition. No basic pattern has been established. Nor has this research been very successful in establishing a domain where the proposition holds. Walt (1987) does not find that under certain circumstances states balance power and in others they balance threat. He maintains that they generally balance threat and do not balance power unless threat is present. Schweller (1997: 928–929) clearly specifies a domain for his hypothesis about bandwagoning (namely revisionist major states), but remains neutral as to whether states balance outside this domain. Christensen and Snyder (1990, 1997) come closest in specifying a domain – namely, multipolar systems when the offensive has the advantage. In this domain, they predict that chain-ganging tends to occur; however, this term has a negative connotation, suggesting something aberrant though not quite pathological. In part, this is because they are concerned with instabilities within multipolarity; yet nowhere do they specify where "normal" (what Morgenthau would call prudent) balancing occurs. Christensen (1997: 69) further delimits this domain to frontline states whose perceived power is not superior to its opponent and the offensive has

---

[28] Lakatos (1970: 137) says the problems scientists choose to work on in powerful research programs are "determined by the positive heuristic of the programme rather than by psychologically worrying . . . anomalies. The anomalies are listed but shoved aside . . . Only those scientists have to rivet their attention on anomalies who are either engaged in trial-and-error exercises or who work in a degenerating phase of a research programme when the positive heuristic ran out of steam."

the advantage. Such an emendation is required because there are many states (like Britain in 1914) that do not balance even under conditions where the offensive is perceived to have the advantage in a multipolar system. Yet, it is far from clear why this further specification of domain is not just a reaction to the discovery of additional discrepant cases; i.e., why is it not a degenerative shift?

We have come a long way from Waltz's (1979: 121) claim that balancing prevails "wherever two, and only two, requirements are met." It would help the field to progress if those who emend a general proposition, like Waltz's, recognize that in certain arenas (and in Waltz's case very large arenas), the proposition does not hold. "De facto recognition" of realism's failings needs to be replaced by "de jure recognition." Then analysts should go on to provide others with some discussion of why a proposition does not hold and what the theoretical implications of that "fact" are for the field. It would also help progress if scholars in addressing the last two questions followed Jervis' (1976) example of not only providing one explanation of the discrepant evidence, but alternative explanations (from the perspective of competing paradigms).

What is also evident from this appraisal of the realist paradigm is that Lakatos's (1970: 119) comment that "There is no falsification before the emergence of a better theory" can play an important role in muting the implications of a degenerating research program, especially when alternative paradigms or competing mid-range theories are ignored, as has been the case in international relations. There have been too many empirical failures and anomalies, and theoretical emendations have taken on an entirely too ad hoc, non-falsifying character for adherents to say that the paradigm cannot be displaced until there is a clearly better theory available. Such a position makes collective inertia work to the advantage of the dominant paradigm and makes the field less rather than more rigorous. Progress will not be made by sticking with the old paradigm and waiting for the new Godot.[29]

---

[29] I do not disagree with Elman and Elman (1997: 925) that judgments about progress should be made with reference to neorealism's rivals, but these rivals must not be just sibling rivals (like classical realism, defensive realism, etc.). This is because a fundamentally flawed paradigm, like alchemy, will not ever produce an adequate theory. Once things appear to be going badly for the dominant theory or paradigm, then critics should only have to search for a different view of the world, and not, in the short run, show that that view is better. The question of which is better should be held in abeyance until there is some research done on the new paradigm.

Conclusion

It would seem that the internal logic of Lakatos' rules requires that a warning flag on the degenerating direction of the research program on balancing be raised. Theorists should be aware of the pitfalls of setting up realist variants that produce a "Heads, I win; tails, you lose" situation that makes realism non-falsifiable. Researchers should construct tests that match realist theories against correctly specified nonrealist theories, rather than just testing realist variants against the null hypothesis. Greater efforts need to be made in specifying testable differences between realist and nonrealist explanations before evidence is assessed so as to limit the use of ex post facto argumentation that tries to explain away discrepant evidence.

The question that needs to be discussed further, if one accepts the general thrust of the analysis that the neotraditional research program on balancing has been degenerating is what the implications of this are for the wider paradigm. Two obvious conclusions are possible – a narrow more conservative conclusion that would try to preserve as much of the dominant paradigm as possible in face of discrepant evidence and a broader more radical conclusion that would take failure in this one research program as consistent with the assessments of other studies and thus an indicator of a much broader problem. It is not really necessary that one conclusion rather than the other be taken by the entire field, since what is at stake here are the research bets individuals are willing to take with their own time and effort. In this light, it is only necessary to briefly outline the implications of two different conclusions.

The narrow conclusion one could draw from this appraisal of the neotraditional research program on balancing is that Waltz's attempt to explain what he regarded as the major behavioral regularity of international politics was premature because states simply do not engage in balancing with anywhere near the regularity he assumed. The defect of his theory may not be so much theoretical as it is empirical. It is the failure of neotraditional researchers and historians to clearly establish the empirical accuracy of Waltz's balancing proposition that so hurts his theory. If the logical connection between anarchy (as a systemic structure) and balancing is what he claims it to be, then this empirical anomaly must indicate some theoretical deficiency, within either the internal logic or the broader paradigmatic view of the world the theory is taking for granted.

The neotraditional approach to date has been to explain away the evidence by bringing to bear new concepts. The argument presented here has been that such changes have been primarily semantic and more clearly conform to what Lakatos calls degenerating theoryshifts than progressive theoryshifts. If this is accepted, then at minimum one would draw the narrow conservative conclusion that the discrepant evidence be accepted (until further research demonstrates otherwise) as showing that states do not balance in the way Waltz thought they did. Realists then could concentrate on other research programs within the paradigm without being susceptible (at least on the basis of this analysis) to the charge of engaging in a degenerating research program. Those who continue to mine realist inquiry, however, should pay more attention to the problem of degeneration in making theoretical reformulations of realism. Specifically, scholars making theoryshifts in realism should take care to make sure that these are not just proteanshifts.

A broader and more radical conclusion would dwell more on why a concept so long associated with realism should do so poorly and so misguide so many theorists. Could not its beguiling quality have something to do with the paradigmatic view of the world it embodies? And could not its failure to pass neotraditional and historical "testing" (or investigation) be an indicator of the distorted view of world politics that the paradigm imposes on scholars? Such questions are reasonable to ask, especially in light of other appraisals that have found other aspects of realism wanting (see Rosecrance and Stein 1993; Lebow and Risse-Kappen 1995; the original text and chapters 9, 12, and 13, in this volume).

Nevertheless, one could argue that the only logically compelling conclusion that can be derived from the analysis in this chapter is that one major research program, which has commanded a great deal of interest, seems to be exhibiting a degenerating tendency. Such a demonstration is important in its own right, particularly if analysts are unaware of the collective impact of their own individual decisions. In addition, it also shows that what admirers of the realist paradigm have often taken as theoretical fertility and a continuing ability to provide new insights is not really that at all, but rather a degenerating process to reformulate itself in light of discrepant evidence.

Yet what is troubling about the narrow conclusion is that if one wants to take the very cautious position that Schroeder's historical evidence affects only Waltz, one should not then be incautious and assume that other research programs within the realist paradigm are doing fine. A more consistent position would be to hold this conclusion in abeyance until all aspects of the paradigm are appraised. The lesson from Schroeder's (1994a, 1994b) and other historians' discrepant evidence should *not* be that his "article leaves the general neo-realist paradigm unscathed" (Elman and Elman 1995: 192), but that a major proposition of the paradigm has failed to pass an important historical test. Nor does the existing research and appraisals of Gilpin indicate that much hope will be found in that quarter for an empirically accurate version of neorealism.

The research program on balancing has been selected for appraisal because it focuses on the major law Waltz tries to explain. If other areas of the research program were satisfying various criteria of adequacy, then there would be no need to entertain the broad conclusion. This, however, is not the case, as can be seen by appraising the neotraditional discourse on the second most important area of Waltz's *Theory of International Politics* – his discussion of polarity.

12 Mearsheimer's multipolar myths and the false promise of realist policy prescriptions: the empirical inaccuracy of the realist paradigm

The previous chapter examined one of the main areas of neorealism that has been researched by neotraditionalists and found it to be a degenerating research program. This chapter will examine a second area of Waltz (1979) that has been a focus of neotraditional attention – his discussion of bipolar and multipolar systems. This aspect of Waltz did not give rise so much to empirical research by neotraditionalists as it did to theorizing about the multipolar future that seemed to be emerging, and deducing from Waltz (1979) the policy implications of a possible system shift to multipolarity. The lack of a sustained research program means this area of inquiry is not susceptible to the charge of being degenerating. This does not imply, however, that all is well with this area of neorealism and the realist paradigm. Such an inference would be obviously fallacious. Rather the work must be appraised on its own terms and with the criteria that are most appropriate.

Theorizing and deducing from an exemplar for policy purposes is one of the hallmarks of realist scholarship, and the major path by which the empirical aspects of realist theory enrich the practical theory of realism. Classical realists, including Morgenthau (1970) himself, did this all the time with *Politics Among Nations*. Nuclear strategists did the same thing with nuclear deterrence theory.[1]

The problem with this kind of deduction (and discourse) is that the empirical theory is often assumed to be true when there may be little evidence to support it. The situation can be made much worse

---

[1] If Brodie (1945) and Kahn (1960) are taken as exemplars, then Kissinger (1957, 1961) Schelling (1960, 1966), and McNamara (1968) can be taken as articulating the theory to solve policy-related problems arising from it.

if there are bodies of evidence that raise serious questions about the empirical accuracy of the paradigm's theories. Typically, realists and neotraditionalists have simply ignored such evidence if it has been of a quantitative sort. Nowhere has this been more evident than the debate over multipolarity and the prospects for peace in the post-Cold War era sparked by Mearsheimer's (1990a, 1994/95) widely read analyses.

Waltz (1979: 161–176) argued for a variety of reasons that multipolarity would be less stable and more dangerous than bipolarity. In the summer of 1990, as the Cold War was ending and the Soviet Union was on the verge of collapsing (although that was not known at the time), John Mearsheimer (1990a, 1990b) wrote two essays arguing that we would soon grow to miss the Cold War. Building on the best theoretical knowledge available, which for him (as well as most of the field) was Waltz, he attempted to deduce what the future would be like. Contrary to the rather commonsense and nonrealist view that this was a time for peace and for celebrating the apparent removal of the nuclear sword of Damocles that had been hanging over the bipolar world, Mearsheimer delineated the (deductive) dangers that lurked ahead. The article and the popularization in *The Atlantic* (Mearsheimer 1990b) generated quite a stir in both the academic and policy communities.

About four years later, Mearsheimer (1994/95) entered the fray again; this time with a broadside on institutionalist theory arguing that global institutions cannot prevent war by changing state behavior. He then went on to argue that realism with its balance-of-power logic would provide the best guide to peace, as it had from roughly 1300–1989, if indeed not longer(!) (Mearsheimer 1994/95: 44–46; see also Wohlforth 1994/95: 126). Such a claim seems almost outlandish in light of the analysis in the previous chapters, and it demonstrates that the issues at stake here are not simply abstract and academic, but go to the heart of the practice of international relations. Realism has always prided itself as a theory of the world that aims to guide practice, and surely this is one of the reasons it has been dominated international relations inquiry since World War II.

This chapter will examine the soundness of that practical guidance by appraising the empirical accuracy of the theorizing that undergrids realist prescriptions for the future. If such an appraisal is to be of any use, it is important that central and specific prescriptions be taken as the basis of the evaluation; otherwise there is a danger of succumbing to vague generalities about the perniciousness of power politics reasoning without clearly showing that there are actual theorists who are seen as speaking for the paradigm that makes such claims. It is for this reason that Mearsheimer's (1990a, 1994/95) work is selected as a case study to appraise the empirical accuracy of realist prescriptions.

Selecting his work as a case study of neotraditional work guided by the realist paradigm is justifiable on three grounds. First, his work is important because it takes international relations theory seriously. Particularly in the 1990a article, Mearsheimer uses theory to carefully deduce broad predictions and policy prescriptions about the future. One of the promises of international relations theory has been precisely this kind of practical knowledge. Mearsheimer's analysis has attracted wide attention because it appeared to fulfill this promise in a manner that most saw as theoretically consistent with Waltz's (1979) neorealism. For this reason, his work is an obvious and natural one to select for appraising the realist paradigm. Not only has it attracted widespread attention and sparked debate, but it also represents, like Waltz, a strong realist theoretical achievement and not some realist straw man. Selecting his work as the basis of a case study is to select work that is central to realism and that is connected directly to the paradigm, in this case both to Waltz and to Morgenthau, since Mearsheimer's assumptions on maximizing power, which he calls "offensive realism," are seen by him as closer to Morgenthau than to the "defensive realism" of Waltz (see Mearsheimer 1994/95: 9–12 especially note 27, but cf. note 20).

Second, Mearsheimer's work is important because it clearly and succinctly makes predictions that provide (before the fact) a body of evidence that is able in principle to falsify or support the underlying theory and hence, indirectly, the paradigm's view of the world. These predictions, especially about the possibility for peace, war, and stability, may constitute (depending on the foreign policy of major states) a psychologically crucial "real world" test of neorealism. Third, his two articles are important because they expose, despite their achievements, one of the fatal weaknesses of the realist tradition. They represent a mode of neotraditionalist realist analysis that goes forth with its theoretical deductions while ignoring evidence, specifically quantitative evidence, that contradicts its main empirical propositions. The tendency to refine and sharpen theory in the absence of solid evidence because of policy needs, can lead a theory to become a doctrine, as happened with nuclear deterrence theory during the 1950s and 1960s. With nuclear deterrence, however, there simply were no data to examine; with multipolarity, this is not the case. Here, there is a body of social science evidence that can be sifted to assess Mearsheimer's empirical propositions. And when this is done, and it will be done here, this body of evidence will stand as an unexplained anomaly for neorealism and the realist paradigm. The theoretical knowledge that Mearsheimer (1990a) has produced will be shown to be a multipolar myth.

The first part of this appraisal will focus on the evidence and delineate how Mearsheimer (1990a) failed to deal with it, and how it shows Waltz's and Mearsheimer's view of multipolarity to be both misleading and simplistic. This evidence along with some suggestive findings from peace research will then be used to show that the possibilities of peace among the strongest major states in the "multipolar" post-Cold War era are much brighter than Mearsheimer believes. These "predictions" are intended to provide a future comparative test between the realist paradigm and a nonrealist issue politics paradigm, as well as showing that there are alternative theories that can, in specific areas, better explain, predict, and prescribe than the dominant realist variants.

The second part of the appraisal will examine Mearsheimer's (1994/95) attack on international institutions as a force for peace in world politics. Again, it will be shown, contrary to Mearsheimer's (1995: 93) claim that "there is little evidence" to show they can produce peace, that there is a substantial body of data-based evidence that is quite relevant to this debate, which has been overlooked by neotraditionalists. This body of evidence, some of which goes back to the early 1970s, shows that international organizations can be a substitute for power politics behavior and may provide a functional equivalent of war in certain circumstances.

The criteria

Unlike the Lakatos (1970) criterion of progressive and degenerating problemshifts, the criteria that will be employed in this chapter are much more conventional and straightforward. The central one is the *criterion of accuracy*. This fundamental criterion says theories should be empirically accurate before they are accepted. Until at least some of their propositions have passed empirical tests adherence to them should be held in abeyance. Once they have passed tests, then they can be seen as satisfying this criterion and can be accepted as, at minimal, not inaccurate.

Sometimes because of the press of events or a predilection against research that does not produce clear unequivocal results, foreign policy scholars will make use of theories that have not been adequately accepted. They do this on the justification that they are using the best theories available, and, since some theory must be used, this is the best solution given the lack of evidence. While this is understandable, there are clear dangers in this practice. One can easily imagine the results if such procedures were taken in bridge building, for example. Indeed, some of the great diplomatic disasters of Western history may not have been so much the product of evil as the result of ignorance (see Singer 1979a: 133–137, 143–144). Diplomats may make poor decisions either because they have no theory and hence do not know what they are doing or because they have a bad theory and make choices that are worse than doing nothing.

All things being equal, it would be preferable to make foreign policy prescriptions on the basis of a theory that had been tested and had some empirical support. Even here, however, one must be very cautious, because the theoretical knowledge still needs to be applied in the real world. A science of physics does not obviate the need for a science of engineering!

In international relations inquiry, things are much more rudimentary. Policy-oriented scholars do not expect a corroborated theory, nor do many seem very troubled or even humbled by that. At any rate, we would not expect serious scholars to employ a theory or set of propositions that was contradicted by a body of empirical evidence, especially if that evidence comes from several different sources and maintains a modicum of scientific rigor in the testing process. The *criterion of empirical soundness* holds that the empirical aspects of a theory used to guide practice must be scientifically sound, i.e., it must be accurate, consistent with existing knowledge, falsifiable, etc. (see ch. 10 above).

If it is not, and used anyway, then we would expect, in the long run, that the prescriptions would have negative consequences and even produce dramatic failures. Practical theories are often judged on the success–failure criterion (see Jervis 1976: 281–282). One of the reasons idealism was rejected was because of the failure of the League and the policy of appeasement to prevent World War II. During the Cold War, realism avoided such a dramatic failure and that is one of the reasons why it still has many adherents.

Nevertheless, an appraisal of a theory need not wait for such dramatic failures. If there is any hope of avoiding them, then it is necessary to assess the prospects for such failures or for negative consequences on the basis of what is empirically known about a theory.

This chapter will appraise the empirical accuracy and soundness of Waltz's propositions about multipolarity as they are utilized by Mearsheimer (1990a) to assess both his and Mearsheimer's policy prescriptions. It will then examine the evidence on international institutions to see if Mearsheimer (1994/95) is correct in his argument that there is little evidence to support the idea that global institutions can prevent war better than traditional power politics.

Such an appraisal is important because it not only provides a comparative assessment between two competing theoretical approaches, but also because it provides a basis for assessing whether the following of one theory incurs important opportunity costs because another theory is not followed. Where we have a chance to compare theories it is important to do so, in order to counter the argument that while the present theory may not be the best, no alternative theory is as plausible (see Elman and Elman 1995: 192). In both parts of this chapter, alternative prescriptions to Mearsheimer's realism will be delineated, which may provide a basis for future assessments as to the relative merits of realist and nonrealist prescriptions.

The multipolar myth – the evidence

Realists have always had a problem with evidence. Typically early realists, like Morgenthau (1960), would support their case by going through history to collect examples that buttressed their points. This procedure, of course, was highly unsystematic in that it did not provide an equal chance for cases that did not support the proposition to emerge. Such an approach was derided by J. David Singer (1969: 79) as "ransacking history" (rather than systematically examining it).

Nevertheless, there are still scholars (neotraditionalists) who eschew data-based findings and see international relations inquiry primarily as making good arguments. The danger of relying on argumentation is that there is now emerging a large number of scholars who actively publish on questions of security, including peace and war, who feel they can write on alliances, crises, bargaining, and the onset of war without dealing with much of the quantitative work on these topics. The only major, and quite, recent exception to this is the attention neotraditionalists have given to the quantitative work on the democratic peace.

Neotraditionalists probably feel they can generally ignore most quantitative analyses on two grounds. First is the notion that this research is contradictory and not very informative, a sentiment best expressed and legitimized by Kenneth Waltz's (1979: 12; 1975: 9) charge that "much pointless work is done" and that "induction leads to a dead end." Second is the belief that quantitative work is not really evidence and can be picked apart by questioning measures, research designs, and theoretical misspecification, and therefore can be safely ignored.

The end result is a failure to come to grips with data-based evidence. To use anecdotal evidence and ignore entire research programs is hardly excusable. The consequences of this failure for just normal discourse, let alone the inter-paradigm debate, are amply illustrated by Mearsheimer (1990a), who fails to discuss any of the relevant empirical research and appears even to be unaware of it. An examination of this research would have shown how much of the debate is misplaced. At one point, Mearsheimer even replied to Stanley Hoffmann's use of anecdotal evidence by saying that it is an empirical question whether bipolarity is more stable than multipolarity and that no historical survey had been done on the question (see Hoffmann et al. 1990: 194–195).

Of course, a literature review of the *Journal of Conflict Resolution* and the *Journal of Peace Research* would have shown that there has been systematic empirical research on the question covering the 1815–1965 period. If this were only a matter of the oversight of one person, then this would not be such a problem. It is equally significant that Hoffmann, the early critic of American social science, also resorted to anecdotal evidence (citing the single case of the Peloponnesian war) rather than systematic evidence. Likewise, Van Evera (1990/91: 10, 26–27), who at least cites some quantitative work, but not always the most relevant of this work, seems not to appreciate fully its import.[2]

---

[2] It is noteworthy, for example, that in the critical section on bipolarity and multipolarity, Van Evera (1990/91: 33–43) does not make use of any of the relevant

This is unfortunate since much of this work, which was published before he wrote, is consistent with his general point that both bipolar and multipolar systems are equally prone to war (Van Evera 1990/91: 34).

Mearsheimer (1990a) argued that bipolarity is more stable than multipolarity and hence the future would be more dangerous than the Cold War past. Following Gaddis (1986), Mearsheimer maintained, in effect, that the presence of nuclear weapons had converted the Cold War into a "long peace." This stability and the long peace associated with it were now about to come to an end.

The first and most important question to ask is: How empirically accurate is this prediction? Concurrent and subsequent events – the Persian Gulf War, the Yugoslav and Bosnian civil wars, Somalia, Rwanda and so forth – seemed to lend credence to his prediction. To look at these wars and the ethnic and border conflicts involving Soviet successor states as indicators of multipolar instability may be psychologically persuasive, but it ignores the violent disturbances of the Cold War – the Czech coup, China, Korea, Hungary, Suez, the Congo, Vietnam, Indonesia, the Middle East, Afghanistan. To these one could add a host of other inter-state wars that occurred in the system such as the India–Pakistan wars, the Iran–Iraq war and the Falklands/Malvinas. There were also numerous instances of civil political violence such as the Nigerian Civil War and the ethnic massacres in Burundi, among others. Thus, once a comparative historical review is conducted, even a cursory one, questions are raised about the accuracy of his prediction.

Of course, the proper way to make this assessment is to examine data on war and count the instances. Two studies have done so. In a systematic review of the two major data sets, Brecher and Wilkenfeld (1991: 86) find 251 international crises from June 1945 to the end of 1985 in their crisis data, as well as eighteen interstate and twelve extra systemic wars from 1945 to 1980 listed in the Correlates of War data (Small and Singer 1982). On the basis of these data, they argue that the absence of direct war between the superpowers is not synonymous with global peace; hence, the idea of a long peace is potentially misleading.

Likewise, Singer (1991) adds more evidence by analyzing Correlates

quantitative studies that will be discussed below. The same is true for his discussion on the "rules of the game" (Van Evera 1990/91: 45).

of War data to 1988 and examining both international wars and internal civil wars to show just how frequent collective warfare was during the Cold War. The data show that there is plenty of instability in the form of warfare in this bipolar period. Nevertheless, what is remarkable about the Cold War for Singer (1991: 83–84) is that the strongest states "managed to prepare for war with a dedication seldom seen in history" without actually fighting one.

This last comment restores a legitimacy to Gaddis' (1986) claim, while fine-tuning it and making it more precise. Does it do the same for Mearsheimer? Not exactly, for what gave Mearsheimer's (1990a) prediction a certain plausibility initially, were inter-state wars in the periphery and ethnic disputes, which the data show were also quite prevalent throughout the entire Cold War period. In light of the evidence, it is now clear that outside the central system of the major states the post-Cold War period is not any less stable or war-prone than the bipolar period that has just passed. The prediction has not been sustained. It may be concluded that, at least to date, multipolarity has not evoked the kind of violent instability that Mearsheimer feared.

There is another aspect to Mearsheimer's analysis that merits scrutiny. Wars in the periphery, despite the early psychological support they provided Mearsheimer's (1990a) analysis, are not exactly what Waltz (1979) had in mind when he was concerned about the instability of multipolar systems. For Waltz and for Mearsheimer, what is critical are relations among the strongest states. For Waltz (1979: ch. 8) such relations become inherently more complicated simply because the number of poles increase. It is this increase in the number of major states that makes Mearsheimer (1990a: 7) expect that the system will become more unstable and lead us soon to miss the Cold War. What seemed odd at the time, and even more so now, is that Mearsheimer discounted, if not outright denied, the importance of the fact that with the end of the Cold War the threat of nuclear war greatly decreased. At best, he seemed to imply this was just a short-term respite before the increase in poles would make the world a much more dangerous place.

For most observers, however, the end of the Cold War seems to mean that the major states (Russia, the United States, Britain, France, Germany, Japan, and China) are now at peace, whereas before they were at risk of nuclear war. Unlike the "long peace" period of 1945–1989, the major states have not been, nor do they seem to be, in danger of becoming involved in a militarized crisis that could escalate to war. In the Cold War, this was always a potential danger (from the Taiwan Straits through Berlin and to Cuba), despite nuclear deterrence. In terms of the more central prediction about relations among major states, Mearsheimer seems again to be quite off the mark. This reflects badly not only on Mearsheimer's analysis, but also on Waltz's (1979) predictions about multipolarity. In fact, one could argue that war among the major states (in any form) is probably at its lowest probability since 1871.

Why does Mearsheimer not see this? He does not see it because his theory does not let him see it. His theory tells him the most significant "fact" about the transition to the post-Cold War era is the emergence of multipolarity, *ergo* this means (deductively) more instability. The perspective of the theory and the paradigm is that the distribution of power is the most important theoretical fact in explaining war and peace. From a nonrealist perspective, however, the distribution of power, or any power variable is at best tangential to the onset of war and the prospects of peace (see Vasquez 1993), so that the shift to multipolarity is simply irrelevant to the question of war/peace.

What is so discouraging about Mearsheimer's analysis is that there existed a body of evidence before he wrote that showed that the polarity of the system is not as theoretically significant for producing war (and peace) as neorealists assume. Instead, the scientific research shows that neither bipolar nor multipolar systems are free from war (cf. Van Evera 1990/91: 34). What this means is that not only do Mearsheimer's (1990a) predictions about multipolarity fail to be sustained, but the larger Waltzian theory from which he makes his deductions appears to be empirically unsound, at least in terms of what it says about bipolarity and multipolarity and war. In addition, and to a certain extent more damning for neotraditionalism, is that their ignoring of an entire body of relevant evidence underlines the risks associated with deducing policy implications from theories without paying adequate attention to scientific tests of those propositions. At best, this reflects a closed-mindedness stemming from an arrogance about one's own mode of analysis. At worse, it reflects a paradigmatic self protection that discounts any method that appears to undercut the central tenets of the paradigm (see ch. 7 above in the original text), unless they do so in such a dramatic fashion (as in the democratic peace) that they cannot be ignored.

What precisely does the quantitative work show and how important is it for the multipolarity debate initiated by Mearsheimer (1990a)? We can begin with one of the least quantitative of these studies. Levy (1985) in an analysis covering five centuries classifies periods (on the basis of historical consensus) in terms of whether they are unipolar, bipolar, or multipolar. He finds that bipolar periods have more frequent wars than multipolar periods, but these are of less severity and lower magnitude.[3] This shows that the two types of systems are different in the kinds of wars they have, but not in terms of one being peaceful and the other more war-prone.

Using a more operationally reliable and precise measure of bipolarity in terms of concentration of power, Wayman (1984) produces findings very similar to Levy's for the 1816–1965 period. He finds that bipolar periods have wars, but these are of lower magnitude (measured by nation-months of war) than multipolar periods, which are associated with the two twentieth-century world wars. He finds that in periods of multipolarity (measured in terms of power concentration) 75 percent of high magnitude wars occur, and in periods of bipolarity, 73 percent of the low magnitude wars occur. These findings make it clear that polarity is not related to the presence of war or peace, but to different *types* of war.[4]

---

[3] Levy also finds unipolar systems having the biggest wars. However, his unipolar systems include periods when a "hegemonic" state is involved in and defeated in a general war involving all leading states. For this reason, some classify such systems as multipolar. Wallace (1985: 109), for example, criticizes Levy's coding of 1797–1815 as unipolar because Britain contested French hegemony.

[4] Some might think that Mansfield (1992) contradicts this general finding in that he finds a curvilinear relationship between power concentration and the frequency of war (see also Mansfield 1994). He concludes that very low and high levels of concentration of power in the system are associated with the onset of few wars, whereas a moderate concentration is associated with a high frequency of war (thereby making for an inverted U-curve relationship).

An examination of the cases that make up these correlations makes one cautious about placing too much theoretical significance on them. Fortunately, Mansfield (1992: 12–13) is committed enough to the scientific enterprise that he discusses these cases in detail. It turns out that the moderate concentration period (1845–1869) coincides with the period of the wars of Italian and German unification. Mansfield (1992: 13; see also Mansfield 1994: 89–90) lists eleven wars for this period of which at least eight are related to the Italian and German Wars, the major one that is not is the Crimean War. If these wars are treated as two wars rather than eight (as the Napoleonic wars or World War I and II have been), much of this relationship would disappear.

Conversely, low concentration of power and few war onsets occur in 1825–1844 and 1875–1919. These are respectively the Concert of Europe and Bismarckian periods (up to 1895), both of which have institutionalized rules of the game. However, the extension of the Bismarckian period to 1895–1919 seems questionable. High con-

This, of course, makes sense historically. The largest wars in terms of the number of states involved and the number of battle deaths, are the big world wars, like the Thirty Years War, the War of Spanish Succession, the Napoleonic Wars, and World War I and II. All these occurred in multipolar periods. Nevertheless, that does not mean that there have not been a host of other kinds of inter-state wars in periods of bipolarity. Indeed, the quantitative evidence is quite consistent with what we know about the Cold War period. One would expect from this research that bipolar periods would have relatively frequent, but not very severe wars, and this is precisely the kind of wars that characterized the Cold War bipolar era – a number of small limited wars occurring fairly frequently over the approximately forty-year period (1947–1989). These would include among others: Korea, Hungary, Arab–Israel, Vietnam, Afghanistan, Ethiopia–Somalia, India–Pakistan, Iran–Iraq, Falklands/Malvinas.

Although Waltz and Mearsheimer define bipolarity in terms of power, there is more to this story than just the association between mutlipolarity and large-scale wars. If polarity is defined in terms of blocs, the relationship is just the opposite of the one found for a bipolarity of power (cf. Morgenthau's [1960: 349–351] distinction between a bipolarity of power and a two-bloc system). Empirical findings show that a bipolarized system of two blocs is associated with severe wars, like the two world wars, while a multipolar system, defined as one of several blocs or no blocs at all, is associated with not very severe wars. Bueno de Mesquita (1978: 259–260), for example, finds that during the period 1816–1965 nearly 80 percent of the multilateral wars (involving at least three states) occur in periods of increasing tightness (i.e. bipolarization) of blocs. Conversely, no multilateral wars occur in periods when bloc tightness is declining. Bueno de Mesquita (1978: 259) also finds for both the nineteenth century (after 1815) and the twentieth century that wars tend to occur after a rise in bloc tightness and rarely occur after a decline in tightness.[5]

centration of power and low warfare is associated with 1920–1924 and 1946–1964. Both of these include periods of war recovery from major world wars as well high concentrations of power due to the defeat of major states in the world wars. Note Mansfield does not do well in finding consistent associations with the two world wars, which is what the thrust of Levy's (1985) and Wayman's (1984) findings are all about.

[5] These findings are very strong for the twentieth century, but still fairly impressive for the nineteenth century, see Bueno de Mesquita (1978: 259).

Wayman (1984, 1985) produces similar findings using a different measure of bloc polarization. He finds that an increase in polarization of alliance blocs in the twentieth century is moderately associated ($r = -0.48$) with an increase in the magnitude of war (Wayman 1985: 135).[6] Specifically, he finds (what we know historically) that prior to the two world wars alliance patterns were becoming more polarized.

These findings seem to indicate that it is not a multipolarity of power alone that is associated with certain types of large wars, but that power multipolarity requires an alliance system that reduces these multiple poles to two hostile blocs to bring about large severe wars. This suggests that not all multipolar periods may be alike, and that some may be much more prone to war contagion and hence world wars than others. As argued in Vasquez (1993: 248), it may be the case that world wars will not occur except in the presence of specific contagion factors and three necessary conditions:

> (1) a multipolar distribution of capability in the system; (2) an alliance system that reduces this multipolarity to two hostile blocs; and (3) the creation of two blocs in which one does not have a clear preponderance of capability over the other.

Kegley and Raymond (1994a, 1994b) build on the work in peace research to show that, in fact, not all multipolar systems are alike. They review the quantitative findings and the historical record to see if they can identify the characteristics that make multipolarity dangerous. Their review of empirical studies suggests that war is associated with systems that have polarized alliances and a permissive norm structure. They also examine six periods of multipolarity (1495–1521, 1604–1618, 1648–1702, 1713–1792, 1815–1914, 1919–1939) for clues about the sources of multipolar instability (Kegley and Raymond 1994b: 72–76). They use this information to delineate possible paths to peace *within* multipolarity, concluding that the two most important things states can do to insure peace are to avoid polarizing alliances and construct a system of binding norms.

Three conclusions can be made on the basis of the above analysis. First, bipolar systems do not seem any more stable than multipolar systems in terms of their proneness to war. Multipolar systems of

---

[6] The negative correlation is due to the fact that Wayman (1985: 128) measures polarization as the number of blocs in the system (by calculating the ratio of actual poles to potential poles among major states). Thus, the more blocs (less polarization), the lower the magnitude of war.

power and bipolar systems of blocs tend to have large world wars. In contrast, periods marked by a bipolarity of power have many inter-state wars, even though they may not always be the most severe wars in history. The Cold War period was no exception to this. In this sense, the idea that bipolar systems are inherently more peaceful is erro-neous.

Second, as the current multipolar system extends in time, there will be an opportunity to test directly Mearsheimer's predictions about the future. This test, if conducted rigorously and objectively, would provide a crucial test for neorealism since, like Waltz's analysis of the balancing of power, it is one of the few instances where neorealism has actually specified, in a clear manner, a body of evidence that would falsify it.

Third, the statistical findings indicate that processes related to war and peace are much more complex than realists generally think. The result is that neorealists make things appear much more determinate than they are. This is especially the case with Mearsheimer's (1990a) predictions about the instability of post-Cold War multipolarity. The extent to which this period will be prone to war is open to the influence of several variables, as Kegley and Raymond (1994a, 1994b) persuasively argue. Conversely, the variable cluster Mearsheimer focuses on, namely the polarity of the system, does not seem to be theoretically significant in terms of questions of peace and war.[7] This complexity identified by peace researchers makes the body of their work, both theoretically and empirically, a much richer source for understanding and dealing with the current period than the single factor emphasis of the realist paradigm.

This last conclusion for most members of the field, and especially neotraditionalists, seems entirely unexpected. How could something as "arcane" as statistical research be more relevant to the future than realism? In no small part, this irony is due to the greater empirical soundness of the nonrealist theory being tested in comparison to the specific neorealist propositions. As demonstrated in the original text of this book, quantitative analysis is a method and by itself has no theory logically connected with it. Only as quantitative work has

---

[7] This does not mean that for other questions, for example the management of foreign policy relations, multipolarity will not be of policy importance. Dealing with six states is going to be different both in management terms and in the unanticipated problems that arise than dealing with one state, as Waltz (1979: 163–170, 194–209) points out. In terms of war probability, however, the differences are statistically insignificant.

turned to more nonrealist hypotheses has it begun to make more progress in generating stronger statistical associations – such has been the case with the studies on multipolarity. This has made these analyses a more empirically sound basis upon which to understand the post-Cold War period we are entering, and thus, in principle, a better guide to practice than a neorealist explanation which has been shown to contradict a body of evidence about patterns of past behavior. But this relevance stems not so much from the statistical techniques, as from the empirical soundness of the theoretical propositions that the techniques have tested.

This means that ignoring relevant quantitative work is not without peril. Nor is this pattern of ignoring quantitative work, which in the aggregate has not given much strong support to realist propositions, been unique to the debate on multipolarity. It repeats itself in the debate over the promise of international institutions.

False promises

One of the main tests of the utility of a practical theory is that it can intellectually grasp and identify the most important policy problems of the day and propose sound solutions or at least some options for dealing with them. This is the test of the criterion of relevance (see ch. 10 above and ch. 13 below). How relevant are realist and nonrealist prescriptions about the post-Cold War era? Does one set of prescriptions appear more promising than the other?

Mearsheimer's (1990a) musings about multipolarity and his subsequent recommendation (Mearsheimer 1993) that nuclear weapons would reduce the danger of war between the Ukraine and Russia (see also Waltz 1981b, 1995) show that the realist paradigm is locked very much into the bipolar nuclear world of the past and is not really apprehending the very changed world of the post-Cold War era, which has its own problems and dangers. The body of theory and findings within peace research, particularly that which takes a more nonrealist bent, paints a very different picture of today's world. It has already been shown that one feasible way of avoiding total wars within multipolarity is to avoid polarizing alliances. Of more importance, of course, would be to avoid handling conflicts of interest in a manner that increases long-term hostility and/or the probability of war. For realists, the latter is an illusion. Such conflicts are inherent (see Carr 1939) either because anarchy will always make states insecure (Waltz 1989: 40) or because international relations is a constant struggle for power (Measheimer 1994/95: 11–12). Yet this position ignores the fact that just because conflict is pervasive, this does not mean that all conflict needs to be resolved violently. One of the lessons of the field of conflict resolution is that violence can be avoided and peace attained in relationships without a harmony of interests (see M. Deutsch 1973; Pruitt and Rubin 1986; Vasquez et al. 1995). Likewise, the fact that harmonies of interest are rare does not mean they never exist; nor does it follow that all conflicts of interest are such that they are equally prone to violent solution. The realist paradigm has a difficult time seeing this, however. Such distinctions make realists nervous; they are like traumatized victims who are quick to see the world as a jungle and would rather be wrong about seeing threats where none exist, than being taken as a "sucker."

From a nonrealist perspective what is critical about the post-Cold War era is not the shift in power – Russia is still the only country that can wipe the United States off the face of the Earth and multipolarity has been emerging since 1964 – but the change in foreign policy goals and with that the radical change in the East–West relationship. With the ideological shift in the former Soviet Union, the United States no longer regards it as a threat. The foreign policy goals of all the major states (including China, which has been gradually adopting market reforms and becoming more integrated into the global economy, especially the United States economy) are now more compatible than they have been since 1871. None of the major states is pursuing goals, in terms of either behavior or rhetoric, that would lead them into a fundamental conflict of interest – real or perceived. Thus, it is possible to build upon and extend the rules of the game that brought about the *modus vivendi* that ended the crisis-prone stage of the Cold War (George 1988). In the post-Cold War era it is much easier for each of the major states to pursue its foreign policy goals without resorting to armed force, because the goals themselves are not that threatening (see Rosecrance 1992; Kupchan and Kupchan 1991).

In this context, an opportunity arises to build a working consensus on rules of the game that can be institutionalized in either informal regimes, like a concert of powers, and/or a host of new or reinvigorated international organizations, like the OSCE, WTO, or the UN Security Council. Mearsheimer (1994/95) questions the utility of such an approach. He argues that the optimistic view that institutions can preserve peace is not warranted on either theoretical or empirical grounds. He states, ". . . institutions are not an important cause of peace . . ." and maintains: "My central conclusion is that institutions have minimal influence on state behavior and thus hold little promise for promoting stability in the post-Cold War world" (Mearsheimer 1994/95: 7). Likewise in his reply to critics, he repeats that the central issue is: ". . . can institutions cause peace by independently affecting state behavior?" (Mearsheimer 1995: 84). He answers with a resounding no.

In doing so, Mearsheimer again ignores quantitative evidence that contradicts his claims. The remainder of this chapter will be devoted to reviewing that evidence and in the process showing that the creation and use of international institutions *are* correlated with periods of peace among major states, whereas the periods in which major states rely on unilateral acts and the use of power politics are associated with wars among major states.

Quantitative research on norms and institutions

The quantitative research is more relevant than the handful of case studies that Mearsheimer (1994/95: 24–26; 1995) and Keohane and Martin (1995: 46–50) discuss in their exchange on institutionalist theory, especially since many of the latter do not focus on security issues involving high politics. The quantitative work in peace research speaks more directly to the security questions with which Mearshemer is primarily concerned. In addition, the evidence it provides is more extensive because it deals with a much larger number of cases and in a more systematic manner that is less prone to selection effects. It is significant that in the exchange between Mearsheimer (1995) and those he criticizes – Keohane and Martin (1995), Kupchan and Kupchan (1995), Ruggie (1995), and Wendt (1995) – that the quantitative evidence is ignored by everyone. In part, this is a function of how Mearsheimer sets the agenda, because only those he attacked are invited to respond, but it also reflects the larger neotraditional tendency of generally ignoring quantitative work outside the democratic peace debate.

The quantitative work has shown that building a set of "rules of the game" or norms among major states is an important correlate of peace. Wallensteen (1984) in a systematic study of the 1816–1976 period found that when major states work out a set of rules of the game to guide their relations, no war occurs between them; even militarized crises are reduced by half. However, when major states are unable to come to some agreement on rules and resort to unilateral acts, especially the practices of power politics (e.g., alliance making, military build-ups, and *realpolitik* tactics), wars break out and crises proliferate (see Vasquez 1993: 269–275 for a full discussion). Likewise, in a set of more operationally precise studies, Kegley and Raymond (1982, 1984, 1990) examine periods in which the dominant tradition in international law considers alliance norms binding and the unilateral abrogation of commitments illegitimate and find that they are less war prone and crisis prone than other periods. While alliance norms and the legal tradition are significant in themselves, these factors are probably an indicator of a much broader consensus on rules of the game that limits unilateral actions (see Kegley and Raymond 1986: 217–224).

Rules and norms are important because they create a way of adjudicating disagreements and do not leave states simply with a choice between stalemate or armed force. Such rules do not have to result in formal institutions, like the League or United Nations Indeed, rules of the game themselves constitute informal institutions and may be more effective than formal organizations because of their flexibility. They provide one means of managing relationships and can be quite successful. Väyrynen (1983), for example, in a study based on historical classifications, finds war less associated with systems of political management that restrain unilateral actions.

Evidence that a rich global institutional context (in terms of inter-governmental organizations) is associated with a reduction in power politics behavior, war, and crises can be found in studies by Wallace (1972) and Faber and Weaver (1984). Wallace's early article is of interest because he identifies a path to war and a path to peace, each separate and fairly distinct from the other. The path to war, for Wallace, begins with status inconsistency brought about by changes in relative capability. This encourages alliance making (and often alliance polarization) and then arms racing. The build-up of arms is highly correlated in Wallace's (1972) model with large amounts of warfare.[8]

In contrast, the path to peace lacks these two power politics

---

[8] See also Wallace's (1979, 1982, 1990) later studies for the tendency of ongoing arms races to increase the probability of escalation of militarized disputes to war and Diehl's (1983) criticism of them. Sample (1997) has resolved much of this controversy by showing that most disputes in the pre-1945 period that do not escalate to war immediately, eventually do so within five years.

practices. Instead, it is characterized by an increased presence of inter-governmental organizations (IGOs). These in turn are negatively correlated with arms races, which indicates that IGOs are negatively correlated (indirectly) with large amounts of warfare in the system. IGOs are also negatively correlated with status inconsistency. This suggests they are created and probably work most effectively when none of the major states experiences any status inconsistency, i.e., when states feel they are accorded the diplomatic status to which they are entitled, given their power.[9] Wallace's (1972) findings indicate that major states can contend over political issues through the use of international organizations and when they do, they do not engage in the practices of power politics.

These findings are particularly interesting because they are quite consistent with Wallensteen's (1984) study, where he finds that, in periods of peace, creating and following rules of the game is prevalent, but in periods associated with major state wars, alliances and arms races tend to be prevalent. This inchoate pattern is further delineated by Faber and Weaver (1984).

Faber and Weaver (1984) examine only European politics from 1815 to 1915, and they concentrate their attention not so much on inter-governmental organizations per se, but on the participation of states in conferences and the signing of treaties to settle issues. They find, not too unsurprisingly, that the more conferences and signed treaties, the less likely war in a given period. They argue that it was through conferences and diplomatic consultations rather than IGOs that most issue settlements in the 1816–1870 period took place. This means that while formal organizations, in and of themselves, may not be essential, rules and norms are. Of course, this is the period of the Concert of Europe, which can be seen as an informal institution. Even though it breaks down at several points, vestiges of the Concert and its conference diplomacy do appear periodically up to the Crimean War (Gulick 1955: 22 [cited in Mearsheimer 1994/95: 36]; cf. Kupchan and Kupchan 1995: 57 note 9). Even more intriguing is Faber and Weaver's (1984) finding that settling certain kinds of issues, namely territorial issues, is negatively correlated with the outbreak of war. Their findings imply that conferences that can settle certain kinds of issues,

---

[9] Status inconsistency is measured in the Correlates of War project by ranking states according to their demographic, economic, and military capability and then comparing that ranking with an index of diplomatic importance based on the exchange of diplomatic representatives. On the latter, see Small and Singer (1973).

may be providing a functional equivalent to war, if one assumes that war is (as Clausewitz 1832 maintained) a way of making binding political decisions.

Overall, the thrust of this research suggests that there are in the international relations of major states two separate worlds – one of power politics that often degenerates into war and one of rules of the game, norms and intergovernmental organizations that is negatively correlated with the power politics practices of alliance making and arms racing. Contrary to what Mearsheimer (1995: 82) believes, it is not so much that global institutions fail to get states to "eschew balance-of-power logic," as it is that the presence of rules of the games, norms, conference diplomacy, and more formal IGOs all reflect a different way of conducting political business. It reflects a different manner of relating to other states (i.e., a different manner of contending over political issues). To avoid war one wants to create nonviolent ways of contending on political issues that are as effective as war. The research of Wallensteen, Wallace and others shows that this is what happens at certain periods within the modern global system, such as the Concert of Europe and the League in the 1920s. Together, the above findings suggest that what is important is not whether the system has two or more major states ("poles"), but the kinds of issues that are on the global political agenda and whether there are rules of the game that exist to manage how states contend over these issues (see Vasquez 1993: ch. 8).

A nonrealist perspective places more emphasis on manipulating the issues on the global agenda and seeking to resolve war-prone issues that are on the agenda through the use of conflict resolution techniques. It also attempts to develop a structure (based on accepting certain rules of the game) that will permit actors to contend and make authoritative decisions over issues through procedures other than just armed force. This set of policy prescriptions (see Vasquez 1994, 1995) is much more optimistic about the prospects for peace in the current period than Mearsheimer's realism and Waltz's neorealism. It predicts that agreement on such rules and the keeping of territorial disputes between major states off the agenda will go a long way in preserving the peace between those states through preventive diplomacy.

There will, of course, still be wars and internal disputes outside the central major state system – precisely because some of the issues over which states are contending (especially territorial issues) do not encourage compromise. Here, the key is to collectively contain and/or attempt to manage such disputes so that a major state is not dragged in. These prescriptions show that a nonrealist issue politics paradigm can offer explanations that are just as powerful and policy relevant as realism, with the advantage of being more consistent with current research findings. Together the predictions and prescriptions, if followed, offer a future comparative test of the two paradigms.

What the findings indicate is that peace, in terms of a low probability of war between major states, is possible. Such periods of peace have not only occurred in the past,[10] but have certain "known" characteristics. Mearsheimer (1994/95: 48) denies all this and derides the false promise of international institutions, claiming that war is basically inevitable. Again, how he does this is of interest, because his position relies heavily on deductive logic and an ignoring of quantitative evidence. Once the latter is examined, there is not much left of his position that there is little empirical evidence to support the view that institutions can preserve peace (Mearsheimer 1995: 93). Let us turn now to his argument that the causal logic of neoliberalism is flawed.

The causal logic of relative gains

It turns out that the major flaw in the causal logic of neoliberalism is that it contradicts the assumptions and deductions of the realist paradigm. Mearsheimer (1994/95: 24–26) argues that liberal institutionalists assume absolute gains, but relative gains actually motivate states. To support this empirical claim he cites (1994/95: 21) three case studies of very specific political economy transactions (Krasner 1991; Grieco 1990; and Mastanduno 1991). What really gives his argument force, however, are the assumptions he brings to the debate. He maintains:

> states in the international system aim to maximize their relative power positions over other states. The reason is simple: the greater the military advantage one state has over other states, the more secure it is. Every state would like to be the most formidable military power in the system because this is the best way to guarantee survival in a world that can be very dangerous.
>
> (Mearsheimer 1994/95: 11–12, see also pp. 9, 20, 48).

[10] Wallensteen (1984) identifies the following periods of peace among major states: Concert of Europe (1816–1848), Bismarck's Order (1871–1895), League of Nations (1919–1932), and Détente (1963–1976) where the study ends.

As with Grieco's (1988) initial article raising the issue, a critique of anything assuming absolute gains is going to appear as strikingly discordant with the above realist view of the world.

The question that is of fundamental importance in this debate is whether states are motivated always by relative or absolute gains. Rather than assuming it is one way or the other, it is equally plausible to think that such concerns might vary by issue area, culture, or historical period (see Snidal 1991; Keohane and Martin 1995: 44). The main point, however, is that this is primarily a research question, and that research has not even started and already conclusions have been reached!

Contrary to expectations (Mearsheimer 1994/95: 15–16; Keohane and Martin 1995: 43) it may turn out to be the case, as Glaser (1994/95: 76) maintains, that security issues are less prone to relative gains thinking than political economy issues involving monetary benefits. As many in the conflict resolution field have shown, security in and of itself is not a zero sum value, but a positive sum value. Increases in my security do not necessarily diminish yours, on the contrary they should increase your security. What conflict resolution practitioners try to do is to frame issues and create bargains that reverse the classic security dilemma (see also Glaser 1994/95: 75–76). Instead of building arms or making alliances to increase my security – which has the effect of increasing the insecurity of the target, thereby leading it to take actions that decrease my security – conflict resolution experts attempt to get both sides to reach agreements where everyone wins something, thus giving each a vested interest in not breaking the agreement.

None of this would be possible if all states behaved the way Mearsheimer thinks they do. Do they *all* really strive "to be the most powerful actor in the system" (Mearsheimer 1994/94: 9)?[11] Nor does it seem that having "the most formidable military in the system . . . is the best way to guarantee survival . . ." (Mearsheimer 1994/95: 12). Only rivals, of which there are many, have these kinds of concerns (see Vasquez 1993: 147–148), and they are primarily the ones who would worry, along with Grieco and Mearsheimer, that unequal economic gains might be translated into military imbalances. Dyads

---

[11] One thinks of poor little Switzerland taking all that money and never letting us know what its real strivings were – not to mention the Swedens, Netherlands, Austrias, Italys, and others who dropped out of the power politics game.

like Canada and the United States or even France and Germany today do not have such concerns, even if they would like to get more than the other in a particular deal. Contrary to Grieco (1988: 497–499), relative gains do not necessarily imply a potential advantage in the survival game and gaining economically does not necessarily mean military gain. This suggests that the entire conceptual frame of the relative/absolute gains debate needs to be broadened with more than just these two concepts being the basis for all discussion.

The debate over relative and absolute gains is rather narrow (if not myopic) given all the issues on the table. What is of importance here is that Mearsheimer ignores the more rigorous peace research on the role of norms and rules of the game of Wallensteen (1984), Kegely and Raymond (1990), and Wallace (1972), for example, who show that such informal institutions are correlated with periods of major state peace. Likewise, Schroeder's (1994a) historical work that shows that major states transcended power politics through the creation of conference diplomacy in the Concert of Europe to create a stable peace will have to be dealt with.

In this light, Mearsheimer's attack on the difficulty of implementing collective security when it faces a specific threat is fine (see also Betts 1992), but this does not in itself refute all nonrealist or even liberal positions. The main focus needs to be on a concert of powers and why the Concert of Europe brought about a modicum of peace (see Rosecrance 1992). From a nonrealist perspective, the concert worked not because each balanced power against the other, as Mearsheimer (1995: 35) claims, but because collectively they attempted to manage their relationship and learn how to resolve disputes non-violently. The latter is just what the aggregate findings from peace research would expect them to do!

To try to explain this away, as Mearsheimer attempts, by saying states did this because it was in their self-interest does not work as it does not explain why the rules were able to get states to put their long-term interests over their short-term interests. To explain behavior as self-interested provides no basis for explaining why long-term interests are selected over short-term interests, or why of the many possible positions that could be in the "interests" of a "state" one is selected. Likewise, an appeal to self-interest does not distinguish the realist paradigm from other paradigms, like the Marxist paradigm that also uses self-interest explanations or the issue politics paradigm that sees costs–benefits as one of three calculi used by decision makers to determine their issue preferences (see Mansbach and Vasquez 1981b: 192–197).

Both theoretically and empirically nonrealist positions are not as easily dismissed as Mearsheimer would like us to believe. Empirically, research on relative vs. absolute gains still needs to accumulate a body of evidence. Conceptually, there appear to be more distinctions than just relative vs. absolute gains that need to be addressed.

The findings from peace research point to where those new conceptualizations might lie. The findings suggest that it is possible to make important political decisions by some mechanism other than war. The research also suggests that it is possible to have some level of governance within the system of major states without resorting to government and impinging greatly on the legal sovereignty of states. The findings reviewed from peace research suggest that there are also political forms of governance that major states use to manage their security relations with each other. This is a point Kupchan and Kupchan (1991, 1995), Rosecrance (1992), and others are trying to make about the concerts of powers – it is a way of governing relations and a mechanism for making decisions. Such a system may not work all the time, nor may it prevent all wars, but it does seem to work some of the time, and it does seem to be very relevant for the time in which we are currently living. Thus, an issue politics paradigm seems to offer more precise policy advice and a clearer path to peace. In contrast, the realist paradigm's promises for peace through strength and deterrence appear to be false.[12] Nowhere is this more apparent than in the recommendation that the spread of nuclear weapons is the best path to peace available under multipolarity.

Nuclear deterrence and multipolar peace

Before beginning this discussion, it should be made clear that no one can complain about Mearsheimer's (1990a: 37–40) position that *if* states are going to get nuclear weapons, then it is better to manage that transition than just permit it to happen. Nor are many going to deny that over the long run states may feel disadvantaged by not having nuclear weapons and hence may seek them (Waltz 1995). These claims may not constitute testable differences between the

---

[12] For general evidence on the inaccuracy of the peace through strength hypothesis, see Wallace (1982) and Bremer (1980).

realist paradigm and other paradigms that incorporate some cost–benefit calculus. The real testable difference has to do with the third assumption of the realist paradigm that sees international politics as a struggle for power and that claims that power can deter war. The objection to Mearsheimer and Waltz is not that nuclear weapons might spread, but that nuclear deterrence will work to keep the peace and because of that a world of major nuclear states will be more stable and less war prone than a world of non-nuclear major states.

There are at least three problems with this position. First, this is a poor prescription because it generalizes to all potential nuclear rivals on the basis of the one-shot case (and perhaps unique experience) of the United States and the Soviet Union with nuclear deterrence. Would deterrence work as well in rivalries with deep-seated territorial conflicts like that between Israel and the Arabs, India and Pakistan, or Iran and Iraq? Research has suggested that territorial disputes have a much higher probability of going to war than other kinds of disputes (Vasquez 1993: ch. 4; Brecher and Wilkenfeld 1989: chs. 9–10). It is significant that the closest the Cold War came to nuclear war was at the territorial frontiers of the two "empires" – Berlin and Cuba (Betts 1987: 98, 116–122). If the United States was willing to risk nuclear war for basically symbolic stakes, what would a state like Israel do to protect its very existence?

Although nuclear weapons have made states more cautious by raising the provocation threshold over which states are willing to go to war, it is not clear that there is no provocation over which nuclear war would not be considered. Indeed, the United States made it clear that it would use nuclear weapons to combat a conventional Soviet attack in Western Europe. Likewise, Israeli nuclear doctrine has maintained that they would use nuclear weapons in extreme circumstances.

Second, there are logical and empirical problems with deterrence theory. One of the main problems is that just because there was no nuclear war in the Cold War does not mean that the presence of the nuclear deterrence doctrine prevented that war. There may have been a variety of other factors that accounted for the absence of war. It may have been just a coincidence. Of course, it may *not* have been, as well. The point is – we do not *know*. Nor is it going to be easy to find out. Given this logical problem how much are we ready to risk on an unsubstantiated theory?

Even if nuclear deterrence had an war-preventing effect in the Cold

War, it worked *with* several other factors that reduced the probability of war. These include the absence of territorial disputes, tolerance of the status quo, the raising of the provocation threshold by the experience of the two world wars (see Mueller 1989), the creation of rules of the game, crisis management (George et al. 1983), and arms control.[13] If several of these factors had been working against deterrence instead of with it, nuclear war may not have been avoided. The experiences of Berlin and Cuba suggest how fragile deterrence can be if just one of these factors is in question. Since war is probably a function of several factors, it is probably erroneous to think that a single factor, like power, could prevent it.

Empirically, statistical studies of extended deterrence has shown that non-nuclear states are not deterred from attacking those protected by nuclear states even when there is an overt threat to use nuclear weapons (Huth 1988: 428, 435; Organski and Kugler 1980: 163–169; Kugler 1984: 476–482). More importantly, it has been shown that often the local conventional balance plays more of a role in deterrence success than the presence of nuclear weapons (see Russett 1963; Huth and Russett 1984; Huth 1988: 435–438). An in-depth set of case studies of American nuclear deterrence by George and Smoke (1974) raises a host of other questions. They show that deterrence theory provided insufficient guidance, that basic prescriptions of deterrence theory were often ignored by US decision makers, and that some of the behavior states engage in during deterrent situations is unexpected (George and Smoke 1974: 130–131, 141–142, 162–172, 200–201, 216–222, 403–409, 421–424, 505, 507; see also Lebow, 1985; 203–204, 211; Garthoff 1987: 110). If deterrence theory cannot predict the actions of Americans, then how well would it do predicting the actions of Russian, Chinese, or Iranian leaders? Yet this is precisely the information that will be needed to make deterrence work in a nuclear crisis and avoid going over the brink.

Third, and most important, the danger with the Mearsheimer's (1993) and Waltz's (1981b, 1995) prescription on the salutary effect of the spread of nuclear weapons is that if it is wrong only once, the fate of the world hangs in the balance.[14] As the number of nuclear states

---

[13] For a full discussion of each and further elaboration of my view on nuclear deterrence, see Vasquez (1991). For a discussion of additional problems with deterrence see Kugler and Zagare (1990).

[14] For specific criticisms of Waltz's and Mearsheimer's positions on the spread of nuclear weapons, see respectively Sagan (1995) and Miller (1993).

grows, the probability for some miscalculation grows. The problem with the nuclear deterrence doctrine is that it has to work not only once or twice, but time after time, through a nuclear eternity. These do not seem like good odds, given the experience of human history.

At least, one would hope that the broader underlying theory on which such a policy was based has the best scientific evidence supporting it. In fact, just the opposite is the case, as chapter after chapter in this book has shown. It is not socially responsible for the field to give policy advice on such a theoretical foundation for questions that could involve the fate of much, if not most, of humanity.

Conclusion

This case study of neotraditional discourse on multipolarity offers some important lessons about the realist paradigm. First, it demonstrates that what has been regarded as one of the pre-eminent strengths of this paradigm – the utility of its practical theory for guiding policy and providing an understanding of the political world in which states operate – may in fact not be a strength at all. The theoretical views of Waltz about multipolarity when used by Mearsheimer to provide an analysis of the immediate post-Cold War era lead to empirical predictions that are not being upheld and to policy recommendations that run counter to common sense and prudence. The latter is particularly true for Waltz's (1995) and Mearsheimer's (1993) position on the sanguine effects of nuclear weapons and nuclear deterrence. Instead, nonrealist prescriptions, particularly those centered around conflict resolution and findings from peace research, offer policy recommendations that seem more relevant to the current historical period and provide a vision of the future that is less prone to self-fulfilling failure.

Second, quantitative tests have shown that much of the neorealist view of multipolarity as unstable and more prone to a breakdown is empirically inaccurate. Crises and war are not associated more with multipolar systems than bipolar systems. The empirical research shows that neither system is more associated with peace than the other. Rather it appears that multipolar systems are associated with large wars of the world war variety, while bipolar systems are associated with more frequent but limited wars. Polarization in terms of the number of alliance blocs has the opposite effect – polarization of the system into two blocs is associated with high magnitude wars, whereas many blocs or no blocs are associated with low magnitude wars.

Neorealists should have been more cautious about their theoretically deduced policy recommendations for the future in light of this evidence, but they were not. And the reason they were not is because they were oblivious of the evidence, because of their biased attitude toward quantitative work. Yet, the work is entirely consistent with what we know about the mulitpolar and bipolar periods of the twentieth century. Ignoring such research has made neorealists prone to give policy advice that appears empirically unsound. This is the third lesson that can be derived from this case study.

Fourth, the empirical unsoundness of neorealist advice must also, in part, reflect negatively on the realist paradigm as a whole, because the main variable used to understand the future focuses on shifts in the distribution of power. The field turns to the realist paradigm to tell it what is the most important theoretical fact that should be studied in international politics to understand the present and the future. From realist perspectives, this fact is always some power-related variable. Yet, the evidence shows repeatedly that power variables are not often as strongly correlated with the onset of war and peace as one would expect given the central focus of them in the paradigm. This is certainly the case with balancing, as was seen in the last chapter. It is also the case with multipolarity as was seen in this chapter. It is also the case with power transitions which by themselves do not provide a sufficient nor a necessary condition for war (see Kim 1992; Kim and Morrow 1992; Vasquez 1996c). This evidence which has been persistent since the mid-1960s should give realists and neorealists more pause.

Fifth, the pattern of ignoring data-based evidence coupled with an over-reliance on theoretical deduction to debunk alternatives to realism has been repeated in the recent debate over the promise of international institutions. Here, the empirical evidence is not as extensive and is more suggestive than definitive. Nevertheless, what evidence there is points to the conclusion that informal institutions centered around a consensus among major states on rules of the game, norms, and a derogation of unilateral acts are correlated with more peaceful periods among major states. Instead of trying to refute this evidence, or better still engaging in data-based research that would show why these correlations do not hold, Mearsheimer (1995: 93) asserts that "there is little evidence that they [institutions] can alter state behavior and cause peace." The reason he says this is that he, like too many neotraditionalists, is oblivious of the findings from peace research. Instead, he goes on to show why, theoretically, the arguments of liberal institutionalists do not hold. In effect, however, all that is really shown is that such liberal arguments are at variance with the paradigm's logic that assumes an inherent struggle for power and hence that actors will always be motivated by relative gains, not absolute gains. While this establishes one testable difference, it is neither a logical nor an empirical refutation of the liberal position.

Again, the nonrealist emphases within peace research seems much more relevant. At the most conservative end, nonrealists identify a path to peace within multipolarity (Kegely and Raymond 1994a, 1994b). At the more radical end, some nonrealists reject the very notion that multipolarity in and of itself is a variable of any great significance. Despite these differences, as well as disagreements over what kind of institutional arrangements or rules would have the most impact, there is agreement among nonrealists that institutions, rules, and norms can have an impact on major states' proneness to war against each other. This basic disagreement with neorealists sets up a future test between the two paradigms that can be used to appraise their relative empirical soundness and historical relevance.

As for the present, current peace research suggests that neorealism and the larger realist paradigm, which it articulates, is not proving to be much of a guide to the contemporary period. It focuses on theoretical facts (multipolarity) that are irrelevant. It makes predictions that are alarmist and obscures the fact that among major states we are more at peace now than at any other time since 1871. By denying the possibility of learning and the role of informal institutional norms for transcending power politics, it misses rare opportunities within history and encourages self-defeating behavior. It lacks a vision of the future, because it sees the immediate past as typical of all the past. It does not understand that peace is possible and has actually occurred in the past among major states.

It is not surprising given the paradigm's world view that various realist theories should have difficulty understanding peace, and therefore should have difficulty understanding our current period. The failings of realism to anticipate change is most dramatically seen in the fact that it was caught unawares about the end of the Cold War – the subject of the next chapter. In addition, the way in which the

Cold War ended and the reaction of the United States to Russia once the Cold War was over pose fundamental anomalies that the paradigm, despite some valiant efforts, cannot explain away as Mearsheimer (1994/95: 46) believes it can. Instead, this literature again provides clues that a paradigm shift would prove more fruitful and more accurate in explaining world politics.

13 Challenging the relevance and explanatory power of the realist paradigm: the debate on the end of the Cold War

The ending of the Cold War is the most dramatic historical event of recent times, and the realist paradigm has failed both to explain and to anticipate it. This is important because in the social sciences such failures have had major psychological impacts on thinking (see p. 73 above). Logically, a single dramatic historical event is only one case, but psychologically, for a discipline that lacks scientific rigor, it is nevertheless unsettling. It raises serious questions about whether the paradigm (and its theoretical variants) are an adequate guide to the world, either intellectually or in terms of policy (see Kratochwil 1993). Such a failure presents dramatic evidence that the paradigm's understanding about the world may be fundamentally wrong. What history is revealing is not simply an incompleteness or lapse, but a piece of evidence so clear and so bald in its contradiction of theory that it cannot be ignored. This naturally makes one wonder whether there may be other historical events of significance that are being ignored or obfuscated by the paradigm.

These are serious concerns for any paradigm, on two grounds. First, if, in fact, a paradigm has failed to anticipate or explain a major historical event, then in what sense is the knowledge it is providing of any great relevance? The failure of scholars guided by realism to anticipate the ending of the Cold War, and particularly the manner in which it would end, speaks volumes about the ability of the paradigm to help understand change. It confirms Ruggie's (1983) charge that one of the theoretical defects of neorealism is its underappreciation of change and its inability to explain it.

Second, the failure to anticipate and explain the end of the Cold War raises questions about the explanatory power of the realist paradigm. The ending of the Cold War did not only catch neorealists offguard, but also the many foreign policy pundits and hard-line Soviet experts who used variants of classical Morgenthauian realism to explain contemporary international affairs. The realist paradigm in this last capacity had always seemed from 1939 until 1989 to score high on the criterion of explanatory power. It had seemed to offer the West a variety of policy options and an intellectual template for understanding the world in which foreign policy actions had to be taken. Indeed, in many ways one could argue that it was this capacity (power) of the paradigm to give plausible explanations of (relevant) historical events that made the paradigm live on despite its failings on other criteria, such as accuracy and falsifiability. If the two pillars on which the paradigm had always rested are now to be called into question, then that would be serious, especially since other paradigms in the past, specifically idealism, had been scuppered because of their failure to anticipate and explain pivotal events.

This chapter will apply the two criteria on which the realist paradigm has traditionally scored the highest – explanatory power and relevance. These are criteria that have been rarely applied to realism in a critical manner. The *criterion of explanatory power* applies to the empirical component of theories. It maintains that theories should be able to offer psychologically plausible explanations of specific events – past, present, and future. By using the general concepts, frame, and propositions of a theory, it should be possible to give an account of why (and often how) the particular occurs. As Morgenthau (1960: 5) says of realism, it:

> allows us to retrace and anticipate, as it were, the steps a statesman – past, present, or future – has taken or will take on the political scene.

Indeed, one of the virtues of the realist concepts of interest and power is that one is able to put oneself into these frames and one is able to "come up with" (but rarely logically deduce) an account of what is, has, or might occur. Marxism, as evinced by Marx's writings on specific historical events, like the 18th Brumaire of Louis Bonaparte, the civil war in France, and the US civil war, has a similar capacity.

The explanatory power of empirical theory determines whether it is a good candidate for becoming a practical theory. Practical theory seeks to guide the practice of foreign policy and international relations. As with empirical theory, it has its own criteria that can be applied to appraise the extent to which it is satisfying its purpose. A key criterion that is employed in appraising practical theory is the *criterion of relevance* (see chapter 10 above). This criterion maintains that the best or most useful practical theory is not one that simply is able to explain events and offer policy guidance, but one that is able to provide guidance on the most difficult and pressing historical events of the day. A good practical theory should be able to unearth and *resolve* the policy dilemmas facing political actors. A good practical theory should speak to the major condition of the day in which political actors find themselves, and it should not only speak to that condition, but in some vein empower them to deal with that condition in a manner that accentuates their particular goals, while making them aware of the perils and pitfalls of human error, both those of intellectual understanding and of implementation. In other words, a practical theory must be *relevant* to the major issues (or key historical forces) of the time.

It was on such grounds that E. H. Carr (1939) and then Morgenthau (1948) were able to argue that realism was superior to Wilsonian utopianism or idealism. Realism was able to anticipate and uncover Hitler's real motives and recommend a good foreign policy to deal with this threat; idealism failed on all three bases. Realists (like Morgenthau 1948, Niehbur 1953, and Kennan 1951) likewise took great pride in providing a frame and advice for how the West should deal with the Soviet Union and the Cold War that emerged at the end of World War II.

It comes as somewhat of surprise, therefore, that realists failed to anticipate the end of the Cold War, were among the last to believe that it was really ending, and were unable to explain what was happening while it was happening. This failing has spilled over to a general questioning of whether the paradigm will be as useful for the future as it was for the past. If the historical factors that helped bring an end to the Cold War were unanticipated and not correctly identified by realists, can we have any confidence that adherents to the paradigm will understand any better the factors that are shaping the new era into which we are moving? More specifically, can a paradigm that has focused so much on conflict, violence, and zero sum games be of much relevance for problems of cooperation, peace, conflict resolution and the creation of positive sum games?

This perceived failing has also raised questions about whether there are other events the paradigm has hidden. As the Cold War came to an end and the idea of a democratic peace caught the imagination of scholars, many began to point out that one of the great successes of the immediate past – the building of a permanent peace in Western Europe after centuries of internecine warfare (see Kegley 1993) – had been ignored by the realist paradigm. Its theoretical and historical signifi-cance had been obfuscated by the paradigm. All of a sudden, it appeared that the nonrealist integrationists like Deutsch et al. (1957), Mitrany (1943) and Haas (1958a) were much more on the mark than any realist theory would have anticipated. Indeed, some still believe that with the absence of an external Soviet threat that the peace of Western Europe will fall apart (see Mearsheimer 1990a: 46–48).

The next section, the heart of the chapter, will look at whether realist theory failed to anticipate the ending of the Cold War and appraise the various attempts by defenders of realism to explain why and how the Cold War ended. This will be seen as the major policy anomaly associated with the Cold War. The third section will outline a nonrealist explanation of the ending of Cold war, pointing out what specific factors (or variable clusters) the realist paradigm has consistently underestimated. The fourth section will examine the second policy anomaly posed by the end of the Cold War for the realist paradigm – the new grand strategy adopted by the United States toward the USSR once it was clear the Cold War was ending. Next, the inadequacies of a liberal explanation, although less egregious, will be highlighted. The concluding section will briefly review the evidence presented in the chapter to appraise the realist paradigm's satisfaction of the criteria of explanatory power and relevance for the historical era that has just ended and for the transition to the new one we are entering.

The *major* policy anomaly

It is generally agreed that a failure of realism to explain the end of the Cold War would reveal a serious theoretical defect. Realists do not say that explaining the end of the Cold War is unimportant or would not be a failing of realism; rather they insist that it can be explained using realist concepts (see Mearsheimer 1994/95: 46). They recognize that an inability to explain an event, even though it is a single case, would have tremendous repercussions. Wohlforth (1994/95: 96), a defender of classical realism, avers that such a failing would damage the policy utility of the paradigm: "If realism can be shown to have nothing to say about the Cold War's end, its relevance to the postwar world can be called into doubt."

Initially, some realists, like Waltz, and others like Keohane, took a strict logical position, that a theory need not be considered very defective for failing to explain a single data point.[1] That position, although having logical merit, obviously grants too much to critics. Since then other realists have been busy trying to reconstruct explanations for what was unanticipated. Before turning to these explanations, it must first be asked how damaging it is that realism failed to anticipate the ending of the Cold War.

John Lewis Gaddis (1992/93) indicts the entire profession of international relations for this failure, saying that it must indicate something fundamentally wrong with the way in which we study the subject. Gaddis, however, is a little too widespread in his blame. He is intent on laying much of the responsibility on scientifically-oriented international relations specialists, when it is not clear that they are the ones who should have first sounded the alarm bells. It seems much more reasonable that Soviet experts and specialists in US–Soviet relations who were closest to the actual events should have been the first to see what was going on. Yet they did not.

In addition, he has a tendency to single out those who employ the scientific method for special castigation when they were not any less successful than those who used traditional methods. Logically, it is theories, not methods, that make predictions about the real world; it is to the dominant theoretical frame of the field that one should turn as a possible source for the failure. One indicator of the theoretical source of this failure is that it seems the more anti-communist the experts, the less likely they were to believe Gorbachev's actions indicated a profound change in relations that might lead to an end of the Cold War. While ideology probably played the major role in blind-siding these experts, the general realist approach upon which these experts often relied to make policy predictions also played a role.[2] The reason why experts in the fields of Soviet studies, of international relations, and American foreign policy may have all failed to predict the end of the Cold War is that they shared the dominant realist approach to international politics.

---

[1] Kratochwil (1993: 66, note 13) attributes this position to Kenneth Waltz, Stephen Walt, and Robert Keohane. Lebow's (1994: 251–252) attributions simply refer to a prominent participant at a conference on the end of the Cold War held at Cornell in October 1991.

[2] See Deudney and Ikenberry (1991: 226–228) for a general discussion of pertinent realist views; see Luttwak (1982) for an example of a realist analysis of Soviet foreign policy.

The failure to anticipate is a serious lapse because it appears that the theoretical frame these scholars employed highlighted certain features of the US–Soviet relationship while hiding others. Both the ideology of anti-communism and the more "objective" realism tended to emphasize the possibilities of conflict, the struggle for power, the inherent conflict of interest (zero sum games and later relative gains), and the risks of appeasement. The possibilities for cooperation, for transcending the Cold War, for the creation of new games, and for escaping the security dilemma were denied or obfuscated. What is significant from the point of view of this appraisal is that *these perceptual failings are precisely those that would have been expected of realism* – particularly the classical realism of Morgenthau discussed in Part I of this book.

As these nonrealist concerns and strategies motivated Gorbachev's new thinking and foreign policy, it was difficult for adherents to the realist paradigm to see and believe that these things were happening. Such actions, like the taking of unilateral initiatives, had long been recommended by nonrealist critics, especially those adopting a social psychological approach, as actions the United States should take (see Osgood 1959; Burton 1982). Realists had opposed such initiatives as unrealistic and naive, so it was difficult to see that the enemy would ever indulge in them. According to their understanding of the world, states engaged in a struggle for power do not engage in such shifts in foreign policy unless it is a trick.[3]

This failure to anticipate poses a serious anomaly for the paradigm because it underlines a theoretical failing in the picture of the world the paradigm is painting. This realist picture made it difficult even to see the new world that was emerging, let alone anticipate it. Thus, while others, like those engaged in statistical analyses or the study of wars in the post-Napoleonic period, might be excused for not paying attention to current policy, no such excuse could be used for Soviet and American foreign policy experts who were using realism as the main theoretical frame to interpret the superpower relationship. The argument here is that it cannot be assumed that the use of realism as a frame and the failure to anticipate is an accident; rather the two seem

---

[3] Among those exemplifying these views and hence distrustful of Gorbachev as late as the Bush administration was Robert Gates, at the time deputy to Brent Scowcroft. Also skeptical were John Sununu, Dan Quayle, and even at times Scowcroft; see Beschloss and Talbott (1993: 47, 72–73, 99, 122, 124). See Gorbachev (1996: 293, 402–403) on his use of these cooperative techniques.

connected, because the paradigm would by its very nature tend to obfuscate the kinds of actions Gorbachev was taking. This is the most damaging explanation that can be made of the failure to anticipate. Even without it, however, there is no doubt that none of the well-known realist variants expected the Cold War to end the way it did.[4]

Conversely, while nonrealist explanations did not forecast the end of the Cold War, they were able to see that Gorbachev's policy would serve as a basis for bringing it to an end, if the United States would respond positively. Their view of world politics was such that for them Gorbachev was for real; it was not a trick. This could be an authentic turning point in history. Indeed, many of the nonrealist explanations that the Cold War was fueled by mirror images, irrational hostility that leads sides to take unwarranted nuclear risks, and the organizational interests of military-industrial complexes in each side suggested that once the conflict was stripped of its ideological fervor, there would be few external reasons (from a strict cost–benefit analysis) to keep the conflict going (see Bronfenbrenner 1961; Rapoport 1964; Rosen 1973; Jervis 1976; Mansbach and Vasquez 1981). While these explanations did not specifically predict Gorbachev's actions, their theory of what fueled the Cold War made them think that given the right political will the actions that were being initiated would create a process that could build peace without coercion. Where they, like Gorbachev, went wrong was in their not anticipating how quickly and easily things could unravel for the Soviet Union, but then neither did the realists see this. All in all, while no explanation forecasted the end of the Cold War, certain nonrealist explanations were caught less unaware than realist explanations, especially hard-line realist explanations. More importantly, certain nonrealist explanations seem to provide more adequate models of why and how it was politically possible for the kind of unilateral cooperative policies taken up by Gorbachev to be adopted by a superpower and to work.

The failure to anticipate the end of the Cold War raises a second point against the realist paradigm; namely, that all subsequent explanations are ex post facto. This is a fairly serious charge because it is so familiar. The great virtue of realism is that it can explain almost any

---

[4] One of the few who actually predicted the collapse of the Soviet Union as early as 1980 was Randall Collins (see Collins and Waller 1992, cited and discussed in Ray and Russett 1996: 462, note 82). They note, however, that Collins also predicted an all-out war between the two rival empires. See also the discussion of Collins in Hopf (1993: 204–205) and in Wohlforth (1994/95: 102).

foreign policy event. Its great defect is that it tends to do this after the fact, rather than before. While such a defect is not always clear because of the myriad of events and the tendency of realist policy advocates to give contradictory advice and/or predictions before the fact, the case of the ending of the Cold War is a documentation of an ex post facto explanation that will stand for all time.

What this means is that even if Gorbachev's actions "can very well be explained by realism" (Mearsheimer 1994/95: 46), it is still after the fact. From a philosophy of science perspective this is a definite weakness. This puts realism in a situation where it must, as has been seen time and again in this book, explain why its theory did not work better.

Ultimately, however, the case must rest in how well realist defenders are able to explain things away. As with neotraditional work on the balancing of power, the intellectual history of realist accounting for the end of the Cold War provides important insights about the dynamics and "logic" of international relations discourse. The set of individual attempts to explain the end of the Cold War using realist concepts provides another case study of its "proteanshifts" (see ch. 11 above). Even more damaging for the paradigm is that all of these ex post facto explanations appear to be less plausible than a nonrealist explanation that centers on leadership changes, domestic politics, and beliefs rather than on power and external coercion.

Ex post facto analysis

Part of the debate over realism and the Cold War centers on which of the many allegedly realist explanations is the authentic realist explanation upon which realist theory and its paradigm should stand or fall. The authentic explanation is the one that is properly derived from the logic of the theory. If several explanations can be derived, this suggests that the theory's predictions are indeterminate, and this is a flaw. If explanations are derived that are contradictory, this raises the question of non-falsifiability and of degenerating proteanshifts. The great risk of ex post facto analysis is that instead of specifying the explanation most consistent with the logic of the theory, explanations will be derived that conform with the known facts.

This danger is particularly evident in the most powerful and popular realist explanation – that the Cold War ended because of a decline in Soviet power. The typical realist explanation of why the

Cold War ended is that the Soviet Union was reacting to its declining economic and military position. This is the explanation Waltz (1990) derives from his theory as the events are unfolding. He stated in a 1990 US Institute of Peace article that the changes taking place in the Soviet Union stemmed "in good part from external causes" and "as the capabilities of the Soviet Union waned, its external behavior dramatically changed" (Waltz 1990: 6–7; cited in Evangelista 1993: 157; see also Waltz 1993: 50).

Similarly, Oye (1995: 58) suggests that a state in economic decline will naturally seek to reverse or halt this trend through a retrenchment in its external commitments, but he couches his explanation within Gilpin's (1981) more broad-ranging analysis. Oye's explanation has attracted a great deal of attention because it is one of the more "realist" in Lebow and Risse-Kappen (1995), which focuses on the ability of international relations theory to account for the end of the Cold War. Nevertheless, despite the emphasis on Gilpin, it must be noted that Oye brings in nonrealist variables, like the role of ideas, and attempts to give a full-textured account of how the Cold War ended and not just a realist explanation of it. Our concern here is on how well the realist aspect of Oye's account, specifically the use of Gilpin's idea of relative decline, explains the end of the Cold War. Wohlforth (1994/95) also takes a realist stance, but emphasizes Soviet *perceptions* of declining power, rather than actual decline as the source of accommodation.

Theoretically, such explanations of foreign policy reversal are logically consistent with what one would expect of both neorealism's emphasis on structure as well as classical realism's emphasis on the distribution of power (see Deudney and Ikenberry 1991: 226–230; 1991/92: 77, 79). It seems to make sense that a state in decline would try to respond to that decline by adjusting its foreign policy (see Friedberg 1988). There are, however, several problems with this explanation of the end of the Cold War.

First, and of no small matter, is that before the fact the opposite was asserted. As Deudney and Ikenberry (1991/92: 81) point out, prior to Gorbachev it was expected that any crisis of decline would spark external aggressiveness not retrenchment, and certainly not accommodation. The former prediction was made theoretically in general and specifically vis-à-vis the Soviet Union. Just before the 1985 rise of Gorbachev, Edward Luttwak (1982) predicted that internal economic pressures would make the Soviet Union more likely to be aggressive against its neighbors, especially in Asia. For hard-line anti-communist realists, the image of the West as an imperial enemy was a core part of the communist belief system and could not be changed internally (Pipes 1984: 41–42).[5] This view was part of the general belief among US conservative academics that the USSR was incapable of internal reform and that the United States must remain vigilant because the internal source of aggression would always be present (see for example, Jeane Kirkpatrick's [1979] essay).

Theoretically, the view that economic crises at home might lead to external aggressiveness rather than retrenchment is the hallmark of the diversionary theory of war (see Levy 1989b). The view that a decline in military power would lead to external aggressiveness is basically the realist theory of preventive war (see Levy 1987; and also Schwaller 1992).[6] Evangelista (1993: 159–160) points out that Waltz (1981a) himself explained on the basis of his theoretical understanding of international politics that relative economic and military weakness made a Soviet military build-up and expansion perfectly understandable. Thus, on theoretical grounds there is a sound basis for a realist prediction that decline in a major state might lead to increased armament and conflict, not retrenchment.

The key, however, is that this prediction was the "widespread expectation in the West" prior to Gorbachev's changes (Deudney and Ikenberry 1991/92: 81). Since this is clearly the case, it should be concluded that the ex ante specification of realism is the authentically derived realist explanation. If this is accurate, and I believe it is, two conclusions seem to follow. First, the way in which the Cold War ended was theoretically unexpected by realist theory, because it should see a relative decline in power as the basis for an increase in conflict and not an ending of the Cold War through accommodation.

---

[5] Both the Luttwak and Pipes examples are taken directly from Deudney and Ikenberry (1991/92: 81, note 20), who summarize and quote each. Wohlforth (1994/95: 103) also states that the few analysts who did think about Soviet decline "tended to assume that Moscow would not face decline gracefully" (i.e., they would be aggressive). He gives the example of Amalrik (1970), who saw the USSR collapsing because of a diversionary war with China (Wohlforth 1994/95: 102, note 24).

[6] Wohlforth objects to the application of this theory to explain Soviet behavior because he says that the USSR was not a hegemon in decline, but a challenger in decline. While this description is historically accurate, there is no reason to predict within the logic of preventive war theory that a challenger might not become more aggressive as a way of stemming its decline, particularly, as in the case with the Soviet Union, where decline is seen primarily in terms of perceptions and prestige. The main point that undercuts Wohlforth's argument, however, is that no realist said that Soviet decline would lead to the kind of accommodation that occurred.

Second, the actual ex post facto explanation of how and why the Cold War ended is really an attempt to change the prediction of the theory in order to fit the subsequent evidence; thereby constituting a move to dismiss falsifying evidence and escape a "real world" test that would be psychologically damaging.

The problem of timing

Another major problem with the decline in power explanation is that it fails to explain why it was precisely at this time that the Soviet Union chose to reverse its policy. Moments of decline had occurred before, why no reversal in foreign policy then? The problem of timing is best exemplified by the fact that the steepest economic decline prior to the end of the Cold War occurred under Brezhnev. As Evangelista (1993: 158–159) documents, the biggest drop in the percentage increase in GNP in the Soviet Union occurred in the early 1970s during the shift from the 1966–1970 period to the 1971–1975 period. The decline after 1975 and until Gorbachev came to power was "less dramatic" (Evangelista 1993: 159). Yet, Brezhnev is not noted for retrenchment as might be predicted by the ex post facto explanation, but as having a policy of building up the military and becoming involved in Afghanistan in 1979.[7] Even if one wants to argue that Brezhnev was an exception to the general decline-retrenchment proposition, this still does not explain why his successors – Andropov and Chernenko – did not move in the direction that Gorbachev did (Stein 1994: 158). If the external situation is as important as structural realism says it is and the power balance as critical as classical realism says it is, then these three other leaders and the entourage around them should have retrenched. They did not.

Since the external power situation was constant from roughly 1975 through 1989, the foreign policy of the Soviet Union should have been comparatively stable and not radically transformed the way it was under Gorbachev. In this sense, Brezhnev and the leaders who followed him, until Gorbachev, were unaffected by the structural factors or the international environment. Therefore, it is not the international environment that brought about the end of the Cold War. To explain that fundamental shift seems to require, logically, the

[7] Note, I do not say, nor believe, that either of these two policies was caused by Soviet "decline."

identification of some other variables. Even Oye (1995: 78), admits that it is the individual variable (of Gorbachev) that is critical and that the international environment did not make these changes inevitable.

It seems that decline in and of itself does not produce a foreign policy shift. What is needed is a change in the foreign policy leadership that produces what Hagan (1994: 146) would call a shift in the orientation of the regime, particularly its ideological orientation (see also Hagan 1993). This tends to happen only when a new party or faction takes over, which is precisely what occurs with Gorbachev's rise. Not only does he reflect an openness and commitment to new ideas, but he eventually brings in with him a new group of individuals who do not share the old way of thinking (see Gorbachev 1996: 180–181, 402).

Another way of illustrating the deficiency of the decline-retrenchment proposition is to show that decline had occurred in the United States, but the Cold War never came close to ending. For instance, it was widely thought that the US was in decline, after the 1973 Arab oil embargo. Indeed, at this time, debate was focused on United States decline; the USSR was not seen as being in any kind of similar situation (Wohlforth 1994/95: 103). Yet, the United States did not end the Cold War. If decline is such a potent variable and had this impact on the USSR in the late 1980s, why did it not have a similar impact on the United States in the early 1970s? Some might say that the Soviet decline was sharper, but US leaders and the public seemed more shocked about the oil embargo than Soviet leaders did about their economic troubles.

True, some have seen Nixon and Kissinger's détente as an effort to deal with relative decline. Some Soviets interpreted détente in this manner and recently some US political scientists have interpreted Carter's foreign policy as adjustment to (economic) hegemonic decline (Skidmore 1996). Yet, Reagan and the hard-liners around him sought to reverse both Carter's policy and the earlier Republican policy of détente. If decline is as important a determinant as is implied, how come this happened? Why did basically the same economic and military position occupied by the United States from 1972 to 1980, lead both to détente and then to Reagan's aggressive foreign policy? Decline of the United States should have had a continuing retrenchment effect, but instead gave rise to Reagan and Cold War II. Again, it seems some domestic political variables must be added to get an accurate explanation of foreign policy shifts.

The magnitude of retrenchment and decline

A third problem with the realist explanation is that what Gorbachev did hardly seems like a retrenchment. Within Gilpin's logic, it makes sense that as the (economic) costs of a specific (foreign) policy increase, a state might retrench, but as Lebow (1994: 262; reprinted in Lebow and Risse-Kappen 1995: ch. 2) rightly contends, what happened under Gorbachev can hardly be characterized as changing peripheral commitments or as retrenchment. This is the main problem with Oye's (1995: 58, 66–68, 72) "prudential realist" argument that economic decline brought about the need for a retrenchment by "shedding peripheral commitments" (see Oye 1995: 58, 66–68, 72; Wohlforth 1994/95: 96–100). Gorbachev could have resurrected and then simply extended, in incremental fashion, Brezhnev's détente policy. Likewise, he could have cut back aid to client states in Eastern Europe without undercutting the very foundation of the communist regimes and without abandoning the Brezhnev doctrine on intervention. What Gorbachev did was way beyond retrenchment. There had been important shifts in Soviet policy before – at Stalin's death, under Khrushchev and even under Brezhnev – but not anything of this magnitude and scope.

Furthermore, no retrenchment of this magnitude would have been predicted beforehand. As Lebow (1994: 264) points out, it is inconceivable that any realist scholar who took Gilpin's general proposition on retrenchment as a guide would have predicted any of the major changes Gorbachev undertook. The explanation of prudential realism, as Oye (1995: 58) terms it, would have more credence if someone had made this prediction about the USSR, but, as shown above, realists were making the opposite prediction. Indeed, "readjustment" was what was being advocated for the United States (Kennedy 1987: 514–535) and not something that was expected from the Soviet Union (see also Nye 1990: 1–22).[8]

Gorbachev was not engaging in retrenchment, but a sea change in

---

[8] Paul Kennedy (1987: 534), for example, stated: "The task facing American statesmen over the next decades, therefore, is to recognize . . . that there is a need to 'manage' affairs so that the *relative* erosion of the United States' position takes place slowly and smoothly, and is not accelerated by policies which bring merely short-term advantage . . ." (emphasis in original). For a realist who sees the United States in a pattern of long-term relative economic decline since the end of World War II, see Mastanduno (1997: 75).

the foreign policy of the Soviet Union intended to end the Cold War. The shift in Soviet foreign policy is simply too radical for the logic of realist theory. To understand the end of the Cold War, one must understand that what was responsible for the shift was a change in the foreign policy beliefs of the Soviet leadership and that this belief system was not preordained by the external power situation that had been relatively constant since 1975.

If the above analysis suggests that the change in the dependent variable (retrenchment) is too great to be explained by the independent variable (relative decline), the fourth criticism of the decline hypothesis that is often made is that the decline was not that severe and certainly not anything to warrant what happened. Here, it is important to distinguish military capability from economic capability. In terms of military capability, even if there had been changes in Soviet conventional forces, the ability of the Soviet nuclear arsenal to destroy the West several times over should not, according to Waltz (1993: 52) and Mearsheimer (1994/95: 46), have affected overall military parity (see Deudney and Ikenberry 1991/92: 90–91).

If we are to take realist theory seriously, then according to it, as well as to the logic of nuclear deterrence, there was *no decline* in Soviet military power. And this of course makes sense; even during the collapse of the Soviet economy under Yeltsin, Russia remained the only state able to utterly destroy the United States and any other nation it might seek to target. It should be very clear that decline did not mean that the Soviet Union need fear for its survival or "national security" (Waltz 1993: 51–52; see also Chernoff 1991). To the extent nuclear weapons brought about the revolution in world politics that Brodie (1945), Herz (1959), Jervis (1989) thought they did, the Soviet Union was just as powerful under Gorbachev as it was under Khrushchev in 1957, and probably much more powerful because its delivery system was better.[9]

A key element in Soviet new thinking on nuclear weapons was that the logic of second strike would permit the saving of a considerable amount of money without any effect on mutual assured destruction. These savings could then be transferred from the defense sector to the

---

[9] Wohlforth (1995) in his reply to Lebow and Mueller (1995) seems to minimize the implications of the impact of nuclear weapons in assessing Soviet power. Certainly, the USSR was much more powerful after Sputnik than before, and more powerful relative to the West after Brezhnev's extensive build-up and deployment of missiles than in 1962.

civilian economy. This basic idea is not that different from what Democrats in the United States had been saying for years in their complaints about "overkill." This led Gorbachev to embrace the idea of "reasonable sufficiency" in the level of Soviet arms that would give it "sufficient defense," which was a shift away from Brezhnev's idea of "equal security," which required the USSR to match the capability of its combined enemies (Oberdorfer 1991: 141, 231). Eventually, this train of thought gave rise to the idea of minimal deterrence – that the USSR could abandon competing with the United States in terms of absolute numbers of different types of nuclear weapons and have a small nuclear arsenal capable of destroying enough US cities so as to deter the United States from a first strike, something not unlike the French idea of deterrence (see Malashenko 1994: 97; Rogov 1994: 121–122; see also Shevardnadze 1991: 95). The latter idea, although never officially implemented, is an indicator of the depths to which some were prepared to cut the military budget. From the perspective of this analysis, what is important about Soviet new thinking and Gorbachev's policies is that they were not motivated by a sense of insecurity due to a decline in power. They bet they could cut costs without any substantial reduction in security benefits.[10]

Motivation is an important issue because, as Wohlforth (1994/95: 95) recognizes, one way of evaluating a theory is to see what causal mechanism or process brings about the postulated effect of the independent variable. For Gilpin's (1981) neorealism as interpreted by Oye (1995), relative decline should produce *insecurity* which would produce retrenchment as a way of recovering power. For classical realism, relative decline should produce a threat to the survival of a state or, at minimum, a threat to its ranking in the power hierarchy. Neither of these motivations seems to have been at work within Gorbachev's circle.

Empirically, there is not much in the existing historical record to indicate that Gorbachev was focusing, in a clear and concentrated manner, on relative decline in terms of fearing for the security of the Soviet Union. The two major American journalistic treatments of this period – Oberdorfer (1991) and Beschloss and Talbott (1993) – do not give this impression. April Carter (1995: 30) maintains that Gorbachev

---

[10] Malashenko (1994: 95), for example, goes so far as to say that Soviet withdrawal from Eastern Europe, Afghanistan, and Mongolia will not affect Soviet ability to deal with a direct attack on its territory because of Soviet nuclear capability.

certainly did not see himself as capitulating to superior strength.[11] If this is the case, then the causal connection between decline and retrenchment simply never occurred. Yet despite the importance of this point, those who advocate the relative decline-retrenchment explanation provide little documentation on Gorbachev's motivation and concentration on questions of relative capability. When Gorbachev did compare the USSR negatively with the United States it was often in terms of the failure of the Soviet system to provide the kinds of non-defense goods (cars and tractors) available in the West (see Gorbachev 1996: 216, for example).

Nor is it clear that the Reagan build-up somehow overwhelmed the USSR with US military superiority. In terms of absolute Soviet military capabilities, Evangelista (1993: 158) shows there was no change (see also Bell 1989: chs. 2 and 4, whom he cites). The major changes in Soviet military and economic capability occurred only after Gorbachev initiated his policies. Wohlforth (1994/95: 127) recognizes that the actual measures of power do not indicate any relative decline: "Critics of realism are right that capabilities, as they are usually measured by political scientists, have little to do with what happened in world politics after 1987." He says outright that there has been a "predictive failure of realist theories" due to the difficulty of assessing power (Wohlforth 1994/95: 105).

This evidence also undercuts the claim of some hard-liners in the Reagan administration that the Cold War ended because the United States was able to push Soviet military spending to the point where it would bankrupt its economy, at least in terms of the US build-up in the 1980s. Chernoff (1991: 118–120) shows that the Soviet Union simply did not respond to the Reagan build-up with an increase in its own military spending. Although the *growth* in US military spending goes up dramatically from 1980 through 1983 and up again in 1985, *growth* in Soviet military spending is constant, despite clear changes in Soviet GNP (see his figure 1). He finds the relationship between the

---

[11] When Gorbachev (1996: 216–218) talks about decline, he does so to emphasize the need for perestroika while simultaneously exuding confidence about the nation's potential to grow and eliminate the gap, if not surpass the West.

Gorbachev explicitly denied to George Shultz in their meeting in Moscow before the Geneva summit that the Soviet Union was economically weaker than the United States and could not compete with the United States in weapons development (Oberdorfer 1991: 135). While some might try to psychologically explain away such a statement, it must be noted that many in the United States, including Brent Scowcroft, did not see the USSR as weak either (Beschloss and Talbott 1993: 12–13, 24).

spending changes in the two states statistically insignificant, even when using a two-year time lag (Chernoff 1991: 119). Likewise, he finds no statistically significant relationship between Soviet GNP growth and military growth (Chernoff 1991: 120). Similarly, Oye (1995: 69) using CIA statistics shows that Soviet military spending was flat from 1978 to 1987. Therefore, the alleged strategy of some Reagan hard-liners never had an impact on the Soviet economy (see also Carter, 1995: 26). Of course, one could argue that the mere prospect of such competition led to Soviet attempts to end the Cold War. This seems a little farfetched because it requires that leaders incur immediate and certain costs in order to prevent future and uncertain losses.[12]

For Wohlforth (1994/95: 108–109; 1993), what matters is not power but perceptions of power. Nevertheless, the argument on the effect of nuclear weapons makes it clear that there could not be, and indeed was not, any perception of military vulnerability. There was no need to give in on Eastern Europe, a united Germany, or the Warsaw Pact because of the perception of decline of relative power. Much more incremental decisions could have been taken (see Rush 1993, cited in Lebow and Mueller 1995: 185). The strategy of accommodation that produced these consequences was not compelled by relative decline. These were consequences of freely made choices that went awry.[13]

The manner in which an analysis of perceptions of power can get one into trouble is illustrated by Wohlforth's (1994/95: 124) argument that "Once Soviet power began to decline . . . it should have been evident that . . . no hegemonic war was in the offing . . . the system

[12] This does not mean that the long-term Soviet emphasis on defense did not have negative economic consequences, some of which may have been severe (see Chernoff 1991). Nevertheless, many reformers did not see these economic problems stemming primarily from the arms competition with the West. Gladkov (1994: 198) states clearly that the Cold War and Soviet military spending did not create the USSR's economic problems; these were the product of central planning, maldistribution, etc. For him, the Cold War effort "made poor economic performance even worse" (see Gorbachev 1996: 179 for a similar view). The reformers' main purpose was to change domestic policy, including economic policy, and to do that they had to confront defense policy. They were not trying to change foreign policy because they were outwitted by a form of "economic warfare" ingeniously implemented by hard-liners in the Reagan administration.

[13] Dobrynin (1995: 636), for example, argues that in the late 1980s the "balance of power" between the USSR and the West was "widely recognized" and could have been the basis of a long-lasting equal cooperation, but instead Gorbachev and his supporters "gave away vital geopolitical and military positions . . ."

was at least temporarily primed for peace." What is ironic about this statement is that most scholars feel the real turning point occurs much earlier, with the 1962 Cuban missile crisis. After this look into the abyss, Kennedy and Khrushchev take initiatives to deal with the danger of nuclear war. It is in 1962 that the Cold War thaws and starts to be primed for peace, and this occurs in a period of rising Soviet capability, not decline, as Wohlforth's logic would lead us to expect. Conversely, Reagan's perception of relative US decline in military capability leads, not to a continuation of détente, but an aggressive Cold War II. It appears that perceptions of power can lead to contradictory policies under different leaders, which implies that it is the leaders' policy preferences and not their perception of power that is crucial.

In terms of economic capability, the situation is a little different. Here Wohlforth (1994/95: 110) is correct that a change in perceptions and specifically a change in the indicators of economic performance from steel and energy production to catching up with the ongoing scientific-technological revolution made Gorbachev and others want to reform the economy more drastically (see for example, Gorbachev 1996: 467). The rapid rise of Japan's GNP and later that of China also pointed out the need to do something about the Soviet economy (Oberdorfer 1991: 215). But it is probably not the case, as it would need to be for the decline-retrenchment to be true, that foreign policy concerns were motivating Gorbachev's economic proposals. From the perspective of the realist explanation, one gets the impression that perestrokia and glasnost were driven by the external situation, when in fact the opposite is the case.[14] Perestrokia and the commitment to reform is what drove Gorbachev to engage in a number of foreign policy acts that produced an end to the Cold War and the bipolar alignment in Europe, a point that will be elaborated in the next section.

The role of domestic politics

The last and one of the most convincing criticisms of realist explanations is made by Evangelista (1993). He maintains that if relative decline was so drastic and so clear, it should have created a consensus

---

[14] There seems to be an emerging consensus on this point; see Stein (1994: 161) and Deudney and Ikenberry (1991: 244; 1991/92: 80).

among Soviet leaders as to what was the rational foreign policy to follow. Instead, disagreement between hard-liners and moderates emerged (see also Stein 1994: 159–160). Furthermore, this disagreement reflected a split between those who followed a more orthodox Marxist–Leninist approach and the new thinkers who wanted to "de-ideologize" foreign policy (see Malensheko 1994: 91, 94–97; Rogov 1994: 120; Gladkov 1994: 199). Soviet foreign policy was determined not by the external environment, but by the outcome of an internal struggle.[15] Domestic politics becomes a critical variable, something which is clearly not easily accommodated by either Waltz's structural realism or the application of Gilpin's decline-retrenchment hypothesis to the end of the Cold War.

Wohlforth (1994/95: 96, 101–102, 126–127) accepts much of this, but then goes on to say that while domestic politics may not be that important for structural realism, it is for classical realism. Indeed, Jack Snyder's (1991) most recent variation of realism, "defensive realism" gives quite a role to domestic determinants of foreign policy. The problem with Wohlforth is that while there may be some room in classical realism for domestic considerations in the evaluation of power (see Morgenthau's [1960: 133–148] notions of national morale and quality of government), he underestimates considerably the extent to which Morgenthau believes that international concerns dominate domestic politics. For Morgenthau (1960: 7–8, 145–148, 561–562, 567–568) domestic politics must be seen as an irrational intrusion on the national interest that could be fatal and (in similar fashion to Waltz 1979: 90–92) lead such states to be selected out. For realists, leaders of states should be able rationally to derive their interests by analyzing the international environment. As Stein (1994: 160) puts it: "realist models . . . assume that changes in international capabilities are obviously and easily read by rational leaders who adapt to changing structures." She goes on to say that within Gorbachev's USSR: "The evidence suggests that feedback was not

---

[15] This does not mean that the external environment is irrelevant. The external variable that is relevant, however, is not the distribution of power or perceptions of it, but the actual interactions of states. From this perspective, Evangelista's (1993: 171, table 7.4) scheme for integrating external and internal would be improved by looking at the level of hostility of interactions and whether they favored accommodationists or hard-liners (see Vasquez 1993: ch. 6). Such concerns are understood by policy makers. The United States, for example, wanted to shape its policy so as not to play into the hands of Gorbachev's hard-line critics (see Beschloss and Talbott 1993: 98–99).

obvious, that it was open to radically different interpretations . . ."
(Stein 1994: 160).

Ultimately, Wohlforth (1994/95: 109) concedes that power is not
necessarily the primary factor, but one of a host of factors:

> This evidence [on Soviet decision making under Gorbachev] suggests
> the importance of many factors: the sense of security provided by
> nuclear weapons; the force of Gorbachev's convictions; the exigencies
> of domestic politics; luck, chance, and caprice. But the available
> evidence also suggests that the story cannot be told . . . without
> according an important causal role to the problem of relative decline.

This is a far cry from Waltz and from classical realism which
maintains that relative power is *the* crucial variable. Similarly, Oye
(1995: 78) concedes:

> Gorbachev and the new thinkers could have chosen to pursue the
> old policies and to defend the old domestic political and economic
> structures. Because there was nothing inevitable about the changes in
> Soviet behavior or morphology, the end of the Cold War is a
> monument to these individuals.

The move to make relative decline one of several variables appears
reasonable, but it still sidesteps three issues: first, does this not imply
that the ex post facto emphasis on relative decline is wrong, as it
stands? Second, does this not constitute a degenerating shift by trying
to come up with a new variant of realism (with Oye it is "prudential
realism"; with Wohlforth an emphasis on perceptions of power rather
than power itself)? Third, does not making relative decline one of
several variables constitute a move that avoids falsifying evidence
because it is difficult (especially in a non-quantitative analysis of a
single case) to determine the relative impact of several variables?
These are all questions that those who wish to stay with realism on
the issue of the ending of the Cold War must ask themselves.

From my perspective, a paradigm shift away from realism would
eliminate many of the theoretical problems realism has encountered in
this historical moment. A nonrealist explanation would look at
leadership shifts, changes in beliefs systems, the role of domestic
politics, and the real possibilities for creating peace out of strategies of
accommodation to explain the end of the Cold War. One of the
distinctive aspects of Gorbachev's foreign policy is that he adopted
many of the recommendations that nonrealists had been urging upon
the West as a way of extending détente and ending the Cold War (see

Mansbach and Vasquez 1981: chs. 10 and 11). From a nonrealist perspective, power shifts or perceptions of power, played a relatively minor role in explaining the shift of Soviet foreign policy from 1985 to 1989.

The outlines of a nonrealist explanation

In separate analyses, large components of a nonrealist explanation are admirably put together by Stein (1994), Lebow (1994) and Risse-Kappen (1994) (all reprinted in Lebow and Risse-Kappen 1995). Janice Stein (1994: 156), in effect, turns Wohlforth (1994/95) and Oye (1995) on their heads, arguing that the end of the Cold War cannot be explained without taking account of Gorbachev and his "representation of the Soviet security problem" and therefore cannot be explained from a realist perspective. For her, the change in "cognitive constructs" or beliefs was not a function of relative decline, but of Gorbachev's "inductive and trial-and-error learning" (Stein 1994: 156ff.). Similarly for Lebow (1994), Gorbachev's restructuring of Soviet foreign policy cannot be explained by changes in the external environment. For Lebow (1994: 268) to explain Gorbachev's most radical decisions, like the abandonment of East European communist regimes, "the analyst must go outside . . . [the realist] paradigm and look at the determining influence of domestic politics, belief systems, and learning." Risse-Kappen (1994) adds to this explanation by showing that many of the intellectual sources of the new thinking in foreign policy came from a transnational coalition which had for years been circulating ideas and concepts that contradicted the dominant (realist and Marxist) thinking on the Cold War (see also Wohlforth 1993: 257; Checkel 1993). Gorbachev picked up ideas from those in his entourage who had had repeated contacts with the West and formulated out of them a new foreign policy approach.[16]

Unlike the realist explanation of relative decline, the theoretical models used in the nonrealist explanation have long been part of the literature on the Cold War (from Osgood 1959 to Mansbach and Vasquez 1981), albeit at the mid-range level. Thus, this explanation is

[16] For instance, Georgi Arbatov, the head of the Institute for the Study of the USA and Canada and part of Gorbachev's inner circle, was a member of the Palme Commission and quite influenced by it. In turn, the Commission's report had a big impact in the USSR (Risse-Kappen 1994: 202; see also Oberdorfer 1991: 160–161; Checkel 1993: 291–294).

not as susceptible to the ex post facto charge made against realism. The purpose of this section, however, is not to address the question of which explanation was better able to anticipate what no one expected, but whether "the facts" the nonrealist explanation would see as most significant for change in world politics were the ones at play in the end of the Cold War. Nonrealists focus not on power variables, but on learning (Jervis 1976; George et al., 1983; Nye 1987; Schroeder 1994b: preface), change in cognitive belief systems (Holsti 1976; Mansbach and Vasquez 1981: 254–280; Mueller 1989), the efficacy of cooperative acts (Kreisberg 1981; Burton 1982, 1984; Pruitt and Rubin 1986), coupled with leadership shifts (Bunce 1981) to explain foreign policy change. Focusing on these variables should offer a more plausible explanation that is more consistent with the historical record than the realist hypothesis on decline and retrenchment. The test, then, is between which of two competing explanations better fits what happened and provides a better analysis of how the variables posited as significant actually produced the outcome in question. The best way to conduct such a test is through "process tracing" (George 1979).

Some might argue that such process tracing could result in a *post hoc, ergo propter hoc* analysis (after this, therefore because of this). The nonrealist explanation might seem susceptible to such a charge because of its emphasis on leadership shifts. Three points need to be made about this criticism. First, leadership change and the other variables that are used to tell a story of how and why the Cold War ended were not just derived from the case material and cobbled together. They were derived from models of learning and cognitive psychology that offered them as more theoretically significant facts than realist power variables (long before the Cold War ended). In particular, the turn to cognitive psychology and to conflict resolution was taken because of perceived deficiencies in realism's rational actor model.

Second, realism generally denies the importance of leadership shifts (domestic politics) and changes in beliefs, arguing for the greater potency of the external structure and relative power ranking of a state, so the nonrealist explanation that is presented is not just some obvious explanation to which everyone would adhere. Realists would expect these variables to be irrelevant and impotent compared to capability variables.

Third, any systematic conclusion about whether the variables in the explanation are of "causal" significance and not just a product of post hoc reasoning can only be determined by examining the role of these variables in comparison to "relative decline-retrenchment" across a series of cases, not just one. The goal of this chapter is more modest. It is to show that a plausible case can be made that the nonrealist cognitive and domestic political variables played a significant role in bringing about the end of the Cold War, but that a similar case cannot be made for the realist-retrenchment hypothesis. The case against realism was presented in the previous section. The remainder of this section presents the case for nonrealism.

Leadership change

From a nonrealist perspective the most important variable is not relative decline, but leadership change. This is consistent with previous evidence both about the Soviet Union (see Bunce 1981) and foreign policy state behavior generally (see Hagan 1994; Chernoff 1994: ch. 7), which shows that sharp shifts in foreign policy tend to occur when leadership changes. What realists ignore is that while the international environment may "rationally favor" certain foreign policy options over others, it is not always (or even necessarily typically) the case that all possible leaders of a state will favor the same basic foreign policy. In other words, domestic politics is crucial because it may give rise to leaders with different ideological perspectives and these differences will not be smoothed out by the external environment, as the realists assume (see Fozouni 1995: 487). Moreover, leadership struggles for power are often determined by domestic policy issues. It may be the case that leaders who have beliefs or predispositions at variance with the dominant foreign policy thinking of a state may come to power (because of positions they take on domestic political issues).

It is my belief that this is precisely what happened with the election of Reagan in 1980. He brought into power with him a set of hard-line foreign policy advisors whose thinking was much sharper to the right than anything that had prevailed in recent times and probably anything since 1945. In addition, Reagan, who was not conversant with the dominant realist discourse, especially on nuclear deterrence, was more open to nonrealist ideas – like nuclear disarmament, as happened in Reykjavik much to the chagrin of some of his conservative advisors (Oberdorfer 1991: 157, 173, 207, 222, 289). While the succession process may typically filter out those who have unusual ideas on foreign policy, it is possible for such leaders to emerge when domestic political issues become the main focus. Leadership shifts can be treated as a stochastic process with the possibility of leaders who are outside a broad foreign policy mainstream periodically coming to power.

Existing evidence on Gorbachev suggests a similar process occurred with his succession; namely, he gained power because of his position on domestic issues, not because of foreign policy (Stein 1994: 161). Indeed, for him foreign policy was ultimately a servant of his domestic program (see, for example, Oberdorfer 1991: 162). As Stein (1994: 161–163, 166–170) points out, Gorbachev did not come to power with a firm set of ideas about changing foreign policy, nor did he necessarily reflect the new foreign policy of a new generation. Instead, he appeared to have had a definite set of ideas of how to reform the economy, and it was this stance that gained him political support.[17] At the same time, he was open to extending this new thinking to foreign policy. Here, he was exposed to those who definitively had new ideas about foreign policy and who through long exposure to a transnational coalition (see Risse-Kappen 1994) thought that the Cold War was a waste of resources and that a strategy of accommodation could end it (see Gladkov 1994: 198–199). In foreign policy, these reformers criticized the old ideological thinking of conventional Marxist-Leninists. Stein (1994: 156) argues that through a trial-and-error process Gorbachev adopted more of this line.

One of the key characteristics of the group supporting a shift in foreign policy was the belief that Soviet foreign policy had been deluded by ideological considerations. This was particularly the case for Soviet foreign policy in the Third World. From the perspective of these "new foreign policy thinkers" the Soviet Union was often used by Third World states (Malashenko 1994: 92, 95). For them, Afghanistan was a symbol of so much that was wrong with Soviet foreign policy. Cuba was a particular irritant as a waste of valuable resources. Time and again these intellectuals called for a the de-ideologization of foreign policy, a theme quickly picked up by Shevardnadze and Gorbachev himself.[18] What is important about the beliefs of this group is that it had multiple sources and that the beliefs themselves had

---

[17] Later, when the reforms provoked criticisms, Gorbachev tried to use foreign policy successes to buttress his domestic support (see Dobrynin 1995: 628, 634–635).

[18] See Gorbachev's major foreign policy speech to the Twenty-Seventh Party Congress in 1986 (Oberdorfer 1991: 159–160, 162).

been percolating within the system for a long time. The beliefs and policy stances were not a direct response to relative decline.

Testable differences

This last claim is a critical testable difference between the cognitive psychological explanation and the realist explanation. For nonrealists, Gorbachev was motivated by domestic policy and had been for most of his career (see for example, Gorbachev 1996: 86, 91–92, 117–121, 127–130, 167–168, 174, 176, 177–178, 231–232). He was interested in cutting military expenditures because he wanted to shift resources to the civilian sector; even Wohlforth (1994/95: 112) says "They all wanted to get their hands on the . . . resources . . . of the defense sector"; see also Gorbachev (1996: 135–136, 173, 178–179, 215, 405) and the example in Beschloss and Talbott (1993: 66).[19] In addition, those who stood for the old Cold War thinking were the ones most in favor of continuing high military expenditures. For Gorbachev, there were both internal economic and political reasons for cutting defense radically.

He was encouraged to do this by those who thought the Cold War had long been a waste of resources (see for example, Malashenko 1994: 92, 97). These individuals, who were Gorbachev's natural constituency both in terms of their sympathies and in terms of their generation, had a domestic political interest in taking advantage of the policy window Gorbachev had opened (Stein 1994: 178). Similarly, Gorbachev (1996: 402) had a political interest in them since they were supportive of perestrokia and glasnost. The old guard in foreign policy was not. So, at a political level one would expect Gorbachev to be less receptive to the old establishment's view on foreign and defense policy.

Questions of political alignments also seem to have played a role in some of the later more radical decisions that Gorbachev took on Eastern Europe. According to Stein (1994: 161, based on an interview with Gorbachev), one of the main factors leading Gorbachev not to support the old guard in Eastern Europe is that they were the allies of his opponents within the Soviet Union (see also Dobrynin 1995: 632). Most East European leaders (with the exception of Kadar of Hungary

---

[19] Even the withdrawal from Afghanistan was couched in this larger policy stance (Oberdorfer 1991: 237).

and Jaruzelski of Poland) opposed perestrokia and glasnost not only at home, but in the Soviet Union itself (see Gorbachev 1996: 483–485). It is this kind of political consideration in the context of his own beliefs that is critical in explaining Gorbachev's decision making.[20] This is very different from the realist tendency to explain Gorbachev's abandonment of Eastern Europe as a function of cutting back commitments because the Soviet Union was losing power. Instead, it seems that Gorbachev hoped that the East European elite would follow his example of perestroika, but whatever they did he was not going to expend economic resources or use the military to prop up their regimes (Gorbachev 1996: 468–469, 486). His rejection of the Brezhnev doctrine and his unwillingness to take an active interventionist role were all part of his official beliefs and constrained him from doing more than remaining neutral. Gorbachev (1996: 484) said:

> I have frequently been asked why the USSR did not intervene in the Romanian drama to assist the dictator's departure. I repeat once more that we did not intervene because to do so would have contradicted the principles of our new policy. The interventions undertaken previously had eventually turned into liabilities, Pyrrhic victories, for us. That was the lesson of Hungary in 1956, Czechoslovakia in 1968, and Afghanistan in 1979.

Shevardnadze was particularly adamant in insisting that the new thinking meant not using force.[21] The end result of this "neutrality" was that things got out of hand throughout Eastern Europe and reformers, as well as the old guard, were quickly thrown out of office, despite, in some cases, support from the United States.[22]

---

[20] Likewise, one of the reasons Gorbachev instituted some democratic procedures, like competitive elections, was that he saw this as a procedure to turn out some of the old guard (Oberdorfer 1991: 215–216; see also Gorbachev 1996: 195–198). It is also clear that one of the main motives behind glasnost was Gorbachev's (1996: 205) belief that it would expose economic inefficiencies and put pressure on bureaucrats and party leaders.

[21] Beschloss and Talbott (1993: 96) report Shevardnadze saying several times to James Baker that "If force is used, it will mean that the enemies of *perestroika* have triumphed. We would be no better than the people who came before us." Shevardnadze maintained the same position even when Baker suggested the Soviets send troops to stabilize the situation in Romania as Ceausescu was under attack (Beschloss and Talbott 1993: 170–171). On Gorbachev's adherence to this principle, see Beschloss and Talbott (1993: 65, 134, 170) and Gorbachev (1996: 293, 464–466, 484–486).

[22] Bush, on his trip to Poland, for example, was so supportive of Jaruzelski, that the latter decided to run for president in the upcoming free elections (Beschloss and Talbott 1993: 88–89).

Another testable difference with realist models (especially the rational actor model) is the way in which changes in foreign policy in the Soviet Union were implemented. These are consistent with empirical findings and mid-range theory on bureaucratic politics. Gorbachev and Shevardnadze went around the bureaucracy to come up with their own proposals (see Dobrynin's [1995: 628–629, 630] complaints).[23] This permitted them to avoid standard operating procedures (Allison and Halperin, 1972; Hermann 1969b), bureaucratic stabilizers that prevent sharp shifts in foreign policy (Goldmann 1988; Hagan 1995), and the dominant mind-set that prevented new ideas from influencing decision making. It is not an accident that both Gorbachev and Shevardnadze lacked extensive foreign policy experience.[24] This "lack of socialization" made them open to new perspectives, especially given that both thought that the Cold War mentality did not deal with the real danger that nuclear weapons posed to humanity and that much of Soviet policy toward the Third World, as exemplified by Afghanistan, had proved to be costly failures that could have been avoided if it were not for the undue influence of ideology.[25]

In order for change to be solidified a purge in personnel associated with or blamed for the failure often occurs (see Vasquez 1985: 662–663), and this was done by Shevardnadze, who revamped the Foreign Ministry, changing 68 of 115 ambassadors (Oberdorfer 1991: 164), as well as by Gorbachev, who removed key individuals associated with the Cold War, including Gromyko and Dobrynin. The landing of a small private airplane in Red Square on May 29, 1987 provided the opportunity for Gorbachev to demand the resignation of Defense Minister Sokolov, thereby permitting him to gain control of the main target of his planned cuts (Dobrynin 1995: 625–626; see also Gorbachev 1996: 232–233, 405).

---

[23] Shevardnadze would sometimes go so far as to present his own ministry's arms control proposals to the Americans, and getting a positive response, bring it directly to Gorbachev; only then would it be presented to the military (Beschloss and Talbott, 1993: 118).

[24] On Shevardnadze's lack of foreign policy experience, see Oberdorfer (1991: 118–123). When Gorbachev (1996: 181) told him of his intention to appoint him foreign minister, Shevardnadze said, "I might have expected anything except this," and went on to say that he was not a foreign policy "professional."

[25] A similar, but considerably muted, effect occurred with Reagan, who was not socialized to US strategic thinking and would entertain radical ideas like zero ballistic missiles and the elimination of nuclear weapons.

The other major testable difference with a realist explanation is that the cognitive approaches see foreign policy choice and change as a function of learning and not simply a "rational" calculation of interests in terms of power (or cost-benefits). Psychology, particularly cognitive psychology, rather than economics becomes the major social science of interest. Instead of a single-factor decision calculus, decision making is analyzed in terms of schemata and changes in them (see Stein 1994: 163–165), images, perceptions (Jervis 1976) and lessons derived from major events in history like wars and crises (May 1973; Jervis 1976; Khong 1992).

External variables

The major gap in the Stein (1994) and Lebow (1994) explanations is some inclusion of external variables. Here the world society-issue politics paradigm proves useful. From this perspective, it is not the structure of the system or the distribution of power that are the key external variables, but the interactions of states (the missing fourth image, see ch. 9, above). Détente provided an important precedent upon which to build. The shift in Gorbachev's belief meant that the inherent conflict of interest (in terms of the absolute differences with the United States) had been reduced dramatically. This implied that possibilities for common interests and for mutual accommodation were, in principle, much higher. Elites in the United States did not recognize this because of their own ideological perspective. Once they did, there was also a tendency to let Gorbachev just negotiate against himself, especially on arms control, which of course did not go unnoticed by Shevardnadze and Gorbachev (Beschloss and Talbott 1993: 116–117, 119). At different points, however, both Reagan and Bush began to reciprocate and tried to get the best deals they could, while Gorbachev remained in power. In addition, both tried to sign agreements with him to support his efforts to stay in power (Beschloss and Talbott 1993: 74–75, 77, 135, 137, 141–144, 180).[26]

Generally, for the world society-issue politics paradigm, the foreign policy stance of a state is a function of a domestic political debate over a new global critical foreign policy issue (see Vasquez 1985: 654–656).

---

[26] Of course, it should not be forgotten that accommodation was also being pushed by US allies and was very popular domestically within the United States, factors which the Soviets rightly saw as pressures upon Reagan and Bush (see, for example, Beschloss and Talbott 1993: 166).

The nature of that foreign policy, e.g., containment, is a function of the interactions of the two states as informed by their prior interactions and by the general lessons they derive from history. A shift in foreign policy is most likely when a leadership with a different ideological perspective or belief system ascends to power (Hagan 1994).

Interactions and relationships occur in the context of existing rules of the game which are constituted by these interactions themselves and the informal institutions (e.g. regimes) they create (Vasquez 1993: ch. 8). The Basic Principles Agreement, Helsinki, and CSCE set up new rules of the game. These institutions provided a forum for nongovernmental actors, like Amnesty International, and for transnational groups to penetrate elites, especially in the USSR (see Risse-Kappen 1994). Realists persistently underestimate the impact of such institutions and the norms that underlie them (see the exchange among Mearsheimer [1995] and Keohane and Martin [1995] and Ruggie [1995]). In part, this is because liberal institutionalists, like Keohane (1984) concede too much conceptual ground by taking a rational choice perspective, rather than basing their views on a "rule following" perspective (see March 1994: ch. 4) or on some of the empirical findings of peace research (see ch. 12, above). The latter show convincingly that when major states attempt to establish rules of the game they are able to manage their relations so as to avoid war and reduce the number of militarized confrontations (see Wallensteen 1984; Kegley and Raymond 1982, 1990; Vasquez 1994). Peace is often associated with the establishment of such a global institutional context and the onset of major state war is associated with the decay of such institutions (Vasquez 1993; Wallace 1972; see also Doran 1971).

Such notions were not new in 1985. Indeed, they had formed the basis of much of the efforts to manage rivalry, adopt confidence building measures, engage in crisis management and even crisis prevention (see in particular Kremenyuk 1994; George et al. 1983; George et al. 1988). Learning to handle crisis situations better through a change in beliefs and behavior became the hallmark of creating détente and extending it.[27] Changes in power were not seen as critical in producing a thaw in the Cold War. Rather the danger of nuclear annihilation was seen as the basis for trying to manage and improve relations. Clearly, the Cuban missile crisis was pivotal in producing

---

[27] On learning in the US–USSR relationship, see Breslauer and Tetlock (1991) and Levy (1994a).

this change. Gorbachev's own investigation into this case helped reinforce his beliefs on the danger of nuclear war (see Lebow and Stein 1994: x–xi). This nuclear learning (Nye 1987; Zubok 1994) provided the impetus for attempting to try to manage crises and wars in the Third World so as to avoid an escalation to the nuclear level (see Gorbachev 1996: 200, 403). This path to nuclear war was recognized by strategic thinkers some time ago (Kahn 1968). Through Pugwash conferences and the informal Dartmouth discussions, ideas about rules and crisis management constantly percolated among academics and policy makers at lower levels.

What changed was not the power of the Soviet Union relative to the United States, but the political will of one side to extend some of the rules that had been the basis of détente, to cut military spending drastically and stop wasteful ideological commitments abroad.[28] Soviet hard-liners were silenced by Gorbachev. Once he could convince Reagan and others of the change in Soviet policy, as well as playing to Reagan's dislike of nuclear weapons, Reagan proved a valuable negotiating partner because he was able to sideline hard-liners in the United States.

Writing just before the 1979 invasion of Afghanistan, Mansbach and Vasquez (1981: 471) argued that the major obstacle preventing détente from being extended was the presence of domestic critics. Once these could be removed, the ending of the Cold War would become a real possibility, because many of the other conditions necessary for its end (the establishment of rules, trust, better interactions, etc.) were now in place. The reduction in the influence of hard-liners and the rise of accommodationists to political power is a key variable (see Vasquez 1993: ch. 6) that brought about the end of the Cold War. This does not mean it was the only variable, but simply the last to be put in proper place. Understanding two-level games becomes critical for understanding the dynamics of the Cold War and how (and why) it ended.

The shift in the domestic political environment was not produced by changes in capability or perceptions of capability, but through a long process of creating and learning new concepts and cognitive maps. Once this had been done, it was simply a matter of waiting until the influence of domestic hard-liners (who had stabilized the Cold War) could be reduced on both sides. The centralized system of

---

[28] See Gorbachev's address to the Politiburo in November 1988 quoted in Wohlforth (1994/95: 114).

the Soviet Union (see Snyder 1991: ch. 6) may have made this happen more quickly there than in the United States.

Even this cursory outline of a nonrealist explanation underlines the main conceptual flaws of the realist paradigm. The nonrealist explanation brings to center stage a number of variables that have been obfuscated if not outrightly ignored by the realist paradigm. These include: (1) the role of domestic politics, (2) the impact of two-level games in light of the relative influence of hard-liners and accommodationists, (3) the importance of cognitive structures and learning, (4) the impact of rules of the game (and informal institutions) on making peace possible, (5) the influence of transnational actors and coalitions, and (6) the relative importance of interactions over systemic structure.[29]

All of these factors were important in bringing about an end to Cold War; yet, none of these has been emphasized by the realist paradigm. Each of these variable clusters deserves investigation and according to the world society-issue politics paradigm will produce better theory than anything coming out of the realist paradigm. This is another way of saying that these factors are going to have a greater causal impact than any power variable. The above analysis of the end of the Cold War suggests that for the most important historical case of our time, this is certainly the case.

The *minor* policy anomaly

The ending of the Cold War and the failure of dominant realist theories to anticipate it and then to clearly explain it, after the fact, has attracted a great deal of attention in the field. For this reason, it poses a major policy anomaly for the paradigm. In focusing on the end of the Cold War, however, scholars should not overlook a second anomaly connected with this case. This has to do with US policy toward Russia in the early post-Cold War era. Not much scholarly attention has been devoted to this question so it can be labeled a minor policy anomaly; yet, it is of equal theoretical interest, because it

---

[29] The realist paradigm also assumes that the issues over which political actors contend are theoretically unimportant, because they can all be reduced to one issue – the struggle for power (Morgenthau 1960: 27). The territorial explanation of war, however, argues that territorial issues are uniquely likely to give rise to war; whereas other issues are considerably less prone to violence. Territoriality constitutes a seventh neglected variable and will be discussed below.

also produces a legitimate test of the ability of the realist paradigm to satisfy the criteria of explanatory power and of relevance.

The test is whether the US policy response toward Gorbachev and Yeltsin, once the Cold War was seen as over, conforms to what the logic of realism would have predicted. From the perspective of classical realism, which sees the world as a struggle for power (Morgenthau 1960) in which relative gains are more of a concern than absolute gains (Grieco 1988), certain predictions follow. Since the world is a struggle for power, it would seem from the logic of realism to behoove any rival of Russia to try to keep it as weak as possible for as long as possible. However, realism would provide two caveats to keep in mind that might change or mute this objective. The first is that Russia should not be so weakened that other potential rivals to the United States would gain an advantage through this disruption of the "balance of power." The second is that in this process, the risk of nuclear war should be reduced to an absolute minimum, i.e., a Russia in decline should not be pushed so far so as to lead it to war with the United States – although conventional wars with other parties that would further destabilize it might not be bad, if this would lead to a further weakening, while not destabilizing the entire system. Because realism is often indeterminate in its foreign policy recommendations, one cannot give precise predictions, but on the whole one would expect that the key focus would be on *relative power and reducing that of Russia in comparison with the United States*. Recognizing that a wide variety of options might be adopted to reach this goal, this seems to be a reasonable expectation one could derive from the paradigm.[30]

Yet, the United States did not seem to react in this manner at all, either under the hard-line Ronald Reagan or the foreign-policy focused George Bush. The major foreign policy goal of the United States and its strategy for peace was to try to make the USSR and then Russia as much like the United States as possible. Instead of a conscious policy of weakening the USSR, it tried to support economic reforms that would make it capitalist and political reforms that would make it democratic, giving the USSR, from the US perspective, the

---

[30] It is also a much fairer test of both realism and nonrealism because it makes a precise prediction that can falsify either. In contrast, Mastanduno's (1997: 57, 60–61, 63) predictions on US security policy, especially on intervention and on trying to preserve the unipolar moment, are too easy a test for realism to pass. Some of these tests' predictions are problematic in that they could also be predicted by other policies, for example, isolationism or attempts to deal with life "after hegemony."

"best" economic and political system possible. By making the USSR capitalist, it would, from the US perspective, make the USSR much stronger and competitive with the United States than the moribund computer/information-age-deficient Soviet socialist economy. If socialism weakened the USSR economically and technologically, as Americans believed it did, then the last thing a realist state that believed in the struggle for power and relative gains should do is make its rival capitalist.

This is a fundamental contradiction that is not easy to explain away. It is a contradiction at the heart of US foreign policy, since it reflects the conflict of three goals recommended by three competing foreign policy philosophies: the advancement of capitalist interests (advocated by economic liberalism), the spread of democracy (advocated by idealism and Wilsonianism), and the successful pursuit of the struggle for power (advocated by realism). Only in rare instances is the most powerful state in the system in a position where it must clearly choose which of these goals to pursue. The United States has not really been in such a situation since the immediate post-World War II period (1945–1947). When the most powerful state chooses one goal over another at critical turning points in history, it permits observers to make certain inferences about the fundamental motivations underlying state behavior and to check these against the predictions of various paradigms.

When push came to shove, the United States sought to make the USSR and then Russia more like itself than to weaken it fundamentally and perhaps irreversibly. It said in its choice that it would be more secure with a powerful capitalist and democratic Russia than it would with an economically weaker communist USSR.[31] Such a choice says that at the most fundamental level the United States (even when led by Republicans) is guided by capitalist and Wilsonian goals, not realist goals. This, of course, should come as no surprise to those familiar with American foreign policy or to realist critics of that policy (see Kennan 1951; Morgenthau 1970), but what this does mean is that the liberal paradigm and Marxist paradigm better predict what the

---

[31] Nor was it the case that Bush was unaware of this kind of realist concern. There were position papers and advisors, like Gates, who advocated a strategy to weaken the USSR and warned that Gorbachev was trying to reform the USSR in order to make it more powerful militarily (see Beschloss and Talbott 1993: 44, 48). On Bush's opting for democracy in the Soviet Union, see Beschloss and Talbott (1993: 150, 158).

United States would do at critical turning points in history than does the realist paradigm.

Nor is this the first time the United States has made such a choice. It did the same thing under Wilson at the end of World War I with the establishment of the Weimar Republic and the creation of new states out of the Austrian–Hungarian Empire. More importantly, it made the same choice in 1945 in how to deal with Germany and Japan. It sought in each instance to create economically powerful states that would be socialized by capitalist and democratic norms into peaceful non-threatening states despite their eventual increase in power (see Ikenberry and Kupchan 1990).[32] Likewise, US support of an integrated Western Europe illustrates a similar choice – the willingness to nourish the creation of a powerful collectivity that may become a rival of major consequence.

These several decisions seem to establish a pattern that is at variance with the thrust of all realist theories, especially those, like Gilpin (1981), that place great emphasis on the uniformity of the behavior of hegemons regardless of who the particular hegemon happens to be. Realism which claims Ancient Greece, Kautilya's India, and "the warring states period" in China as cases illustrating its universal applicability should be able to explain twentieth-century US foreign policy and cannot take refuge in the claim of American exceptionalism.[33]

The claim of American exceptionalism is undercut by looking at Gorbachev's foreign policy initiatives, which also run counter to realist expectations. As Lebow (1994: 261) points out, several of his

---

[32] While military limitations were placed on these states (thus perhaps conforming to realist expectations), producing an economically vibrant state would seem to make inevitable that economic power would be eventually converted to political and military power. The latter, of course, is a major prediction of Gilpin's (1981) neorealist theory, as well as Organski's (1958) power transition thesis (see also Organski and Kugler 1980; 1977). At any rate, such military restrictions could not be imposed on the USSR, since it was not defeated, so that the Cold War case is a purer choice.

[33] This is the argument that the United States is unique and different from all other countries. For an early refutation of this claim, see Rosecrance (1976). Even if this ad hoc explanation were introduced, it would still be damaging because it would be an admission that some kinds of countries who become hegemons would behave differently than theoretically expected. Elsewhere (Vasquez 1993: 115–116), I have argued, on the basis of Gochman's (1980) empirical findings, that the practices of power politics are learned social constructions that more obviously guide the behavior of European states than they have those outside Europe, especially the United States and China.

initiatives seem to be totally oblivious of relative gains concerns. Even US Secretary of State, George Shultz, admitted at the time (on background to the press) that Gorbachev's April 1987 proposal to unilaterally eliminate Shorter-Range Intermediate Nuclear Force missiles (SRINF) was very one-sided in favor of the West, so much so that he did not think that, if the USSR had had a democratic legislature, it would survive ratification (Oberdorfer 1991: 228).

These examples show that the conceptual deficiencies of realism's attempt to explain foreign policy in terms of the national interest and power have come home to roost. The United States when forced to choose at the critical historical turning point of our time, chose to achieve security by making the USSR more in its image rather than trying to weaken it as a way of winning a realist struggle for power. Such things should not happen if Morgenthau's (1960: 4) objective laws of international politics are laws. And if they do, then the United States should suffer, yet to date the United States seems to have been correct – that trying to help the Soviet Union and integrate it into the global economy will build a foundation for further cooperation and not lead to the rise of a new more powerful rival. Of greater certainty are American decisions vis-à-vis Japan, Germany, and especially an integrated Western Europe (see Kegely 1993) which have stood the test of time. These have been paths to peace which like the current policy of the US pose an anomaly for the realist paradigm both in terms of why such policies were initiated in the first place and why they seem to have worked in the second.

In fact, the success of the Schuman plan to end war in Western Europe raises the question of whether liberalism and idealism is a better paradigm. Likewise, the choices of the United States in 1945–1947 and 1989–1992 seem better explained by liberalism and idealism. This inference should not be made too quickly, but should be examined in light of other possible nonrealist explanations and the ability of liberalism to give a full accounting of the ending of the Cold War.

A brief note on liberal explanations

Liberalism and neoliberalism have enjoyed a great resurgence of interest in recent years. Because they are not realist, they are by definition an example of a nonrealist paradigm. Liberalism, however, is not the paradigm I have in mind as the best alternative to realism.

Indeed, framing the paradigm debate in international relations as one of realism vs. liberalism (as is often done in the United States) is not from my perspective a progressive shift. Here, I wish only to note that the above nonrealist explanation of the Cold War should not be taken as a liberal explanation, even though it may share certain propositions with it (like the importance of institutions and transnational actors). More important, some of the quintessential aspects of the liberal explanation are called into question by the end of the Cold War.

Deudney and Ikenberry (1991/92) draw upon ideas associated with the democratic peace to help explain the end of the Cold War. In doing so they lend credence to the liberal paradigm and its explanatory power even though they indicate that the most important factors bringing about the end of the Cold War "have not been central" to liberalism (Deudney and Ikenberry 1991/92: 117; 1991: 244). They suggest, for example that one of three major background factors that permitted Gorbachev to end the Cold War is that he learned that democratic states are generally pacific and hence provide a benign external environment for the USSR (see Deudney and Ikenberry 1991/92: 78, 83, 85). While this is part of a larger complex explanation and hardly a single-factor explanation, I want to focus here on whether the pacific nature of democracy really had that much impact on bringing about the end of the Cold War, because that is the aspect of their explanation most relevant to liberalism.[34]

There are three problems with the liberal aspect of their explanation. First, it is far from clear that democratic states were pacific or provided a benign environment for the USSR (because of their democratic nature). Second, as with realism, there is a problem of timing. The United States and Western states were democratic during the entire post-1945 period; why did this effect take about forty-four years to work? Third, when the effect did occur, it occurred under Reagan, one of the least pacific and least "benign" administrations in terms of its orientation toward communism and the Soviet Union.

One of the basic tenets of liberalism is the democratic peace, i.e.,

---

[34] Deudney and Ikenberry (1991: 244) describe their complete explanation of the end of the Cold War as the industrial modernization theory. This maintains that a main cause of the end of the Cold War was economic stagnation, which produced the need to change domestically. Such reform was permitted by the nuclear environment that made the USSR secure from attack and by the less threatening nature of liberal states. For them, reform was also encouraged by comparisons with the more efficient and successful capitalist system.

democratic liberal states do not wage war against each other. Deudney and Ikenberry (1991, 1991/92) incorporate this idea into their larger analysis in an imaginative fashion by implying that the leaders of the Soviet Union gradually learned that democratic states are not prone to initiate wars against other powerful states (Deudney and Ikenberry 1991/92: 85). They go on to say that: "The internal pluralism and structure of the Western system largely forecloses the formation and implementation of an offensive grand strategy" and that the liberal states' "extensive system of deliberation and consultation tends to filter out rash and extreme ideas" (Deudney and Ikenberry 1991/92: 84–85; see also Snyder 1991).

The main question arising from these claims is whether they are true in general and specifically with regard to Western Cold War relations with the USSR. The answer in both instances seems to be no. Most of the quantitative analysts try to avoid the broader claim that democratic states are more pacific than other states (Maoz and Abdolali 1989; Russett 1993), even Rummel (1995: 458–59) does not say that democratic states will be involved in war less frequently than other states. A number of the above findings show that democratic states can be quite belligerent in terms of involvement and initiation of war, although Ray (1995: 18–21) reviews evidence to show that the mere presence of a democratic state can reduce the frequency of war, even if it does not eliminate the possibility of war. Thus, according to these statistically based generalizations, one can infer, contrary to Deudney and Ikenberry that the Soviet Union was quite reasonable in feeling threatened by democratic states, because it was not itself a democratic state.

In additon, it is a bit far-fetched to think that Soviet leaders gradually learned that democracies, unlike other states, are inherently peaceful, when such a proposition was not even widely accepted by Western scholars until 1992 or so, long after Gorbachev initiated his reforms. Prior to that the field generally accepted Waltz's (1959) realist argument that the nature of states does not explain war. Waltz rejected the idea that evil states cause war (from Wilson's perspective dictatorships, from Lenin's perspective capitalist states). Similarly, peace researchers, like Small and Singer (1976), rejected the idea that democratic states were less war prone on the basis of their findings. Rummel's (1983) early claim that libertarian states were inherently more peaceful was not accepted, in part, because it was seen as ideological. Doyle (1986) effectively resurrected the liberal democratic peace proposition, but only with extensive statistical testing by Maoz and Abdolali (1989) and by Russett (1993) did the proposition gain wide currency. Still, despite this evidence, it remains controversial among traditionalists, especially realists (e.g., Mearsheimer 1990a: 48–51; Spiro 1994; and Mansfield and Snyder 1995; but see also quantitative scholars like Thompson 1996 and Senese 1997). If American political scientists have been resistant to the claim, why should we assume that Gorbachev and his entourage would accept it before it even gained currency in the United States?

What really happened in the USSR was much more modest – some advisors began to argue that the USSR's behavior made the United States more hostile than it needed to be and that a change to a less threatening foreign policy and a more defensive nuclear strategy could have important policy benefits (Wohlforth 1993: 258). Deudney and Ikenberry (1991/92) do not want to claim that Gorbachev consciously knew that democratic states were pacific (though they imply that), but that the relationship was more subtle. Somehow the Soviets gleaned the pacific nature of democratic states from their behavior over the course of the Cold War. This is what all Deudney and Ikenberry's talk about the inability of democratic states to come up with an offensive grand strategy and the tendency of democratic states to filter out rash and extreme ideas is meant to convey.

Yet, it is not clear that any of this is true. Without doubt, democratic France and Britain had no trouble formulating the ideology (and offensive grand strategy) of imperialism and the "white man's burden." The United States had its grand strategy of manifest destiny. Likewise, even though democratic systems can filter out some extreme (or even the most extreme) ideas that does not mean that some do not get through or that non-democratic systems cannot filter out risky policies. Snyder (1991: ch. 6) says that the Soviet system was less prone to overexpansion than Germany's or Japan's systems in the 1930s. Certainly, the American system has been prone to messianic crusades both internally and externally from Puritan times on. The expulsion of Roger Williams from the Massachusetts Bay Colony, the Salem witch trials, John Brown's Raid, the Mexican War, "fifty-four forty or fight," the Philippine war, making the world safe for democracy, the temperance movement and prohibition, the communist purges of the 1950s, CIA covert operations against Third World countries and interventions in democratic elections like those in France and Italy in 1948 and Chile in 1970, the Bay of Pigs, the

Vietnam War, Reagan's Cold War II, and even the recent hysteria about drugs, alcohol, and "sexual" harassment all have an edge to it, reflecting a highly aggressive and bellicose tendency to mobilize forces of repression to cleanse the system. Nathaniel Hawthorne's *Scarlet Letter* and Melville's Ahab capture something deep and dark about the American spirit. Concerns about morality are more noble and generous than *realpolitik* self-interest, but they also have another side to them – intolerance of sin, the willingness to employ force to eliminate evil, the castigation of the different.

The liberal paradigm tends to ignore its own pitfalls and exaggerate its merits. It tends to extol its own pacific character when at its very heart it is not very pacific at all. What is so troubling about the liberal explanation is that it seems so ideological.[35] It puts the entire *blame* of the Cold War from beginning to end on the communists, and this is contrary to what most international relations analyses of the Cold War would say (see, for example, George et al. 1983; Gaddis 1987; Jervis 1976; Bronfenbrenner 1961; Larson 1985).[36] Liberalism does this because, like realism, it is fundamentally not a scholarly or scientific paradigm, but an ideology. As such, it raises a host of dangers, not only for the conduct of foreign policy, but to scientific inquiry itself.[37]

---

[35] The same is true of Deudney and Ikenberry's (1991: 247–248; 1991/92: 84, 97–106) view that the collapse of the Soviet Union vindicates capitalism in that the end of the Cold War was brought about because capitalism was more dynamic and generally a superior economic system than communism.

[36] Of course, this would not be the conclusion of many American Kremlinologists who specialize in Soviet foreign policy, like Ulam (1974) or Rubenstein (1972), but then these scholars make no secret of their anti-communism.

[37] I define ideology in the Marxist sense of a set of political beliefs that grow out of and serve one's interests. Political philosophies, if they are broad and detailed enough, are ideologies in that they offer a framework for interpreting the world and a basis for action to bring about one's preferences. Ideology takes on the negative connotation I have given it here when it strives to hold onto its beliefs regardless of their truth (empirical accuracy and consistency with the evidence). Scientific inquiry involves a commitment to test beliefs according to a specific set of procedures and to accept the outcome of these tests as determining whether a claim should be accepted as true or false. Given these distinctions between science and ideology, it is possible to judge to what extent any given scholarly paradigm is scientific or ideological (in both its positive and negative connotations). As with Mannheim (1955), I share the view that it is the responsibility of scholars (especially scientific scholars) to take empirical truth as the highest standard by which to judge empirical claims. Ideologues often accept ideas not on the basis of their consistency with criteria for truth, but on the basis of whether the ideas serve their interests and/or have beneficial consequences. Liberalism has a tendency to be ideological because it is a full blown

Some of these are exhibited in the debate over the ending of the Cold War. For instance, despite the best attempts by rigorous peace researchers like Russett (1993), Maoz and Abdolali (1989), and Ray (1995) to separate the empirical hypothesis (that democratic states do not fight each other) from the larger normative political philosophy of liberalism and Wilsonianism, Deudney and Ikenberry (1991/92) bring the idea of a democratic peace to bear on the end of the Cold War in a manner that makes the West appear to be not responsible and relatively innocent. Most political conflicts are not this simple and morally straightforward. History is not a struggle between good and evil with progressive tendencies. From a scientific perspective (as well as a post-modernist one), this view of history appears as a highly dubious assumption produced by ideological self-delusion.

The danger of liberalism to scientific inquiry is that because it is a normative philosophy for making foreign policy there is a constant risk that its ideological tendencies will swallow up any scientifically neutral attempt to test its empirical components. Such testing is best done within a nonrealist paradigm that remains consciously separate from any political ideology, including liberalism. In adopting a political ideology as a scholarly paradigm, there is always the danger that the commitment to the normative goals will distort the empirical analysis, that the scholar will be committed first to the normative goals and strategies of the ideology and not to appraising its (empirical) truth claims on the basis of explicit criteria. These, of course, are fundamental issues that are not unique to liberalism and take us far afield from the Cold War, so discussion of them will be deferred. Suffice it to say here that while aspects of liberalism provide better explanations both for US foreign policy toward the Soviet Union and for the absence of war within Western Europe, other aspects of US bellicosity and aggressiveness are ignored, if not distorted. One of the merits of the world society-issue politics paradigm explanation is that Western bellicosity is not ignored, but brought into the very heart of explaining the origins and dynamics of the Cold War (see Mansbach and Vasquez 1981: ch. 10 for a detailed exposition).

The major flaw with the liberal explanation is that the ideological nature of the paradigm leads it to emphasize the benign aspects of democratic state behavior in a way that distorts the historical record

normative political philosophy with clear political preferences on a wide range issues.

in a manner that is politically self-serving. In terms of the specific history of relations, Soviet leaders had few reasons to see the West as pacific. Their ideology did not permit for this possibility and there was much in reality to confirm this expectation beginning right in 1917 when the West, including the United States, intervened militarily to help the White Russians try to overthrow the Bolsheviks. Likewise, reluctance by the British in the 1930s to make an alliance against Hitler, coupled later with talk by Churchill and other conservatives of the benefits of a war between Germany and the USSR, hardly made Soviet leaders trustful of democratic states. Finally, the virulent anti-communism within the United States in the 1920s and the McCarthy era, Dulles' ringing the USSR with alliances, the nuclear arms race, and the unwillingness to pursue Malenkov's overtures for peace after Stalin's death, as well as a host of other crises, all made it perfectly reasonable to assume that the United States was a threat to Soviet communism.

In addition to this major flaw, there are two technical problems that cast doubt on the liberal explanation. If democratic states were that pacific, it seems that the Cold War should have ended much earlier than it did. There were several missed opportunities to end the Cold War (see Larson 1997), and some of these were missed because the United States failed to respond to Soviet overtures, like those associated with the 1955 Austrian State Treaty. Others were missed because the United States dismissed them as Soviet propaganda, like some of the early proposals on arms control (see Clemens 1968, esp. ch. 1). Likewise, attempts at United States accommodation, like détente, had difficulty culminating in their logical conclusion because hard-line critics, like Reagan and Senator Henry Jackson, hamstrung Kissinger and Ford.

One of the patterns that emerges in the dynamics of the Cold War is that democratic systems have a difficult time controlling hard-line appeals, and this seems to have limited the ability of United States leaders to respond to Soviet overtures, as well as to make accommodative initiatives. Kennedy, for example, wanted to delay recognition of "Red China" until the second term to avoid criticism. Johnson feared that failure to do something about Vietnam would lead to a charge of losing another China. Democrats generally were put at an electoral disadvantage because Republicans would accuse them of being soft on communism. But even Democrats could play this card as when Carter scored a major tactical point against Ford in a presidential debate when Ford was insufficiently vocal in opposing Soviet domination of Eastern Europe and seemed to accept the current status quo, which had long been United States practice, but never officially expressed as such.

To those within the United States, like myself (see Mansbach and Vasquez 1981: 471–472), who have long thought that the Cold War could be ended on the basis of a mutual accommodation and hence end a wasteful use of resources, it comes as something of a disappointment that the Soviet system was able to produce a set of leaders committed to ending the Cold War before the United States did. The fact that this happened more quickly in the USSR than in the United States does not speak well for the allegedly pacific tendencies of democracies. Nor, if the Cold War and nuclear arms race are seen as irrational in the long term, even though they may be rational in the short term (Marcuse 1964: ix), does this speak well of the nature of democratic government. Indeed, it is one of the great ironies of the Cold War that such a dangerous and wasteful ideological struggle was ended by the side that was seen as closed, unopen, unaccountable to its people, and unable to reform itself.

The problem of timing, then, is not simply that the long time-lag raises questions about the causal significance of this variable. The problem also harks back to the first criticism of the liberal explanation; namely, that democratic government is not as pacific as liberals think. One of the reasons for the time lag may have something to do with the very nature of democratic processes that limit accommodative responses in situations of rivalry, which is a very serious criticism undermining the very logic of the idea that democracies are inherently peaceful.

In addition, the actual ending of the Cold War in the twilight of the Reagan administration and the beginning of the Bush administration provides the coup de grâce to the liberal explanation, while simultaneously reinforcing the explanation of the world society-issue politics paradigm. Reagan's rapid military build-up and Cold War II was one of the least pacific responses to the Soviet Union in the post-1945 period.[38] He did not exhibit the benign image that Deudney and Ikenberry (1991/92: 83) talk about. They explicitly recognize this as a

---

[38] Indeed, some conservatives, like Caspar Weinberger (1990) and Richard Perle (1991) (see Deudney and Ikenberry 1991/92: 79; Summy 1995: 4) identify this very belligerence (and not the pacific nature of democracies) as the reason the Cold War ended.

flaw in the liberal explanation, but try to minimize it by saying that Western allies undercut this belligerence (Deudney and Ikenberry (1991/92: 87). Taken alone Reagan's policy could be seen as ironic, but in conjunction with the other flaws in the liberal explanation it really indicates that the idea of the West being benign simply does not hold.

Even more damaging is that the world society-issue politics paradigm can explain – by looking at the balance between hard-liners and accommodationists – why Reagan was able to engage Gorbachev and begin the process that ended the Cold War. Reagan was able to deal with Gorbachev better than accommodationists like Carter would have, because as a hard-liner he was able to undercut criticisms by those to his right. Such observations have been common in recent years, but of the three explanations under consideration – liberal, realist, and world society-issue politics – only the latter has a fully developed dynamic model of the role hard-liners and accommodationists play vis-à-vis external interactions and domestic politics (see Vasquez 1993: ch. 6; see also Hagan 1994; Putnam 1988).

While it is difficult in light of the above arguments to argue that Soviet leaders were not threatened by democratic capitalist states in the Cold War, and by Reagan in particular, this does not mean that the nature of the threat was as great as that facing Stalin in the 1930s. It is true that the United States posed a less direct threat than did Nazi Germany or militarist Japan, as Deudney and Ikenberry (1991/92: 83–84) assert, but the reason for this is not that the United States was democratic, but because it did not have territorial ambitions toward the Soviet Union.

Here, Deudney and Ikenberry's (1991/92: 90–92) analysis on nuclear weapons is much more on the mark than their analysis on democracy. They suggest that in addition to the presence of democratic states, the presence of nuclear weapons made the Soviet Union more secure in its boundaries than at any time in its history. Because of its second strike ability the Soviet Union need not have feared invasion. A similar argument is made by Oye (1995: 76), who states that Soviet advocates of new thinking saw nuclear weapons as providing an end to the "old specter of Western encirclement" and the danger of attack. For this reason, Soviet leaders could reach an accommodation with the West. Indeed, the territorial security provided by second strike often played a large role in Gorbachev's desire to cut defense (see Oye 1995: 74–76). At the same time the danger of total annihilation and the risk of nuclear war – either through accident or more likely through mismanagement of a crisis – provided a real incentive to accommodate (see Mansbach and Vasquez 1981: 270–271).

Deudney and Ikenberry correctly derive these effects from the logic of nuclear strategic thinking; nevertheless, they overlook a confounding variable that may better explain why there was no war between the USSR and the United States; i.e., there was no territorial dispute between the United States and the USSR, nor has there ever really been one. As Gaddis (1987: 4–5, 223) pointed out during the Cold War, the United States and the Soviet Union are one of the few pairs of major states never to have fought each other in their history.[39]

From the perspective of the territorial explanation of war (see Vasquez 1993: ch. 4), the main reason the USSR and the United States did not find each other too threatening and never went to war was that neither claimed the territory of the other. Contrary to realism not all issues are equally likely to give rise to war (see Vasquez 1996b; Sample 1996; Hensel 1996; Huth 1996; Gibler 1996; Senese 1996); territorial disputes are much more war prone than disputes over other types of issues. This means that it would be easier to resolve peacefully the ideological issues under contention between the United States and USSR than it would have been to resolve the territorial issues between Nazi Germany and the USSR.

The Cold War was primarily an ideological struggle, and so long as each was willing to respect the status quo and not threaten territory, the danger of war was minimal. In such circumstances nuclear deterrence could work, in part, because it was not placed under great stress (see Vasquez 1991), as noted in the previous chapter. The two occasions when territory on the border frontiers of the two empires became a point of contention and crisis bargaining – Cuba and Berlin – were precisely the two instances in which the two superpowers came closest to nuclear war (see Betts 1987: 98, 116–122; and page 311 above).

The absence of territorial issues between the two superpowers goes a long way to explaining why the Cold War remained cold, and as such needs to be added as a seventh variable to the nonrealist

---

[39] The only possible exception is the 1917 intervention, which Gaddis does not regard as a war. Small and Singer (1982: 80, 202, 227) list this as an intervention in an ongoing civil war and not as an interstate war.

explanation given earlier in the chapter. With nuclear weapons raising the provocation threshold, the ideological issues under contention were simply not of sufficient material importance to warrant direct fighting, let alone the risk of escalation to nuclear war.[40] The absence of territorial issues meant that the ideological rivalry would be stalemated. The presence of second strike capability meant that gaining adherents to one side would not change the power of either side. This made the ideological struggle take on an unreal quality, especially as Third World states would play each side against the other. In this context, the struggle for influence and the arms race began to be seen as a waste of resources by accommodationists on both sides. Attempts to cut military spending, however, hit up against those who had a vested economic and/or organizational interest in that spending, as well as those guiding the prevailing Cold War ideology on either side. Nevertheless, the repetition of crises and the risk of nuclear war provided a constant spur for accommodation.

Eventually, the right mix of leaders in the two countries emerged so that the Cold War could be ended. This right mix involved the ascension of a leader on one side who could initiate accommodation and control internal criticism, and the presence of a leader on the other who could respond positively without receiving overwhelming criticism. It turned out that the centralized system of the USSR was, whether it be coincidence or not, able to produce the first type of leader, while the United States could only produce an open-minded hard-liner able to respond, but unwilling to initiate. In either case, each leader came to power for domestic reasons and was primarily concerned with domestic political questions so there is a certain stochastic element to this process in terms of having to wait for the right mix of leaders.

From the theoretical perspective of the world society-issue politics paradigm, once this mix is present, the ability of leaders to learn and be open-minded is critical in changing the dominant foreign policy belief system of a side and thereby the goals that are pursued. Attempts at accommodation eventually produce, on aggregate, agreements that increase the use of positive acts, which in turn reduce hostility (see Mansbach and Vasquez 1981: ch. 7). These *interactions*, in

---

[40] This implies that nuclear rivals who have highly salient territorial issues at stake – like Israel and the Arabs or India and Pakistan – would be much more prone to deterrence failures and hence nuclear war (see Vasquez 1991).

turn, strengthen accommodationists on each side and reduce the number and influence of hard-liners (see Vasquez 1993: ch. 6). Other elements of the external environment played a much more limited role – in terms of both the impact of power variables and the pacific quality of democracies – in ending the Cold War than the realist or liberal paradigms would postulate.

Conclusion

One of the main strengths of the realist paradigm has been to give rise to theories that have a great deal of relevance to the pressing political questions of the day. It has achieved this relevance by providing a frame that permits analysts and policy makers to explain theoretically what has happened, is happening, and might happen in the world. This capacity to offer plausible explanations, however, should not be confused with the ability to provide *accurate* explanations. Explanatory power is a theoretical quality not an empirical quality. The realist paradigm has never scored well on accuracy, as has been seen throughout this book. Yet, its ability to score high on explanatory power and relevance has made it quite useful to scholars and policy makers alike. The ambiguity of evidence, the lack of rigor, and the tendency of adherents to act as debaters trying to win an argument, rather than scientists or judges trying to get at an impartial determination of the truth, adds to the difficulty of rejecting a paradigm on the basis of the criterion of accuracy, especially when it seems to be performing well on the basis of the criteria of explanatory power and relevance.

In this light, the assessment of this chapter should be disturbing to those who believe that the realist paradigm best captures "the essentials" of international politics. The appraisal in this chapter has shown that for the major case of our time – the ending of the Cold War – the realist paradigm has failed to satisfy the criteria of explanatory power and relevance. Relevance can be assessed on a day-by-day basis, but its greatest test comes at critical turning points in history. These are often few and far between. In the twentieth century one can think of 1914–1918, 1933–1945, 1945–1947, and 1989–1991. Not since the end of World War II and the origins of the Cold War has there been a time of transition and change like this one. In such a time, theory is at a premium and its mettle is tested. Can it rise to the occasion? Can it provide a sound explanation of what is going on and a guide to the future? Can it anticipate the transition, or explain it only after the fact?

On all these questions the theories of the realist paradigm did not score very well. The more committed analysts and foreign policy experts were to the realist approach, the harder time they had believing that Gorbachev was for real. The failure to anticipate the end of the Cold War was not, as Gaddis (1992/93) avers, a failure of method, but a failure of theory. Those who adhered to very different methodological approaches – country experts in Soviet studies, traditional international relations scholars, policy analysts, quantitative scholars, historians, journalists – failed equally to anticipate the end of the Cold War regardless of the method they employed. Yet most of these did share the dominant realist frame for explaining the world they were studying.

The realist paradigm failed because it obfuscated the very factors and behavior that were now becoming critical for understanding what was going on – accommodation, absolute gains and cooperation, transcending power politics, the creation of new games. The ending of the Cold War is a major anomaly for the paradigm because it underlines the incompleteness of the picture of the world the paradigm paints and its distortion of "reality." Realist American observers could not understand Gorbachev and did not expect his behavior, because in their realist world of the struggle for power, such a leader of such a powerful state should not exist. Realism in its various guises failed to be relevant to the immediate crisis. It could not provide a guide, first because adherents to the paradigm could not understand what was happening. Once they understood what was happening, they could not believe it was actually happening. Then once they did believe it, they had little guidance to offer. Liberals and other nonrealists who had long advocated accommodation, escaping the security dilemma, building institutions for peace and conflict resolution were much quicker to grasp what was going on. They had plenty of policy advice to offer. Realism became irrelevant – practically and intellectually – for the every day affairs of the period.

Scholars, however, do not need to deal with the press of events. They have time to regroup and rethink. Adherents to the paradigm worked quickly and claimed that realist concepts and propositions could explain what had happened. Gorbachev ended the Cold War, they maintained, because the relative decline of the Soviet Union compelled it to retrench. The end of the Cold War was not an anomaly, even though unexpected. While the immediate relevance of the paradigm might have suffered, the explanatory power of the paradigm could be held intact.

This effort to explain the end of the Cold War, however, suffers from both logical and empirical problems. Logically, the relative decline-retrenchment proposition is an ex post facto explanation. Before the fact, realists, including Waltz, were predicting the opposite – relative decline would make the Soviet Union more aggressive and perhaps expansionistic. Explaining something after the fact in a manner directly opposite to what was said before the fact gives the distinct impression that adherents are unconsciously succumbing to the tendency of misspecifying the theory to fit subsequent events. Instead of deriving the authentic realist explanation most consistent with the logic of the paradigm, they have derived the explanation most consistent with the evidence. This impression is reinforced by the fact that, as Lebow (1994: 264) says, no realist would have predicted anything like this beforehand.

Empirically, there are numerous problems. First, there is the matter of timing. The Soviet Union had experienced other periods of decline yet there had never been such a sharp shift in its foreign policy. In addition, the sharpest decline in economic capability had occurred under Brezhnev in the early 1970s, not during the transition to Gorbachev. Second, if relative decline produces retrenchment, then the widely discussed decline of the United States after the Arab oil embargo should have produced a shift in US foreign policy. While détente may be interpreted in that light, Reagan's Cold War II cannot. This means that relative decline in the United States was associated with both accommodation and a hard-line policy. Similarly, within the Soviet Union relative decline was associated with both Brezhnev's stability and Gorbachev's radical change. It seems relative decline can be associated with several policies.

Third, the amount of decline the Soviet Union was posited as having undergone does not seem to warrant the extent to which Gorbachev changed Soviet foreign policy. What Gorbachev engaged in hardly seems to be retrenchment or the "shedding of peripheral commitments." It was a sea change. Fourth, and this gets to the heart of the matter, there was *no decline* in the area the realist paradigm sees as most important – political and military power. The Soviet Union was still a nuclear superpower equal to the United States, with the Soviet second strike capability clearly unimpaired. If one is to take realist nuclear theory seriously, then one cannot take the decline-retrenchment proposition seriously.

Fifth, if relative decline was a cause of the shift in Soviet foreign policy, then this external phenomenon should figure prominently in Gorbachev's motivation. Not only is there not much evidence that relative decline concentrated his attention, but his main concerns were domestic not international. He came to power on the basis of his domestic concerns and these shaped his foreign policy, rather than vice versa. There is plenty of evidence to show that Gorbachev and his advisors wanted to cut military spending so they could divert resources to the civilian economy. Conversely, there is little evidence to support the idea that Gorbachev and his advisors wanted to cut military spending and accommodate the United States because they felt they could no longer compete with a superior foe.

Lastly, if relative decline was so powerful as an external force, it should give rise, according to realist theory, to a consensus on a rational foreign policy response. Disagreement should be over details or options, not over fundamentals. Instead, as Evangelista (1993) shows, the leadership was sharply split along ideological lines with advocates of "the new thinking" opposing the old guard (see also Wohlforth 1994/95: 124). Gorbachev systematically eliminated the latter from positions of authority, as did Shevardnadze.

Taken together these empirical problems are considerable. They indicate that at its heart the explanatory deficiency of the realist paradigm stems from its basic inaccuracy. A shift to a nonrealist explanation better captures and explains the transition.

From the perspective of the nonrealist explanation given in this chapter, the end of the Cold War was not brought about by the external situation the Soviet Union was facing, but by a domestic leadership change that brought to power new individuals with new belief systems. Gorbachev's main purpose was domestic reform, and he sought to use Soviet foreign policy to help him in this purpose. In particular, he thought that by cutting back military spending he could transfer resources to the civilian sector. Through a trial-and-error process he developed a new cognitive map of Soviet foreign policy. In this process he was influenced by intellectuals who had been long exposed to Western critics of the Cold War, who saw it as a waste of resources. These intellectuals were encouraged by Gorbachev's new thinking and rode his agenda of change to increased influence. They advocated a de-ideologization of foreign policy and cutbacks to Third

World states, as well as a host of arms control measures aimed at the West. These foreign policy intellectuals were Gorbachev's domestic allies at home. Abroad, he became, with Shevardnadze at the helm, committed to the non-use of force. Since most of the leaders in Eastern Europe opposed his program of perestroika and glasnost and were seen by him as allies of his domestic opponents, Gorbachev had no incentive to intervene to save them as things began to unravel.

The Cold War came to an end because a leader (Gorbachev) eventually emerged on one side that was able to initiate a series of actions that could break the cycle of arms racing and competing for client states, as well as the hostility and propaganda to which each side had grown inured. These actions which often took on the characteristic of unilateral unreciprocated actions, eventually produced a positive response by a leader (Reagan) who was able to control hard-line critics who had previously undermined accommodation. This magic combination of a strong accommodative leader interacting with a responsive formerly hard-line leader permitted all the other factors that had been previously in place to finally bring the Cold War to an end.

Getting the domestic political environment of each side in order proved critical, but other factors were of equal importance. Of these, prior interactions that established the basis of accommodation were particularly important. Previous efforts at détente and the emerging global institutional structure established by Helsinki, CSCE, crisis management and crisis prevention techniques had made each side learn that they could establish and live by certain rules of the game that would manage their rivalry and make it less prone to war. The combination of the absence of territorial issues and the nuclear raising of the provocation threshold also reduced greatly the probability of war. Ideological disagreement it turned out was not worth the risk of major war (Mueller 1989; Vasquez 1991), let alone nuclear war.

With positive responses by Reagan and by Bush, the United States developed a vested interest in, first, Gorbachev and, then, Yeltsin and used its foreign policy to undercut Gorbachev's and Yeltsin's hard-line critics. When the United States finally believed the Cold War was over, it moved beyond containment toward a new grand strategy for dealing with its former rival. Instead of trying to weaken its rival, as might be expected by a state guided by the realist assumption of international politics as a perennial and deadly struggle for power, the United States opted to remake the USSR and later Russia in its own image. It sought to strengthen the Russian economy by making it capitalist and improve the efficiency of Russian government by making it democratic. If these reforms accomplished what the United States thought they would, then some day Russia would emerge both more powerful and more peaceful than it currently was.

Such a foreign policy contradicted everything realism posited about the sweep of history. A realist would not try to build up a former rival, and once having done so, would not expect that rival to be more peaceful than it was when it was weak. American foreign policy in the post-Cold War era posed another anomaly for the realist paradigm, particularly since it appears to be choosing – when push comes to shove – ideological goals over power concerns.

A shift to a new paradigm emphasizes a number of factors (variables) that have been long ignored by the realist paradigm. These include the importance of domestic politics and leadership shifts for inter-state interactions, of learning and cognitive structures for changing foreign policy, of the creation of rules of the game and institutions for building peace, and of the role of territorial issues for bringing about war. All of these factors turned out to be critical in ending the Cold War. Nonrealists were better able to see these factors at work and better able to explain the Cold War, because they were tracking these factors. Realists were not; they were focused primarily on power.

There is a certain overlap between the world society-issue politics paradigm and the liberal paradigm, especially since both are still being defined. There are also differences, however, especially with regard to explaining the end of the Cold War. The world society-issue politics paradigm focuses on the effect of cooperative actions, the redefining of issues, and the role of learning. The liberal paradigm places more emphasis on the pacific nature of democratic states and the benign face they presented to the Soviet Union. This emphasis, however, can lead to distortions of the historical record, which appear to be politically self-serving. One of the main problems with liberalism as a scholarly paradigm is that it is primarily an ideology with a strong normative component. Its explanation of the Cold War tends to put the blame all on one side and this contradicts most of what we know about politics and the dynamics of rivalry.

The ending of the Cold War and the new challenges for foreign policy in the post-Cold War era pose anomalies for international relations inquiry. The realist paradigm has failed at this important turning point in history to be relevant and to exhibit the kind of theoretical explanatory power that has long been its strong suit. Driving this failure has been the fundamental empirical inaccuracy of the paradigm, which has been a persistent problem. Even with all the epistemological evasions and ambiguities it has had in its intellectual arsenal, it can not adequately explain away its failure to account for the end of the Cold War. A nonrealist approach provides a much better account of why and how it ended.

14 Conclusion: the continuing inadequacy of the realist paradigm

One of the major conclusions of the original text was that research guided by the realist paradigm was not producing strong statistical findings. Continual research was not resulting in a cumulation of knowledge. One of the reactions to this was to reinforce the already existing belief (see Bull 1966) that quantitative analysis was a technique that would not yield much of significance. The legitimacy of the messenger was questioned and the message's authenticity rejected.

As noted in the concluding chapter of the original text, this is an ad hoc explanation that serves to protect the paradigm by dismissing discrepant evidence of a certain sort. While persuasive to those who do not like quantitative analysis, the argument in itself does not provide an adequate test of the claim the ad hoc explanation is making. To do that, two obvious tests logically need to be conducted: one that would control for the paradigm to see if nonrealist hypotheses did as poorly as realist hypotheses and a second that would control for the method to see if realist hypotheses investigated by traditional analysis produced research conclusions markedly different from those produced by quantitative analysis. The original text did provide a preliminary test of the first, which found that nonrealist hypotheses do proportionately better, albeit the sample size for nonrealist hypotheses was small.

The study in Part II has been intended to see whether using traditional analyses provides better research results for realist propositions. One of the major conclusions of this study is that the neo-traditional theorizing and policy analysis since Waltz's *Theory of International Politics* (1979) has proven no more able to provide clear evidence in favor of the realist paradigm than did the earlier quantitative research that tested the paradigm. Doing research by hard thinking and confronting theory with the "real world" of events has not necessarily made the paradigm look any better.

The criteria of adequacy and the case studies

The analysis in Part II conducted a series of case studies, each providing one or more criteria for appraising a central aspect of the realist paradigm. This chapter will examine how well the realist paradigm fared on the entire set of criteria with an eye to whether a nonrealist paradigm promises to do any better. It is important to examine the case studies collectively, because it is always possible that while the realist paradigm might do poorly on one criterion, it might excel on another. Likewise, while research on one variant of realism might suggest falsification, research on another variant might suggest confirmation. Failure to compare performance across the criteria would simply invite a series of ad hoc explanations every time a realist theory did poorly – such as the response of Elman and Elman (1995) to Schroeder's (1994a) review of historical evidence.

Part II has applied the most important criteria of adequacy to those research areas where one would expect the realist paradigm in its neorealist and neotraditional variants to do particularly well. The first criterion applied was the one set forth by Lakatos (1970) explicitly to deal with a situation where a series of theories is formulated to deal with discrepant evidence. This criterion maintains that research programs that reformulate theories must do so in a manner that results in progressive problemshifts (or theoryshifts) and not degenerating problemshifts. Since realism is often lauded for its theoretical robustness and its ability to offer new explanations, the application of this criterion was seen as perfectly legitimate and appropriate. Indeed, some argued that one of the main reasons for the realist paradigm's staying power is its ability to provide new theoretical insights (Hollis and Smith 1990: 66). Although this perception is certainly present within the discipline, such a conclusion could be *logically* made only if the theoretical shifts were in fact progressive and not degenerative. Hence the rationale for applying this criterion in chapter 11 to one of the more extensively developed neotraditional research programs – the investigation of Waltz's balancing proposition.

Another of the major assets of the realist paradigm that is lauded by many – and not just by adherents to the paradigm – is its ability to provide a theoretical understanding of the current world in which we live, so as to provide a sound guide to practice. The ability of neorealism to satisfy this expectation was dramatically revealed in 1990 with John Mearsheimer's analysis of the coming multipolar world. Deducing policy warnings and prescriptions from Waltz's (1979) neorealist analysis of multipolarity and bipolarity, he demonstrated the theoretical power of the realist paradigm to guide practice. He later went on in 1994/95 to attack the empirical soundness of nonrealist institutionalist prescriptions to provide a guide to peace in the new era we are entering.

Realism has always prided itself on its ability to guide practice, but such guidance should only be accepted if there is some assurance that the advice is empirically sound; i.e. if there is some evidence to reasonably assume that the theory underlying the advice is empirically accurate. The criteria of empirical accuracy and empirical soundness are therefore clearly appropriate to apply to this body of work, both to Mearsheimer's own prescriptions and to his charge that liberal institutionalist prescriptions are not sound. This case study was presented in chapter 12.

The final area that was examined, in which one would expect the realist paradigm to excel, concerned its explanatory power, particularly its ability to explain historical events of great significance. It was this ability that permitted realism to supersede idealism after the collapse of the League and the coming of World War II. Realism appeared to explain why the League (and the theory underlying it) had to fail, and why realism would provide a better explanation of the forces shaping international politics. For Morgenthau (1960: 5), understanding that politics was a struggle for power and using the concept of national interest to analyze that struggle would permit observers to explain past actions and anticipate future ones. Until recently, no one had severely challenged realism's ability to come up with plausible explanations of historical events, albeit much of their plausibility comes from their familiarity. Instead, the focus has been on whether these explanations are empirically accurate. Similarly, no one had criticized the relevance of the realist paradigm to speak to the major political issues of the day. Realism clearly has had much to say about the two World Wars and the Cold War; what is debated is the *soundness* of what has been said, not its *relevance*.

The criteria of explanatory power and relevance, therefore, are criteria that realism has always appeared to satisfy, and because of this, no one would question their appropriateness. Indeed, any

successful challenger to the realist paradigm would have to demonstrate that it would be able to provide greater explanatory power by
being able to explain things the paradigm was unable to explain or
explained incorrectly. Likewise, given the tight grip realism has had
on practice, it is unlikely that any challenger would be able to displace
it in this arena, unless it showed that it had more relevance than
realism for dealing with the critical issues of our time.

The only problem with applying these criteria is that history
provides few openings for testing them. We understand enough about
the sociology of knowledge to know that ideas about politics are
rarely tested in the real world except at major cataclysms or turning
points in history. Eventually, however, turning points come, and in
our own time, it has been the end of the Cold War that has provided
the turning point.

The selection of the case study on the end of the Cold War was
clearly based on an opportunity provided by history and as such can
be seen as a kind of natural experiment. It is nevertheless a fair test,
because if realism could prove to be as relevant to this new era as it
appeared to be to the previous one, then its mettle would have been
tested and strengthened. Examining this debate also provided an
opportunity to shift the focus away from Waltz and to Gilpin (1981)
whose explanation of change in international history provided the
basis of one of the main, but not the only, realist attempts to explain
the end of the Cold War.

The findings of the case studies

What have these case studies revealed? From the days of E. H. Carr
(1939) on, realists have claimed that their theories are empirically
accurate, robust and fruitful, empirically sound guides to practice,
and explanatorily powerful. An appraisal that insisted on the realist
paradigm's doing well on all of these criteria would be quite stringent.
But what has been found is that the realist paradigm has not done
well on any of these criteria.

The central core of the paradigm on balancing and power still has
difficulty on both logical and empirical grounds. Much of the theoretical richness and "growth" in the paradigm's theories has, as was seen
in chapter 11, really been an attempt to emend theories in light of
discrepant evidence. Rather than being a healthy sign, this is an
indicator of the degenerating nature of the core of the realist research

program. The proliferation of "realisms," from offensive and defensive realism (Mearsheimer 1994/95: 11–12, note 27; Snyder 1991: 10–13), contingent realism (Glaser 1994/95: 52), and prudential realism (Oye 1995: 58) to balance of threat (Walt 1987) and balance of interests (Schweller 1994), reflects both the indeterminate logic of power politics, as well as its tendency to protect itself from empirical falsification by chameleon proteanshifts that camouflage its nonconformity with the evidence.

Some realists would have us believe that such criticisms may be telling for Waltz (1979) and even for the entire neotraditional research program on balancing (see Elman and Elman 1995), but that there is more to realism than just Waltz's neorealism – and the rest of realism is left unscathed. The latter inference is not necessarily true. Each realist variant will have to be systematically appraised in turn, but those other variants that have been touched upon here, or reviewed systematically elsewhere, do not seem to be any more empirically accurate, even though they do not have degenerative research programs.

Elman and Elman's (1995) shift to Gilpin to show that not all of neorealism is undermined by Schroeder's (1994a) historical analysis, for example, does not seem to do the trick; for while work on Gilpin is not degenerating, it is far from clear that his explanations of political phenomena, like war, are any more accurate than Waltz's (1979, 1959) (see chs. 9 and 11, above). The most difficult problem in using Gilpin to save realism in light of Waltz's failures is the seeming implausibility of neotraditional attempts to explain the end of the Cold War in terms of a Gilpin decline thesis.

The shift back to classical realism, which is frequently taken to save the paradigm from criticisms made of Waltz, likewise proves no better (see, for example, the moves by Mearsheimer [1994/95] and by Schweller [1994]). First, such shifts are clearly degenerating because they do not show that the shift back has greater empirical content; i.e., that these early propositions have clear empirical support – in terms of either case studies or systematic historical investigation. Second, such shifts sometimes entail theoretical elaboration with, at best, only cursory historical surveys serving as evidence. Quantitative evidence is often ignored.

The time is long past when adherents to realism can go on assuming the empirical accuracy of the paradigm because not every aspect of it has been fully tested and only parts have been falsified by both quantitative and non-quantitative evidence. Realism is too indeterminate and too old for such a move to be taken seriously. Adherents to the paradigm must specify what will falsify specific realist variants. They must then go on to show that these variants can pass tests. Until then the field should not take it as a rebuttal presumption that the realist paradigm is going to satisfy the criterion of empirical accuracy. What seems more likely is what was suggested in the original text – i.e., that the realist paradigm has failed to satisfy the criterion of empirical accuracy because it is empirically inaccurate.

The fundamental inaccuracy of the paradigm has come home to roost in two major areas – the attempt to deal with the multipolar future and the inability to anticipate and explain the end of the Cold War. The intellectual costs of neotraditional ignoring of quantitative analysis were delineated in chapter 12 in the review of Mearsheimer's arguments on mulitipolarity and the false promise of international institutions. The deductive logic he used to demonstrate the perils of multipolarity was seen as empirically unsound. Contrary to what he thought, multipolar periods are not less peaceful than bipolar periods; rather, each seems associated with different types of war. Careful and systematic quantitative analysis by Wayman (1984) and others established that finding long before Mearsheimer (1990a) wrote. The quantitative analysis also conforms to what we know historically about the nuclear bipolar period that has just ended. It supports Van Evera's (1990/91) position over that of Mearsheimer (1990a), although the latter has received considerably more attention, undoubtedly because of its closer conformity to neorealist logic.

Ultimately, logic is only as good as the empirical accuracy of the premises used to establish the conclusion. For realism, the premise that power is the key determinate of international politics has proven to be the source of many of its problems. Mearsheimer (1990a: 5–6), as a good realist and neorealist, issued a warning about the future everyone was celebrating because for him the shift in the distribution of power indicated, theoretically, that the system would be more unstable and war prone. Yet, what the quantitative research showed is that the difference in power distribution between bipolar and multipolar systems has no effect on the occurrence of war. One distribution of power is not more associated with war than the other. This specific research on polarity is highly consistent with the general trend of the early quantitative research discussed in the original text that shows that power variables are not strongly correlated with the occurrence of war. The key factor on which the realist paradigm focuses – power –

led one of its chief advocates to make predictions about future multi-polarity that unbeknown to him and other neotraditionalists would not hold for past periods of multipolarity. Nevertheless, in doing so, he has laid out a crucial future test where these neorealist predictions can be compared to those based on nonrealist peace research.

This tendency to use realist logic to make prescriptions on the basis of theoretical predictions about the future, while ignoring the relevant quantitative evidence, was repeated in Mearsheimer's (1994/95) attack on the importance of international institutions for promoting peace. Here the evidence is more suggestive than the evidence on polarity; nevertheless, it consistently runs counter to Mearsheimer's position. It shows that when states do make concerted efforts to establish rules of the game to guide their relations, peace is more likely. The findings of peace research suggest, contrary to Mear-sheimer, that norms and informal institutions do make a difference and that it has been possible to establish periods of peace among major states within the post-Napoleonic era.

In addition, it was argued that the neorealist belief in the potency of nuclear deterrence (Mearsheimer 1993; Waltz 1995) appears to advocate risky policies on the basis of theoretical deductions that are untested and based on a paradigm that has had a very poor empirical record. Conversely, the policy implications of nonrealist peace research findings seem more prudent, more relevant to the problems of the post-Cold War era, and more empirically sound.

The relevance and the explanatory power of the realist paradigm was further undermined by the unanticipated ending of the Cold War, as was seen in chapter 13. Adherents to the paradigm were surprised by the events of 1989–1991. Realists of all stripes did not anticipate the Cold War to end in the way it did. Once the foreign policy objectives of the Soviet Union began to change, hard-line realists denied the reality of these shifts. After it was clear the Cold War had ended and a new historical era had begun, adherents to the realist paradigm developed an ex post facto explanation of the end of the Cold War based on Gilpin's neorealist analysis of decline. This explanation, however, is very problematic logically because it would never have been seriously entertained by realists before the fact; indeed, many realists argued that Soviet decline would, then, result in increased conflict and aggression, not accommodation. In addition, the explanation was found to suffer from several other empirical and theoretical problems. For example, it has difficulty seeing that in the mid-1980s there emerged from the ranks of the Communist Party of the USSR a leader who through a series of unilateral actions opted his country out of the struggle for power in the belief that peace was possible and that zero sum games could be converted into positive sum games. Furthermore, he did this with seemingly little concern about relative gains. At the same time, nonrealist approaches that emphasize cognitive psychology and learning and de-emphasize power seem to offer a more plausible explanation.

The failure to anticipate and adequately explain the end of the Cold War is not the first time the realist paradigm has had difficulty with an event of major historical significance. The realist belief that the use of alliances to balance power would prevent war did not work in the twentieth century. It led to "chain-ganging" and a rapid spread of the Austro-Hungarian/Serbian war in the late summer of 1914. In 1939, the major states failed to balance against Hitler's hegemonic bid in accordance with one of realism's and neorealism's fundamental "laws" of international politics. At best, it can be said they engaged in "buck-passing." Nor did the host of power politics practices that states engaged in prior to 1914, 1939, or 1941 prevent war by a strategy of peace through strength. Instead, the practices of alliance making, military build-ups, and *realpolitik* tactics seem to increase the probability of war.

All of the above historical events pose fundamental anomalies for the realist paradigm. If the major propositions of the various realist theories are correct, then the events depicted above should not have happened. It is difficult to have much confidence in a paradigm when the three major events of the twentieth century – World War I, World War II, and the ending of the Cold War – do not conform to its central theoretical expectations.

The three case studies of neotraditionalism have produced three conclusions: (1) that one of the oldest and most central research programs of the realist paradigm (and of neorealism) – that dealing with the balancing of power – has a marked tendency toward degenerating problemshifts; (2) that the neorealist analysis of the relationship between polarity and war is empirically inaccurate, thereby making Mearsheimer's theoretical pronouncements and prescriptions about the future empirically unsound; and (3) that the end of the Cold War, particularly the way in which it ended, has muted the explanatory power of the realist paradigm while the development of a new world order has raised questions about the paradigm's relevance. In each instance, the case studies suggest that elements of a nonrealist paradigm can do better. The use of nonrealist perspectives that have been critical of realism help identify the major problem areas that the realist paradigm must overcome to become an adequate guide to research. These are also the problems a nonrealist paradigm would need to resolve in order to produce better and more accurate theories than the realist paradigm has produced.

Prolegomenon to any future adequate paradigm

International relations research has suggested several areas where neorealism (but also classical realism) has been deficient or incorrect. Criticism, including neotraditional criticism, has centered on the following: (1) domestic politics plays an important role and cannot be ignored in the hopes that structural or power conditions will shape foreign policy behavior; (2) Waltz's emphasis on the systemic level of analysis, while useful, must be supplemented by work on other levels; in particular there is a pressing need for a theory of foreign policy; (3) realist predictions are frequently indeterminate; (4) balancing behavior does not seem to be a modal response to anarchy and does not occur in the conditions one would expect it, nor does it have the consequences that are always anticipated; and (5) there appear to be zones of peace, like that consisting of democratic liberal states, that the realist paradigm does not expect to occur. To these problem areas can be added one from the findings of quantitative research: (6) whether a system is multipolar or bipolar is not a very important variable for predicting the probability of war within a system, and therefore concerns about the dangers of current multipolarity are greatly exaggerated.

The need to look at domestic politics in order to fully understand and explain world politics has been a persistent theme among neotraditionalists, even among those quite sympathetic to neorealism. Snyder and Jervis (1993) examine the deficiencies of the systemic perspective for accounting for key elements in international behavior. Snyder (1991) himself sees the internal structure of the state as a key factor in the failure of some states to be restrained by the power of other states. Posen (1984: 7–9) seeks to develop a theory of foreign policy to complement Waltz. The need to look at beliefs is also a persistent theme (Van Evera 1984; Snyder 1984; Jervis 1976; Lebow 1981; Stein 1994).

Domestic politics seems to be important because of its impact on foreign policy and subsequent behavior. The classical realist tendency to black box the domestic arena, which is exemplified in its most extreme form in Waltz's systemic emphasis, leads to incomplete and inaccurate explanations. The general nature of the system and the external situation in which states find themselves do not adequately predict what the foreign policy of a state will look like. What this means is that the national interests of the state defined in terms of power are not so clear that one can, as Morgenthau thought, retrace and anticipate the actions of decision makers. As a result, leadership shifts can produce sharp changes in foreign policy, as was seen in the study of the end of the Cold War. All this points scholars toward a study of belief systems, learning, and the effect of the pulling and hauling of domestic politics on foreign policy and undermines the realist assumption of the state as a unitary rational actor (see chapter 8 in the original text).

Criticism of the lack of emphasis on domestic politics leads naturally to a criticism of neorealism's emphasis on the system level to the exclusion of other levels. The attention given in the field to Putnam's (1988) analysis of two-level games perhaps best reflects the consensus on the need to look beyond system variables. Putnam's analysis is important because it demonstrates that on issues of "low politics" like economic negotiations, domestic politics have an impact on the issue position of leaders. Studies of "high politics" also find domestic considerations important, as for example Levy and Barnett (1991) and Larson (1991) do in alliance making (see chapter 11, above) and Huth (1996) and Roy (1997) do in analyzing why territorial issues give rise to war even when the power differentials would suggest the contrary.

An adequate paradigm, therefore, must have a theory of foreign policy that can account not only for the actual policy of a state (its goals, objectives, and strategy, including grand strategy), but also its foreign policy behavior (the actions it takes vis-à-vis others). The issue politics paradigm attempts to deal with this problem by coming up with a new set of concepts to replace the emphasis on national interest and power. It discusses the "issue position" of actors as the main dependent variable to tap "policy" and offers a set of propositions for explaining how issue positions are determined, as well as new concepts for explaining the cooperative and conflictive interactions of actors (see Mansbach and Vasquez 1981b). Such an approach suggests the need for a general social science mid-range theory of decision making. Nonrealists have emphasized the value of studying cognitive psychology, models of learning, and even animal behavior as a source of ideas about collective choice, rather than relying solely on more "rational choice" oriented approaches common in economics.

In addition to a theory of decision making, a theory of foreign policy will need an explanation of foreign policy change. This is where Waltz's neorealism was criticized early on (see Ruggie 1983; Ashley 1984), but it should be pointed out that Gilpin's (1981) attempt to provide a neorealist explanation of change in history, while plausible within the logic of the realist paradigm, did not seem able to provide an accurate account of the end of the Cold War. This is because, as with classical realism, the emphasis on power as the key factor for explaining politics just does not seem as important as realists assume. Nor does it often tell us all we need to know. For realism and for the field generally, there is a need to develop an explanation of how domestic politics affects foreign policy (see Kapstein 1995). Here the work of Hagan (1993) provides a number of suggestive answers (see also Rosati et al. 1994), especially for nonrealists.

One of the key insights substantiated by quantitative research is that the dyad (or interaction) level of analysis is the most important for explaining foreign policy behavior and world politics. Quantitative work in comparative foreign policy did not begin to make much headway until it shifted away from the "monad" (trying to explain the foreign policy of a single state, like France or the United States) to an analysis of the dyad (explaining the foreign policy of a state vis-à-vis another state, controlling for issue area) (see Rummel 1972; Kegley and Skinner 1976: 308–311). Scholars, particularly quantitative scholars, who tried to study the foreign policy behavior of a single state fell into a "monad trap" from which conceptually it was difficult to escape and from which few strong statistical findings were produced. Likewise, in the study of war, only as there was a shift from the system level to the dyad level did stronger statistical findings become more common (see Singer 1982: 37–38; Bueno de Mesquita and Lalman 1988; Bremer 1992). As was discussed in chapter 9, it appears that the dyad (or more appropriately the interaction level) is the key level of analysis (or image) on which scholars should focus.

One of the difficulties in realizing this and why it took so long in coming is that neither Singer (1961) nor Waltz (1959) included this

level in their treatment of the question. Scholars were simply conceptually unaware of this level of analysis and needed to stumble
painfully upon it, even though it is certainly embodied within the
very label of the field – international *relations* – and Morgenthau's
(1960: ch. 10) analysis of how to evaluate a nation's power. Nevertheless, it is Burton et al. (1974) with his nonrealist emphasis on *relationships* that appears to provide a key to future progress – first in terms of
getting away from the idea that all relationships are a struggle for
power, and second in his opening up the possibility of changing
relationships so that conflict might be resolved (and even actively
prevented before it starts – what he calls conflict *provention* (Burton
1990). It is this shift away from the zero-sum-relative-gain world of
realism that marks the distinctive quality of nonrealist approaches,
particularly the world society-issue politics paradigm and neoliberalism. And it will no doubt be on this question that the inter-paradigm
debate will turn (see chapter 8 in the original text).

The third problem area for realism is that in too many instances it is
indeterminate (Rosecrance and Stein 1993; Evangelistia 1993). The
paradigm's logic of power politics is such that it can accommodate a
variety of explanations. The articulation of the paradigm thus has
been quite fruitful and theoretically robust. The negative side,
however, has been when the logic provides contradictory explanations, such as states will balance power (Waltz 1979) or they will not
balance (Schweller 1994), or a balance of power is associated with
peace (Dehio 1961) or is associated with war (Organski 1958; Kugler
and Lemke 1996). In terms of the ability of realism to guide foreign
policy, this indeterminacy does not tell decision makers which of the
many policies or options they might pursue is most consistent with
the logic of realism. From a theoretical perspective, this makes it
difficult to determine the adequacy of realist explanations of current
foreign policy and of the past. Even those very sympathetic to realism
recognize the seriousness of this problem and can become quite
frustrated (see Oye 1995: 77).

This means that it is often possible for realism to avoid falsification
by coming up with a variety of explanations one of which is more apt
to fit the evidence than another. This poses the problem of determining what is the authentic realist explanation. Scholars think of this
as a problem of non-falsifiability, but as was seen in chapter 11, it is
really a problem of degenerating research programs. This is especially
the case with the realist paradigm, because what is at issue is not

simply a handful of differing realist explanations, but a series of realist theories (a number of which are created in the light of discrepant historical evidence). It is always possible, as Lakatos (1970: 116–117) says, to come up with an auxiliary proposition or conceptual change that will save a research program – the problem is how to determine whether such changes are ad hoc or actually getting at the truth. Thus, if Walt (1987) finds that states do not balance against power, but against threat, is this a falsification of realism and neorealism or the legitimate basis for creating a new realist theory? Lakatos' rules on progressive and degenerating problemshifts seek to provide a rigorous procedure for answering such questions.

In the meantime, the most difficult problem for the realist paradigm is to determine which of its many possible variants are its authentic representatives. Another way of putting this is that, if realism is to be considered scientific, it must specify (before tests) what will count as evidence for falsifying it. After the fact, it is, logically, too late. This is the potential problem with Wayman and Diehl's (1994: 22–23) suggestion that realism be reconstructed on the basis of strong statistical findings. While such an inductive strategy can be useful, it is necessary to specify what evidence, beyond that already marshalled, will serve as an adequate test of this new realism.

Likewise, a nonrealist paradigm will have to do the same thing. Now it may turn out that fundamental assumptions of any given paradigm are just so broad that their "logic" does not compel a single set of non-contradictory propositions to be derived. This can happen for two basic reasons: because the assumptions are quite broad and because the empirical premises may shift. In such instances, which are probably typical, it is necessary for theorists to make their case as to why a given variant is the authentic representative of the paradigm before the evidence is examined, because what is at issue in such a question is not whether the variant is empirically accurate, but whether it is the best theoretical specification of the paradigm's view of the world. Once that is determined, then it is possible for the test of that variant to be also a test of the paradigm's view of the world. Without that theoretical specification, degeneration and non-falsifiability will carry the day.

The last three problems that have been delineated – the lack of balancing, zones of peace, and the seeming unimportance of polarity for conflict – are unexpected research outcomes that the realist paradigm must explain away. If a nonrealist paradigm can better explain these outcomes or identify patterns related to the dependent variables in question, then it will appear more adequate. The first and last of these outcomes suggests that power is not as key a variable for explaining behavior as adherents to the realist paradigm think. There is a wealth of evidence to suggest that variables other than power or power-related concerns are more important for explaining international relations. Such propositions, including further tests on balancing and on multipolarity, provide crucial future empirical tests to assess the relative accuracy of realist and nonrealist propositions.

The finding on the zones of peace forms a different kind of an anomaly for the realist paradigm. First, it is very unexpected and inconsistent with the notion that international politics is a perennial struggle for power. Second, it is damaging to the realist paradigm because it was a finding predicted by the nonrealist liberal paradigm. If there are zones of peace based on factors other than the democratic liberal nature of states, then this would be evidence in favor of nonrealist competitors to the liberal paradigm; i.e., in favor of the world society-issue politics paradigm.

Whether realism will be able to solve these problems and whether new Waltzes and Gilpins will emerge remains to be seen. In the meantime, it is important to briefly address whether the Liberal Kantian paradigm that is associated with the democratic peace finding is currently the best nonrealist alternative.

Where do we go from here?

The analyses in both the original text and the set of case studies present arguments and evidence for abandoning the realist paradigm and working to construct a nonrealist alternative. For most people, especially within North America, the main alternative they think of is some form of liberalism. It should be obvious from the preceding chapters (especially ch. 13) that my reading of the major intellectual events in the history of the field provides a different and much broader view of what has been going on than the conventional American interpretation that sees international relations discourse primarily in terms of a debate between realism and liberalism. I want to emphasize that the alternative to realism that I have in mind is not the Liberal Kantian paradigm that has attracted so much attention in recent years.

This is especially important because the kind of theoretical work I have done on issue politics (Mansbach and Vasquez 1981b) and that Burton has done on conflict resolution has often been subsumed under "pluralism" (see Banks 1985a). Yet it is not the insistence on non-state actors that is the more radical aspect of this paradigm, although Mansbach, Ferguson, and Lampert (1976) emphasized that. Rather it has been the rejection of the third assumption on politics as a struggle for power. Here the work on conflict resolution is closer to the mark, even though it is possible to integrate such techniques into a more social engineering liberal approach.

My main concerns with the Liberal Kantian paradigm are threefold. First, it is not clear, as already discussed in chapter 13, that the reason democratic states tend not to wage war against each other is that there is something about their joint governmental structure that makes them inherently peaceful toward one another. Even if this were to be found to be the case, it would still be possible to supersede the Kantian paradigm if some other paradigm could explain not only the democratic zone of peace, but other zones of peace as well. From my own perspective, it is the resolution of territorial issues coupled with a set of norms for handling territorial disputes that is critical in preventing war between democratic states. There is no reason why these factors cannot also work when societies are non-democratic. This is an important testable difference between the liberal paradigm and a world society-issue politics paradigm. On the theoretical level, then, the Kantian paradigm, although rich in insights about the conditions of peace, is somewhat narrow. Its propositions on international organization and on increasing wealth can be incorporated in nonrealist paradigms that are not grounded so centrally on the question of democracy. Increasing wealth, for example, is seen as a solution to war by Marx as well as a number of other thinkers.

Second, and more fundamental, is that the Liberal Kantian paradigm is closely tied with liberalism as a political philosophy. Going from realism to liberalism in many ways will be replacing one ideology with another. There are real dangers in this for the practicing of science. The most important is that this would tie empirical work much more closely with normative work than has usually been the case in the English-speaking world. Critical theorists have often advocated such a unity (see Cox 1981) and post-modernists and post-positivists have questioned whether it is ever possible to make such a separation. Still, one does not usually think that uniting empirical and normative theory so that it is more of a handmaiden to American liberalism is what critical theorists and post-modernists really have in mind.

Third, there is good reason for them and others to worry about such a "partnership." Rather than making science a critical institution within global society, it would make it much more so than it was under realism the kind of homogenizing-social-engineering-global culture that Ashley (1983a) worried about. Whenever empirical and normative work are closely tied together as critical theorists like to do, there is always the danger that one's idea of normative goodness (or political interests) will weigh too heavily in one's thinking about what is empirically true and theoretically adequate. Such dangers are greatest when the normative theory guiding empirical analysis is a full-blown political philosophy, as liberalism is. It should be noted that despite realism's ties with conservativism, it is sufficiently independent intellectually for democratic liberals, like a Kennedy or a Lyndon Johnson, to embrace it.

For me, the answer is to move in a different direction – one that would build upon the attempt to keep a scientific study of inter-national politics (broadly defined) independent from normative inquiry, while also introducing the normative concerns of post-moder-nists and critical theorists that will make space for such inquiry within the field and encourage a normative pluralism that positivism has choked off. This pluralism should also extend to empirical analyses focusing on some of the topics of inquiry that were closed off by the rise of realism such as the study of international law and diplomatic history. In addition, there also should be a greater pluralism with regard to method. There is no reason why the field cannot encourage those who embrace philosophical techniques like hermeneutics and deconstruction. At the same time, there needs to be more communi-cation and comparison of empirical analyses, regardless of their method, for the purpose of appraising theories and for determining what is being learned about a particular subject. Without that, there is no real engagement with those who take a different approach and no real learning. A pluralism that allows each little sect to go off and form its own little subfield may be tolerant, but it is not really opening up the dominant discourse to new ideas and challenges. It also poses the danger of fracturing the discipline into schools of thought that can avoid evidence and criticism.

How discourse is opened up is crucial for the inter-paradigm debate. Debate implies communication, not separation and indifference. Debate, however, is not an end in itself. Despite the limitations of the scientific spirit and the social engineering dangers it has posed, the idea that there is an empirical truth and that it is both possible and noble to search for it, regardless of one's own philosophical, ethical, religious, and political beliefs, is still a value well worth preserving and institutionalizing. Such a value, as post-modernists rightly point out, means at certain points making debate come to a resolution. It is not wrong or intolerant to determine through a collective process (so long as it does not coerce belief) that some explanations appear to be false and others on the right track. For a variety of reasons, scholars feel they are on more solid ground for making judgments like this on empirical questions than on normative ones. What needs to be done is not to give up on this quest, but to work to make theory appraisal as rigorous and as open a process as possible.

There are two strategies worth considering for increasing such cumulation of knowledge about international relations. The first is to make theory appraisal more systematic, especially as it relates to the paradigm debate. The second is to take a more mid-range theory approach and concentrate on what Guetzkow (1950) called islands of theory. These strategies are not necessarily contradictory, but they are sufficiently different so as to spread out the risks if one turns out to be wrong.

One of the main themes of the original text is that international relations inquiry is much more cumulative and focused than it initially appears. One reason for this is that there is a dominant paradigm that sets the research agenda and ranks the priorities. In many ways, international relations is a coherent discipline because it has had a paradigm. Even when it has had a tendency to divide along methodological lines, shared theoretical interests have kept scholars in contact with each other.

The inter-paradigm debate can provide the same function, as the realist paradigm is increasingly challenged by competitors. It is important that such a debate be conducted on as rigorous a plane as possible. No matter what one thinks of Kuhn, one does not want such decisions to be made on the basis of a political struggle. One of the purposes of this book has been to present reasonable criteria (i.e., decision rules) for conducting and resolving the debate. Because they are generally not controversial, it should be possible for adherents to different paradigms to agree that such criteria would provide a fair set of tests for theory and paradigm appraisal. Collectively, the field needs to be much more rigorous in applying these criteria at two specific points during inquiry: (1) before tests in the construction of research designs, and (2) after tests in the appraising of theories. Only by being more rigorous both in testing the existing dominant paradigm and in building a new paradigm that can explain the growing body of counterevidence, as well as produce new non-obvious findings of its own, will progress be made.

One of the problems with this strategy is that while some attention needs to be paid to grand theory, if too much attention is paid to this endeavor, then research may never deepen and grow within a particular subject area. Some, like Jack S. Levy, have argued that greater effort be placed on constructing mid-range theories on fairly specific topics like decision making, perception and learning, war, peace, alliance behavior, negotiation and bargaining, conflict resolution, international political economy, and so forth. Without such specialization, there is a danger that the inter-paradigm debate will orient research to such grand questions that no real new knowledge will be generated, thereby giving the field a superficial quality. Research on mid-level theories will also aid discussion of the inter-paradigm debate by increasing the knowledge base and helping to inform theory construction, thereby eventually feeding into a paradigm-oriented theory appraisal strategy.

Although the attempt to study world politics systematically has not produced quick answers, rigor has made a difference. One of the problems with traditional theorizing has been the attempt to explain empirical generalizations that were never fully documented. This has been the main flaw in Waltz's (1979) and Gilpin's (1981) elegant analyses. Generating empirical findings (through quantitative analysis and the careful examination of historical evidence) is still essential. Nevertheless, until the findings are put together and integrated into a theory, they are of limited use. Therefore, the creation of a scientific theory, whether through induction or deduction, remains a pressing task. Such an enterprise is best done at the mid-range level using important research in each of the specific areas to develop islands of theory. Guetzkow's (1950) vision that such islands of theory could be cumulated and eventually connected remains a project worth pursuing. What is needed in a post-modern and post-positivist era is not less science, but more theoretically critical science. This is particularly the case in a field that has been dominated by a flawed paradigm.

References

Abolfathi, Farid (1980) "Threat, Public Opinion, and Military Spending in the United States, 1980–1990" in P. McGowan and C. Kegley, Jr. (eds.) *Sage International Yearbook of Foreign Policy Studies*, vol. 5, Beverly Hills: Sage, pp. 83–133.

Abolfathi, Farid, John J. Hayes, and Richard Hayes (1979) "Trends in United States Response to International Crises" in C. Kegley, Jr. and P. McGowan (eds.) *Sage International Yearbook of Foreign Policy Studies*, vol. 4, Beverly Hills: Sage, pp. 57–85.

Alcock, Norman, and Keith Lowe (1969) "The Vietnam War as a Richardson Process," *Journal of Peace Research* 6 (2): 105–112.

Alger, Chadwick F. (1965) "Personal Contact in Intergovernmental Organizations" in H. C. Kelman (ed.) *International Behavior: A Social Psychological Analysis*, New York: Holt, Rinehart, and Winston, pp. 523–547.

(1966) "Interaction and Negotiation in a Committee of the United Nations General Assembly," *Peace Research Society (International) Papers* 5: 141–159.

(1968) "Interaction in a Committee of the UN General Assembly" in J. D. Singer (ed.) *Quantitative International Politics*, New York: Free Press, pp. 51–84.

(1970) "Research on Research: A Decade of Quantitative and Field Research on International Organizations," *International Organization* 24 (Summer): 414–450.

Alger, Chadwick F., and Steven J. Brams (1967) "Patterns of Representation in National Capitals and Intergovernmental Organizations," *World Politics* 19 (July): 646–663.

Alker, Hayward R., Jr. (1964) "Dimensions of Conflict in the General Assembly," *American Political Science Review* 58 (September): 642–657.

(1971) "Research Paradigms and Mathematical Politics." Paper presented at the 1971 International Political Science Association Roundtable on "Quantitative Methods and Political Substance," Mannheim, Germany.

(1996) "The Presumption of Anarchy in World Politics" in H. R. Alker

Rediscoveries and Reformulations, Cambridge: Cambridge University Press, pp. 355–393.

Alker, Hayward R., Jr. and P. F. Bock (1972) "Propositions about International Relations" in *Political Science Annual*, vol. 3, Indianapolis: Bobbs-Merrill, pp. 385–490.

Alker, Hayward R., Jr., and Donald Puchala (1968) "Trends in Economic Partnership: The North Atlantic Area, 1928–1963" in J. D. Singer (ed.) *Quantitative International Politics*, New York: Free Press, pp. 287–316.

Alker, Hayward R., Jr., and Bruce M. Russett (1965) *World Politics in the General Assembly*, New Haven: Yale University Press.

Allison, Graham T. (1971) *Essence of Decision: Explaining the Cuban Missile Crisis*, Boston: Little, Brown.

Allison, Graham T., and Morton H. Halperin (1972) "Bureaucratic Politics: A Paradigm and Some Policy Implications," *World Politics* 24 (Supplement): 40–89.

Amalrik, Andrei (1970) *Will the Soviet Union Survive Until 1984?* New York: Harper and Row.

Angell, Robert C. (1965) "An Analysis of Trends in International Organizations," *Peace Research Society (International) Papers* 3: 185–195.

   (1967) "The Growth of Transnational Participation," *Journal of Social Issues* 23 (January): 108–129.

Armor, Daniel, Joseph Giacquinta, R. Gordon McIntosh, and Diana Russell (1967) "Professors' Attitudes Toward the Vietnam War," *Public Opinion Quarterly* 31 (2): 159–175.

Aron, Raymond (1966) *Peace and War*, New York: Doubleday.

Ashby, W. Ross (1952) *Design for a Brain*, New York: John Wiley.

Ashley, Richard K. (1976) "Noticing Pre-paradigmatic Progress" in J. Rosenau (ed.) *In Search of Global Patterns*, New York: Free Press, pp. 150–158.

   (1981) "Political Realism and Human Interests," *International Studies Quarterly* 25 (June): 204–236.

   (1983a) "The Eye of Power: The Politics of World Modeling," *International Organization* 37 (Summer): 495–535.

   (1983b) "Three Modes of Economism," *International Studies Quarterly* 27 (December): 463–496.

   (1984) "The Poverty of Neorealism," *International Organization* 38 (Spring): 225–286.

   (1987) "The Geopolitics of Geopolitical Space: Toward a Critical Social Theory of International Politics," *Alternatives* 12 (October): 403–434.

   (1988) "Geopolitics, Supplementary Criticism: A Reply to Professors Roy and Walker," *Alternatives* 13 (January): 88–102.

Ashley, Richard K., and R. B. J. Walker (1990) "Speaking the Language of Exile: Dissident Thought in International Studies," *International Studies Quarterly* 34 (September): 259–266.

Austin, J. L. (1962) *How to Do Things with Words*, New York: Oxford University Press.

Axelrod, Robert (ed.) (1976a) *Structure of Decision*, Princeton: Princeton University Press.

(1976b) "Decision for Neo-imperialism: The Deliberations of the British Eastern Committee in 1918" in R. Axelrod (ed.) *Structure of Decision*, Princeton: Princeton University Press, pp. 77–95.

(1984) *The Evolution of Cooperation*, New York: Basic Books.

Ayer, A. J. (1946) *Language, Truth, and Logic*, London: Victor Gollancz.

Azar, Edward E. (1970) "Analysis of International Events," *Peace Research Reviews* 4: 1–113.

(1972) "Conflict Escalation and Conflict Reduction in an International Crisis: Suez, 1956," *Journal of Conflict Resolution* 16 (June): 183–201.

(1980) "The Conflict and Peace Data (COPDAB) Project," *Journal of Conflict Resolution* 24 (March): 143–152.

Azar, Edward E., and Joseph D. Ben-Dak (eds.) (1975) *Theory and Practice of Events Research*, London: Gordon and Breach.

Azar, Edward, and T. Havener (1976) "Discontinuities of the Symbolic Environment: A Problem in Scaling Events, *International Interactions* 2 (4): 231–246.

Baldwin, David A. (ed.) (1993) *Neorealism and Neoliberalism: The Contemporary Debate*, New York: Columbia University Press.

Ball, Margaret (1951) "Bloc Voting in the General Assembly," *International Organization* 5 (February): 3–31.

Banks, Arthur S. (1971) *Cross-Polity – Series Data*, Cambridge, Mass.: MIT Press.

(1973) *Cross-National Data Analysis*, Syracuse: Syracuse University International Relations Program.

Banks, Arthur S., and Robert B. Textor (1963) *A Cross-Polity Survey*, Cambridge, Mass.: MIT Press.

Banks, Michael (1985a) "The Inter-Paradigm Debate," in M. Light and A. J. R. Groom (eds.) *A Handbook of Current Theory*, London: Frances Pinter, pp. 7–26.

(1985b) "Where We Are Now," *Review of International Studies* 11 (July): 215–233.

Barrera, Mario, and Ernst B. Haas (1969) "The Operationalization of Some Variables Related to Regional Integration: A Research Note," *International Organization* 23 (Winter): 150–160.

Barringer, Richard (1972) *War: Patterns of Conflict*, Cambridge, Mass.: MIT Press.

Baudrillard, Jean (1990) *Seduction*, New York: St. Martin's.

Beal, Richard Smith (1976) "A Contra-Kuhnian View of the Discipline's Growth" in J. Rosenau (ed.) *In Search of Global Patterns*, New York: Free Press, pp. 158–161.

Bell, Cora (1989) *The Reagan Paradox*, New Brunswick: Rutgers University Press.

Bell, P. M. H. (1986) *The Origins of the Second World War in Europe*, London: Longman.

References

Bell, Wendell (1960) "Images of the United States and the Soviet Union Held by Jamaican Elite Groups," *World Politics* 12 (January): 225–248.

Berger, Peter L., and Luckmann, Thomas (1966) *The Social Construction of Reality*, New York: Doubleday.

Bernstein, Robert A., and Peter Weldon (1968) "A Structural Approach to the Analysis of International Relations," *Journal of Conflict Resolution* 12 (June): 159–181.

Beschloss, Michael R., and Strobe Talbott (1993) *At the Highest Levels*, Boston: Little, Brown.

Betts, Richard K. (1987) *Nuclear Blackmail and Nuclear Balance*, Washington, DC: Brookings.

 (1992) "Systems of Peace or Causes of War? Collective Security, Arms Control and the New Europe," *International Security* 17 (Summer): 5–43.

Bhaskar, Roy (1989) *Reclaiming Reality*, London: Verso.

Bingham, June (1961) *Courage to Change: An Introduction to the Life and Thought of Reinhold Niebuhr*, New York: Scribner's.

Blachowicz, James A. (1971) "Systems Theory and Evolutionary Models of the Development of Sciences," *Philosophy of Science* 38 (June): 178–199.

Blalock, Hubert M., Jr. (1960) *Social Statistics*, New York: McGraw-Hill.

Blechman, Barry M. (1972) "Impact of Israeli Reprisals on Behavior of the Bordering Arab Nations Directed at Israel," *Journal of Conflict Resolution* 16 (June): 155–182.

Blechman, Barry M., and Stephen S. Kaplan (1978) *Force Without War*, Washington, DC: Brookings.

Bobrow, Davis B., Steve Chan, and John A. Kringen (1977) "Understanding How Others Treat Crises," *International Studies Quarterly* 21 (March): 199–224.

 (1979) *Understanding Foreign Policy Decisions: The Chinese Case*, New York: Free Press.

Bonham, G. Matthew, and Michael Shapiro (1973) "Simulation in the Development of a Theory of Foreign Policy Decision-Making" in P.J. McGowan (ed.) *Sage International Yearbook of Foreign Policy Studies*, vol. 1, Beverly Hills: Sage, pp. 55–71.

 (1976) "Explanation of the Unexpected: the Syrian Intervention in Jordan in 1970" in R. Axelrod (ed.) *Structure of Decision*, Princeton: Princeton University Press, pp. 113–141.

Boswell, Terry, and Mike Sweat (1991) "Hegemony, Long Waves, and Major Wars: A Time Series Analysis of Systemic Dynamics, 1496–1967," *International Studies Quarterly* 35 (June): 123–149.

Brady, Linda P. (1975) "Explaining Foreign Policy Behavior Using Transitory Qualities of Situations." Paper presented at the annual meeting of the American Political Science Association, San Francisco.

Brams, Steven (1966a) "Transaction Flows in the International System," *American Political Science Review* 60 (December): 880–898.

 (1966b) "Trade in the North Atlantic Area: An Approach to the Analysis of

Transformation in a System," *Peace Research Society (International) Papers* 6: 143–164.

(1968) "A Note on the Cosmopolitanism of World Regions," *Journal of Peace Research* 5 (1): 87–95.

(1969a) "The Search for Structural Order in the International System: Some Models and Preliminary Results," *International Studies Quarterly* 13 (September): 254–280.

(1969b) "The Structure of Influence Relationships in the International System" in J. Rosenau (ed.) *International Politics and Foreign Policy*, rev. edn. New York: Free Press, pp. 583–599.

Braybrook, Daniel, and Charles E. Lindblom (1963) *A Strategy of Decision: Policy Evaluation as a Social Process*, New York: Free Press.

Braybrook, Daniel, and Alexander Rosenberg (1972) "Comment: Getting the War News Straight: The Actual Situation in the Philosophy of Science," *American Political Science Review* 66 (September): 818–826.

Brecher, Michael (1977) "Toward a Theory of International Crisis Behavior," *International Studies Quarterly* 21 (March): 39–75.

Brecher, Michael, Blema Steinberg, and Janice Stein (1969) "A Framework for Research on Foreign Policy Behavior," *Journal of Conflict Resolution* 13 (March): 75–101.

Brecher, Michael, and Jonathan Wilkenfeld (1989) *Crisis, Conflict and Instability*, Oxford: Pergamon.

(1991) "International Crises and Global Instability: The Myth of the 'Long Peace'" in C. Kegley, Jr. (ed.) *The Long Postwar Peace*, New York: HarperCollins, pp. 85–104.

Bremer, Stuart A. (1980) "National Capabilities and War Proneness" in J. D. Singer (ed.) *The Correlates of War: II*, New York: Free Press, pp. 57–82.

(1992) "Dangerous Dyads: Conditions Affecting the Likelihood of Interstate War, 1816–1965," *Journal of Conflict Resolution* 36 (June): 309–341.

Bremer, Stuart A., Cynthia Cannizzo, Charles W. Kegley, Jr., and James Lee Ray (1975 [1992]) "The Scientific Study of War: A Learning Package," New York: Learning Resources in International Studies. Reprinted and adapted by Marie T. Henehan in J. Vasquez and M. Henehan (eds.) (1992) *The Scientific Study of Peace and War*, Lexington: Lexington Books, pp. 373–437.

Breslauer, George W., and Philip E. Tetlock (1991) *Learning in U.S. and Soviet Foreign Policy*, Boulder: Westview.

Brewer, Thomas L. (1973) "Issue and Context Variation in Foreign Policy," *Journal of Conflict Resolution* 17 (March): 89–115.

Brickman, Philip, Philip Shaver, and Peter Archibald (1968) "American Tactics and American Goals in Vietnam as Perceived by Social Scientists," *Peace Research Society (International)* 10: 79–104.

Brodie, Bernard (1945) "The Atomic Bomb and American Security," Memorandum No. 18, Yale Institute of International Studies.

Brody, Richard A. (1972) "Problems in the Measurement and Analysis of International Events" in E. Azar, R. Brody, and C. McClelland (eds.)

International Events Interaction Analysis, Sage Professional Papers in International Studies, 02–001, Beverly Hills: Sage, pp. 45–58.

Bronfenbrenner, Urie (1961) "The Mirror Image in Soviet-American Relations," *Journal of Social Issues* 17 (3): 45–56.

Bryce, James (1922) *International Relations*, New York: Macmillan.

Bueno de Mesquita, Bruce (1975) "Measuring Systemic Polarity," *Journal of Conflict Resolution* 19 (June): 197–216.

(1978) "Systemic Polarization and the Occurrence and Duration of War," *Journal of Conflict Resolution* 22 (June): 241–267.

(1981) "Risk, Power Distributions, and the Likelihood of War," *International Studies Quarterly* 25 (December): 541–568.

(1989) "The Contribution of Expected-Utility Theory to the Study of International Conflict" in M. Midlarsky (ed.) *Handbook of War Studies*, Boston: Unwin Hyman, pp. 143–169.

Bueno de Mesquita, Bruce, and David Lalman (1988) "Empirical Support for Systemic and Dyadic Explanations of International Conflict," *World Politics* 41 (October): 1–20.

(1992) *War and Reason*, New Haven: Yale University Press.

Bull, Hedley (1966) "International Theory: The Case for a Classical Approach," *World Politics* 18 (April): 361–377.

(1972) "The Theory of International Politics, 1919–1969" in B. Porter (ed.) *The Aberystwyth Papers: International Politics, 1919–1969*, London: Oxford University Press, pp. 30–56.

(1977) *The Anarchical Society*, New York: Columbia University Press.

Bunce, Valerie (1981) *Do New Leaders Make a Difference?* Princeton: Princeton University Press.

Burgess, Philip M. (1970) "Nation-typing for Foreign Policy Analysis: A Partitioning Procedure for Constructing Typologies" in E. Fedder (ed.) *Methodological Concerns in International Studies*, St. Louis: University of Missouri Center for International Studies.

Burgess, Philip M., and James E. Harf (1975) *Global Analysis: A Data Scheme and Deck for Univariate and Bivariate Analysis*, New York: Consortium for International Studies Education of the International Studies Association.

Burgess, Philip M., and Richard Lawton (1972) *Indicators of International Behavior: An Assessment of Events Data Research*, Sage Professional Papers in International Studies, 02–010, Beverly Hills: Sage.

Burrowes, Robert (1974) "Mirror, Mirror, on the Wall . . . : A Comparison of Events Data Sources" in J. Rosenau (ed.) *Comparing Foreign Policies*, New York: Halsted/John Wiley, pp. 383–406.

Burrowes, Robert, and Bertram Spector (1973) "The Strength and Direction of Relationships Between Domestic and External Conflict and Cooperation: Syria, 1961–67" in J. Wilkenfeld (ed.) *Conflict Behavior and Linkage Politics*, New York: David McKay.

Burton, John W. (1972) *World Society*, Cambridge: Cambridge University Press.

(1982) *Dear Survivors*, London: Frances Pinter.

(1984) *Global Conflict*, Brighton: Wheatsheaf.

(1990) *Conflict: Resolution and Provention*, Basingstoke: Macmillan.

(1995) "Conflict Provention as a Political System" in J. Vasquez et al. (eds.) *Beyond Confrontation: Learning Conflict Resolution in the Post–Cold War Era*, Ann Arbor: University of Michigan Press, pp. 115–127.

Burton, John W., A. J. R. Groom, Chris R. Mitchell, and A. V. S. de Reuck (1974) *The Study of World Society: A London Perspective*, Occasional Paper No. 1, International Studies Association.

Butterfield, Herbert (1953) *Christianity, Diplomacy and War*, London: Epworth Press.

Butterworth, Robert Lyle (1976) *Managing Interstate Conflict: Data with Synopses*, Pittsburgh: University Center of International Studies, University of Pittsburgh.

(1978) "Do Conflict Managers Matter?" *International Studies Quarterly* 22 (June): 195–214.

Buzan, Barry (1993) "From International System to International Society," *International Organization* 47 (Summer): 327–352.

Buzan, Barry, Charles Jones, and Richard Little (1993) *The Logic of Anarchy: Neorealism to Structural Realism*, New York: Columbia University Press.

CACI (1975) Crisis Inventory, Final Technical Report. Arlington, Va.: CACI, Inc.

Callahan, Patrick, Linda Brady, and Margaret Hermann (eds.) (1982) *Describing Foreign Policy Behavior*, Beverly Hills: Sage.

Campbell, David (1989) Security and Identity in United States Foreign Policy, Ph.D. Dissertation, Australian National University.

(1992) *Writing Security*, Minneapolis: University of Minnesota Press.

Campbell, Joel, and Leila Cain (1965) "Public Opinion and the Outbreak of War," *Journal of Conflict Resolution* 9 (September): 318–328.

Caporaso, James A. (1978) "Dependence, Dependency, and Power in the Global System: A Structural and Behavioral Analysis," *International Organization* 32 (Winter): 13–43.

Caporaso, James A., and Michael D. Ward (1979) "The United States in an Interdependent World: The Emergence of Economic Power" in C. Kegley, Jr., and P. McGowan (eds.) *Sage International Yearbook of Foreign Policy Studies*, vol. 4, Beverly Hills: Sage, pp. 139–169.

Carnap, Rudolf (1952) *The Continuum of Inductive Methods*, Chicago: University of Chicago Press.

(1962) *The Logical Foundations of Probability*, Chicago: University of Chicago Press.

Carr, Edward Hallett (1939, 1964) *The Twenty Years' Crisis*, New York: Harper and Row.

(1947) *The Soviet Impact on the Western World*, New York: Macmillan.

(1951) *The Bolshevik Revolution*, New York: Macmillan.

Carter, April F. (1995) "Did Reagan 'Win' the Cold War?" in R. Summy and M. Salla (eds.) *Why the Cold War Ended*, Westport: Greenwood Press, pp. 19–31.

Chadwick, Richard N. (1969) "An Inductive Empirical Analysis of Intra- and International Behavior and Aimed at a Partial Extension of Inter-Nation Simulation Theory," *Journal of Peace Research* 6 (3): 193–214.

Chan, Steve (1978) "Chinese Conflict Calculus and Behavior: Assessment from a Perspective of Conflict Management," *World Politics* 30 (April): 391–410.

(1979) "Rationality, Bureaucratic Politics and Belief System: Explaining the Chinese Policy Debate, 1964–66," *Journal of Peace Research* 16 (4): 333–348.

Chan, Steve, John A. Kringen, and Davis B. Bobrow (1979) "A Chinese View of the International System" in J. D. Singer and M. D. Wallace (eds.) *To Augur Well*, Beverly Hills: Sage, pp. 271–289.

Charlesworth, James C. (ed.) (1967) *Contemporary Political Analysis*, New York: Free Press.

Checkel, Jeffrey (1993) "Ideas, Institutions, and the Gorbachev Foreign Policy Revolution," *World Politics* 45 (January): 271–300.

Chernoff, Fred (1991) "Ending the Cold War: the Soviet Retreat and the U.S. Military Buildup," *International Affairs* 67 (1): 111–126.

(1994) *After Bipolarity: The Vanishing Threat, Theories of Cooperation, and the Future of the Atlantic Alliance*, Ann Arbor: University of Michigan Press.

Choucri, Nazli (1969a) "The Perceptual Base of Non-alignment," *Journal of Conflict Resolution* 13 (March): 57–74.

(1969b) "The Non-Alignment of Afro-Asian States: Policy, Perception, and Behavior," *Canadian Journal of Political Science* 2 (March): 1–17.

(1972) "In Search of Peace Systems: Scandinavia and the Netherlands, 1870–1970" in B. M. Russett (ed.) *Peace, War, and Numbers*, Beverly Hills: Sage, pp. 239–299.

Choucri, Nazli, and Robert C. North (1969) "The Determinants of International Violence," *Peace Research Society (International) Papers* 12: 33–63.

(1975) *Nations in Conflict: National Growth and International Violence*, San Francisco: Freeman.

Christensen, Thomas J. (1997) "Perceptions and Alliances in Europe, 1865–1940," *International Organization* 51 (Winter): 65–97.

Christensen, Thomas J., and Jack Snyder (1990) "Chain Gangs and Passed Bucks: Predicting Alliance Patterns in Multipolarity," *International Organization* 44 (Spring): 137–168.

(1997) "Progressive Research on Degenerate Alliances," *American Political Science Review* 91 (December): 919–922.

Cimbala, Stephen J. (1969) "Foreign Policy as an Issue Area: A Roll Call Analysis," *American Political Science Review* 63 (March): 148–156.

Claude, Inis L., Jr. (1956, 1964) *Swords into Plowshares*, New York: Random House.

(1962) *Power and International Relations*, New York: Random House.

Clausewitz, Carl von (1832) *On War*, J. J. Graham translation, 1874 (1966 edn) London: Routledge and Kegan Paul.

Clemens, Walter C., Jr. (1973) *The Superpowers and Arms Control*, Lexington: Lexington Books.

Cobb, Stephen A. (1969) "Defense Spending and Foreign Policy in the House of Representatives," *Journal of Conflict Resolution* 13 (September): 358–369.

Coddington, Alan (1965) "Policies Advocated in Conflict Situations by British Newspapers," *Journal of Peace Research* 2 (4): 398–404.

Cohen, Bernard C. (1967) "Mass Communication and Foreign Policy" in J. Rosenau (ed.) *Domestic Sources of Foreign Policy*, New York: Free Press, pp. 195–212.

Cohn, Carol (1987) "Sex and Death in the Rational World of Defense Intellectuals," *Signs* 12 (4): 687–718.

Collins, Randall, and David Waller (1992) "What Theories Predicted the State Breakdowns and Revolutions of the Soviet Bloc?" in L. Kriesberg and David R. Segal (eds.) *Research in Social Movements, Conflicts, and Change*, vol. 14, Greenwich: JAI Press, pp. 31–47.

Coplin, William D. (1966) *The Functions of International Law*, Chicago: Rand McNally.

(1968) "The World Court in the International Bargaining Process" in R. W. Gregg and M. Barkun (eds.) *The United Nations System and Its Functions*, Princeton: Van Nostrand, pp. 317–333.

(1974) *Introduction to International Politics*, 2nd edn. Chicago: Rand McNally.

Coplin, William D., Stephen Mills, and Michael K. O'Leary (1973) "The PRINCE Concepts and the Study of Foreign Policy" in P. J. McGowan (ed.) *Sage International Yearbook of Foreign Policy Studies*, vol. 1, Beverly Hills: Sage, pp. 73–103.

Coplin, William D. and Michael K. O'Leary (1971) "A Simulation Model for the Analysis and Explanation of International Interactions." Paper Presented at the annual meeting of the International Studies Association, San Juan, Puerto Rico.

Copson, William (1973) "Foreign Policy Conflict among African States, 1964–1969" in P. J. McGowan (ed.) *Sage International Yearbook of Foreign Policy Studies*, vol. 1, Beverly Hills: Sage, pp. 189–217.

Cox, Robert W. (1981) "Social Forces, States and World Orders: Beyond International Relations Theory," *Millennium* 10 (Summer): 126–155.

(1986) "Postscript 1985" to reprint of Cox (1981) in R. Keohane (ed.) *Neorealism and Its Critics*, New York: Columbia University Press, pp. 239–249.

Crow, Wayman J., and Robert C. Noel (1965) "The Valid Use of Simulation Results," La Jolla, Calif.: Western Behavioral Sciences Institute.

Dean, P. Dale, and John A. Vasquez (1976) "From Power Politics to Issue Politics: Bipolarity and Multipolarity in Light of a New Paradigm," *Western Political Quarterly* 29 (March): 7–28.

Dehio, Ludwig (1961) *The Precarious Balance*, New York: Vintage.

Denton, Frank H. (1966) "Some Regularities in International Conflict, 1820–1949," *Background* 9 (February): 283–296.

Der Derian, James (1987) *On Diplomacy: A Genealogy of Western Estrangement*, Oxford: Basil Blackwell.

Der Derian, James, and Michael J. Shapiro (eds.) (1989) *International/Intertex-*

tual Relations: Postmodern Readings of World Politics, Lexington: Lexington Books.

Dessler, David (1989) "What's At Stake in the Agent-Structure Debate?" *International Organization* 43 (Summer): 441–473.

(1991) "Beyond Correlations: Toward a Causal Theory of War," *International Studies Quarterly* 35 (September): 337–355.

Deudney, Daniel and G. John Ikenberry (1991) "Soviet Reform and the End of the Cold War: Explaining Large-scale Historical Change," *Review of International Studies* 17 (July): 225–250.

(1991/92) "The International Sources of Soviet Change," *International Security* 16 (Winter): 74–118.

Deutsch, Karl W. (1953) *Nationalism and Social Communication*, Cambridge, Mass.: MIT Press.

(1956) "Shifts in the Balance of Communication Flows: A Problem of Measurement in International Relations," *Public Opinion Quarterly* 20 (Spring): 143–160.

(1964) *The Nerves of Government*, New York: Free Press.

(1966) "Integration and Arms Control in the European Political Environment: A Summary Report," *American Political Science Review* 60 (June): 354–365.

(1968) *The Analysis of International Relations*, Englewood Cliffs: Prentice-Hall.

Deutsch, Karl W., Sidney Burrell, Robert Kann, Maurice Lee, Jr., Martin Lichterman, Raymond Lindgren, Francis Lowenheim, and Richard Van Wagenen (1957) *Political Community and the North Atlantic Area*, Princeton: Princeton University Press.

Deutsch, Karl W., and Alexander Eckstein (1961) "National Industrialization and the Declining Share of the International Economic Sector," *World Politics* 13 (January): 267–299.

Deutsch, Morton (1973) *The Resolution of Conflict*, New Haven: Yale University Press.

Diehl, Paul F. (1983) "Arms Races and Escalation: A Closer Look," *Journal of Peace Research* 20 (5): 205–212.

Diesing, Paul (1992) *How Does Social Science Work? Reflections on Practice*, Pittsburgh: University of Pittsburgh Press.

Dobrynin, Anatoly (1995) *In Confidence*, New York: Times Books.

Doran, Charles F. (1971) *The Politics of Assimilation*, Baltimore: Johns Hopkins University Press.

Doran, Charles F., Robert Pendley, and George Antunes (1973) "A Test of Cross-National Event Reliability, *International Studies Quarterly* 12 (June): 175–203.

Dougherty, James E., and Robert L. Pfaltzgraff, Jr. (1971) *Contending Theories of International Relations*, Philadelphia: Lippincott.

Doyle, Michael (1986) "Liberalism and World Politics," *American Political Science Review* 80 (December): 1151–1169.

Driver, M. J. (1965) "A Cognitive Structure Analysis of Aggression, Stress, and

Personality in an Inter-Nation Simulation," Lafayette, Indiana: Purdue University.

Dunn, Frederick S. (1949) "The Present Course of International Relations Research," *World Politics* 2 (October): 80–95.

East, Maurice (1975) "Explaining Foreign Policy Behavior Using National Attributes." Paper Presented at the annual meeting of the American Political Science Association, San Francisco.

East, Maurice, and Philip Gregg (1967) "Factors Influencing Cooperation and Conflict in the International System," *International Studies Quarterly* 11 (September): 244–269.

East, Maurice, and Charles F. Hermann (1974) "Do Nation-types Account for Foreign Policy Behavior?" in J. Rosenau (ed.) *Comparing Foreign Policies,* New York: Halsted/John Wiley, pp. 269–303.

East, Maurice, Stephen A. Salmore, and Charles F. Hermann (eds.) (1978) *Why Nations Act: Theoretical Perspectives for Comparative Foreign Policy Studies,* Beverly Hills: Sage.

Easton, David (1965) *A Framework for Political Analysis,* Englewood Cliffs: Prentice-Hall.

Eckhardt, William (1965) "War Propaganda, Welfare Values, and Political Ideologies," *Journal of Conflict Resolution* 9 (September): 345–358.

Ellis, William, and John Salzberg (1965) "Africa and the UN: A Statistical Note," *American Behavioral Scientist* 8 (April): 30–32.

Elman, Colin (1996) "Horses for Courses: Why *Not* Neorealist Theories of Foreign Policy?" *Security Studies* 6 (Autumn): 7–53.

Elman, Colin, and Miriam Fendius Elman (1995) "History vs. Neo-realism: A Second Look," *International Security* 20 (Summer): 182–193.

(1997) "Lakatos and Neorealism: A Reply to Vasquez," *American Political Science Review* 91 (December): 923–926.

Etheredge, Lloyd S. (1978) *A World of Men: The Private Sources of American Foreign Policy,* Cambridge, Mass.: MIT Press.

Evangelista, Matthew (1993) "Internal and External Constraints on Grand Strategy: The Soviet Case" in R. Rosecrance and A. Stein (eds.) *The Domestic Bases of Grand Strategy,* Ithaca: Cornell University Press, pp. 154–178.

Evans, Peter, Harold Jacobson, and Robert Putnam (eds.) (1993) *Double-Edged Diplomacy: International Bargaining and Domestic Politics,* Berkeley: University of California Press.

Faber, Jan, and R. Weaver (1984) "Participation in Conferences, Treaties, and Warfare in the European System, 1816–1915," *Journal of Conflict Resolution* 28 (September): 522–534.

Feldstein, Helen S. (1967) "A Study of Transaction and Political Integration: Transnational Labour Flow Within the European Economic Community," *Journal of Common Market Studies* 6 (1): 24–55.

Ferguson, Yale H., and Richard W. Mansbach (1988) *The Elusive Quest: Theory and International Politics,* Columbia: University of South Carolina Press.

References

(1991) "Between Celebration and Despair: Constructive Suggestions for Future International Theory," *International Studies Quarterly* 35 (December): 363–386.

Ferris, Wayne (1973) *The Power Capabilities of Nation-States*, Lexington: D. C. Heath.

Feyerabend, Paul K. (1976) "On the Critique of Scientific Reason," in R. S. Cohen et al. (eds.) *Boston Studies in the Philosophy of Science*, vol. 39, Dordrecht, Holland: D. Reidel, pp. 109–143.

Finnegan, Richard B. (1970) "Patterns of Influence in International Relations Research," *Journal of International and Comparative Studies* 3: 84–106.

(1972a) "The Field of International Relations: The View from Within," *Towson State Journal of International Affairs* 7: 1–24.

(1972b) "International Relations: The Disputed Search for Method," *Review of Politics* 34 (January): 40–66.

Fischer, Markus (1992) "Feudal Europe, 800–1300: Communal Discourse and Conflictual Practices," *International Organization* 46 (Spring): 427–466.

Fisher, William E. (1969) "An Analysis of the Deutsch Social-Causal Paradigm of Political Integration," *International Organization* 23 (Spring): 254–290.

Fleming, William G. (1969) "Sub-Saharan Africa: Case Studies of International Attitudes and Transactions of Ghana and Uganda" in J. Rosenau (ed.) *Linkage Politics*, New York: Free Press, pp. 94–161.

Foucault, Michel (1972) *The Archaeology of Knowledge*, New York: Pantheon.

(1977) *Discipline and Punish: The Birth of the Prison*, New York: Pantheon.

(1979) *Language, Counter-Memory, Practice*, Oxford: Blackwell.

(1980) "Truth and Power" in M. Foucault, *Power/Knowledge*, edited by C. Gordon, New York: Pantheon.

Fox, William T. R. (1949) "Interwar International Relations Research: The American Experience," *World Politics* 2 (October): 67–80.

Fozouni, Bahman (1995) "Confutation of Political Realism," *International Studies Quarterly* 39 (December): 479–510.

Freeman, Linton (1965) *Elementary Applied Statistics*, New York: John Wiley.

Friedberg, Aaron L. (1988) *The Weary Titan: Britain and the Experience of Relative Decline, 1895–1905*, Princeton: Princeton University Press.

Frohock, Fred M. (1974) *Normative Political Theory*, Englewood Cliffs: Prentice-Hall.

Gaddis, John Lewis (1986) "The Long Peace: Elements of Stability in the Postwar International System," *International Security* 10 (Spring): 99–142.

(1987) *The Long Peace: Inquiries into the History of the Cold War*, New York: Oxford University Press.

(1992/93) "International Relations Theory and the End of the Cold War," *International Security* 18 (Winter): 5–58.

Galtung, Johan (1964a) "A Structural Theory of Aggression," *Journal of Peace Research* 1 (2): 95–119.

(1964b) "Summit Meetings and International Relations," *Journal of Peace Research* 1 (1): 36–54.

(1966) "East-West Interaction Patterns," *Journal of Peace Research* 3 (2): 146–177.

(1971) "A Structural Theory of Imperialism," *Journal of Peace Research* 8 (2): 81–119.

Galtung, Johan, and Mari Ruge (1965a) "Patterns of Diplomacy," *Journal of Peace Research* 2 (2): 101–135.

(1965b) "The Structure of Foreign News," *Journal of Peace Research* 2 (1): 64–91.

Gamson, William A., and André Modigliani (1968) "Some Aspects of Soviet-Western Conflict," *Peace Research Society (International) Papers* 9: 9–24.

(1971) *Untangling the Cold War*, Boston: Little, Brown.

Garthoff, Raymond L. (1987) *Reflections on the Cuban Missile Crisis*, Washington, DC: Brookings.

Geller, Daniel S. (1992) "Capability Concentration, Power Transition, and War," *International Interactions* 17 (3): 269–284.

George, Alexander L. (1969) "The Operational Code: A Neglected Approach to the Study of Political Leaders and Decision-making," *International Studies Quarterly* 13 (June): 190–222.

(1979) "Case Studies and Theory Development: The Method of Structured, Focused Comparison" in P. G. Lauren (ed.) *Diplomacy: New Approaches in History, Theory, and Policy*, New York: Free Press.

(1988) "U.S.–Soviet Efforts to Cooperate in Crisis Management and Crisis Avoidance" in A. George, P. Farley, and A. Dallin (eds.) *U.S.–Soviet Security Cooperation*, New York: Oxford University Press, pp. 581–599.

George, Alexander L., et al. (1983) *Managing U.S.–Soviet Rivalry: Problems of Crisis Prevention*, Boulder: Westview.

George, Alexander L., David K. Hall, and William Simons (1971) *The Limits of Coercive Diplomacy*, Boston: Little, Brown.

George, Alexander L., and Richard Smoke (1974) *Deterrence in American Foreign Policy*, New York: Columbia University Press.

George, Alexander L., Philip J. Farley, and Alexander Dallin (eds.) (1988) *U.S.–Soviet Security Cooperation*, New York: Oxford University Press.

George, Jim (1993) "Of Incarceration and Closure: Neo-Realism and the New/Old World Orders," *Millennium* 22 (Summer): 555–592.

(1994) *Discourses of Global Politics: A Critical (Re)Introduction to International Relations*, Boulder: Lynne Rienner.

George, Jim, and David Campbell (1990) "Patterns of Dissent and the Celebration of Difference: Critical Social Theory and International Relations," *International Studies Quarterly* 34: (September): 269–293.

Gibler, Douglas M. (1996) "Alliances That Never Balance: The Territorial Settlement Treaty," *Conflict Management and Peace Science* 15 (1): 75–97.

Gilpin, Robert (1981) *War and Change in World Politics*, Cambridge: Cambridge University Press.

References

(1987) *The Political Economy of International Relations*, Princeton: Princeton University Press.

(1989) "The Theory of Hegemonic War" in R. Rotberg and T. Rabb (eds.) *The Origin and Prevention of Major Wars*, Cambridge: Cambridge University Press, pp. 15–37.

Gladkov, Peter V. (1994) "Superpowers No More: The United States and Russia in Post-Cold War Europe" in M. Midlarsky, J. Vasquez, and P. Gladkov (eds.) *From Rivalry to Cooperation: Russian and American Perspectives on the Post-Cold War Era*, New York: HarperCollins, pp. 193–207.

Glaser, Charles L. (1994/95) "Realists as Optimists: Cooperation as Self-Help," *International Security* 19 (Winter): 50–90.

Gleditsch, Nils Petter (1967) "Trends in World Airline Patterns," *Journal of Peace Research* 4 (4): 366–408.

(1969) "The International Airline Network: A Test of the Zipf and Stouffer Hypotheses," *Peace Research Society (International) Papers* 11: 123–153.

Gochman, Charles S. (1980) "Status, Capabilities, and Major Power Conflict" in J. D. Singer (ed.) *The Correlates of War: II*, New York: Free Press, pp. 83–123.

Gochman, Charles S., and James Lee Ray (1979) "Structural Disparities in Latin America and Eastern Europe, 1950–1970," *Journal of Peace Research* 16 (3): 231–254.

Goertz, Gary (1994) *Contexts of International Politics*, Cambridge: Cambridge University Press.

Goldmann, Kjell (1988) *Change and Stability in Foreign Policy: The Problems and Possibilities of Detente*, Princeton: Princeton University Press.

Gorbachev, Mikhail (1996) *Memoirs*, New York: Doubleday.

Graber, Doris A. (1969) "Perceptions of Middle East Conflict in the U.N., 1953–1965," *Journal of Conflict Resolution* 13 (December): 454–484.

Green, Donald P., and Ian Shapiro (1994) *Pathologies of Rational Choice Theory: A Critique of Applications in Political Science*, New Haven: Yale University Press.

Greenstein, Fred I., and Nelson W. Polsby (eds.) (1975) *International Politics, Handbook of Political Science*, vol. 8, Reading, Mass.: Addison-Wesley.

Gregg, Robert (1965) "The Latin American Bloc in United Nations Elections," *Southwestern Social Science Quarterly* 46 (September): 146–154.

Grieco, Joseph M. (1988) "Anarchy and the Limits of International Cooperation: A Realist Critique of the Newest Liberal Institutionalism," *International Organization* 42 (Summer): 485–507.

(1990) *Cooperation among Nations: Europe, America, and Non-Tariff Barriers to Trade*, Ithaca: Cornell University Press.

Guetzkow, Harold (1950) "Long Range Research in International Relations," *American Perspective* 4 (Fall): 421–440. Reprinted in J. Vasquez (ed.) *Classics of International Relations*, 3rd edn, Upper Saddle River, New Jersey: Prentice-Hall, 1996, pp. 67–75.

(1968) "Some Correspondences Between Simulations and Realities in International Relations" in M. Kaplan (ed.) *New Approaches to International Relations*, New York: St. Martin's, pp. 202–269.

Guetzkow, Harold, and Joseph J. Valadez (1981) "International Relations Theory: Contributions of Simulated International Processes" in H. Guetzkow and J. Valadez (eds.) *Simulated International Processes*, Beverly Hills: Sage, pp. 197–151.

Gulick, Edward V. (1955) *Europe's Classical Balance of Power*, New York: Norton.

Haas, Ernst B. (1953) "The Balance of Power: Prescription, Concept, or Propaganda?" *World Politics* 5 (April): 442–477.

(1958) *The Uniting of Europe*, Stanford: Stanford University Press.

(1962) "System and Process in the International Labor Organization: A Statistical Afterthought," *World Politics* 14 (January): 339–352.

Haas, Ernst B., Robert Butterworth, and Joseph Nye, Jr. (1972) "Conflict Management by International Organizations," Morristown, New Jersey: General Learning Press.

Haas, Michael (1965) "Societal Approaches to the Study of War," *Journal of Peace Research* 2 (4): 307–323.

(1968) "Social Change and National Aggressiveness, 1900–1960" in J. D. Singer (ed.) *Quantitative International Politics*, New York: Free Press, pp. 215–244.

(1969) "Communication Factors in Decision Making," *Peace Research Society (International) Papers* 12: 65–86.

(1970) "International Subsystems: Stability and Polarity," *American Political Science Review* 64 (March): 98–123.

(1974) *International Conflict*, Indianapolis: Bobbs-Merrill.

Habermas, Jürgen (1984, 1988) *The Theory of Communicative Action*, vols. I and II, Boston: Beacon Press.

Hagan, Joe D. (1993) *Political Opposition and Foreign Policy in Comparative Perspective*, Boulder: Lynne Rienner.

(1994) "Domestic Political Regime Change and Foreign Policy Restructuring" in J. Rosati, J. Hagan, and M. Sampson, III (eds.) *Foreign Policy Restructuring: How Governments Respond to Change*, Columbia: University of South Carolina Press, pp. 138–163.

Hall, Rodney Bruce, and Friedrich V. Kratochwil (1993) "Medieval Tales: Neorealist 'Science' and the Abuse of History," *International Organization* 47 (Summer): 479–491.

Halperin, Morton H. (1974) *Bureaucratic Politics and Foreign Policy*, Washington, DC: Brookings Institution.

Halperin, Morton H., and Arnold Kanter (eds.) (1973) *Readings in American Foreign Policy: A Bureaucratic Perspective*, Boston: Little, Brown.

Handelman, John R., John A. Vasquez, Michael K. O'Leary, and William D. Coplin (1973) "Color It Morgenthau: A Data-based Assessment of Quantitative International Relations." Paper presented at the annual meeting of the International Studies Association, New York.

References

Hanson, Norwood Russell (1965) *Patterns of Discovery*, Cambridge: Cambridge University Press.

Hawkesworth, Mary (1992) "The Science of Politics and the Politics of Science" in M. Hawkesworth and M. Kogan (eds.) *Encyclopedia of Government and Politics*, London: Routledge, pp. 5–39.

Hazlewood, Leo, John J. Hayes, and James R. Brownell (1977) "Planning for Problems in Crisis Management," *International Studies Quarterly* 21 (March): 75–105.

Healy, Brian, and Arthur Stein (1973) "The Balance of Power in International History: Theory and Reality," *Journal of Conflict Resolution* 17 (March): 33–62.

Hempel, Carl G. (1968) "Explanation in Science and History" in P. H. Nidditch (ed.) *The Philosophy of Science*, New York: Oxford University Press, pp. 54–79.

Henehan, Marie T. (1981) "A Data-based Evaluation of Issue Typologies in the Comparative Study of Foreign Policy." Paper presented at the annual meeting of the International Studies Association, Philadelphia.

Hensel, Paul R. (1996) "Charting a Course to Conflict: Territorial Issues and Interstate Conflict, 1816–1992," *Conflict Management and Peace Science* 15 (Spring): 43–73.

Heradstveit, Daniel (1979) *The Arab-Israeli Conflict: Psychological Obstacles to Peace*, Olso: Universitesforlaget.

Hermann, Charles F. (1969a) *Crises in Foreign Policy*, Indianapolis: Bobbs-Merrill.

(1969b) "International Crisis as a Situational Variable" in J. Rosenau (ed.) *International Politics and Foreign Policy*, 2nd edn, New York: Free Press, pp. 409–421.

(1971) "What is a Foreign Policy Event?" in W. Hanrieder (ed.) *Comparative Foreign Policy*, New York: David McKay, pp. 295–321.

(1972a) (ed.) *International Crises: Insights from Behavioral Research*, New York: Free Press.

(1972b) "Threat, Time, and Surprise: A Simulation of International Crisis" in C. Hermann (ed.) *International Crises*, New York: Free Press, pp. 187–216.

(1978) "Decision Structure and Process Influences on Foreign Policy," in M. East, S. Salmore, and C. Hermann (eds.) *Why Nations Act*, Beverly Hills: Sage, pp. 69–102.

Hermann, Charles F., Maurice East, Margaret Hermann, Barbara Salmore, and Stephen Salmore (1973) *CREON: A Foreign Events Data Set*, Sage Professional Papers in International Studies, 02–024. Beverly Hills: Sage.

Hermann, Margaret G. (1974) "Leader Personality and Foreign Policy Behavior," in J. Rosenau (ed.) *Comparing Foreign Policies*, New York: Halsted/John Wiley, pp. 201–234.

Hermann, Margaret G., Charles F. Hermann, and William J. Dixon (1979) "Decision Structures and Personal Characteristics in Comparative

Foreign Policy." Paper presented at the annual meeting of the Midwest Political Science Association, Chicago.

Herz, John H. (1959) *International Politics in the Atomic Age*, New York: Columbia University Press.

Hilton, Gordon (1973) *A Review of the Dimensionality of Nations Project*, Sage Professional Papers in International Studies, 02–015, Beverly Hills: Sage.

Hobbes, Thomas (1651 [1950]) *Leviathan*, New York: E. P. Dutton.

Hoffman, Frederik (1967) "The Functions of Economic Sanctions," *Journal of Peace Research* 4 (2): 140–160.

Hoffmann, Stanley (1959) "Long Road to International Relations Theory," *World Politics* 11 (April): 346–378.

(1960) (ed.) *Contemporary Theory in International Relations*, Englewood Cliffs: Prentice-Hall.

Hoffmann, Stanley, Robert O. Keohane, John J. Mearsheimer (1990) "Correspondence: Back to the Future, Part II" *International Security* 15 (Fall): 191–199.

Hoggard, Gary D. (1974) "Differential Source Coverage in Foreign Policy Analysis" in J. Rosenau (ed.) *Comparing Foreign Policies*, New York: Halsted/John Wiley, pp. 353–381.

Hollis, Martin, and Steve Smith (1990) *Explaining and Understanding International Relations*, Oxford: Oxford University Press.

(1991) "Beware of Gurus: Structure and Action in International Relations," *Review of International Studies* 17 (October): 393–410.

(1994) "Structure and Action: Further Comment," *Review of International Studies* 18 (April): 187–188.

Holsti, Kalevi J. (1966) "Resolving International Conflict: A Taxonomy of Behavior and Some Figures on Procedure," *Journal of Conflict Resolution* 10 (September): 272–296.

Holsti, Ole R. (1965) "Perceptions of Time, Perceptions of Alternatives, and Patterns of Communication as Factors in Crisis Decision-Making," *Peace Research Society (International) Papers* 3: 79–120.

(1966) "External Conflict and Internal Consensus: The Sino-Soviet Case" in P. Stone et al. (eds.) *General Inquirer*, Cambridge, Mass.: MIT Press, pp. 343–358.

(1967) "Cognitive Dynamics and Images of the Enemy: Dulles and Russia" in D. Findlay, O. Holsti, and R. Fagen (eds.) *Enemies in Politics*, Chicago: Rand McNally, pp. 25–96.

(1970) "The 'Operational Code' Approach to the Study of Political Leaders: John Foster Dulles' Philosophical and Instrumental Beliefs," *Canadian Journal of Political Science* 3 (March): 123–157.

(1972) *Crisis Escalation War*, Montreal: McGill-Queens University Press.

(1976) "Foreign Policy Formation Viewed Cognitively," in R. Axelrod (ed.) *Structure of Decision*, Princeton: Princeton University Press, pp. 18–54.

Holsti, Ole R., Richard A. Brody, and Robert C. North (1965) "Measuring Affect and Action in International Reaction Models: Empirical Materials from the 1962 Cuban Crisis," *Peace Research Society (International) Papers* 2: 170–190.

Holsti, Ole R., and Alexander L. George (1975) "The Effects of Stress on the Performance of Foreign Policy-Makers," in *Political Science Annual*, vol. 6, Indianapolis: Bobbs-Merrill, pp. 255–319.

Holsti, Ole R., P. Terrence Hopmann, and John D. Sullivan (1973) *Unity and Disintegration in International Alliances: Comparative Studies*, New York: John Wiley.

Holsti, Ole R., Robert C. North, and Richard A. Brody (1968) "Perception and Action in the 1914 Crisis," in J. D. Singer (ed.) *Quantitative International Politics*, New York: Free Press, pp. 123–158.

Holsti, Ole R., and John D. Sullivan (1969) "National-International Linkages: France and China as Non-Conforming Alliance Members" in J. Rosenau (ed.) *Linkage Politics*, New York: Free Press, pp. 147–195.

Hopf, Ted (1993) "Getting the End of the Cold War Wrong," *International Security* 18 (Fall): 202–208.

Hopkins, Raymond and Donald J. Puchala (eds.) (1978) "The Global Political Economy of Food," *International Organization* 32 (Winter, special issue).

Hopmann, P. Terrence (1967) "International Conflict and Cohesion in the Communist System," *International Studies Quarterly* 11 (September): 212–236.

Horvath, William J. (1968) "A Statistical Model for the Duration of Wars and Strikes," *Behavioral Science* 13 (January): 18–28.

Horvath, William J., and Caxton Foster (1963) "Stochastic Models of War Alliances," *Journal of Conflict Resolution* 7 (June): 110–116.

Houweling, Henk W., and Jan G. Siccama (1985) "The Epidemiology of War, 1816–1980," *Journal of Conflict Resolution* 29 (December): 641–663.

Huth, Paul K. (1988) "Extended Deterrence and the Outbreak of War," *American Political Science Review* 82 (June): 423–443.

(1996) *Standing Your Ground: Territorial Disputes and International Conflict*, Ann Arbor: University of Michigan Press.

Huth, Paul K., and Bruce M. Russett (1984) "What Makes Deterrence Work? Cases from 1900 to 1980," *World Politics* 36 (December): 496–526.

Ikenberry, G. John, and Charles A. Kupchan (1990) "Socialization and Hegemonic Power," *International Organization* 44 (Summer): 283–315.

Jacobsen, Kurt (1969) "Sponsorship in the U.N.," *Journal of Peace Research* 6 (3): 235–256.

Janis, Irving L. (1972) *Victims of Groupthink*, Boston: Houghton Mifflin.

Janis, Irving L., and Leon Mann (1977) *Decision Making*, New York: Free Press.

Jensen, Lloyd (1965) "Military Capabilities and Bargaining Behavior," *Journal of Conflict Resolution* 9 (June): 155–163.

(1966) "American Foreign Policy Elites and the Prediction of International Events," *Peace Research Society (International) Papers* 5: 199–209.

(1968) "Approach-Avoidance Bargaining in the Test-ban Negotiations," *International Studies Quarterly* 12 (June): 152–160.

(1969) "Postwar Democratic Politics: National-International Linkages in the

Defense Policy of the Defeated States" in J. Rosenau (ed.) *Linkage Politics*, New York: Free Press, pp. 304–323.

Jervis, Robert (1976) *Perception and Misperception in International Politics*, Princeton: Princeton University Press.

(1978) "Cooperation under the Security Dilemma," *World Politics* 30 (January): 167–214.

(1989) *The Meaning of the Nuclear Revolution*, Ithaca: Cornell University Press.

Johnson, James Turner (1995) "International Law and the Peaceful Resolution of Interstate Conflicts" in J. Vasquez et al. (eds.) *Beyond Confrontation: Learning Conflict Resolution in the Post-Cold War Era*, Ann Arbor: University of Michigan Press, pp. 155–177.

Jones, Susan, and J. David Singer (1972) *Beyond Conjecture in International Politics: Abstracts of Data-based Research*, Itasca, Ill.: F. E. Peacock.

Kacowicz, Arie M. (1995) "Explaining Zones of Peace: Democracies as Satisfied Powers?" *Journal of Peace Research* 32 (August): 265–276.

Kahn, Herman (1960) *On Thermonuclear War*, Princeton: Princeton University Press.

(1968) *On Escalation: Metaphors and Scenarios*, rev. edn, Baltimore: Penguin.

Kaiser, David (1990) *Politics and War: European Conflict from Philip II to Hitler*, Cambridge, Mass.: Harvard University Press.

Kaiser, Karl (1971) "Transnational Politics: Toward a Theory of Multinational Politics," *International Organization* 25 (Autumn): 790–818.

Kant, Immanuel (1795) [1991] *Perpetual Peace*, translated by H. B. Nisbet, reprinted in Hans Reiss (ed.) *Kant: Political Writings*, Cambridge: Cambridge University Press.

Kaplan, Morton A. (1957) *System and Process in International Politics*, New York: John Wiley.

Kapstein, Ethan B. (1995) "Is Realism Dead? The Domestic Sources of International Politics," *International Organization* 49 (Autumn): 751–774.

Kato, Masakatsu (1968) "A Model of U.S. Foreign Aid Allocation: An Application of a Rational Decision-Making Scheme" in J. Mueller (ed.) *Approaches to Measurement in International Relations*, New York: Appleton-Century-Crofts, pp. 198–215.

Katz, P. (1972) "Psyop Automated Management Information Systems PAMIS." Foreign Media Analysis File. Kensington, Md.: American Institute for Research.

Katz, P., M. M. Lent, and E. J. Novotny (1973) "Survey of Chinese News Media Content in 1972: A Quantitative Analysis." Kensington, Md.: American Institute for Research.

Kaufman, Robert R., Harry I. Chernotsky, and Daniel S. Geller (1975) "A Preliminary Test of the Theory of Dependency," *Comparative Politics* 7 (April): 303–330.

Kay, David A. (1969) "The Impact of African States on the United Nations," *International Organization* 23 (Winter): 20–47.

Kegley, Charles W., Jr. (1973) *A General Empirical Typology of Foreign Policy*

Behavior, Sage Professional Papers in International Studies, 02–014 Beverly Hills: Sage.

(1991) "The New Containment Myth: Realism and the Anomaly of European Integration," *Ethics and International Affairs* 5: 99–114.

(1993) "The Neoidealist Moment in International Studies? Realist Myths and the New International Realities," *International Studies Quarterly* 37 (June): 131–146.

Kegley, Charles W., Jr. (ed.) (1995) *Controversies in International Relations Theory: Realism and the Neoliberal Challenge*, New York: St. Martin's.

Kegley, Charles W., Jr., and Gregory A. Raymond (1982) "Alliance Norms and War: A New Piece in an Old Puzzle," *International Studies Quarterly* 26 (December): 572–595.

(1986) "Normative Constraints on the Use of Force Short of War," *Journal of Peace Research* 23 (September): 213–227.

(1990) *When Trust Breaks Down*, Columbia: University of South Carolina Press.

(1994a) *A Multipolar Peace? Great-Power Politics in the Twenty-First Century*, New York: St. Martin's.

(1994b) "From Detente to Entente: Prospects for Establishing a Multipolarity of Peace" in M. Midlarsky, J. Vasquez, and P. Gladkov (eds.) *From Rivalry to Cooperation: Russian and American Perspectives on the Post-Cold War Era*, New York: HarperCollins, pp. 100–115.

Kegley, Charles W., Jr., Stephen A. Salmore, and David J. Rosen (1974) "Convergences in the Measurement of Interstate Behavior" in P. J. McGowan (ed.) *Sage International Yearbook of Foreign Policy Studies*, vol. 2, Beverly Hills: Sage, pp. 309–339.

Kegley, Charles W., Jr., and Richard J. Skinner (1976) "The Case-for-Analysis Problem" in J. Rosenau (ed.) *In Search of Global Patterns*, New York: Free Press, pp. 303–318.

Kelman, Herbert C. (ed.) (1965) *International Behavior: A Social-Psychological Analysis*, New York: Holt, Rinehart and Winston.

Kennan, George F. (1951) *American Diplomacy, 1900–1950*, Chicago: University of Chicago Press.

Kennedy, Paul (1987) *The Rise and Fall of the Great Powers: Economic Change and Military Conflict from 1500 to 2000*, New York: Random House.

Keohane, Robert O. (1969) "Who Cares about the General Assembly?" *International Organization* 23 (Winter): 141–149.

(1983 [1989]) "Theory of World Politics: Structural Realism and Beyond" in Ada W. Finifter (ed.) *Political Science: The State of the Discipline*, Washington, DC: American Political Science Association. Reprinted in Robert O. Keohane, *International Institutions and State Power*, Boulder: Westview.

(1984) *After Hegemony*, Princeton: Princeton University Press.

(1986a) (ed.) *Neorealism and Its Critics*, New York: Columbia University Press.

(1986b) "Realism, Neorealism and the Study of World Politics" in Robert O. Keohane (ed.) *Neorealism and Its Critics*, New York: Columbia University Press, pp. 1–26.

(1988) "International Institutions: Two Approaches," *International Studies Quarterly* 32 (December): 379–396.

Keohane, Robert O., and Lisa L. Martin (1995) "The Promise of Institutionalist Theory," *International Security* 20 (Summer): 39–51.

Keohane, Robert O., and Joseph S. Nye, Jr. (eds.) (1971, 1972) *Transnational Relations and World Politics.* Cambridge, Mass.: Harvard University Press.

(1974) "Transgovernmental Relations and International Organizations," *World Politics* 27 (October): 39–62.

(1977) *Power and Interdependence: World Politics in Transition,* Boston: Little, Brown.

Khong, Yuen Foong (1992) *Analogies at War: Korea, Munich, Dien Bien Phu, and the Vietnam Decisions of 1965,* Princeton: Princeton University Press.

Kihl, Young W. (1971) *Conflict Issues and International Civil Aviation Decisions: Three Cases,* Monograph Series in World Affairs 8/1. Graduate School of International Studies, University of Denver.

Kim, Woosang (1992) "Power Transitions and Great Power War from Westphalia to Waterloo," *World Politics* 45 (October): 153–172.

(1996) "Power Parity, Alliance, and War from 1648 to 1975" in Jacek Kugler and Douglas Lemke (eds.) *Parity and War,* Ann Arbor: University of Michigan Press, pp. 93–105.

Kim, Woosang, and James D. Morrow (1992) "When Do Power Shifts Lead to War?" *American Journal of Political Science* 36 (November): 896–922.

King, Gary, Robert O. Keohane, and Sidney Verba (1994) *Designing Social Inquiry: Scientific Inference in Qualitative Research,* Princeton: Princeton University Press.

Kirk, Grayson (1947) *The Study of International Relations in American Colleges and Universities,* New York: Council on Foreign Relations.

Kirkpatrick, Jeane (1979) "Dictatorships and Double Standards," *Commentary* 68 (November): 34–45.

Kissinger, Henry A. (1957) *Nuclear Weapons and Foreign Policy,* New York: Harper.

(1961) *The Necessity for Choice,* New York: Harper.

(1994) *Diplomacy,* New York: Simon & Schuster.

Klein, Bradley S. (1994) *Strategic Studies and World Order,* Cambridge: Cambridge University Press.

Klingberg, Frank L. (1952) "The Historical Alternation of Moods in American Foreign Policy," *World Politics* 4 (January): 239–273.

(1966) "Predicting the Termination of War: Battle Casualties and Population Losses," *Journal of Conflict Resolution* 10 (June): 129–171.

Knorr, Klaus, and James N. Rosenau (eds.) (1969a) *Contending Approaches to International Politics,* Princeton: Princeton University Press.

Knorr, Klaus, and James N. Rosenau (1969b) "Tradition and Science in the Study of International Politics" in K. Knorr and J. Rosenau (eds.) *Contending Approaches to International Politics,* Princeton: Princeton University Press, pp. 3–19.

Kocs, Stephen A. (1994) "Explaining the Strategic Behavior of States: International Law as System Structure," *International Studies Quarterly* 38 (December): 535–556.

Koertge, N. (1978) "Towards a New Theory of Scientific Inquiry" in G. Radnitzky and G. Anderson (eds.) *Progress and Rationality in Science*, Dordrecht, Holland: D. Reidel, pp. 253–278.

Koslowski, Rey, and Friedrich V. Kratochwil (1994) "Understanding Changes in International Politics: The Soviet Empire's Demise and the International System," *International Organization* 48 (Spring): 215–247.

Krasner, Stephen D. (1978) *Defending the National Interests*, Princeton: Princeton University Press.

(1991) "Global Communications and National Power: Life on the Pareto Frontier," *World Politics* 43 (April): 336–366.

Kratochwil, Friedrich V. (1993) "The Embarrassment of Changes: Neo-realism as the Science of *Realpolitik*," *Review of International Studies* 19 (January): 63–80.

Kremenyuk, Victor A. (1994) "The Cold War as Cooperation" in M. Midlarsky, J. Vasquez, and P. Gladkov (eds.) *From Rivalry to Cooperation: Russian and American Perspectives on the Post-Cold War Era*, New York: HarperCollins, pp. 3–25.

Kriesberg, Louis (1981) "Noncoercive Inducements in US-Soviet Conflicts: Ending the Occupation of Austria and Nuclear Weapons Tests," *Journal of Political and Military Sociology* 9 (Spring): 1–16.

(1995) "Applications and Misapplications of Conflict Resolution Ideas to International Conflicts," in J. Vasquez et al. (eds.) *Beyond Confrontation: Learning Conflict Resolution in the Post-Cold War Era*, Ann Arbor: University of Michigan Press, pp. 87–102.

Kugler, Jacek (1984) "Terror without Deterrence: Reassessing the Role of Nuclear Weapons," *Journal of Conflict Resolution* 28 (September): 470–506.

Kugler, Jacek, and Douglas Lemke (eds.) (1996) *Parity and War*, Ann Arbor: University of Michigan Press.

Kugler, Jacek, and A. F. K. Organski (1989) "The Power Transition: A Retrospective and Prospective Evaluation" in M. Midlarsky (ed.) *Handbook of War Studies*, Boston: Unwin Hyman, pp. 171–194.

Kugler, Jacek, and Frank C. Zagare (1990) "The Long-term Stability of Deterrence," *International Interactions* 15 (3–4): 255–278.

Kuhn, Thomas S. (1957) *The Copernican Revolution*, Cambridge, Mass.: Harvard University Press.

(1962, 1970a) *The Structure of Scientific Revolutions*, 1st edn, 2nd edn, enlarged. Chicago: University of Chicago Press.

(1970b) "Reflections on My Critics" in I. Lakatos and A. Musgrave (eds.) *Criticism and the Growth of Knowledge*, Cambridge: Cambridge University Press, pp. 231–278.

(1971) "Second Thoughts on Paradigms" in F. Suppe (ed.) *The Structure of Scientific Theories*, Urbana: University of Illinois Press, pp. 459–517.

(1977) *The Essential Tension*, Chicago: University of Chicago Press.

Kupchan, Charles A. (1994) *The Vulnerability of Empire*, Ithaca: Cornell University Press.

Kupchan, Charles A., and Clifford A. Kupchan (1991) "Concerts, Collective Security, and the Future of Europe," *International Security* 16 (Summer): 114–161.

(1995) "The Promise of Collective Security," *International Security* 20 (Summer): 52–61.

Lakatos, Imre (1970) "Falsification and the Methodology of Scientific Research Programmes" in I. Lakatos and A. Musgrave (eds.) *Criticism and the Growth of Knowledge*, Cambridge: Cambridge University Press, pp. 91–196.

Lakatos, Imre, and Alan Musgrave (eds.) (1970) *Criticism and the Growth of Knowledge*, Cambridge: Cambridge University Press.

Lamb, Curtis, and Bruce M. Russett (1969) "Politics in the Emerging Regions," *Peace Research Society (International) Papers* 12: 1–31.

Lancaster, F. W. (1916) *Aircraft in Warfare: The Dawn of the Fifth Arm*, London: Constable.

Lapid, Yosef (1989) "The Third Debate: On the Prospects of International Theory in a Post-Positivist Era," *International Studies Quarterly* 33 (September): 235–254.

Larson, Deborah Welch (1985) *Origins of Containment: A Psychological Explanation*, Princeton: Princeton University Press.

(1991) "Bandwagon Images in American Foreign Policy: Myth or Reality?" in Robert Jervis and Jack Snyder (eds.) *Dominoes and Bandwagons*, New York: Oxford University Press, pp. 85–111.

(1997) *Anatomy of Mistrust*, Ithaca: Cornell University Press.

Laudan, Larry (1977) *Progress and Its Problems: Towards A Theory of Scientific Growth*, Berkeley: University of California Press.

Laulicht, Jerome (1965a) "An Analysis of Canadian Foreign Policy Attitudes," *Peace Research Society (International) Papers* 3: 121–136.

(1965b) "Public Opinion and Foreign Policy Decisions," *Journal of Peace Research* 2 (2): 147–160.

Layne, Christopher (1993) "The Unipolar Illusion: Why New Great Powers Will Rise," *International Security* 17 (Spring): 5–51.

Lebow, Richard Ned (1981) *Between Peace and War: The Nature of International Crisis*, Baltimore: Johns Hopkins University Press.

(1985) "Conclusions" in R. Jervis, R. N. Lebow, and J. Stein (eds.) *Psychology and Deterrence*, Baltimore: Johns Hopkins University Press, pp. 202–232.

(1994) "The Long Peace, the End of the Cold War, and the Failure of Realism," *International Organization* 48 (Spring): 249–277.

Lebow, Richard Ned, and John Mueller (1995) "Correspondence: Realism and the End of the Cold War," *International Security* 20 (Fall): 185–186.

Lebow, Richard Ned, and Thomas Risse-Kappen (eds.) (1995) *International Relations Theory and the End of the Cold War*, New York: Columbia University Press.

References

Lebow, Richard Ned, and Janice Gross Stein (1994) *We All Lost the Cold War*, Princeton: Princeton University Press.

Leng, Russell J. (1980) "Influence Strategies and Interstate Behavior," in J. D. Singer (ed.) *The Correlates of War: II*, New York: Free Press, pp. 125–157.

Leng, Russell J., and Robert A. Goodsell (1974) "Behavioral Indicators of War Proneness in Bilateral Conflicts" in P. J. McGowan (ed.) *Sage International Yearbook of Foreign Policy Studies*, vol. 2, Beverly Hills: Sage, pp. 191–226.

Leng, Russell J., and Hugh B. Wheeler (1979) "Influence Strategies, Success and War," *Journal of Conflict Resolution* 23 (December): 655–684.

Lerner, Daniel, and Marguerite N. Kramer (1963) "French Elite Perspectives on the United Nations," *International Organization* 17 (Winter): 54–75.

Levy, A. (1977) "Coder's Manual for Identifying Serious Inter-Nation Disputes, 1816–1965." Correlates of War Project, Ann Arbor, Michigan (internal memo).

Levy, Jack S. (1984) "The Offensive/Defensive Balance of Military Technology: A Theoretical and Historical Analysis." *International Studies Quarterly* 28 (June): 219–238.

    (1985) "The Polarity of the System and International Stability: An Empirical Analysis" in A. Sabrosky (ed.) *Polarity and War*, Boulder: Westview, pp. 41–66.

    (1987) "Declining Power and the Preventive Motivation for War," *World Politics* 40 (October): 82–107.

    (1989a) "The Causes of War: A Review of Theories and Evidence" in Philip E. Tetlock et al. (eds.) *Behavior, Society, and Nuclear War*, vol. 1, New York: Oxford University Press, pp. 209–333.

    (1989b) "The Diversionary Theory of War: A Critique" in M. Midlarsky, (ed.) *Handbook of War Studies*, Boston: Unwin Hyman, pp. 259–288.

    (1990/91) "Preferences, Constraints, and Choices in July 1914," *International Security* 15 (Winter): 151–186.

    (1994a) "Learning from Experience in U.S. and Soviet Foreign Policy" in M. Midlarsky, J. Vasquez, and P. Gladkov (eds.) *From Rivalry to Cooperation: Russian and American Perspectives on the Post-Cold War Era*, New York: HarperCollins, pp. 56–86.

    (1994b) "The Theoretical Foundation of Paul W. Schroeder's International System," *The International History Review* XVI (November): 715–744.

Levy, Jack S. and Michael N. Barnett (1991) "Domestic Sources of Alliances and Alignments: The Case of Egypt, 1962–1973," *International Organization* 45 (Summer): 369–395.

    (1992) "Alliance Formation, Domestic Political Economy, and Third World Security," *Jerusalem Journal of International Relations* 14 (December): 19–40.

Levy, Marion J., Jr. (1969) " 'Does It Matter If He's Naked?' Bawled the Child" in Klaus Knorr and James N. Rosenau (eds.) *Contending Approaches to International Politics*, Princeton: Princeton University Press, pp. 87–109.

Lijphart, Arend (1963) "The Analysis of Bloc Voting in the General Assembly:

A Critique and a Proposal," *American Political Science Review* 57 (December): 902–917.

(1964) "Tourist Traffic and Integration Potential," *Journal of Common Market Studies* 2 (March): 251–262.

(1974) "The Structure of the Theoretical Revolution in International Relations," *International Studies Quarterly* 18 (March): 41–74.

Little, Richard (1995) "Neorealism and the English School," *European Journal of International Relations* 1 (March): 9–34.

(1996) "The Growing Relevance of Pluralism?" in S. Smith, K. Booth, and M. Zalewski (eds.) *International Theory: Positivism and Beyond*, Cambridge: Cambridge University Press, pp. 66–86.

Luard, Evan (1976) *Types of International Society*, New York: Free Press.

Lustick, Ian S. (1997) "Lijphart, Lakatos, and Consociationalism," *World Politics* 50 (October): 88–117.

Luttwak, Edward (1982) *The Grand Strategy of the Soviet Union*, New York: St. Martin's.

Lyotard, Jean-François (1984) *The Post-Modern Condition*, Minneapolis: University of Minnesota Press.

Mahoney, Robert B., Jr. (1976) "American Political-Military Operations and the Structure of the International System, 1946–1975." Paper presented to the annual meeting of the Section on Military Studies of the International Studies Association, Ohio State University.

Mahoney, Robert B., Jr., and Richard Clayberg (1980) "Images and Threats: Soviet Perceptions of International Crises, 1946–1975" in P. McGowan and C. Kegley, Jr. (eds.) *Sage International Yearbook of Foreign Policy Studies*, vol. 5, Beverly Hills: Sage, pp. 55–81.

Malashenko, Igor Y. (1994) "Back to Realism: The End of the Cold War and the Collapse of the Soviet Union" in M. Midlarsky, J. Vasquez, and P. Gladkov (eds.) *From Rivalry to Cooperation: Russian and American Perspectives on the Post-Cold War Era*, New York: HarperCollins, pp. 89–99.

Mannheim, Karl (1955) *Ideology and Utopia*, New York: Harcourt Brace.

Manno, C. S. (1966) "Majority Decision and Minority Response in the U.N. General Assembly," *Journal of Conflict Resolution* 10 (March): 1–20.

Mansbach, Richard W., Yale H. Ferguson, and Donald E. Lampert (1976) *The Web of World Politics*, Englewood Cliffs: Prentice-Hall.

Mansbach, Richard W., and John A. Vasquez (1981a) "The Effect of Actor and Issue Classifications on the Analysis of Global Conflict-Cooperation," *Journal of Politics* 43 (August): 861–875.

(1981b) *In Search of Theory: A New Paradigm for Global Politics*, New York: Columbia University Press.

Mansfield, Edward D. (1992) "The Concentration of Capabilities and the Onset of War," *Journal of Conflict Resolution* 36 (March): 3–24.

(1994) *Power, Trade, and War*, Princeton: Princeton University Press.

Mansfield, Edward D., and Jack Snyder (1995) "Democratization and the Danger of War," *International Security* 20 (Summer): 5–38.

References

Maoz, Zeev, and Nasrin Abdolali (1989) "Regime Types and International Conflict, 1816–1976," *Journal of Conflict Resolution* 33 (March): 3–35.

March, James (1994) *A Primer on Decision Making*, New York: Free Press.

Marcuse, Herbert (1964) *One Dimensional Man: Studies in the Ideology of Advanced Industrial Society*, Boston: Beacon Press.

Mastanduno, Michael (1991) "Do Relative Gains Matter? America's Response to Japanese Industrial Policy," *International Security* 16 (Summer): 73–113.

(1997) "Preserving the Unipolar Moment: Realist Theories and U.S. Grand Strategy after the Cold War," *International Security* 21 (Spring): 49–88.

Masterman, Margaret (1970) "The Nature of a Paradigm" in Imre Lakatos and Alan Musgrave (eds.) *Criticism and the Growth of Knowledge*, Cambridge: Cambridge University Press, pp. 59–89.

May, Ernest R. (1973) *"Lessons" of the Past: The Use and Misuse of History in American Foreign Policy*, New York: Oxford University Press.

McClelland, Charles A. (1961) "The Acute International Crisis," *World Politics* 14 (October): 182–204.

(1967) "The World/Interaction Survey: A Research Project on Theory and Measurement of International Interaction and Transaction," University of Southern California (mimeographed).

(1968) "Access to Berlin: The Quantity and Variety of Events, 1948–1963" in J. D. Singer (ed.) *Quantitative International Politics*, New York: Free Press, pp. 159–187.

(1970) "International Interaction Analysis in the Predictive Mode," University of Southern California (mimeographed).

(1972a) "The Beginning, Duration and Abatement of International Crises: Comparisons in Two Conflict Arenas" in C. Hermann (ed.) *International Crises*, New York: Free Press, pp. 83–111.

(1972b) "Some Effects on Theory from the International Event Analysis Movement" in E. Azar, R. Brody, and C. McClelland (eds.) *International Events Interaction Analysis: Some Research Considerations*, Sage Professional Papers in International Studies, 02–001, Beverly Hills: Sage, pp. 15–43.

(1976) "An Inside Appraisal of the World Event Interaction Survey" in J. Rosenau (ed.) *In Search of Global Patterns*, New York: Free Press, pp. 105–110.

(1977) "The Anticipation of International Crises," *International Studies Quarterly* 21 (March): 15–38.

McClelland, Charles A., and Gary D. Hoggard (1969) "Conflict Patterns in the Interactions among Nations" in J. Rosenau (ed.) *International Politics and Foreign Policy*, New York: Free Press, pp. 711–724.

McCormick, James M. (1975) "Evaluating Models of Crisis Behavior: Some Evidence from the Middle East," *International Studies Quarterly* 19 (March): 17–45.

McGowan, Patrick J. (1968) "Africa and Non-alignment," *International Studies Quarterly* 12 (September): 262–295.

412

(1969) "The Pattern of African Diplomacy: A Quantitative Comparison," *Journal of Asian and African Studies* 4 (July): 202–221.

(1974) "A Bayesian Approach to the Problem of Events Data Validity" in J. Rosenau (ed.) *Comparing Foreign Policies*, New York: Halsted/John Wiley, pp. 407–444.

McGowan, Patrick J., and T. H. Johnson (1979) "The AFRICA Project and the Comparative Study of African Foreign Policy" in M. Delaney (ed.) *Aspects of International Relations in Africa*, Bloomington: African Studies Program, Indiana University, pp. 109–124.

McGowan, Patrick J., and Dale Smith (1978) "Economic Dependency in Black Africa: An Analysis of Competing Theories," *International Organization* 32 (Winter): 179–235.

McNamara, Robert S. (1968) *The Essence of Security*, New York: Harper and Row.

Mearsheimer, John J. (1990a) "Back to the Future: Instability In Europe After the Cold War," *International Security* 15 (Summer): 5–56.

(1990b) "Why We Will Soon Miss the Cold War," *The Atlantic* 266 (August): 35–50.

(1993) "The Case for a Ukrainian Nuclear Deterrent," *Foreign Affairs* 72 (Summer): 50–66.

(1994/95) "The False Promise of International Institutions, *International Security* 19 (Winter): 5–49.

(1995) "A Realist Reply," *International Security* 20 (Summer): 82–93.

Meyer, Donald B. (1960) *The Protestant Search for Political Realism, 1919–1941,* Berkeley and Los Angeles: University of California Press.

Meyers, Benjamin (1966) "African Voting in the U.N. General Assembly," *Journal of Modern African Studies* 4 (2): 213–227.

Midlarsky, Manus I., and Raymond Tanter (1967) "Toward a Theory of Political Instability in Latin America," *Journal of Peace Research* 4 (3): 209–227.

Miller, Steven E. (1993) "The Case Against a Ukrainian Nuclear Deterrent," *Foreign Affairs* 72 (Summer): 67–80.

Milner, Helen (1991) "The Assumption of Anarchy in International Relations Theory," *Review of International Studies* 17 (January): 67–85.

Milstein, Jeffrey S. (1972) "American and Soviet Influence, Balance of Power, and Arab-Israeli Violence" in B. M. Russett (ed.) *Peace, War, and Numbers,* Beverly Hills: Sage, pp. 139–164.

Milstein, Jeffrey S., and William Mitchell (1968) "Dynamics of the Vietnam Conflict: A Quantitative Analysis and Predictive Computer Simulation," *Peace Research Society (International) Papers* 10: 163–213.

(1969) "Computer Simulation of International Processes: The Vietnam War and the pre-World War I Naval Race," *Peace Research Society (International) Papers* 12: 117–136.

Mitrany, David (1943 [1966]) *A Working Peace System*, Chicago: University of Chicago Press.

References

Moll, Kendall D., and Gregory M. Luebbert (1980) "Arms Race and Military Expenditure Models," *Journal of Conflict Resolution* 24 (March): 153–185.

Morgan, Patrick M. (1977) *Deterrence: A Conceptual Analysis*, Beverly Hills: Sage.

Morgenthau, Hans J. (1948, 1960, 1978) *Politics Among Nations: The Struggle for Power and Peace*, 1st, 3rd and 5th rev. edns. New York: Knopf.

— (1951) *In Defense of the National Interest*, New York: Knopf.

— (1952) "Another Great Debate: The National Interest of the United States," *American Political Science Review*, 46 (December): 961–988.

— (1958) *Dilemmas of Politics*, Chicago: University of Chicago Press.

— (1967) "Common-sense and Theories of International Relations," *Journal of International Affairs* 21 (2): 207–214.

— (1970) *Truth and Power: Essays of a Decade, 1960–70*, New York: Praeger.

Morgenthau, Hans J., and Kenneth W. Thompson (eds.) (1950) *Principles and Problems of International Politics*, New York: Knopf.

— (1993) *Politics Among Nations: The Struggle for Power and Peace*, Brief Edition, revised by Kenneth W. Thompson, New York: McGraw-Hill.

Morrow, James D. (1993) "Arms versus Allies: Trade-offs in the Search for Security," *International Organization* 47 (Spring): 207–233.

Morse, Edward L. (1976) *Modernization and the Transformation of International Relations*, New York: Free Press.

Moses, L. E., R. A. Brody, O. R. Holsti, J. B. Kadane, and J. S. Milstein (1967) "Scaling Data on Inter-nation Action," *Science* 156 (26 May): 3778.

Moskos, Charles, and Wendell Bell (1964) "Emergent Caribbean Nations Face the Outside World," *Social Problems* 12 (Summer): 24–41.

Mueller, John E. (1989) *Retreat from Doomsday: The Obsolescence of Major War*, New York: Basic Books.

Musgrave, Alan (1976) "Method or Madness?" in R. Cohen et al. (eds.) *Boston Studies in the Philosophy of Science*, vol. 39, Dordrecht, Holland: D. Reidel, pp. 457–491.

— (1978) "Evidential Support, Falsification, Heuristics, and Anarchism" in G. Radnitzky and G. Andersson (eds.) *Progress and Rationality in Science*, Dordrecht: D. Reidel, pp. 181–201.

Nagel, Ernest (1961) *The Structure of Science*, New York: Harcourt, Brace, & World.

Nameworth, Zvi, and Thomas L. Brewer (1966) "Elite Editorial Comment on the European and Atlantic Communities in Four Continents" in P. Stone et al. (eds.) *General Inquirer*, Cambridge, Mass.: MIT Press, pp. 401–427.

Naroll, Raoul (1968) "Imperial Cycles and World Order," *Peace Research Society (International) Papers* 7: 83–102.

Nicholson, Michael (1983) *The Scientific Analysis of Social Behavior: A Defence of Empiricism in Social Science*, New York: St. Martin's.

— (1992) "Imaginary Paradigms: A Sceptical View of the Inter-Paradigm Debate in International Relations," Kent Papers in Politics and International Relations, Series 1, No. 7, Canterbury.

414

(1996a) *Causes and Consequences in International Relations: A Conceptual Study*, London: Frances Pinter.

(1996b) "The Continued Significance of Positivism?" in S. Smith, K. Booth, and M. Zalewski (eds.) *International Theory: Positivism and Beyond*, Cambridge: Cambridge University Press, pp. 128–145.

Nicolson, Harold (1939) *Diplomacy*, London: Oxford University Press.

Niebuhr, Reinhold (1940) *Christianity and Power Politics*, New York: Scribner's.

(1953) *Christian Realism and Political Problems*, New York: Scribner's.

Niou, Emerson, Peter C. Ordeshook, and Gregory F. Rose (1989) *The Balance of Power: Stability in International Systems*, New York: Cambridge University Press.

North, Robert C., and Nazli Choucri (1968) "Background Conditions to the Outbreak of the First World War," *Peace Research Society (International) Papers* 9: 125–137.

Nye, Joseph, S., Jr. (1987) "Nuclear Learning and U.S.–Soviet Security Regimes," *International Organization* 41 (Summer): 371–402.

(1988) "Neorealism and Neoliberalism," *World Politics* 40 (January): 235–251.

(1990) *Bound to Lead: The Changing Nature of American Power*, New York: Basic Books.

(1993) *Understanding International Conflicts*, New York: HarperCollins.

Oberdorfer, Don (1991) *The Turn: From the Cold War to a New Era*, New York: Poseidon Press.

Ohlstrom, Bo (1966) "Information and Propaganda," *Journal of Peace Research* 3 (1): 75–88.

O'Leary, Michael K. (1969) "Linkages between Domestic and International Politics in Underdeveloped Nations" in J. Rosenau (ed.) *Linkage Politics*, New York: Free Press, pp. 324–346.

(1976) "The Role of Issues" in J. Rosenau (ed.) *In Search of Global Patterns*, New York: Free Press, pp. 318–325.

Olson, William C. (1972) "The Growth of a Discipline" in B. Porter (ed.), *The Aberystwyth Papers: International Politics 1919–1969*, London: Oxford University Press, pp. 1–29.

Olson, William C., and A. J. R. Groom (1991) *International Relations Then and Now: Origins and Trends in Interpretation*, London: HarperCollins Academic.

Onuf, Nicholas Greenwood (1989) *World of Our Making*, Columbia: University of South Carolina Press.

Organski, A. F. K. (1958, 1968) *World Politics*, 1st and 2nd edns. New York: Knopf.

Organski, A. F. K., and Jacek Kugler (1977) "The Costs of Major Wars: The Phoenix Factor," *American Political Science Review* 71 (December): 1347–1366.

(1980) *The War Ledger*, Chicago: University of Chicago Press.

Osgood, Charles E. (1959) "Suggestions for Winning the Real War with Communism," *Journal of Conflict Resolution* 3 (December): 295–325.

References

Ostrom, Charles W., and Francis W. Hoole (1978) "Alliances and War Revisited: A Research Note," *International Studies Quarterly* 22 (June): 215–236.

Oye, Kenneth A. (1995) "Explaining the End of the Cold War: Morphological and Behavioral Adaptations to the Nuclear Peace?" in Richard Ned Lebow and Thomas Risse-Kappen (eds.), *International Relations Theory and the End of the Cold War*, New York: Columbia University Press, pp. 57–83.

Paige, Glenn D. (1969) *The Korean Decision: June 24–30, 1950*, New York: Free Press.

Perle, Richard (1991) "Military Power and the Passing Cold War" in C. Kegley, Jr., and K. Schwab (eds.) *After the Cold War: Questioning the Morality of Deterrence*, Boulder: Westview, pp. 33–38.

Peterson, Sophia (1975) "Research on Research: Events Data Studies, 1961–1972" in P. J. McGowan (ed.) *Sage International Yearbook of Foreign Policy Studies*, vol. 3, Beverly Hills: Sage, pp. 263–309.

Peterson, V. Spike (ed.) (1992) *Gendered States: Feminist (Re)Visions of International Relations Theory*, Boulder: Lynne Rienner.

Phillips, Warren R., and Robert C. Crain (1974) "Dynamic Foreign Policy Interactions: Reciprocity and Uncertainty in Foreign Policy" in P. J. McGowan (ed.) *Sage International Yearbook of Foreign Policy Studies*, vol. 2, Beverly Hills: Sage, pp. 227–266.

Phillips, Warren R., and Richard V. Rimkunas (1979) "A Cross-Agency Comparison of U.S. Crisis Perception" in J. D. Singer and M. D. Wallace (eds.) *To Augur Well*, Beverly Hills: Sage, pp. 237–270.

Pipes, Richard (1984) *Survival is Not Enough*, New York: Simon & Schuster.

Platig, E. Raymond (1967) *International Relations Research: Problems of Evaluation and Advancement*, Santa Barbara: Clio Press.

Popper, Karl (1935, 1959) *The Logic of Scientific Discovery*, London: Hutchinson.
    (1970) "Normal Science and Its Dangers" in I. Lakatos and A. Musgrave (eds.) *Criticism and the Growth of Knowledge*, Cambridge: Cambridge University Press, pp. 51–58.

Porter, Brian (ed.) (1972) *The Aberystwyth Papers: International Politics 1919–1969*, London: Oxford University Press.

Posen, Barry R. (1984) *The Sources of Military Doctrine: France, Britain, and Germany Between the World Wars*, Ithaca: Cornell University Press.

Pruitt, Dean G. (1965) "Definition of the Situation as a Determinant of International Action" in Herbert C. Kelman (ed.) *International Behavior: A Social-Psychological Analysis*, New York: Holt, Rinehart and Winston, pp. 343–432.
    (1995) "The Psychology of Social Conflict and Its Relevance to International Conflict" in J. Vasquez et al. (eds.) *Beyond Confrontation: Learning Conflict Resolution in the Post-Cold War Era*, Ann Arbor: University of Michigan Press, pp. 103–114.

Pruitt, Dean G., and Jeffrey Z. Rubin (1986) *Social Conflict: Escalation, Stalemate, and Settlement*, New York: Random House.

Puchala, Donald J. (1991) "Woe to the Orphans of the Scientific Revolution" in

R. Rothstein (ed.) *The Evolution of Theory in International Relations,* Columbia: University of South Carolina Press, pp. 39–60.

Putnam, Robert D. (1988) "Diplomacy and Domestic Politics: The Logic of Two-Level Games," *International Organization* 42 (Summer): 427–460.

Quester, George H. (1977) *Offense and Defense in the International System,* New York: Wiley.

Quine, W. V. O. (1961) *From a Logical Point of View,* New York: Harper and Row.

Rapoport, Anatol (1964) *Strategy and Conscience,* New York: Schocken Books.

Ray, James Lee (1980) "The Measurement of System Structure" in J. D. Singer (ed.) *The Correlates of War: II,* New York: Free Press, pp. 36–54.

(1995) *Democracy and International Conflict,* Columbia: University of South Carolina Press.

Ray, James Lee, and Bruce Russett (1996) "The Future as Arbiter of Theoretical Controversies: Predictions, Explanations, and the End of the Cold War," *British Journal of Political Science* (October): 441–470.

Ray, James Lee, and J. David Singer (1973) "Measuring the Concentration of Power in the International System," *Sociological Methods and Research* 1 (May): 403–437.

Ray, James Lee, and Thomas Webster (1978) "Dependency and Economic Growth in Latin America," *International Studies Quarterly* 22 (September): 409–434.

Reinton, Per Olav (1967) "International Structure and International Integration: The Case of Latin America," *Journal of Peace Research* 4 (4): 334–365.

Richardson, Lewis F. (1960a) *Arms and Insecurity,* Chicago: Quadrangle Books.

(1960b) *Statistics of Deadly Quarrels,* Chicago: Quadrangle Books.

Rieselbach, Leroy N. (1960a) "The Basis of Isolationist Behavior," *Public Opinion Quarterly* 24 (Winter): 645–657.

(1960b) "Quantitative Techniques for Studying Voting Behavior in the U.N. General Assembly," *International Organization* 14 (Spring): 291–306.

(1964) "The Demography of the Congressional Vote on Foreign Aid, 1939–1958," *American Political Science Review* 58 (September): 577–588.

Risse-Kappen, Thomas (1994) "Ideas Do Not Float Freely: Transnational Coalitions, Domestic Structures, and the End of the Cold War," *International Organization* 48 (Spring): 185–214.

Robinson, James A., and Richard C. Snyder (1965) "Decision-making in International Politics" in H. Kelman (ed.) *International Behavior: A Social-Psychological Analysis,* New York: Holt, Rinehart and Winston, pp. 435–463.

Robinson, Thomas W. (1967) "A National Interest Analysis of Sino-Soviet Relations," *International Studies Quarterly* 11 (June): 135–175.

Rock, Stephen R. (1989) *Why Peace Breaks Out,* Chapel Hill: University of North Carolina Press.

Rogov, Sergey M. (1994) "The Changing Perspective of Russian-American Relations" in M. Midlarsky, J. Vasquez, and P. Gladkov (eds.) *From Rivalry to Cooperation: Russian and American Perspectives on the Post-Cold War Era,* New York: HarperCollins, pp. 116–125.

Rosati, Jerel A., Joe D. Hagan, and Martin W. Sampson, III (eds.) (1994) *Foreign Policy Restructuring: How Governments Respond to Global Change*, Columbia: University of South Carolina Press.

Rosecrance, Richard (ed.) (1976) *America as an Ordinary Country*, Ithaca: Cornell University Press.

(1992) "A New Concert of Powers," *Foreign Affairs* 71 (Spring): 64–82.

(1995) "Overextension, Vulnerability, and Conflict," *International Security* 19 (Spring): 145–163.

Rosecrance, Richard, Alan Alexandroff, Brian Healy, and Arthur Stein (1974) *Power, Balance of Power, and Status in Nineteenth Century International Relations*, Sage Professional Papers in International Studies, 02–029, Beverly Hills: Sage.

Rosecrance, Richard, and Chih-Cheng Lo (1996) "Balancing, Stability, and War: The Mysterious Case of the Napoleonic International System," *International Studies Quarterly* 40 (December): 479–500.

Rosecrance, Richard, and Arthur A. Stein (eds.) (1993) *The Domestic Bases of Grand Strategy*, Ithaca: Cornell University Press.

Rosecrance, Richard, and Zara Steiner (1993) "British Grand Strategy and the Origins of World War II," in Richard Rosecrance and Arthur Stein (eds.) *The Domestic Bases of Grand Strategy*, Ithaca: Cornell University Press, pp. 124–153.

Rosen, J. Steven (ed.) (1973) *Testing the Theory of the Military-Industrial Complex*, Lexington: Lexington Books.

Rosenau, James N. (ed.) (1961, 1969) *International Politics and Foreign Policy*, 1st and rev. edns. New York: Free Press.

(1962) "Consensus-building in the American National Community: Some Hypotheses and Some Supporting Data," *Journal of Politics* 24 (November): 639–661.

(1966) "Pre-theories and Theories of Foreign Policy" in R. B. Farrell (ed.) *Approaches to Comparative and International Politics*, Evanston, Ill.: Northwestern University Press, pp. 27–93.

Rosenau, James N., and Ernst-Otto Czempiel (eds.) (1992) *Governance without Government*, Cambridge: Cambridge University Press.

Rosenau, Pauline Marie (1992) *Post-Modernism and the Social Sciences*, Princeton: Princeton University Press.

Rosenberg, Justin (1994) *The Empire of Civil Society: A Critique of the Realist Theory of International Relations*, London: Verso.

Rowe, Edward T. (1964) "The Emerging Anti-Colonial Consensus in the U.N.," *Journal of Conflict Resolution* 8 (September): 209–230.

(1969) "Changing Patterns in the Voting Success of Member States in the U.N. General Assembly, 1945–1966," *International Organization* 23 (Spring): 231–253.

Roy, A. Bikash (1997) "Intervention Across Bisecting Borders," *Journal of Peace Research* 34 (August): 303–314.

Rubenstein, Alvin Z. (1972) *Foreign Policy of the Soviet Union*, 3rd edn. New York: Random.

Rubin, Jeffrey, and Bert R. Brown (1975) *The Social Psychology of Bargaining and Negotiation*, New York: Academic Press.

Ruge, Mari (1964) "Technical Assistance and Parliamentary Debates," *Journal of Peace Research* 1 (2): 77–94.

Ruggie, John Gerard (1983) "Continuity and Transformation in the World Polity: Toward a Neorealist Synthesis," *World Politics* 35 (January): 261–285.

(1995) "The False Premise of Realism," *International Security* 20 (Summer): 62–70.

Rummel, Rudolph J. (1963) "Dimensions of Conflict Behavior Within and Between Nations," *General Systems Yearbook* 8: 1–50.

(1964) "Testing Some Possible Predictors of Conflict Behavior Within and Between Nations," *Peace Research Society (International) Papers* 1: 79–111.

(1966a) "A Social Field Theory of Foreign Conflict Behavior," *Peace Research Society (International) Papers* 4: 131–150.

(1966b) "Some Dimensions in the Foreign Behavior of Nations," *Journal of Peace Research* 3 (3): 201–224.

(1967a) "Dimensions of Dyadic War, 1820–1952," *Journal of Conflict Resolution* 11 (June): 176–184.

(1967b) "Some Attributes and Behavioral Patterns of Nations," *Journal of Peace Research* 4 (2): 196–206.

(1968) "The Relationship Between National Attributes and Foreign Conflict Behavior" in J. D. Singer (ed.) *Quantitative International Politics*, New York: Free Press, pp. 187–214.

(1969) "Indicators of Cross-National and International Patterns," *American Political Science Review* 63 (March): 127–147.

(1972) "U.S. Foreign Relations: Conflict, Cooperation, and Attribute Distances" in B. M. Russett (ed.) *Peace, War, and Numbers*, Beverly Hills: Sage, pp. 71–113.

(1976) "The Roots of Faith" in J. Rosenau (ed.) *In Search of Global Patterns*, New York: Free Press, pp. 10–30.

(1977) *Field Theory Evolving*, Beverly Hills: Sage.

(1979) *War, Power, Peace, Understanding Conflict and War*, vol. 4. Beverly Hills: Sage.

(1995) "Democracies ARE less Warlike Than Other Regimes," *European Journal of International Relations* 1 (December): 457–479.

Rush, Myron (1993) "Fortune and Fate," *The National Interest* 31 (Spring): 19–25.

Russett, Bruce M. (1962a) "International Communication and Legislative Behavior: The Senate and the House of Commons," *Journal of Conflict Resolution* 6 (December): 291–307.

(1962b) "Cause, Surprise and No Escape," *Journal of Politics* 24 (February): 3–22.

(1963) "The Calculus of Deterrence," *Journal of Conflict Resolution* 7 (June): 97–109.

(1964) "Measures of Military Effort," *American Behavioral Scientist* 7 (February): 26–29.

(1966) "Discovering Voting Groups in the U.N.," *American Political Science Review* 60 (June): 327–339.

(1967) *International Regions and the International System*, Chicago: Rand McNally.

(1968a) "Components of an Operational Theory of International Alliance Formation," *Journal of Conflict Resolution* 12 (September): 285–301.

(1968b) "Delineating International Regions" in J. D. Singer (ed.) *Quantitative International Politics*, New York: Free Press, pp. 317–352.

(1968c) "Regional Trading Patterns, 1938–1963," *International Studies Quarterly* 12 (December): 360–379.

(1969) "The Young Science of International Politics," *World Politics* 22 (October); 87–94.

(1970) "Methodological and Theoretical Schools in International Relations" in N. D. Palmer (ed.) *A Design for International Relations Research: Scope, Methods, and Relevance*, Monograph 10, American Academy of Political and Social Sciences, Philadelphia, October, pp. 87–106.

(1993) *Grasping the Democratic Peace*, Princeton: Princeton University Press.

(1995) "The Democratic Peace: 'And Yet It Moves'," *International Security* 19 (Spring): 164–184.

Russett, Bruce M., and Hayward R. Alker, Jr., Karl W. Deutsch, and Harold D. Lasswell (1964) *World Handbook of Political and Social Indicators*, New Haven: Yale University Press.

Russett, Bruce M., and Curtis Lamb (1969) "Global Patterns of Diplomatic Exchange, 1963–64," *Journal of Peace Research* 6 (1): 37–55.

Sagan, Scott D. (1995) "More Will Be Worse" in S. Sagan and K. Waltz, *The Spread of Nuclear Weapons: A Debate*, New York: W. W. Norton, pp. 47–91.

Salmore, Barbara G., and Stephen A. Salmore (1975) "Regime Constraints and Foriegn Policy Behavior." Paper presented at the annual meeting of the American Political Science Association, San Francisco.

Salmore, Stephen A. (1972) National Attributes and Foreign Policy: A Multivariate Analysis. Ph.D. Dissertation, Princeton University.

Salmore, Stephen A., and Donald Munton (1974) "An Empirically Based Typology of Foreign Policy Behaviors" in J. Rosenau (ed.) *Comparing Foreign Policies*, New York: Halsted/John Wiley, pp. 329–352.

Sample, Susan G. (1996) Arms Races and the Escalation of Disputes to War. Ph.D. Dissertation, Vanderbilt University.

(1997) "Arms Races and Dispute Escalation: Resolving the Debate," *Journal of Peace Research* 34 (February): 7–22.

Sawyer, Jack (1967) "Dimensions of Nations: Size, Wealth, and Politics," *American Journal of Sociology* 73 (September): 145–172.

Scheffler, Israel (1967) *Science and Subjectivity*, Indianapolis: Bobbs-Merrill.

Schelling, Thomas C. (1960) *The Strategy of Conflict*, New York: Oxford University Press.

(1966) *Arms and Influence*, New Haven: Yale University Press.

Schmidt, Brian C. (1994) "The Historiography of Academic International Relations," *Review of International Studies* 4 (October): 349–367.

Schmitter, Philippe C. (1969) "Further Notes on Operationalizing Some Variables Related to Regional Integration," *International Organization* 23 (Spring): 327–336.

Schroeder, Paul, W. (1994a) "Historical Reality vs. Neo-realist Theory," *International Security* 19 (Summer): 108–148.

(1994b) *The Transformation of European Politics, 1763–1848*, Oxford: Clarendon Press.

Schuman, Frederick L. (1933) *International Politics*, New York: McGraw-Hill.

Schwarzenberger, Georg (1941) *Power Politics*, New York: Prager.

Schweller, Randall L. (1992) "Domestic Structure and Preventive War: Are Democracies More Pacific?" *World Politics* 44 (January): 235–269.

(1994) "Bandwagoning for Profit: Bringing the Revisionist State Back In," *International Security* 19 (Summer): 72–107.

(1997) "New Realist Research on Alliances: Refining, Not Refuting, Waltz's Balancing Proposition," *American Political Science Review* 91 (December): 927–930.

Senese, Paul D. (1996) "Geographical Proximity and Issue Salience: Their Effects on the Escalation of Militarized Interstate Conflict," *Conflict Management and Peace Science* 15 (Fall): 133–161.

(1997) "Between Dispute and War: The Effect of Joint Democracy on Interstate Conflict Escalation," *Journal of Politics* 59 (February): 1–27.

Shapere, Dudley (1964) "The Structure of Scientific Revolutions," *Philosophical Review* 73 (July): 383–394.

(1971) "The Paradigm Concept," *Science* 172: 706–709.

Shapiro, Michael J. (1966) "Cognitive Rigidity and Perceptual Orientations in an Inter-Nation Simulation," Evanston, Ill.: Northwestern University (mimeographed).

(1981) *Language and Political Understanding*, New Haven: Yale University Press.

Shaw, Martin (1992) "Global Society and Global Responsibility: The Theoretical, Historical and Political Limits of 'International Society'," *Millennium* 21 (Winter): 421–434.

Shevardnadze, Eduard (1991) *The Future Belongs to Freedom*, New York: Free Press.

Shimony, A. (1976) "Comments on Two Epistemological Theses of Thomas Kuhn" in R. S. Cohen et al. (eds.) *Boston Studies in Philosophy of Science*, vol. 39, Dordrecht, Holland: D. Reidel, pp. 569–588.

Sigler, John H. (1969) "News Flow in the North African International Subsystem," *International Studies Quarterly* 13 (December): 381–397.

(1972a) "Reliability Problems in the Measurement of International Events in the Elite Press" in J. Sigler, J. Field, and M. Adelman (eds.) *Applications of Event Data Analysis*, Sage Professional Papers in International Studies, 02–002, Beverly Hills: Sage, pp. 9–30.

(1972b) "Cooperation and Conflict in the United States-Soviet-Chinese Relations, 1966–1971," *Peace Research Society (International) Papers* 19: 107–128.

Simon, Herbert (1957) *Administrative Behavior*, 2nd edn. New York: Macmillan.

Simowitz, Roslyn, and Barry L. Price (1990) "The Expected Utility Theory of Conflict: Measuring Theoretical Progress," *American Political Science Review* 84 (June): 439–460.

Singer, J. David (1958) "Threat-Perception and the Armament-Tension Dilemma," *Journal of Conflict Resolution* 2 (March): 90–105.

(1961) "The Level of Analysis Problem in International Relations," in K. Knorr and S. Verba (eds.) *The International System: Theoretical Essays*, Princeton: Princeton University Press, pp. 72–92.

(1964) "Soviet and American Foreign Policy Attitudes: A Content Analysis of Elite Articulations," *Journal of Conflict Resolution* 8 (December): 424–485.

(1965) "Data-Making in International Relations," *Behavioral Science* 10 (January): 68–80.

(1966) "The Behavioral Science Approach to International Relations: Payoff and Prospects," *SAIS Review* 10: 12–20.

(1968) (ed.) *Quantitative International Politics*, New York: Free Press.

(1969) "The Incompleat Theorist: Insight without Evidence" in K. Knorr and J. Rosenau (eds.) *Contending Approaches to International Politics*, Princeton: Princeton University Press, pp. 62–86.

(1972a) "The 'Correlates of War' Project: Interim Report and Rationale," *World Politics* 24 (January): 243–270.

(1972b) *The Scientific Study of Politics: An Approach to Foreign Policy Analysis*, Morristown, New Jersey: General Learning Press.

(1976) "The Correlates of War Project: Continuity, Diversity, and Convergence" in F. Hoole and D. Zinnes (eds.) *Quantitative International Politics: An Appraisal*, New York: Praeger, pp. 21–42.

(1979a) (ed.) *The Correlates of War: I*, New York: Free Press.

(1979b) "The Management of Serious International Disputes: Historical Patterns since the Congress of Vienna." Paper presented to the 11th World Congress of the International Political Science Association, Moscow.

(1980) (ed.) *The Correlates of War: II*, New York: Free Press.

(1982) "Confrontational Behavior and Escalation to War, 1816–1980," *Journal of Peace Research* 19 (1): 37–48.

(1991) "Peace in the Global System: Displacement, Interregnum, or Transformation?" in C. Kegley, Jr. (ed.) *The Long Postwar Peace*, New York: HarperCollins, pp. 56–84.

Singer, J. David, Stuart A. Bremer, and John Stuckey (1972) "Capability

Distribution, Uncertainty, and Major Power War, 1820–1965" in B. M. Russett (ed.) *Peace, War, and Numbers,* Beverly Hills: Sage, pp. 19–48.

Singer, J. David, and Melvin Small (1966a) "National Alliances Commitments and War Involvement, 1815–1945," *Peace Research Society (International) Papers* 5: 109–140.

(1966b) "The Composition and Status Ordering of the International System, 1815–1940," *World Politics* 18 (January): 236–282.

(1968) "Alliance Aggregation and the Onset of War, 1815–1945" in J. D. Singer (ed.) *Quantitative International Politics,* New York: Free Press, pp. 247–286.

(1972) *The Wages of War, 1816–1965: A Statistical Handbook,* New York: John Wiley.

Singer, J. David, and Michael D. Wallace (1970) "Intergovernmental Organization and the Preservation of Peace, 1816–1965: Some Bivariate Relationships," *International Organization* 24 (Summer): 520–547.

Singer, Marshall R., and Barton Sensenig III (1963) "Elections within the United Nations," *International Organization* 17 (Autumn): 901–925.

Siverson, Randolph M., and Joel King (1980) "Attributes of National Alliance Membership and War Participation, 1815–1965," *American Journal of Political Science* 24 (February): 1–15.

Siverson, Randolph M., and Ross A. Miller, (1996) "The Power Transition: Problems and Prospects" in Jacek Kugler and Douglas Lemke (eds.) *Parity and War,* Ann Arbor: University of Michigan Press, pp. 57–73.

Siverson, Randolph M., and Harvey Starr (1991) *The Diffusion of War,* Ann Arbor: University of Michigan Press.

Skidmore, David (1996) *Reversing Course: Carter's Foreign Policy, Domestic Politics, and the Failure of Reform,* Nashville: Vanderbilt University Press.

Small, Melvin, and J. David Singer (1969) "Formal Alliances, 1816–1965: An Extension of the Basic Data," *Journal of Peace Research* 6 (3): 257–282.

(1973) "The Diplomatic Importance of States, 1816–1970: An Extension and Refinement of the Indicator," *World Politics* 25 (July): 577–599.

(1976) "The War Proneness of Democratic Regimes 1816–1965," *Jerusalem Journal of International Relations* 1 (Summer): 50–69.

(1979) "Conflict in the International System, 1816–1977: Historical Trends and Polity Futures" in C. Kegley, Jr. and P. McGowan (eds.) *Sage International Yearbook of Foreign Policy Studies,* vol. 4, Beverly Hills: Sage, pp. 89–115.

(1982) *Resort to Arms: International and Civil Wars, 1816–1980,* Beverly Hills: Sage.

Smith, Raymond (1969) "On the Structure of Foreign News: Comparison of the *New York Times* and the Indian White Papers," *Journal of Peace Research* 6 (1): 123–136.

Smith, Steve (1987) "Paradigm Dominance in International Relations: The Development of International Relations as a Social Science," *Millennium* 16 (Summer): 189–206.

(1995) "The Self-Images of a Discipline: A Genealogy of International Relations Theory" in Ken Booth and Steve Smith (eds.) *International Relations Theory Today*, Cambridge: Polity Press, pp. 1–37.

(1996) "Positivism and Beyond" in S. Smith, K. Booth, and M. Zalewski (eds.) *International Theory: Positivism and Beyond*, Cambridge: Cambridge University Press, pp. 11–44.

Smoker, Paul L. (1963) "A Mathematical Study of the Present Arms Race," *General Systems Yearbook* 8: 51–59.

(1964a) "Fear in the Arms Race: A Mathematical Study," *Journal of Peace Research* 1 (1): 55–64.

(1964b) "Sino-Indian Relations: A Study in Trade, Communication and Defense," *Journal of Peace Research* 1 (2): 65–76.

(1965a) "A Preliminary Empirical Study of an International Integrative Subsystem," *International Association* 17 (November): 638–646.

(1965b) "Trade, Defense, and the Richardson Theory of Arms Races," *Journal of Peace Research* 2 (2): 161–176.

(1966) "The Arms Race: A Wave Model," *Peace Research Society (International) Papers* 4: 151–192.

(1967) "Nation-State Escalation and International Integration," *Journal of Peace Research* 4 (1): 61–75.

Snidal, Duncan (1991) "Relative Gains and the Pattern of International Cooperation," *American Political Science Review* 85 (September): 701–726.

Snyder, Glenn H., and Paul Diesing (1977) *Conflict Among Nations: Bargaining, Decision Making, and System Structure*, Princeton: Princeton University Press.

Snyder, Jack (1978) "Rationality at the Brink: The Role of Cognitive Processes in Failures of Deterrence," *World Politics* 30 (April): 345–365.

(1984) *The Ideology of the Offensive*, Ithaca: Cornell University Press.

(1991) *Myths of Empire: Domestic Politics and International Ambition*, Ithaca: Cornell University Press.

(1995) "Myths, Modernization, and the Post-Gorbachev World" in Richard Ned Lebow and Thomas Risse-Kappen (eds.) *International Relations Theory and the End of the Cold War*, New York: Columbia Univesity Press, pp. 109–126.

Snyder, Jack, and Robert Jervis (eds.) (1993) *Coping with Complexity in the International System*, Boulder: Westview.

Snyder, Richard C., H. W. Bruck, and Burton Sapin (1954) *Decision-Making as an Approach to the Study of International Politics*, Princeton: Foreign Policy Analysis Project, Princeton University.

(1962) (eds.) *Foreign Policy Decision-Making*, New York: Free Press.

Snyder, Richard C., and Glenn D. Paige (1958) "The United States Decision to Resist Aggression in Korea: The Application of an Analytic Scheme," *Administrative Science Quarterly* 3 (December): 342–378.

Spegele, Roger D. (1996) *Political Realism in International Theory*, Cambridge: Cambridge University Press.

Spiezio, K. Edward (1990) "British Hegemony and Major Power War, 1815–1935: An Empirical Test of Gilpin's Model of Hegemonic Governance," *International Studies Quarterly* 34 (June): 165–181.

Spiro, David E. (1994) "The Insignificance of the Liberal Peace," *International Security* (Fall): 50–86.

Spykman, Nicholas (1942) *America's Strategy in World Politics: The United States and the Balance of Power*, New York: Harcourt, Brace & World.

Starr, Harvey (1974) "The Quantitative International Relations Scholar as Surfer: Riding the Fourth Wave," *Journal of Conflict Resolution* 18 (June): 336–368.

Stein, Janice Gross (1994) "Political Learning by Doing: Gorbachev as Uncommitted Thinker and Motivated Leader," *International Organization* 48 (Spring): 155–183.

Steinbruner, John D. (1974) *The Cybernetic Theory of Decision*, Princeton: Princeton University Press.

Stephens, Jerome (1973) "The Kuhnian Paradigm and Political Inquiry: An Appraisal," *American Journal of Political Science* 17 (August): 467–488.

Stinchcombe, Arthur (1968) *Constructing Social Theories*, New York: Harcourt, Brace & World.

Stockholm International Peace Research Institute (SIPRI) (1968/69) *Stockholm International Peace Research Institute Yearbook of World Armaments and Disarmament*, New York: Humanities Press.

Stoessinger, John G. (1961, 1975) *The Might of Nations*, 1st and 5th edns. New York: Random House.

(1971) *Nations in Darkness: China, Russia, and America*, New York: Random House.

Strauss, Barry S. (1991) "Of Balances, Bandwagons, and Ancient Greeks" in Richard Ned Lebow and Barry S. Strauss (eds.) *Hegemonic Rivalry: From Thucydides to the Nuclear Age*, Boulder: Westview, pp. 189–210.

Suganami, Hidemi (1996) *On the Causes of War*, Oxford: Clarendon Press.

Sullivan, Michael P. (1972) "Symbolic Involvement as a Correlate of Escalation: The Vietnam Case" in B. M. Russett (ed.) *Peace, War, and Numbers*, Beverly Hills: Sage, pp. 185–213.

(1979) "Foreign Policy Articulations and U.S. Conflict Behavior" in J. D. Singer and M. D. Wallace (eds.) *To Augur Well*, Beverly Hills: Sage, pp. 215–235.

Summy, Ralph (1995) "Introduction: Challenging the Emergent Orthodoxy" in R. Summy and M. Salla (eds.) *Why the Cold War Ended*, Westport: Greenwood Press, pp. 1–15.

Suppe, Frederick (1977) "Afterword" in F. Suppe (ed.) *The Structure of Scientific Theories*, Urbana: University of Illinois Press.

Sylvester, Christine (1994) *Feminist Theory and International Relations in a Postmodern Era*, Cambridge: Cambridge University Press.

Taagepara, Rein (1968) "Growth Curves of Empires," *General Systems Yearbook* 13: 171–175.

References

Tanter, Raymond (1966) "Dimensions of Nations, 1958–60," *Journal of Conflict Resolution* 10 (March): 41–64.

(1974) *Modelling and Managing International Conflicts*, Beverly Hills: Sage.

Tarski, A. (1949) "The Semantic Conception of Truth" in H. Feigl and W. Sellars (eds.) *Readings in Philosophical Analysis*, New York: Appleton-Century-Crofts, pp. 52–84.

Taylor, Charles (1985) *Philosophy and the Human Sciences*, Cambridge: Cambridge University Press.

Taylor, Charles Lewis, and Michael Hudson (1972) *World Handbook of Political and Social Indicators*, 2nd edn. New Haven: Yale University Press.

Taylor, Trevor (1978a) "Power Politics" in T. Taylor (ed.) *Approaches and Theory in International Relations*, London: Longman, pp. 122–140.

(1978b) *Approaches and Theory in International Relations*, London: Longman.

Teune, Henry, and S. Synnestvedt (1965) "Measuring International Alignment," *Orbis* 9 (Spring): 171–189.

Thompson, E. P. (1978) *The Poverty of Theory and Other Essays*, New York: Monthly Review Press.

Thompson, James (1968) "How Could Vietnam Happen? An Autopsy," *Atlantic Monthly* (April): 47–53.

Thompson, Kenneth W. (1952) "The Study of International Politics: A Survey of Trends and Developments," *Review of Politics* 14 (October): 433–443.

(1960) *Political Realism and the Crisis of World Politics: An American Approach to Foreign Policy*, Princeton: Princeton University Press.

Thompson, William R. (1996) "Democracy and Peace: Putting the Cart Before the Horse," *International Organization* 50 (Winter): 141–174.

Thompson, William R., Robert D. Duval, and Ahmed Dia (1979) "Wars, Alliances, and Military Expenditures," *Journal of Conflict Resolution* 23 (December): 629–654.

Thompson, William R., and Gary Zuk (1986) "World Power and the Strategic Trap of Territorial Commitments," *International Studies Quarterly* 30 (September): 249–267.

Tickner, J. Ann (1992) *Gender in International Relations: Feminist Perspectives on Achieving Global Security*, New York: Columbia University Press.

Tornebohm, H. (1976) "Inquiring Systems and Paradigms" in R. S. Cohen et al. (eds.) *Boston Studies in Philosophy of Science*, vol. 39, Dordrecht: D. Reidel, pp. 635–654.

Toulmin, Stephen (1950) *The Place of Reason in Ethics*, Cambridge: Cambridge University Press.

(1953) *Philosophy of Science: An Introduction*, New York: Harper and Row.

(1967) "Conceptual Revolutions in Science" in R. S. Cohen and M. W. Wartofsky (eds.) *Boston Studies in Philosophy of Science*, vol. 3, Dordrecht: D. Reidel, pp. 331–347.

(1970) "Does the Distinction Between Normal and Revolutionary Science Hold Water?" in I. Lakatos and A. Musgrave (eds.) *Criticism and the Growth of Knowledge*, Cambridge: Cambridge University Press, pp. 39–47.

(1972) *Human Understanding*, vol. 1. Princeton: Princeton University Press.

Tucker, Robert W. (1952) "Professor Morgenthau's Theory of Political Realism," *American Political Science Review* 46: 214–224.

Ulam, Adam B. (1974) *Expansion and Coexistence*, rev. edn. New York: Praeger.

Urmson, J. O. (1968) *The Emotive Theory of Ethics*, New York: Oxford University Press.

Van Evera, Stephen (1984) "The Cult of the Offensive and the Origins of the First World War," *International Security* 9 (Summer): 58–107.

(1990/91) "Primed for Peace: Europe After the Cold War," *International Security* 15 (Winter): 7–57.

(forthcoming) *The Causes of War*, Ithaca: Cornell University Press.

Vasquez, John A. (1974a) The Power of Paradigms: An Empirical Evaluation of International Relations Inquiry. Ph.D. Dissertation, Syracuse University.

(1974b) "Alternative Perspectives on the U.N. Conference on the Human Environment," in J. R. Handelman, H. B. Shapiro, J. A. Vasquez, *Introductory Case Studies for International Relations: Vietnam, the Middle East, and the Environmental Crisis*, Chicago: Rand McNally, pp. 60–83.

(1976a) "A Learning Theory of the American Anti-Vietnam War Movement," *Journal of Peace Research* 13 (4): 299–314.

(1976b) "Statistical Findings in International Politics," *International Studies Quarterly* 20 (June): 171–218.

(1983) *The Power of Power Politics: A Critique*, New Brunswick: Rutgers University Press.

(1985) "Domestic Contention on Critical Foreign Policy Issues: The Case of the United States," *International Organization* 39 (Autumn): 643–666.

(1991) "The Deterrence Myth: Nuclear Weapons and the Prevention of Nuclear War" in C. Kegley, Jr. (ed.) *The Long Postwar Peace*, New York: HarperCollins, pp. 205–223.

(1992) "World Politics Theory" in M. Hawkesworth and M. Kogan (eds.) *Encyclopedia of Government and Politics*, London: Routledge, pp. 839–861.

(1993) *The War Puzzle*, Cambridge: Cambridge University Press.

(1994) "Building Peace in the Post-Cold War Era" in M. Midlarsky, J. Vasquez, and P. Gladkov (eds.) *From Rivalry to Cooperation: Russian and American Perspectives on the Post-Cold War Era*, New York: HarperCollins, pp. 208–218.

(1995) "Why Global Conflict Resolution Is Possible," in J. Vasquez et al. (eds.) *Beyond Confrontation: Learning Conflict Resolution in the Post-Cold War Era*, Ann Arbor: University of Michigan Press, pp. 131–153.

(1996a) "The Causes of the Second World War in Europe: A New Scientific Explanation," *International Political Science Review* 17 (April): 161–178.

(1996b) "Territorial Issues and the Probability of War: A Data-Based Analysis." Paper presented at the annual meeting of the Peace Science Society (International), Rice University, Houston, October 26.

(1996c) "When are Power Transitions Dangerous? An Appraisal and Reformulation of Power Transition Theory" in Jacek Kugler and Douglas Lemke (eds.) *Parity and War*, Ann Arbor: University of Michigan Press, pp. 35–56.

References

(1997) "The Realist Paradigm and Degenerative versus Progressive Research Programs: An Appraisal of Neotraditional Research on Waltz's Balancing Proposition," *American Political Science Review* 91 (December): 899–912.

(1998) "The Evolution of Multiple Rivalries Prior to the Second World War in the Pacific" in P. Diehl (ed.) *The Dynamics of Enduring Rivalries*, Urbana/Champaign: University of Illinois Press, pp. 191–224.

Vasquez , John, James Turner Johnson, Sanford Jaffe, and Linda Stamato (eds.) (1995) *Beyond Confrontation: Learning Conflict Resolution in the Post-Cold War Era*, Ann Arbor: University of Michigan Press.

Vasquez, John A., and Richard W. Mansbach (1984) "The Role of Issues in Global Co-operation and Conflict," *British Journal of Political Science* 14 (September): 411–433.

Väyrynen, Raimo (1983) "Economic Cycles, Power Transitions, Political Management and Wars Between Major Powers," *International Studies Quarterly* 27 (December): 389–418.

Vincent, Jack E. (1968) "National Attributes as Predictors of Delegate Attitudes at the United Nations," *American Political Science Review* 62 (September): 916–931.

(1969) "The Convergence of Voting and Attitude Patterns at the United Nations," *Journal of Politics* 31 (November): 952–983.

Voevodsky, John (1969) "Quantitative Behavior of Warring Nations," *Journal of Psychology* 72 (July): 269–292.

Walker, R. B. J. (1993) *Inside/Outside: International Relations as Political Theory*, Cambridge: Cambridge University Press.

Wallace, Michael D. (1970) Status Inconsistency, Vertical Mobility, and International War, 1825–1964. Ph.D. Dissertation, University of Michigan.

(1971) "Power, Status and International War," *Journal of Peace Research* 8 (1): 23–36.

(1972) "Status, Formal Organization, and Arms Levels as Factors Leading to the Onset of War, 1820–1964" in B. M. Russett (ed.) *Peace, War, and Numbers*, Beverly Hills: Sage, pp. 49–69.

(1973a) *War and Rank among Nations*, Lexington: D. C. Heath.

(1973b) "Alliance Polarization, Cross-Cutting, and International War, 1815–1964," *Journal of Conflict Resolution* 17 (December): 575–604.

(1979) "Arms Races and Escalation: Some New Evidence," *Journal of Conflict Resolution* 23 (March): 3–16.

(1981) "Old Nails in New Coffins: The Para Bellum Hypothesis Revisited," *Journal of Peace Research* 18 (1): 91–96.

(1982) "Armaments and Escalation: Two Competing Hypotheses," *International Studies Quarterly* 26 (March): 37–51.

(1985) "Polarization: Towards a Scientific Conception" in A. Sabrosky (ed.) *Polarity and War*, Boulder: Westview, pp. 95–113.

(1990) "Racing Redux: The Arms Race-Escalation Debate Revisited" in C. Gochman and A. Sabrosky (eds.) *Prisoners of War*, Lexington: Lexington Books, pp. 115–122.

Wallensteen, Peter (1981) "Incompatibility, Confrontation, and War," *Journal of Peace Research* 18 (1): 57–90.

(1984) "Universalism vs. Particularism: On the Limits of Major Power Order," *Journal of Peace Research* 21 (3): 243–257.

Wallerstein, Immanuel (1974) *The Modern World System*, New York: Academic Press.

Walt, Stephen M. (1987) *The Origins of Alliances*, Ithaca: Cornell University Press.

(1988) "Testing Theories of Alliance Formation: The Case of Southwest Asia," *International Organization* 42 (Spring): 275–316.

(1992) "Alliances, Threats, and U.S. Grand Strategy: A Reply to Kaufman and Labs," *Security Studies* 1 (Spring): 448–482.

(1997) "The Progressive Power of Realism," *American Political Science Review* 91 (December): 931–935.

Waltz, Kenneth N. (1959) *Man, the State, and War*, New York: Columbia University Press.

(1975) "Theory of International Relations" in F. Greenstein and N. Polsby (eds.) *Handbook of Political Science*, vol. 8, Reading, Mass.: Addison-Wesley, pp. 1–85.

(1979) *Theory of International Politics*, Reading, Mass.: Addison-Wesley.

(1981a) "Another Gap?" (Commentary on Robert E. Osgood, "Containment, Soviet Behavior, and Grand Strategy,") *Policy Papers in International Affairs* (16): 79–80. Berkeley: Institute of International Studies.

(1981b) *The Spread of Nuclear Weapons: More May Be Better*, Adelphi Paper 171. London: International Institute for Strategic Studies.

(1989) "The Origins of War in Neorealist Theory" in R. Rotberg and T. Rabb, (eds.) *The Origin and Prevention of Major Wars*, Cambridge: Cambridge University Press, pp. 39–52.

(1990) "On the Nature of States and Their Recourse to Violence," *United States Institute of Peace Journal* 3 (June): 6–7.

(1993) "The Emerging Structure of International Politics," *International Security* 18 (Fall): 44–79.

(1995) "More May Be Better" in S. Sagan and K. Waltz, *The Spread of Nuclear Weapons: A Debate*, New York: W. W. Norton, pp. 1–45.

(1997a) "Evaluating Theories," *American Political Science Review* 91 (December): 913–917.

(1997b) "International Politics Is Not Foreign Policy," *Security Studies* 6 (Autumn): 54–57.

Watkins, John (1970) "Against Normal Science" in I. Lakatos and A. Musgrave (eds.) *Criticism and the Growth of Knowledge*, Cambridge: Cambridge University Press, pp. 25–37.

Wayman, Frank Whelon (1984) "Bipolarity and War: The Role of Capability Concentration and Alliance Patterns among Major Powers, 1816–1965," *Journal of Peace Research* 21 (1): 61–78.

(1985) "Bipolarity, Multipolarity, and the Threat of War" in A. Sabrosky (ed.) *Polarity and War*, Boulder: Westview, pp. 115–144.

Wayman, Frank W., and Paul F. Diehl (1994) "Realism Reconsidered" in F. Wayman and P. Diehl (eds.) *Reconstructing Realpolitik*, Ann Arbor: University of Michigan Press, pp. 3–26.

Weigert, Kathleen, and Robert Riggs (1969) "Africa and United Nations Elections: An Aggregate Data Analysis," *International Organization* 23 (Winter): 1–19.

Weinberger, Caspar (1990) *Fighting for Peace*, New York: Warner Books.

Weiss, H. K. (1963) "Stochastic Models for the Duration and Magnitude of a 'Deadly Quarrel,'" *Operations Research* 11 (January–February): 101–121.

Weissberg, Robert (1969) "Nationalism, Integration, and French and German Elites," *International Organization* 23 (Spring): 337–347.

Wendt, Alex (1987) "The Agent-Structure Problem in International Relations Theory," *International Organization* 41 (Summer): 335–370.

(1992) "Anarchy is What States Make of It: The Social Construction of Power Politics," *International Organization* 46 (Spring): 391–425.

(1995) "Constructing International Politics," *International Security* 20 (Summer): 71–81.

Werner, Suzanne, and Jacek Kugler (1996) "Power Transitions and Military Buildups" in Jacek Kugler and Douglas Lemke (eds.) *Parity and War*, Ann Arbor: University of Michigan Press, pp. 187–207.

White, Ralph K. (1949) "Hitler, Roosevelt, and the Nature of War Propaganda," *Journal of Abnormal and Social Psychology* 44 (2): 157–175.

(1965) "Images in the Context of International Conflict: Soviet Perceptions of the U.S. and U.S.S.R" in Herbert C. Kelman (ed.), *International Behavior: A Social-Psychological Analysis*, New York: Holt, Rinehart and Winston, pp. 236–276.

(1966) "Misperception and the Vietnam War," *Journal of Social Issues* 22 (July): 1–164.

(1970) *Nobody Wanted War*, Garden City, New York: Doubleday.

Wiener, Norbert (1954) *The Human Use of Human Beings*, Boston: Houghton Mifflin.

Wight, Martin (1946) *Power Politics*. "Looking Forward" Pamphlet No. 8. London: Royal Institute of International Affairs.

(1966) "Why Is There No International Theory?" in H. Butterfield and M. Wight (eds.) *Diplomatic Investigations*, London: George Allen & Unwin, pp. 17–34.

Wilkenfeld, Jonathan (1968) "Domestic and Foreign Conflict Behavior of Nations," *Journal of Peace Research* 5 (1): 56–69.

(1975) "A Time-Series Perspective on Conflict Behavior in the Middle East" in P. J. McGowan (ed.) *Sage International Yearbook of Foreign Policy Studies*, vol. 3, Beverly Hills: Sage, pp. 177–212.

Wilkenfeld, Jonathan, Gerald W. Hopple, and Paul J. Rossa (1979) "Sociopolitical Indicators of Conflict and Cooperation" in J. D. Singer and M. D. Wallace (eds.) *To Augur Well*, Beverly Hills: Sage, pp. 109–151.

Williams, L. Pearce (1970) "Normal Science, Scientific Revolutions and the

History of Science" in I. Lakatos and A. Musgrave (eds.) *Criticism and the Growth of Knowledge*, Cambridge: Cambridge University Press, pp. 49–50.

Wilson, John (1956) *Language and the Pursuit of Truth*, Cambridge: Cambridge University Press.

Winch, Peter (1965) *The Idea of a Social Science*, New York: Humanities Press.

Wohlforth, William C. (1993) *The Elusive Balance: Power and Perceptions During the Cold War*, Ithaca: Cornell University Press.

(1994/95) "Realism and the End of the Cold War," *International Security* 19 (Winter): 91–129.

(1995) "Correspondence: Realism and the End of the Cold War," *International Security* 20 (Fall): 186.

Wolfers, Arnold (1949) "Statesmanship and Moral Choice," *World Politics* 1 (January): 175–195.

(1951) "The Pole of Power and the Pole of Indifference," *World Politics* 4 (October): 39–63.

(1959) "The Actors in International Politics" in W. T. R. Fox (ed.) *Theoretical Aspects of International Relations*, South Bend, Indiana: University of Notre Dame Press, pp. 83–106.

(1962) *Discourd and Collaboration*, Baltimore: Johns Hopkins University Press.

Wolin, Sheldon, T. (1968) "Paradigms and Political Theories" in P. King and B. C. Parekh (eds.) *Politics and Experience*, Cambridge: Cambridge University Press, pp. 125–152.

Worrall, John (1978) "The Ways in Which the Methodology of Scientific Research Programmes Improves on Popper's Methodology" in G. Radnitzky and G. Andersson (eds.) *Progress and Rationality in Science*, Dordrecht: D. Reidel, pp. 45–70.

Wright, Quincy (1942, 1965a) *A Study of War*, 1st and 2nd edns. Chicago: University of Chicago Press.

(1955) *The Study of International Relations*, New York: Appleton-Century-Crofts.

(1965b) "The Escalation of International Conflicts," *Journal of Conflict Resolution* 9 (December): 434–449.

Wright, Quincy, and C. J. Nelson (1939) "American Attitudes Toward Japan and China, 1937–38," *Public Opinion Quarterly* 3 (Spring): 46–62.

Young, Oran R. (1968) *The Politics of Force*, Princeton: Princeton University Press.

(1969) "Professor Russett: Industrious Tailor to a Naked Emperor," *World Politics* 21 (April): 486–511.

(1980) "International Regimes: Problems of Concept Formation," *World Politics* 37 (April): 331–356.

Zahar, Elie (1973) "Why Did Einstein's Programme Supersede Lorentz's? (I)," *British Journal for the Philosophy of Science* 24 (June): 95–123.

Zakaria, Fareed (1992) "Realism and Domestic Politics: A Review Essay," *International Security* 17 (Summer): 177–198.

Zaninovich, George A. (1962) "Pattern Analysis of Variables within the

International System: The Sino-Soviet Example," *Journal of Conflict Resolution* 6 (September): 253–268.

Zimmern, Alfred (1936) *The League of Nations and the Rule of Law*, London Macmillan.

(1939) (ed.) *University Teaching of International Relations*, Paris: International Institute of Intellectual Co-operation, League of Nations.

Zinnes, Dina A. (1966) "A Comparison of Hostile State Behavior in Simulate and Historical Data," *World Politics* 18 (July): 474–502.

(1968) "Expression and Perception of Hostility in Pre-war Crisis: 1914" in J. D. Singer (ed.) *Quantitative International Politics*, New York: Free Press, pp. 85–119.

(1976) *Contemporary Research in International Relations*, New York: Free Press.

Zinnes, Dina A., Robert C. North, and Howard E. Koch (1961) "Capability, Threat and the Outbreak of War" in J. Rosenau (ed.) *International Politics and Foreign Policy*, New York: Free Press, pp. 469–482.

Zubok, Vladislav (1994) "Soviet Nuclear Learning – Peculiar Patterns" in M. Midlarsky, J. Vasquez, and P. Gladkov (eds.) *From Rivalry to Cooperation: Russian and American Perspectives on the Post-Cold War Era*, New York: HarperCollins, pp. 40–55.

Name index

Abdolali, Nasrin, 353–354, 356
Abolfathi, Farid, 100
Alcock, Norman, 110
Alger, Chadwick F., 108n, 110–111, 128, 144
Alker, Hayward R., Jr., 22, 23n, 83, 87, 110–111, 148, 186, 198, 212
Allison, Graham T., 159–160, 165, 343
Amalrik, Andrei, 326n
Andropov, Yuri V., 327
Angell, Robert C., 110
Antunes, George, 97
Arbatov, Georgi A., 337n
Archibald, Peter, 111
Aristotle, 25
Armor, Daniel, 111
Aron, Raymond, 65–66, 68
Ashby, W. Ross, 40
Ashley, Richard K., 22, 23n, 186, 193, 195–197, 199, 212, 217, 220–221, 379, 384
Austin, J. L., 88n
Axelrod, Robert, 159, 196
Ayer, A. J., 22
Azar, Edward E., 85n, 96, 162

Baker, James, 342n
Baldwin, David A., 6, 192n, 193
Ball, Margaret, 87, 110
Banks, Arthur S., 83–84
Banks, Michael, 184, 187, 195, 229, 383
Barnett, Michael N., 253, 264, 280, 378
Barrera, Mario, 110
Barringer, Richard, 99–100
Baudrillard, Jean, 215, 220–221
Beal, Richard Smith, 21
Bell, Cora, 332
Bell, P. M. H., 260
Bell, Wendell, 111

Ben-Dak, Joseph D., 85n
Berger, Peter L., 218
Bernstein, Robert A., 110
Beschloss, Michael R., 322n, 331–332, 335n, 341–344, 349n
Betts, Richard K., 309, 311
Bhaskar, Roy, 224
Bingham, June, 36n
Bismarck, Otto von, 208, 297n, 307n
Blachowicz, James A., 27
Blalock, Hubert M., Jr., 112n, 126
Blechman, Barry M., 97, 100
Bobrow, Davis B., 85n, 95–97, 100
Bonham, G. Matthew, 159
Boswell, Terry, 206, 275
Boulding, Kenneth E., 65
Brady, Linda P., 92, 95, 98
Brams, Steven J., 110
Braybrook, Daniel, 28, 179
Brecher, Michael, 100, 110, 294, 311
Bremer, Stuart A., 86, 94, 172–173, 195, 209, 310n, 379
Breslauer, George W., 345n
Brewer, Thomas L., 98, 110
Brezhnev, Leonid Ilich, 327, 329, 331, 342, 364
Brickman, Philip, 111
Brodie, Bernard, 287n, 330
Brody, Richard A., 85n, 87, 110, 164
Bronfenbrenner, Urie, 161, 323, 355
Brown, Bert B., 170
Brownell, James R., 100
Bruck, H. W., 68
Bryce, James, 34, 38
Brezhnev, Leonid Ilich, 327, 329, 331, 342, 364
Bueno de Mesquita, Bruce, 94, 155, 171, 195, 247n, 252, 256, 298, 379

433

Subject index

absolute gains, 192n, 259, 307–310, 348, 363
  see also relative gains
actors in international relations, 37, 48–53, 68, 87, 89, 91–95, 97–98, 100, 109–112, 138, 140–142, 156, 188
ad hoc explanations, 210, 370
  in research programs, 26, 30, 232–233, 238, 241, 244–245, 247n, 248, 268, 270–272, 276, 281, 283, 381
  of this analysis, 124–125, 150–152, 178–179, 369
Afghanistan, 327, 331n, 340–343, 346
alliances, 68, 85–86, 94, 210n, 265–266, 268–269, 271, 279, 299, 301, 306, 357, 376
  formation of, 255, 261, 264–265, 304, 308
  as a realist topic, 53–54, 58, 93–94, 116–118, 134–143, 147, 149
  and war, 147, 171–174, 304, 306
  see also balancing of power, buck-passing, chain-ganging
anarchy, 191, 203–204, 212, 252–254, 266, 270–271, 273, 275, 278, 281, 284, 301, 377
anomalies, 3, 9, 26, 32, 35–37, 62, 73, 75, 153–154, 162, 168, 173–174, 178, 180, 196, 205, 210, 213, 231, 238, 240, 255, 261–262, 264, 266, 269, 271, 282–284, 316, 320, 322, 351, 364, 367, 382
Arab-Israeli conflict, 311, 361n
arms control, 14, 148, 339, 343n, 344, 351, 357, 366
arms races, 23n, 99, 101, 146, 173–174, 279, 304–306, 308, 357, 361, 366

balance of power, 37, 74, 83, 86–87, 168, 172, 191, 200, 249–250, 252–255, 264,
267, 269n, 280, 288, 306, 308–309, 327, 333, 348, 376
  as a realist topic, 39, 53–54, 133–143, 174
  see also balancing of power
balance of threat, 254–260, 262–264, 269n, 273, 279–280, 282, 373, 381
balancing of power, 5–6, 8, 184, 196n, 232, 249–276, 278–286, 314, 370, 373, 376–377, 380–382
  defined, 254
bandwagoning, 5, 249, 254, 261–265, 271, 273–274, 276–277, 279–280, 282
  defined, 254n, 263
bargaining, 162–164, 170–171
  as a subfield, 39, 70, 156
behavioralism, 21, 33, 39–47, 69, 73, 80, 82–87, 105, 176–177, 186–187, 189
  defined, 39–41
billiard ball model, 165
bipolarity, 86–87, 184, 191, 249, 287–288, 293–301, 313–314, 334, 371, 374, 377, 381
  balancing under, 266, 278
  findings on, 171–172, 297–300
buck-passing, 5, 249, 253, 265–272, 376
  defined, 265
bureaucratic politics, 159–163, 167, 343

capitalism, 198–199, 201, 212, 216, 219, 260, 348–349, 353, 355n, 359
case studies, xiv, 2–3, 5–9, 22, 64, 166, 231, 263, 272–273, 289, 323, 370–377, 382
chain-ganging, 5, 249, 265–266, 268–272, 282, 376
  defined, 265
China, 87, 97, 100, 255n, 295, 302, 312, 326n, 334, 350n, 357
coercion, 72, 101, 163, 168, 170

world society-issue politics paradigm,
188, 197, 203–204, 207, 211, 344, 347,
356, 359–361, 367, 380, 382–383
World War I, 6, 33, 78, 86, 146, 168,
273–274, 297–298, 312, 350, 371
and alliances, 265, 267–269, 278–279,
283, 376
World War II, 6, 32, 35–37, 73, 168, 196,
235–236, 260, 273–274, 297–298, 312,
350, 354, 359–360, 371

and alliances, 210n, 257n, 262n, 265–266,
268–269, 278–280, 359, 376

youthfulness of the field, 124, 150–151,
153, 178–180

zero-sum games, 164, 308, 319, 322, 376,
380

CAMBRIDGE STUDIES IN INTERNATIONAL RELATIONS